CHURCH-STATE ISSUES IN AMERICA TODAY

CHURCH-STATE ISSUES IN AMERICA TODAY

Volume 1: Religion and Government

Edited by
Ann W. Duncan and Steven L. Jones

PRAEGER PERSPECTIVES

PRAEGER

Westport, Connecticut
London

Ref
BR
516
C4925
2008
v.1

Library of Congress Cataloging-in-Publication Data

Church-state issues in America today / edited by Ann W. Duncan and Steven L. Jones.
   p. cm.
   Includes bibliographical references and index.
   ISBN 978-0-275-99367-2 (set : alk. paper)—ISBN 978-0-275-99368-9 (vol. 1 : alk. paper)—ISBN 978-0-275-99369-6 (vol. 2 : alk. paper)—ISBN 978-0-275-99370-2 (vol. 3 : alk. paper)
   1. Church and state—United States.   2. United States—Church history.
   I. Duncan, Ann W., 1978–   II. Jones, Steven L., 1971–
BR516.C4925   2008
322′.10973—dc22   2007030692

British Library Cataloguing in Publication Data is available.

Copyright © 2008 by Ann W. Duncan and Steven L. Jones

All rights reserved. No portion of this book may be
reproduced, by any process or technique, without the
express written consent of the publisher.

Library of Congress Catalog Card Number: 2007030692
ISBN: 978-0-275-99367-2 (set)
      978-0-275-99368-9 (vol. 1)
      978-0-275-99369-6 (vol. 2)
      978-0-275-99370-2 (vol. 3)

First published in 2008

Praeger Publishers, 88 Post Road West, Westport, CT 06881
An imprint of Greenwood Publishing Group, Inc.
www.praeger.com

Printed in the United States of America

The paper used in this book complies with the
Permanent Paper Standard issued by the National
Information Standards Organization (Z39.48–1984).

10 9 8 7 6 5 4 3 2 1

Contents

   Preface   vii
   Ann W. Duncan and Steven L. Jones

   Introduction: Church and State in Context   1
   Barbara A. McGraw

1   Historical Perspectives on Church and State   41
   Richard Bowser and Robin Muse

2   Religion, Rhetoric, and Ritual in the U.S. Government   63
   Ann W. Duncan

3   Public Expression of Faith by Political Leaders   103
   W. Jason Wallace

4   The Internationalization of Church-State Issues   135
   Zachary R. Calo

5   The Status of Faith-Based Initiatives in the Later
   Bush Administration   167
   Douglas L. Koopman

6   Political Endorsements by Churches   195
   Mary C. Segers

7   The Relevance of State Constitutions to Issues of Government
   and Religion   227
   David K. Ryden

8 The Limits of Free Exercise in America 257
Timothy J. Barnett

Appendix: Selected Cases 291

About the Editors and Contributors 301

Index 305

Preface

Ann W. Duncan and Steven L. Jones

At first glance, the separation of church and state in the United States seems a rather straightforward and clear-cut concept. The U.S. government should neither establish a certain religion nor limit the free exercise of religion by its citizens. However, the broad spectrum of church and state issues hotly debated in Washington, D.C., and in American communities suggests that this separation carries with it a bit of ambiguity. The most recognized applications of this doctrine come when religion surfaces in our schools or specific policy decisions that affect the lives of ordinary Americans. Yet, it is in the context of the government itself that some of the most interesting tensions arise in negotiating the relationship between religion and politics in the American government.

Indeed, the complexities of church and state issues in the United States of America began with the founding of the nation. While the founding fathers are remembered for their particular insistence on maintaining a separation between religion and the government, they were also very religious men who would never have denied the importance of faith in God for a just government. In this time of increasing diversity, the question arises: in a nation still primarily Christian, to what extent is latent influence or traditional reference to God acceptable? Clearly, the government cannot establish a national church, but can it incorporate prayer into its regular rituals? Clearly, the government cannot endorse a particular religion, but can a president express particular doctrinal beliefs? What are the limits of establishment? How do the state and national governments rectify sometimes conflicting views on the subject? To what extent can or should the United States seek to spread its ideas about morality and the proper relations between church and state throughout the world?

It is to these questions that the first volume of this three-volume collection turns by focusing on intersections of religion and politics in the federal, state, and local governments. Covering topics including international relations, the rhetoric of political leaders, and the use of religion to support governmental candidates and programs, this volume demonstrates the difficulties in defining establishment of religion. Barbara McGraw's introduction provides a theoretical framework for understanding the variety of particular issues presented in these three volumes. Examining the role of religion in American identity and at its founding, McGraw suggests an inclusive yet deeply meaningful foundation on which to build the national identity. The first chapter, by Richard Bowser and Robin Muse, discusses strategies of interpretation of the Establishment and Free Exercise Clauses of the Constitution. Bowser and Muse outline the surprisingly varied perspectives on the meanings of these clauses and the ramifications of these perspectives for public policy and judicial decision. Ann Duncan's chapter highlights some of the subtle and, in many cases, unlegislated intersections of church and state in the U.S. government. Elaborating on one such intersection, W. Jason Wallace focuses on expressions of faith by political leaders. Taking a historical and sociological approach, Wallace surveys the changes in such expressions and their reception by the American public. Zachary Calo then moves beyond the domestic legal issues addressed in other chapters to take an international perspective on issues of church and state through a discussion of U.S. policy regarding international religious freedom and human rights laws. Douglas Koopman discusses faith-based initiatives by examining their effectiveness in comparison to their secular counterparts and presents an overview of the recent controversies and court cases. In a chapter on political endorsement by churches, Mary Segers surveys the varieties of ways in which religious leaders can and have issued endorsements of politicians through voting instructions from the pulpit, voting guides, and allowing political candidates access to church directories. Segers discusses the competing rights of individuals, religious or not, to express political preference and engage in free religious expression and the constitutional constraints of the Establishment Clause. In his chapter on the future of federalism, David Ryden highlights what he anticipates to be a central issue in the realm of church and state for the future: the applicability of state constitutional religion clauses to church/state issues and the interplay between state and federal constitutions in this arena. In an interesting turn from chapters dealing primarily with either free exercise or establishment issues, Tim Barnett delves into those cases in which these two American ideals appear to conflict. Through a discussion of theoretical points of controversy and specific case studies of intersections of religion and politics, the chapters in this volume highlight many of the key debates and issues relevant to the specific case studies in Volumes 2 and 3.

Introduction: Church and State in Context

Barbara A. McGraw

Today, there is a battle over the hearts and minds of the American people about the meaning and purpose of the nation and its legacy of the past for America's future. As a consequence, contemporary debates about society's issues abound with arguments about the relevance of the founding era, in particular the founders' original intentions for the nation. Debates about the meaning and reach of the "religion clauses" of the First Amendment to the Constitution (that is, church and state issues) often take center stage: "Congress shall make no law respecting an establishment of religion, or prohibiting the free exercise thereof..."[1] One might frame the issue this way: to what degree has or should religion inform the underlying values, symbols, structures, laws and public policies of the nation? Hence the question: is our nation a nation under God? One side in the debate, the religious right, answers "yes." The other side, the secular left, answers "no." And confusingly both sides claim the mantle of the American founders.

It is no wonder, then, that there is a "culture war" involving debates about history as foundational to the meaning of the American founding for its own time as for our time. In fact, the stories we tell ourselves about our history are imparted in court briefs and opinions from the U.S. Supreme Court on down, where various historical narratives are repeated as support for one argument or another,[2] and in the public schools, from which future generations gain their understanding of what it means to be an American.

Those stories also are recounted in public policy debates and election politics, on television and radio talk shows, in films and other media, and even at the "kitchen table" and the "water cooler."

On one hand, the Christian right, which often includes other religious people on the right, claims that the nation was founded on Christian or Judeo-Christian principles. The argument is that although there is no specific reference to Christianity in the nation's founding documents, it was the founders' understanding and assumed context that the nation's moral referent for its basic political framework and laws was Christianity. Any conception of a "separation" of the state from the church was meant to protect the church from the intrusions of government, not the government from the church. Those on this side of the debate often support this point by quoting the founder of Rhode Island, Roger Williams (c.1603–1684), who wrote in 1644:

When they have opened a gap in the hedge or wall of separation between the garden of the church and the wilderness of the world, God hath ever broke down the wall itself, removed the Candlestick, etc., and made His Garden a wilderness as it is this day. And that therefore if He will ever please to restore His garden and Paradise again, it must of necessity be walled in peculiarly unto Himself from the world, and all that be saved out of the world are to be transplanted out of the wilderness of the World.[3]

Accordingly, the Christian right contends that the "garden" of the church is to remain unspoiled by the "wilderness" of the world. But nevertheless the world is in the purview of Christians and their religion.

Those holding this view point to the Declaration of Independence, which credits our "Creator" with having "endowed" human beings with their "unalienable rights," and refers to "Nature's God"—all religious tenets derived from Christianity, they claim. In addition, they note that the words "separation of church and state" do not appear in the religion clauses or anywhere else in the Constitution. They conclude, therefore, that religion, in particular Christianity, is the ultimate foundation of our nation. This "side" of the debate has its heroes, for example, John Adams, who said, "Our Constitution was made only for a moral and religious people. It is wholly inadequate to the government of any other."[4] They conclude that not only does Christianity serve as the nation's foundation, but it is also the bulwark against the exercise of ever-increasing state power. That is, Christians and their churches can be better trusted with the preservation of our liberties than can the state.

On the other hand, the secular left, which includes religious people who believe that a secular nation is conducive to liberty, claims that the founders distrusted religion and therefore established the nation on "secular," meaning non-religious, foundations.[5] They point to historical events involving abuses on account of religion combined with state power, including the Catholic Spanish Inquisition and the abuses of Protestant John Calvin's Geneva city-state (where, in both cases, burning heretics at the stake was the order of the day); the age of religious wars in Europe from 1559 to 1715; and similar abuses and conflicts in colonial America as reasons for keeping religion and government separate so as to ensure the freedom of the people.

Consequently, those holding this view conclude that the founders sought to separate church and state not only to protect the church from the state, but also to protect the state, and therefore the liberty of people it represents, from the church. They point to the U.S. Constitution, noting that it contains no references to God. Accordingly, the religion clauses mean, as Thomas Jefferson (1743–1826) said in 1802, that there is a "wall of separation between church and state,"[6] regardless of the fact that the phrase itself is not in the Constitution. This "side" also has its heroes. For example, James Madison expressed considerable reservations about religion when he said

The conduct of every popular Assembly, acting on oath, the strongest of religious ties, shews that individuals join without remorse in acts agst. which their consciences would revolt, if proposed to them separately in their closets. When Indeed Religion is kindled into enthusiasm, its force—like that of other passions—is increased by the sympathy of a multitude.[7]

They quote Jefferson, as well, who rejected the notion that any civil or ecclesiastical "legislators and rulers" have any legitimate authority over "the faith of others." He stated that the imposition of "their own opinions and modes of thinking" has "established and maintained false religions over the greatest part of the world and through all time . . . "[8] This side believes that secular sources serve as the foundation of our nation and that the state's legal and political procedures are the bulwark against the potential for state encroachments on individual liberty and against creeping ecclesiastical power aligned with the state. That is, the state, as established by the founders, can be better trusted with the preservation of our liberties, than can the church.

Still others hold a third view: the founders' original intent is not particularly relevant today. According to this view, looking back more than 200 years to a time very different from our own in order to surmise the founders' original intent is an exercise in futility. New times require us to solve today's problems with new ideas. Among those with this view are those who contend that all morally foundational claims, whether on the left-progressive liberal side or right-conservative traditional side, threaten the existence of the plurality of views we now enjoy, many of which arise out of the various multicultural perspectives that thrive in the nation today.[9] I submit, in response to this argument, that the failure to take account of our place today in the overall historical context that led America to its founding can only lead to the potential for history to repeat itself—and it is not a history we are likely to wish to repeat.

It very well may be that we all have a lot to argue about. Perhaps we always have. However, while we are not likely to settle the debate once and for all here, there is no doubt that it is helpful to take a broader view than perhaps has any particular "side" in the contentious culture war debates. Accordingly, let us take a brief look at the historical context for the founding of America, specifically as it relates to ideas about the relationship of state and religion, that is, the contested concept of the "separation of church and state" and religious liberty, including the role of religion in public life. But let us not begin with a favored resolution of a particular issue as our goal and then read back into history what would support that resolution. Instead, let us take into account the evidences of history that various "sides" in the debate have proffered and consider them as a whole in an effort to gain guidance for what should be the context of the discussion today. That is, rather than tracking through history and choosing a secular or religious narrative as a lens through which to consider church and state issues today, let us consider them together as they appear in history: a complex combined narrative that both includes and transcends polarized views. Then we can answer the fundamental question—What grounds the American system?—so that the various arguments and debates about church/state issues can take place without undermining what makes all of the conversations possible in the first place.

SEPARATION OF CHURCH AND STATE AND RELIGIOUS LIBERTY IN CONTEXT

The idea of a boundary between church and state did not begin in the founding era. It did not begin with Thomas Jefferson's Danbury Letter reference to the "wall of separation between church and state." It did not even begin with Roger Williams's reference to the need for a wall to protect "the garden of the church" from "the wilderness of the world." In fact, many supporters and detractors of the concept embodied in the much aligned and praised phrase "separation of church and state," if not the "wall" metaphor itself, might be surprised that it has a long history that predates the colonial period and the founding of the United States and the states by centuries—and can be found in both theological and secular sources. One could reasonably conclude, in fact, that it was the convergence of theology and secular philosophy in the thinking of the founding generation that made founding a nation on the principles of "life, liberty and the pursuit of happiness" possible, and that to attempt to separate them today obscures the foundations of the nation, distorts its purpose, and undermines the promise of the nation for its own future and its legacy for the world.

For most of human history there was no conception of religion being something that could even be thought of as separate from culture as a whole and, therefore in turn, from the governing authorities and structures of a particular society. We even see this today in tribal communities around the world. That which appeals to the spiritual in society—the "other world" and its transcendent or immanent being or beings—is all of one piece with daily rituals, work, community life, life passages, and so on.[10] When agriculture was discovered and the great civilizations of Egypt and China arose, the state and religion functioned as one entity with the emperor or pharaoh as the head of governing authorities *and* as either a god or as the gods' representative on earth. The idea was one of a grand hierarchy with the ruler at the top as a god with inherent authority or with the gods at the top, providing the sanction of divine authority to the ruler. In either case, the ruler would then wield state power in exercise of divine authority over the people.[11] Thus "church" and state not only were joined, they were not even thought of as two things combined; they were one.

As Christendom developed in Europe, however, the idea of religion and state as one was challenged. During the medieval period, the Catholic Church, growing in power, opposed the sovereignty of the rulers, who previously had claimed the mantle of authority over matters temporal and religious.[12] The Church, in the person of the pope, claimed universal supremacy over the weak states of the period as "divine right" to absolute sovereignty vested in the pope by God, and asserted that canon law superceded secular law and that the authority of the emperor or king derived from the Church.[13] This political theology held, consequently, that God's law is the higher law over even the king.[14] That is, the king's actions could be adjudged in error by reference to the divine law of God, as interpreted by the pope.[15] As a result, the king's law and divine law were no longer understood as being one and the same, but separate—with God's law as the ultimate sovereign referent. Thus, resistance against such supreme spiritual power is resistance against God and therefore was prohibited as a mortal sin.[16]

In response, temporal rulers also claimed "divine right." This counterclaim took shape as "the Divine Right of the Emperors" in the fourteenth century[17] and emerged in the seventeenth century as the "Divine Right of Kings."[18] There the idea was that the emperor or king has divine sanction to come into power and therefore derives his authority directly from God. Moreover, it was held that sovereignty, which cannot be divided between secular and religious authorities, must be unified in the king.[19]

Hence, the church stood apart from the state and interpreted state authority according to the church's interpretation of God's law, while the state claimed authority directly from God according to the state's own interpretations, thus standing apart from the church. Of course the application of the authority of church or state was uneven in practice, as power struggles persisted and various entitles (monarchy, parliament, barons/nobles, and various ecclesiastical authorities after the Protestant Reformation) pressed their claims. Still, although in one sense church and state were separated, they were joined in one thing: regardless of who is sovereign over earthly realms, such sovereignty derives from God and divine law reigns over all.[20] Each, then, in its own view stood as a "check" on the power of the other. Nevertheless, they worked together, particularly in England after the Protestant Reformation there made the king the head of the Anglican Church.

Christian political theory combined the two in a joint effort to create a uniform moral order in society, using state authority to enforce church doctrine, while the state used church doctrine to justify its punishments.[21] This justification for the exercise of absolute power over the people was based on the doctrine of original sin, which holds that human beings are inherently sinful.[22] Consequently, this reasoning continues, the state must enforce the moral order on the people as a whole to prevent them from straying from accepted religious doctrine—all in an effort to create a uniform society based on religious moral precepts. That is, government's role is to restrain the sinful nature of human beings to help ensure their salvation for the eternal realm and for an orderly society in the world. Moreover, it was believed that because state and church would not tolerate deviance from established norms, discord would be stifled and peace would prevail.

However, the seeds of the concept of the separation of religious authority and state authority had previously been planted, which would prove to have far-reaching implications. As a consequence, further theological developments came to the fore that stood at odds with the prevailing arrangement between church and state and their claims for absolute authority. These involved the nature of human beings and their relationship to God and society. First was the belief that human beings have inherent dignity and worth because they are made in the image of God and they are God's children. Consequently, there is something inviolable in every human being's nature, and that inviolability is at the very center of what it means to be a human being. Because this is equally so in all human beings, human beings have equal dignity; ultimately, no one is more worthy than another—not even the king. Some people may put on vestments or gain the power of armies, but in the beginning and in the end, they all are of equal dignity before God. Second was the belief that God created human beings with free will. Consequently, human beings are free to conduct their lives as they will. There also developed a great faith in human beings' capacity for knowledge and reason, potential for understanding, and a consequent ability to improve themselves and their world.[23]

Moreover, because of human beings' freedom and equal inherent dignity and the accountability of everyone to the law of God, a strain in Christian theology held that the people can legitimately resist the state when the state strays from a right course and fails to adhere to God's law.[24] In other words, no longer were the people bound by the laws of the state by virtue of its absolute authority. Instead, it was deemed to be the people's prerogative, even duty, to hold the state accountable, if the state violated the law of God. In other words, the conscience of the people was separated from the authority of state and church.

Still, the notion of a grand hierarchy that ruled over the masses persisted in most quarters. Now, however, another view emerged to challenge that hierarchical order. Liberty and inherent dignity and all that implied gave rise to what were viewed as legitimate claims—that is, rights—superior to state *and* church authority.[25] But questions remained: Should the ultimate protector of these rights be an all-powerful autocratic ruler charged with the obligation, as Hobbes (1588–1679) advocated? Should the "general will" of the people as gleaned by those in power serve to accomplish the goal, as Rousseau (1712–1778) believed? These questions were much debated at the time of the founding and during its immediately preceding history. The American founders found their answer primarily in the writings of John Locke (1632–1704). Through Locke, the idea of God's law as the ultimate authority persisted and was very influential in the political philosophy that eventually would make its way into the ideas that formed the basis for the American founding and beyond. Now, however, the sovereignty derived from God would be vested not in the king or any church but in the people.

LOCKE'S "ENLIGHTENMENT" POLITICAL THEOLOGY

Locke is known as a pivotal Enlightenment Era (c.1650–1800) philosopher. Enlightenment philosophers eschewed tradition and custom (thought to be based on superstition and ignorance) in favor of the use of human reason in each individual's "search and study"[26] and "argument and debate"[27] to discover the true and the good in all areas of human endeavor, including religion, law, and politics. Often enlightenment philosophers are characterized as secular philosophers because they eschewed religious dogma, in particular its bases for government. However, as we shall soon see, Locke's writings can be seen as a clear articulation of the line of thinking outlined briefly in the previous section, but taken further. That is, Locke did not leave religion behind. Rather, the ground that began with religion and governing authorities as one and then shifted to place God's law over state and church had shifted once again in Locke's works.

Locke began his political philosophy by returning, metaphorically, to the "state of nature," a state prior to the formation of societies. Locke asserted that in the state of nature the people are free and equal as created by God; that is they inherently have free will and equal dignity as human beings. For Locke, the liberty and equal dignity of the people constitute, then, the fundamental natural law—the law of the state of nature. And Locke concluded that, because freedom and equality are the natural state of human beings in the state of nature, freedom and equality are legitimate claims against the state. Consequently, those claims should be secured as civil rights when societies are formed—so as not to thwart the essential nature of human beings as God intended.[28]

However, Locke noted that there is a significant problem in the state of nature that must be solved when societies are formed so as to preserve the natural rights of the people: in the state of nature there is no impartial judge of disputes between various people. As a result, when violations of the natural law occur or there are other disputes, there is no one to arrive at an unbiased resolution.[29] Without a way to provide unbiased resolutions of disputes, there is only the "state of war"—battles among those making various claims.[30] Locke concluded that the eventual result of this is either an anarchistic and violent chaos or, more likely, a powerful ruler rises to the top—the winner of the battles.[31]

Locke challenged the monarchy on this basis, concluding that the king was merely the descendent of the brute who rose to power in the battles of the "state of war" in the state of nature. In other words, there was no "divine right" of kings—only the assertion of power. And that power was not likely to be exercised in an unbiased way to preserve the natural rights of the people, as history had shown. Europe's own history was filled with battles for power and religious wars, as well as the torture, hanging, and burning at the stake of those deemed to be heretics by the dictates of whomever came to power at any particular time. Thus, Locke rejected outright the state's and ecclesiastical authorities' claims that using the coercions of the state to impose a church dictated uniform moral order on the people as a whole would produce a good and peaceful society.[32] Locke concluded that a different approach was needed. Government must be established on laws that affirm the natural rights of the people and provide an unbiased legal and political system—the impartial judge.[33] That is, God's law—the natural law—should be over the state *and* the churches and be preserved and interpreted through an unbiased political and legal system established by and for the benefit of the people.[34] No longer was the ultimate authority the king or any church. Now the people would ensure that God's natural law would rule.

Central to Locke's approach to government was the need to secure the people's civil right to tolerance of their religious beliefs, which he believed requires "just bounds" between the state and religion.[35] One reason was practical and secular. Locke saw religious tolerance as the means to creating a more peaceful society than had been the case when uniformity was imposed on the people from the top down through the sanction of the church and the power of the state. However, another reason rested on Locke's adoption of a line of thought that opposed on theological grounds top-down governing authority. That is, it was not a rejection of religion that led Locke to religious toleration, as some have concluded. Instead, Locke shifted to a different religious idea. Consequently, Locke rejected traditional political theory based on the doctrine of original sin and the whole idea of uniformity derived from it.[36] He held instead that a moral and peaceful society is not more likely to come from the top down through religious doctrine enforced by the state over the people. Rather, it is more likely to come through the people, whose good will is not corrupted by power and who therefore are more likely to hear the voice of God.[37]

Locke's approach to government and religious toleration was based on a simple theology: there is God and God communicates with the people. Hence, God's relationship is not with the elites of religious institutions and the state who then tell everyone what to do and persecute those who do not follow their attempts at uniformity. Instead, God's relationship is with each individual human being through conscience informed by revelation, spiritual or other insight, nature and reason.[38] Thus, freedom of conscience was fundamental to Locke's approach to government. The people must be free to listen for the voice of God, however they understand that, and answer that call. Locke said, in effect, that the only way that it is even possible for a good society to be realized is to trust the people.[39]

Accordingly, Locke concluded that government should be a "social contract."[40] Under the social contract the people would consent to a government to which they would give up their right to punish violators of the natural law in exchange for an impartial legal and political system that would secure their natural rights (freedom, especially freedom of conscience and its expression, and equal dignity, which requires equal justice) and would ensure their safety and general welfare. The purpose of this form of government is not only to secure the people's best chance for a just and peaceful society. Locke held that his proposed legal/political system, his social contract, also is central to the search for the true and the good, which he reasoned could never be attained through the auspices of the powerful, be they state or ecclesiastical authorities. As Locke said

> For truth certainly would do well enough, if she were once left to shift for herself. She seldom has received, and I fear never will receive, much assistance from the power of great men, to whom she is but rarely known, and more rarely welcome. She is not taught by laws, nor has she any need of force to procure her entrance into the minds of men. Errors indeed prevail by the assistance of foreign and borrowed succours, but if truth makes not her way into the understanding by her own light, she will be but the weaker for any borrowed force violence can add to her.[41]

Thus, Locke put his trust in the people over the powerful, believing that history had shown that the powerful are prone to corruption and therefore violate the natural rights of the people. While there is no guarantee, Locke said, the only way it is even *possible* for a good society to be realized is to limit the power of the state and eliminate the power of the churches. A free people of inherent dignity, equal to that of kings and popes, would be able to be and do good in society because the "social contract" would provide a secure framework within which freedom could be exercised.

But while Locke sought to limit the power of the state and eliminate the power of any church over the people, he did not argue against religion *per se*. In fact, be believed that his approach would strengthen religion, curtail the potential for religion to be corrupted by power, and make it possible for true faith to flourish.[42] To accomplish this, Locke turned the old hierarchical order (God → church/state → the people) on its head. Locke did not abandon the idea that God's law should prevail, but now it would be given effect in society by the people who would build the good society not via a top-down hierarchy, as had been the previous approach, but from the ground up (God → the people → the social contract → limited government by the people and for the people by their consent → creating an open space for the freedom to be and do good).

It follows, then, that Locke never intended religion to be relegated to a private sphere in the sense that it is irrelevant to common concerns and therefore should remain out of sight. Rather, it was to take part, through the people—through their own individual activities and through the voluntary societies that the people formed and joined. Moreover, religion was to be welcomed as a contributor to discussions about law and public policy, but the resulting law and public policy could go only as far as the limited authority of the unbiased political/legal system extended and only so far as those contributions were consistent with all of the people's natural rights. And those natural rights had a very far reach in Locke's political thought.[43]

Asserting that toleration is "the chief characteristical mark of the true church,"[44] Locke claimed the right to toleration for those in all of the most controversial Protestant sects of his day, as well as Catholics,[45] Jews,[46] Muslims (Mahometans),[47] Native Americans,[48] and pagans,[49] and consequently said,

[I]f solemn assemblies, observations of festivals, public worship be permitted to any one sort of professors [i.e., religious people], all these things ought to be permitted to the Presbyterians, Independents, Anabaptists, Arminians, Quakers, and others, with the same liberty. Nay, if we may openly speak the truth, and as becomes one man to another, neither pagan, nor Mahometan, nor Jew ought to be excluded from the civil rights of the commonwealth because of his religion.[50]

Locke even concluded that true toleration requires that those practicing "idolatry, superstition, and heresy" and "heathens" should be given their civil right to freedom of conscience.[51] Unlike those who came before him, Locke eschewed any sort of enforced conformity, holding instead that toleration reflects the natural law, that is, the religious values that form the foundations for a political system based on the liberty and equal dignity of the people.

Thus, the "just bounds" between church and state would be achieved. God, including reason (which, according to Locke, is "natural revelation"[52]), would inform the people's consciences directly, rather than through the dictates of the state armed with the sanction of church authority, and the people would be free to answer that call. As a result, there would be an open space where the people could pursue the good society from the perspective conscience gives them. The people would form and join voluntary associations (including churches)[53] to pursue their individual, group, and common ends beyond governmental interference, not only in their effort to find way to live together in society in peace, considering their differences, but also in their ultimate search for the true and the good.

FOUNDING A NATION BY THE PEOPLE AND FOR THE PEOPLE

In the founding era, developments within Christianity rose to meet Lockean fundamentals and merged religious faith with political aspirations to inspire a nation. Because of this, it was no longer "church" that stood as a check on the state. The people, persuaded by Locke's arguments and principles and motivated by faith, joined fundamental religious ideas about the nature of man and man's relationship with God to ideas about how to constrain power so that its potential for corruption would be severely limited, if not eliminated altogether.[54] The ultimate purpose: a free people of equal inherent dignity who could bring the good into the world through their participation in a government by and for the people and in their daily lives.

Mid-eighteenth century America was in the grip of a profound religious revival. Traveling preachers such as George Whitefield (1714–1770) galvanized large segments of the population through emotional sermons, which called the people to "new birth" in Christ.[55] Those involved in this "great awakening" believed that authentic religion was exhibited not through church membership, but through one's own profound conversion experience.[56] Status and power were leveled as Christ-centered converts gathered in revival meetings that inspired these members of the founding generation. They rejected ecclesiastical authorities and their doctrines and discovered a faith, not grounded in unconfirmed belief, but in the experience of being embraced by God. At the same time, Locke's much quoted phrase "life, liberty, and property," as well as the "laws of nature," the "state of nature," and the "social compact," inspired church sermons that awakened the people to their natural rights and galvanized them to take up the political cause against oppressive arbitrary government.[57]

This great awakening had a counterpart that shared its antiauthoritarianism and its focus on individual religion, though this was a movement that came from a significantly different direction—"rational religion." Contrary to the usual narrative, the founders who believed in rational religion were not adherents of a kind of "deism" that held that God was a divine Creator who then absented the world, leaving it to run like a finely tuned clock.[58] Instead, rational religion involved real faith. (Even Jefferson, often thought of as one of the most "deist" of the founders, was known to practice regular private devotions.[59]) Here, however, the emotionalism of "new birth" evangelical revivals was eschewed in favor of reasoned reflection. The light of reason was believed to be more authentic than emotions, which might be flamed into a passion that could irrationally spur a "mob" to infringe the inalienable natural rights of others.[60] That is, rational religion was deemed by its adherents to be a more reliable source of inspiration consistent with "Nature's God" and therefore God's natural law[61] than the emotional religion of revivals.

Nevertheless, despite differences, the two religious impulses were closer cousins than one might think at first blush. The reason is that both eschewed authority that sought to limit human beings' ability to find happiness and godliness in their own way. Thus both espoused limitations on governmental power and eschewed church authorities aligned with government in state establishments.[62] Consequently, although they were strange bedfellows in some respects, they were bedfellows nevertheless in the struggle for liberty as the revolutionary period was upon them. Locke's influence was pervasive in both, and therefore clearly he was not merely the most influential political philosopher of the age; he was "the head and heart of the Revolution."[63]

As a consequence, the founders adopted Locke's approach to the basic foundations of government and formed a nation by the people and for the people to secure their natural "unalienable rights."[64] They established a legal and political system designed to provide the greatest chance for securing the people's "safety and happiness."[65] This was a nation founded not on the dictates of any particular religious sect, but on God's law—"nature and nature's God"[66]—and all that that implied: the inherent equal dignity and liberty of the people and their potential to bring their best forward, to be and do good as they understood it. They could build a good society from the ground up. Therefore, this was not a wholly "secular" endeavor, as some argue. Rather, it built upon centuries of political philosophy and theology, both of which found their expression in the political theology of John Locke and were given effect by the American founders in the political/legal system of the new nation. The Declaration of Independence, which begins by referencing "the Laws of Nature and of Nature's God," is based on that political theology:

We hold these truths to be self-evident, that all men are created equal that they are endowed by their Creator with certain unalienable rights Rights, that among these are Life, Liberty and the pursuit of Happiness. That to secure these rights, Governments are instituted among Men, deriving their just powers from the consent of the governed. That whenever any Form of Government becomes destructive of these ends, it is the Right of the People to alter or to abolish it . . . And for the support of this Declaration, with a firm reliance on the protection of Divine Providence, we mutually pledge to each other our Lives, our Fortunes, and our sacred Honor.

The U.S. Constitution and the constitutions of the states established a political/legal system that was to be unbiased—to provide the "impartial judge" of which Locke had spoken, a system where, as Thomas Paine famously declared, "the law is king."[67] That is, the governments were designed to be, in the words of John Adams (1735–1826), "government of laws and not men."[68] The law, then, became the ultimate ruler; hence the oft-cited phrase "the rule of law." Embodied in that phrase is the whole notion that the ultimate law is the law of nature—God's law, which requires liberty of the people and respect for the inherent equal dignity of every human being. That is, no matter how revered or powerful any persons or groups may be, their decisions may not be substituted legitimately in place of the law. Moreover, the unbiased legal/political system is based on equal justice. Hence, no one, no matter how exemplary she or he is thought to be, is exempt from—that is, "above"—the law.

To best ensure that the law, and not men, shall be and remain the ruler, Locke had advocated the idea of the consent of the governed through a social contract. However, his approach did not necessarily require democratic processes. The founders, on the other hand, took Locke's social contract a step further. Looking back into history and discovering there the concepts of democracy and republicanism, the founders combined the two to form what can be termed a "democratic republic." That is, they established a government whereby the people elect representatives through a democratic process that makes those representatives beholden to the people.

Further, to provide the best chance for the political/legal system to be unbiased, it was deemed necessary to check power because, as history had shown, it has great potential to corrupt. Consequently, the founders, following Locke and others,[69] decided that the government of the new nation should provide for the separation of powers: legislative, judicial, and executive. The separation of powers also included the separation of ecclesiastical—that is, church—authority from the government, as well.

Second, the founders established national and state governments that were limited in their authority and thus acknowledged and secured the people's liberties. The "first liberty" is the right to religious liberty, and that liberty was understood to be far-reaching, where "everyone," as George Washington said, "shall sit in safety under his own vine and fig tree, and there shall be none to make him afraid."[70] Thus, following Locke, the founders understood religious liberty to extend far beyond the various sects of Protestant Christianity. As Samuel Adams's "The Rights of Colonists and a List of Infringements and Violations of Rights" (1772) stated:

In regard to Religeon, mutual toleration in the different professions thereof, is what all good and candid minds in all ages have ever practiced; and both by precept and example inculcated on mankind: And it is now generally agreed among christians that this spirit of toleration in the fullest extend consistent with the being of civil society "is the chief characteristical mark of the true church" & In so much that Mr. Lock [sic] has asserted, and proved beyond the possibility of contradiction on any solid ground, that such toleration ought to be extended to all whose doctrines are now subversive of society.[71]

In this regard, Richard Henry Lee was even more explicit when he said: "I fully agree with the Presbyterians, that true freedom embraces the Mahomitan [Muslim] and the Gentoo [Hindu] as well as the Christian religion."[72] Thomas Jefferson's "Notes on Religion" stated: "Shall we suffer a Pagan to deal with us and not suffer him to pray to his god? . . . It is the refusing toleration to those of different opinion which has produced all the bustles and wars on account of religion."[73] And regarding the debate about the Virginia Act for Religious Freedom, Jefferson said: "The insertion [of Jesus Christ in the preamble] was rejected by the great majority, in proof that they meant to comprehend, within the mantle of its protection, the Jew and the Gentile, the Christian and the Mohammedan, the Hindoo and the Infidel of every denomination."[74] In fact, the founders went further than Locke to provide liberty of conscience rights to atheists and even to the intolerant. For example, Jefferson said:

Locke denies tolerance to those who entertain opinions contrary to those moral rules necessary for the preservation of society; as for instance . . . [those] who will not own and teach the duty of tolerating all men in matters of religion; or who deny the existence of god (it was a great thing to go so far—as he himself says of the parliament which framed the act of toleration but where he stopped short we may go on. . . .)[75]

But perhaps Richard Henry Lee put it best when he said in 1787: "It is true, we are not disposed to differ much, at present, about religion; but when we are making a constitution, it is to be hoped, for ages and millions yet unborn . . ."[76] Thus, Lee contemplated a nation for "ages and millions" that would be more diverse, perhaps even much more diverse, than the nation for whom he and others were "making a constitution."

These are but a few of the many statements in the founding era that proclaimed religious liberty for all. Clearly, the founders intended the widest possible freedom of conscience.

The founders' political/legal system was designed to create a space for the exercise of liberty, in particular liberty of conscience and its expression. And it was understood that liberty of conscience would serve in large part as the means to building the good society. How would a government that ensured freedom of conscience and its expression foster a society that is good? The people would listen for the voice of God, however understood (including the voice of reason) and would answer that call. They would then participate in argument and debate, not only in the search for the best ways to live together considering their differences, but also in the search for the true and the good. As Thomas Jefferson said, echoing Locke:

[S]he [truth] is the proper and sufficient antagonist to error, and has nothing to fear from conflict unless by human interposition [she is] disarmed of her natural weapons, free argument and debate; errors ceasing to be dangerous when it is permitted freely to contradict them.[77]

In other words, there was to be a public forum in which a great conversation would take place, where the people and their elected representatives and those appointed by them would deliberate from all of their various perspectives about the issues of the day.

However, as perhaps is now clear, that great conversation was never meant to exclude religious voices. As a matter of fact, religion continued to be a participant in public debate from the founding era and forward because the "separation of church and state" did not mean that all religious principles were abandoned. It meant that certain general principles—those on which the natural law of freedom and equal dignity, and in turn the rule of law, were based—would prevail over the various sectarian doctrines of the religions of the new nation. Some held that those natural law foundations of the nation are based on the general principles of Christianity. Others held that those principles followed the political philosophy of the Enlightenment Era secular thinkers. Clearly, however, it was both.[78] As John Dickenson (1732–1808) wrote in 1788:

[A] constitution is the organization of the contributed rights in society. Government is the exercise of them. It is intended for the benefit of the governed; of course [it] can have no just powers but what conduce to that end: and the awfulness of the trust is demonstrated in this—that it is founded on the nature of man, that is, on the will of his Maker, and is therefore sacred. It is an offence against Heaven, to violate that trust.[79]

On these bases, the American founders formed a nation by the people and for the people to secure their natural rights, provide an impartial legal and political system, and ensure the safety and general welfare of the people. This was given effect in the U.S. Constitution and its Bill of Rights, and in the constitutions and declarations of rights of the states, all of which made freedom of conscience and its expression central tenets for the new nation, and all of which recognized that there were bounds between church and state.

RELIGION AND TRADITION: WORKING OUT THE MEANING AND EXTENT OF ESTABLISHMENT AND LIBERTY

The religion clauses and their counterparts in state constitutions have been at the center of debates about American identity from the beginning. The reason is that while there was a general consensus about the foundations of our first freedom in the founding era, there was not agreement about the implications of those foundations for American law and culture.[80] It was clear that the founders sought to secure the rights of those in a vast diversity of Christian sects, as well as those in myriad minority religions at the time. At the same time, however, there was an understanding among many generally that society must be based on shared values. Debates about what is or should be the source of those values ensued early on.

The antiauthoritarianism of rational religion and evangelical awakenings prevailed in both, as each saw tyranny from state or church authority as the antithesis of a government by and for the people. After all, the founders and those who followed were well aware of the dangers involved in the exercise of power by either. However, deciding which governmental prerogatives encroach on liberties or risk religious establishments was not as easily accomplished in practice, as the general principles suggested. Consequently, the salient question of the time was: what is the meaning of liberty and establishment in a society framed by laws that derive from culturally "established" customs and traditions? After the founding and since, the courts and legislatures have been charged with determining the answer to this question.

As we have seen, debates about natural rights and the demise of tyranny did not begin with the founding generation. That conversation began long before and was reflected in the English common law tradition, which had given early voice to the concept of natural rights and liberties.[81] The founding generation had appealed to English common law tradition as providing the "rights of Englishmen,"[82] and then extended those rights based in large part on the political philosophy of John Locke.

As we all know, however, the founders did not extend them far enough. Clearly, America did not live up to its ideal at the founding: those without property were denied the right to vote; slavery was promoted by the south and tolerated by the north; women did not gain full rights as free human beings; and Native Americans were robbed of their land and liberty. As a consequence, while the founding generation broke with customs and traditions in some respects, it continued them in others. That is, while the new nation held out the promise of liberty, it also was steeped in a traditional culture influenced by preexisting law and public policy, which predated the new nation and which, consequently, often was at odds with the general principles enunciated in the Declaration of Independence and the constitutions, bills of rights, and declarations of rights of the nation and the states.

Boundaries of Liberty: The Blasphemy Cases and State Constitutions

The traditional culture of the founding generation was reflected in the English common law, on which state and federal courts continued to rely well after the founding, and was persuasive to jurists and others regarding challenges to prior law on constitutional grounds. Blasphemy cases are illustrative. While a detailed account and analysis of blasphemy jurisprudence is well beyond the scope of this introductory chapter,[83] the issue nevertheless reveals an early attempt to mediate between traditional culture reflected in the common law and the new constitutional regime of the United States and the states, the language of which, of course, provides broad liberty protections.[84]

William Blackstone's *Commentaries on the Laws of England*[85] remained authoritative for those making and interpreting state and federal law in the new nation. "Blasphemy," Blackstone wrote, "against the Almighty is denying his being or providence, or uttering contumelious reproaches on our Savior Christ. It is punished, at common law by fine and imprisonment, for Christianity is part of the laws of the land."[86] Relying on Blackstone and the English common law, the states continued to prosecute offenders, who claimed, in a failed attempt to avert punishment, that liberty rights granted under U.S. and state constitutions in effect repealed blasphemy laws.

The liberty issue at stake in the blasphemy cases was, of course, freedom of speech, but the cases also raised the issue of religious establishment—the joining of church and state—because of the reasoning adopted by the courts. For example, in *Updegraph v. The Commonwealth of Pennsylvania* (1824), Abner Updegraph sought to have his conviction for blasphemy overturned on the grounds that the blasphemy law under which he had been indicted was no longer valid because it contravened the clear prohibition against freedom of speech in both the state and federal constitutions. Updegraph's misconduct had been

> not having the fear of God before his eyes ... contriving and intending to scandalize, and bring into disrepute, and vilify the Christian religion and the scriptures of

truth, in the presence and hearing of several persons . . . did unlawfully, wickedly and premeditatively, despitefully and blasphemously say . . . : "That the Holy Scriptures were a mere fable: that they were a contradiction, and that although they contained a number of good things, yet they contained a great many lies." To the great dishonor of Almighty God, to the great scandal of the profession of the Christian religion.[87]

Interestingly, Updegraph was a member of a debating association and claimed that his statement was made in the context of a debate on a religion question. Nevertheless, the Pennsylvania Supreme Court rejected Updegraph's claim that reliance on Christianity to legitimize blasphemy laws violates the U.S. Constitution and the Pennsylvania constitution. The court upheld Updegraph's conviction and sentence, which included a fine of $500 and a two year prison sentence, stating that "Christianity is part of the common law; the act against blasphemy is neither obsolete nor virtually repealed; nor is Christianity inconsistent with our free governments or the genius of the people."[88]

The *Updegraph* court was correct: Christianity was a part of the common law. After all, the common law against blaspheming Christianity traced back to England's established church. Neither the U.S. nor Pennsylvania constitutions invoked by blasphemers had established Christianity, Pennsylvania being one of the states that never had a religious establishment. Yet the Pennsylvania Supreme Court based its holding on common law foundations in England's established Christianity. Hence the court reasoned that Christianity provided the basis for civil law, and therefore to blaspheme Christianity was to blaspheme the nation's foundations.

We will first dispose of what is considered the grand objection—the constitutionality of Christianity—for, in effect that is the question. Christianity, general Christianity, is and always has been a part of the common law . . . not Christianity founded on any particular religious tenets; not Christianity with an established church . . . but Christianity with liberty of conscience to all men . . . In this the constitution of the United States has made no alteration, nor in the great body of the laws which was an incorporation of the common-law doctrine of Christianity . . . without which no free government can long exist.[89]

This line of reasoning, rather than being an aberration, was consistent with much of the thinking at the time. The idea was that Christianity provided the foundation of the nation and the states.

Similarly, founding era constitutions and declarations of rights, while providing broad liberty rights, including of course freedom of religion, contained references to Christianity, Christian virtues, or belief in God as foundational, as well. For example, the Delaware Declaration of Rights (1776) provided:

[A]ll men have a natural and unalienable right to worship Almighty God according to the dictates of their own consciences and understandings; and that no man ought or of right can be compelled to attend any religious worship or maintain any ministry contrary to or against his own free will and consent, and that no authority can or ought to be vested in, or assumed by any power whatever that shall in any case interfere with, or in any manner controul the right of conscience in the free exercise of religious worship . . . [A]ll persons professing the Christian religion ought forever to enjoy equal rights and privileges in this state, unless under colour of religion, any man disturb the peace, the happiness or safety of society.[90]

Clearly, many in the founding generation believed that the liberties they revered and secured derived in large part from their long-held traditions—including their Christian tradition. The natural law tradition had developed in large part from a genus of Christian theology, many believed, and therefore its preservation as the foundation of the country's culture and tradition was wise. Consequently, while the general principle of liberty, especially religious liberty, was included in every state constitution, several permitted state funding of their nominally established churches[91] and had religious tests for office,[92] requiring an oath in the belief in Christianity or at least God. It was Christianity, many felt, that had inspired them to travel the path of resistance and liberty in the first place; Christianity had been Locke's own religious ground.

What did all this mean, however, in the face of an immediate history that reflected some of the most severe abuses that had been the consequence of the combination of religion and government—even Christianity and government? The answer was that it was not the authoritarian version of Christianity to which they appealed. It was not even all of anyone's *particular* Christianity to which they appealed. It was the "general principles" or "first precepts" of a "true" or "genuine" Christianity, which informed the foundations of the new nation.[93] The general principles of that true and genuine Christianity were understood to be the font of liberty on which the nation was founded. In other words, the true and genuine general principles of Christianity were those that were consistent with the natural law tradition of inalienable rights that Locke had advocated. As the *Updegraph* court said, it was "Christianity with liberty of conscience to all men" that prevailed. Not Christianity opposed to liberty.

Thus, many in the founding generation relied on the religiously grounded conception of human beings and their relationship with God, the roots of which in large part were in the Christian theology discussed earlier. Accordingly, it was understood that the governments of the states and the United States did not *grant* the people their civil rights. Rather, those rights were endowed by the Creator and merely *secured* in the founding documents; those rights were understood to be a part of what it is to be a human being. That is why those rights are "natural" and "inalienable." In other words, what often is thought to be the "secular" foundations of the nation involve a "religious" imperative for equal liberty as well, and together they constitute what can be termed the nation's "sacred ground." As Noah Webster said of the founding:

[T]he religion which has introduced civil liberty, is the religion of Christ and his apostles, which enjoins humility, piety and benevolence; which acknowledges in every person a brother, or a sister, and a citizen with equal rights. This is *genuine Christianity*, and to this we owe our free constitutions of government.[94]

Similarly, John Adams famously stated:

The *general principles*, on which the fathers achieved independence, were the only principles in which that beautiful Assembly of young men could unite, and these principles only could be intended by them in their address, or by me in my answer. And what were these general principles? I answer, the general principles of Christianity, in which all those sects were united: and the general principles of English and American Liberty, in which all those young men united, and which had united all parties in America, in majorities sufficient to assert and maintain her Independence.[95]

Likewise, John Quincy Adams said a generation later:

[T]he Declaration of Independence first organized the social compact [i.e., Locke's social contract] on the foundation of the Redeemer's mission on earth [and] laid the corner stone of human government upon the *first precepts* of Christianity.[96]

In other words, the privileged place for Christianity in the language of the era was *because* the general principles and first precepts of genuine Christianity were believed to support liberty.

In this regard, it is important to note that, even in those states with "establishments" and "tests," the role of church authority over the government institutions of those states was essentially nil, as the enforcement of orthodoxy had been abandoned by the end of the revolutionary period, and religious toleration was the norm.[97] That is, whatever pronouncements in the founding era regarding the importance of Christianity to the foundations of the nation, they did not imply an authority role for churches and their doctrines; just bounds between church and state prevailed. Furthermore, the existing weak state religious "establishments" were abolished for the most part by the end of the founding era. The Connecticut, New Hampshire, and Massachusetts establishments were abolished by 1818, 1819, and 1833, respectively. Religious tests for office were abandoned in more than a majority by 1800 and several states expressly prohibited them.[98]

Still, laws that later would be found to violate constitutional principles, such as blasphemy laws, and some states' religious tests for office continued to be upheld until much later.[99] That does not mean, however, that today we should consider returning to the ways of the past in its entirety in order to regain a former cultural hegemony, as some have argued.[100] Nor does it mean that references to Christianity from the past should dictate what should be the law of the land today. Rather, the founding generation set in motion a conversation about the meaning and extent of America's sacred ground: what customs and traditions from English common law and Christianity embedded in federal and state law are consistent with constitutional essentials and which are not? The institution of slavery provides an instructive case.[101]

Abolition: Christianity at the Crossroads of Liberty and Equal Dignity

Remnants of an old order prevailed in the new nation. Top-down authoritarian theologies that were inconsistent with the sacred ground of the nation justified oppression in some parts. Consequently, traditional religion and culture steeped in an ideology of hierarchical societal roles in a state enforced social order ran headlong into ideals enunciated in the founding era over the issue of slavery. However, the debate about slavery that took place in America before and during the founding era, and which was only resolved finally with a civil war, did not occur at the divide between secular and religious camps. Rather, religious arguments based on Christianity were made for and against the institution of slavery.

On one hand, abolitionists argued that slavery was contrary to fundamental laws of justice that originally derived from the belief in the liberty and equal dignity of every human person. Therefore, the enslavement of one man by another, making the former the "property" of the latter to be bought and sold, was thought to violate not only the legal principle of equal justice, but the moral tenets of Christianity, as well. For example, at their General Assembly in 1818, Presbyterians declared unanimously:

We consider the voluntary enslaving of one part of the human race by another as a gross violation of the most precious and sacred rights of human nature; as utterly inconsistent with the law of God . . . and as totally irreconcilable with the spirit and principles of the Gospel of Christ."[102]

On the other hand, an authoritarian Christianity bolstered the argument for slavery. The Bible was cited as evidence that slavery is legitimate. George D. Armstrong wrote in *The Christian Doctrine of Slavery* only a few years before the Civil War in 1857 that although wrongdoing may be found in the practice of slavery, the institution itself is not sinful because arguing otherwise would require "mak[ing] the Bible declare that slave-holding is a sin, when it plainly teaches just the contrary."[103] The continuance of the institution of slavery was consistent with the appropriate ordering of society, others argued. In a well-ordered society, when each plays his or her proper role, all are blessed. As Thomas Bacon said in a sermon to slaves in Maryland in 1749:

God hath appointed several offices and degrees in his family, as they are dispersed and scattered all over the face of the earth. Some he hath made masters and mistresses, for taking care of their children, and others that belong to them. . . . Some he hath made servants and slaves to assist and work for the masters and mistresses that provide for them; and others he hath made ministers and teachers to instruct. . . . [A]s Almighty God hath sent each of us into the world for some or other of these purposes, so, from the King, who is his head servant in a country, to the poorest slave, we are all obliged to do the business he hath set us about . . . And while you, whom he hath made slaves, are honestly and quietly doing your business, and living as poor Christians ought to do, you are serving God, in your low station, as much as the greatest prince alive, and will be as much favor shown you at the last day.[104]

Echoing this sentiment, Presbyterian James H. Thornwell (1812–1862) called abolitionists "Atheists, Socialists, Communists, Red Republicans, [and] Jacobins," while arguing that those who support the institution of slavery are "friends of order and regulated freedom . . . [who understand] the principles upon which the security of the social order and the development of humanity depend" because "the spirit of true obedience is universally the same."[105]

Slavery proponents even asserted that the separation of church and state should preserve the right to hold slaves. Because there were varying religious views, the state could not legitimately "impose" one view, that is abolition, on others, they argued. For example, Armstrong argued:

We object to the course proposed by [abolitionists], for dealing with slavery, because it requires the Church to obtrude herself into the province of the State, and this, in direct violation of the ordinance of God. . . . [Is it] right for the preacher, in the pulpit on the Sabbath, to discuss the claims of rival candidates, and the Church, in her councils to direct her members how to vote? The Church and State has each its own appropriate sphere of operation assigned it of God, and neither can innocently intrude herself into the province of the other.[106]

Yet what was at issue in this debate was not the state's authority to legislate on moral issues that also are in the purview of religion. Such a limitation was never the meaning of "just bounds" between, or "separation of," church and state. Most laws necessarily have moral dimensions that tread on religious territory. As we have seen, the foundational legal principles of the nation are religiously grounded, while serving secular, that is, "this worldly," purposes. These always were intended to be "imposed" on the people. What was at stake were the nation's sacred ground itself and the degree to which authoritarian claims on the basis of Christian precedent would be allowed to continue to supersede it.

Arriving at the answer tore the nation apart. But through speech, debate, and eventually war, the nation rejected all bases for enslavement and relied instead on the core principles of equal inherent dignity and liberty enunciated in the Declaration of Independence. An understanding of what the founders had set in motion reached a new consensus, however uneasy it was at first.

That understanding was not new, of course, and a similar story could be told regarding the rights of other minorities and the rights of women—and other stories are being written still. We have continued to refer back to the beginning and trace the development of our understanding from then to now as we have found our way through all of the crucibles, where America's sacred ground has been challenged and survived, and finds us where we are today: not devoid of all values as some would argue, and not full of all the Christian values of a particular authoritarian Christian ideology. Changing times and evolving policies have clarified the principled foundations of the nation. Those principles have not been rejected in favor of a conception of an authoritarian social order that trumps natural rights. Rather, it has been the appeal to those principles that has led America to "a more perfect union." By reaching back to the past, we have continued to forge the future on our sacred ground.

UNDERSTANDING THE FRAMEWORK, PRINCIPLES, AND PURPOSE OF OUR SACRED GROUND

It is often said that the U.S. Constitution does not provide any positive values on which to build the common good. Those holding this view note, for example, that the Bill of Rights, including the religion clauses, merely states what the government may *not* do—not what the people *should* do. However, based on what has been written here, it is not difficult to see that those holding that view really have missed the point: the religious ground of a system secured by "negative rights" is also a moral ground that serves the good.

Ours is not a nation with God at the top of a grand hierarchy speaking through ecclesiastical authorities aligned with the state to impose the law on the people from the top down. Ours is a nation with a sacred ground derived from the enlightened and religious conception of the relationship of the people to the ultimate. That is, God's relationship is not with society as a whole or with any particular organization in it. Rather, the idea and belief that stand behind the founding documents of the nation are that God and reason speak to individual people through conscience, and accordingly the people must be free to answer that call. Then, as individuals of conscience freely express themselves from the perspective conscience gives them, they participate in dialogue and debate—a great conversation—in the search for the true and the good. They find a way to work together to create the good society from the ground up.

To give effect to this, the American founders formed a social contract, which established a government by the people and for the people. Founded on the rule of law—the "higher law" from which the liberty and equal inherent dignity of the people derive, such government necessarily must be limited in its reach; absolute government is its antithesis. As a consequence, the intent and effect of such a government was the establishment of an open and free public space—a "public forum." To ensure that the public forum does not devolve into a Lockean "state of war—a "free-for-all" of competing interests where the powerful rise to the top and use their "freedom" to oppress and therefore limit the freedom of others—the public forum has a framework and principles. The people must honor these, if the system is to remain free for *all*. It is this framework and these principles to which we should turn in order to account for and mediate our differences if the system is going to fulfill its intended purpose: to make a better world.

As I have written in more detail elsewhere,[107] the public forum established by the founders has a framework that, in effect, consists of two tiers, each of which has certain basic moral precepts. Each tier creates a space for public participation of different scopes, and together the two tiers of the public forum make possible the people's pursuit of a good society as they continually strive toward a "more perfect union."[108]

The first tier of the public forum involves matters that are appropriate for law and public policy incorporated as fundamental through America's founding documents. These are matters appropriate for governmental action and, therefore, involve not only discussion about and promulgation of public policy, laws and regulations, but also adjudication of disputes and enforcement of the law. This tier, which I refer to as the "civic public forum," gives effect to John Locke's "impartial judge" of disputes. That is, it is the basis for the unbiased legal and political system that secures the people's natural rights and provides for the safety and general welfare of the people in a way that is consistent with their natural rights.

The civic public forum has, in effect, two foundational principles, which are grounded in liberty and equal inherent dignity. Because they are principles of the civic public forum, they can be thought of as being fundamental "laws." First is the law of no harm, which is derived from the overall principles of liberty and inherent dignity. That is, there is something inviolable about human beings that cannot legitimately be infringed, not even for the benefit of the commons. Consequently, the first law of the civic public forum is that no one may harm another in his or her life, liberty, or property. Now, of course, there may be differing views of the meaning of "harm," but the principle remains as an anchor for debates about law and public policy in the civic public forum. The non-harming law has a companion principle: the law of consistency/no hypocrisy. That is, do not do unto others what you would not want done unto you." This is Locke's reversed statement of the golden rule.[109] Law and public policy, their enforcement, and the adjudication of disputes involving them should strive for consistency in their application to everyone. In other words, they should recognize the equal inherent dignity of every human being and therefore serve equal justice.

The second tier of the public forum does not involve the authority and power of the state. It is the open and free space for persuasion and voluntary actions and acceptance regarding matters that do not involve law or public policy, or enforcement by the state. Nevertheless, matters for this forum are "public" in that they involve speech, debates, and actions that very much are, and were always intended to be, in the public eye.[110] That said, because they do not involve law or public policy, or enforcement by the state, they belong to an arena of persuasion and the voluntary activities of the people. This tier, which I refer to as the "conscientious public forum," creates the space for the exercise of the people's liberty of conscience beyond the purview of the state, and because government is limited, this is the greater of the two tiers of the public forum.

This conscientious public forum also has two fundamental principles. They are "duties" because they are not enforced by the state. That is, they are moral principles that must be adhered to voluntarily if the system is going to work the way it was intended and fulfill its purpose. First is the duty to raise conscience beyond one's own wants and desires to that higher someone or something—to God, to Universal Compassion, or Universal Reason, the Divine (however understood)—in a sincere effort to glean what conscience directs, not only for oneself, but for the betterment of one's society and even the world. Second, there is a duty to participate. After all, the system is based on trusting the people. Consequently, participation is central to the whole process conceived by Locke and the founders. But that participation should be accomplished not only by one's own speech and activity, but also by listening to the views of others, all with honesty and respect.

Moreover, as we have seen, religious voices were never meant to be suppressed in the great conversations of a legal/political system based on liberty and equal inherent dignity. The idea that society is divided into two spheres, one public and one private, with religion delegated to the private sphere where it is in effect hidden, is a wholly erroneous way to think about the participation of religion in the lives of the people. On the contrary, religious and non-religious voices alike were always meant to be welcomed in the two tiers of the public forum, and historically they have been. However, in both cases, to be legitimate, the participation must be consistent with the framework and principles of the legal/political system. That is, neither religious nor secular participants may legitimately invade the rights of others. Yet there is much room in the conscientious public forum for individuals and the communities they form and join—"communities of conscience"—to set what they believe are even higher standards than what mere law requires.[111]

We can see, then, that even though the founders created a limited government and, as a consequence, the Bill of Rights was framed in negative terms (i.e., what the government cannot do legitimately), when the founders framed the Constitution, they nevertheless grounded it in a framework and set of principles, which have a purpose: to make it possible for the people to build a good society. It is, then, a values-based constitution.

Accordingly, the founders' legal/political system, following Locke, does not produce a state that consists of an absolute authority. Locke and the founders well knew that authoritative governments never produce a society that in any way could be thought of as good. First of all, absolute government breeds corruption because absolute power tends to corrupt. Second, it results in discord because the oppressed always rise up in an effort to right the harms against them. As Jefferson said, "[It is] no wonder the oppressed should rebel, and they will continue to rebel and raise disturbance until their civil rights are full[y] restored to them and all partial distinctions, exclusions and incapacitations removed."[112] This had been Locke's thinking as well when he said, "[W]hat else can be expected but that these men, growing weary of the evils under which they labour, should in the end think it lawful for them to resist with force, and to defend their natural rights . . . with arms as well as they can?" In other words, absolute authority and its exercise of power often are the direct cause of unrest. Third, when absolute authority is based on religion, it necessarily involves a usurpation of God's authority, which, Locke and the American founders believed, is much more likely to be known by individuals through conscience than by authorities who often are corrupted by power.[113]

Still, government is not to be so limited that it provides no structure or values at all. Rather, there is what has been described here as the sacred ground, which is what creates the space for liberty and thereby becomes the framework of the two-tiers of the public forum and their corresponding principles. That is, the view that currently permeates large segments of American culture today that *no* values should be "imposed" on anyone in our multicultural society is misplaced. This is, of course, the idea that all morals are relative and that everyone is entitled to a morality unto himself. Instead, what has been shown here is that while it is true that the American legal/political system was designed to promote liberty and embrace diversity, it was never meant to promote an absolute moral relativity. Rather, it was meant to create the space where the exercise of virtue would be possible. Such a system has grounding principles, as we have seen. It is not a comprehensive moral order imposed on the people *in toto*. Yet, nevertheless, it has a moral framework that creates the public forum for debate about the moral good. Consequently, the system does not involve a complete free-floating moral relativism, on one hand, nor does it involve an absolute freedom-limiting moral absolutism, on the other hand. This system, with its values-based constitution, is a middle way.

In effect, then, what the founders wrought was a compromise between those who believed in the essential good nature of humankind and those suspicious of human beings' potential to be led astray by the intoxication of power. Consequently, no longer was trust placed in the rule of an absolute king through the auspices of the state; no longer was trust placed in the hands of ecclesiastical authorities. Now a government by the people and for the people would place its trust in the people engaged in the great conversations of the civic and conscientious public forums, anchored in the framework, principles, and purpose of the nation, not only about how to live together in peace considering their differences, but also in the ultimate search for the true and the good.

Hence, beyond its own values, the constitution and the legal/political system it established anticipate that a free people will use their freedom well. Released from the fetters of an authoritarian government, the people no longer are forced by the government into societal patterns at odds with conscience. The people are free to live a full life according to the "true faith," whatever that may be, and answer its call; the people can be and do all that they believe reflects the true and the good, so long as they do not violate the sacred ground of the nation. That is, the founders' legal/political system places the virtue of a free people at the heart of a nation that makes the pursuit of virtue possible. As James Madison said, "To suppose that any form of government will secure liberty or happiness without any virtue in the people is a chimerical idea."[114] That is, it is *an illusion*. And John Adams said, "Our constitution was made only for a moral and religious people. It is wholly inadequate to the government of any other." In other words, it is *because* the government is limited—not dictating a unified conception of the true and the good—that the true and the good must come from the people. Otherwise, as I have said elsewhere:

If enough of us do not [fulfill] the conscientious moral principles, then we will end up proving our founders wrong: a society of free individuals does not promote the good—not even as separately conceived by society's various constituents; it promotes a licentious society where individuals have no regard for their nation and its future, only themselves. When that happens—when we have lost sight of what freedom was for—we will surely be in danger of losing the liberties that the founders and all of our forbears fought so hard to give to "ages and millions yet unborn."[115]

Unless the people are raising their minds and hearts to something greater than themselves—to God or Universal Reason or Universal Compassion or the Divine (however they each understand that)—and discerning what conscience wants of them and bringing that to the public forum, the system cannot fulfill its intended purpose: to make a better world. In other words, freedom is not for our own happiness; it is for the happiness of everyone.

CONCLUSION

Clearly, America did not live up to its ideal at the founding. Yet it is an ideal worth keeping, because it has not been the rejection of the original sacred ground of the nation that has led us through the trials of our nation. The abolition of slavery, gaining women's rights, the civil rights movement and its resulting historic legislation, and more have been accomplished by *appealing* to our sacred ground. Accordingly, today the issue regarding the founders' original intentions and American identity is not: how do we return to the way things were or were understood to be at the time of the founding? Surely, we do not want to return to the days of oppressive laws that supported slavery and subjugated women and others. The issue is: how do we identify and keep what is essential to our sacred ground—the framework, principles, and purpose of our nation—while taking account of new insights and new or newly understood circumstances?

Unfortunately, however, rather than having a conversation about this question, the debate itself has been framed in other terms, terms that undermine the foundations of the legal/political system the founders bequeathed to the nation. On one hand, many argue that the U.S. Constitution is a Christian document and that ours is a Christian nation. On the other hand, others argue that it is wholly secular. Yet it is a mistake to think that references to Christianity at the time of the founding mean that there were no bounds between church and state; it is also a mistake to appeal to an absolutist secular authority that eschews and marginalizes religion and therefore undermines religious liberty. Both tend toward the top-down absolute authority that the American founders repudiated.

Rather, the way we should understand the debate today is that we are continuing to have the conversation we always have had in America—a debate about the line between governing authority, on the one hand, and the authority of conscience, on the other hand. But what grounds those authorities should not be in dispute: it is our sacred ground founded by the people and for the people. Consequently, rather than arguing about whether or not the nation is based on Christianity or secular Enlightenment Era sources, we ought to understand that it is both, but at the same time neither in absolute terms. In other words, the debate is really about the line between the civic and conscientious public forums. And we can only negotiate that line legitimately by reference to our fundamental values: liberty, equal inherent dignity, non-harming, consistency/no hypocrisy (i.e., impartiality and equal justice), raising conscience, and participation with honesty and respect. Surely, debates on the line are difficult, but not more difficult today than they always have been.

Is our nation a nation under God? Perhaps so, if by that we mean that historically our nation is grounded in certain principles that derive from religion as well as secular ideas. Perhaps not, if we mean that God is at the top of a grand hierarchy with a Christian president as the nation's interpreter of God's will. Should the Ten Commandments be posted on public property? Perhaps so, if we mean that there are general moral principles on which the nation stands. Perhaps not, if we mean that the law of the land includes the injunction that "you shall have no other gods before me" or that the law must be based on the Bible. Should minority religions' practices receive exceptions to laws that are generally applicable to everyone? Perhaps not, when those "laws of general applicability" are truly neutral and are necessary to secure the natural rights of the people and to ensure their safety and general welfare. Perhaps so, if those laws involve traditions and customs that stem from majoritarian religious beliefs. Should homosexuals be permitted to become legally married? Should abortion be legal? Should political leaders use religious language and metaphor to make their points? Should religious schools receive public funds?

Whatever the issue facing us today, as the conversations proceed we have a responsibility to refer back again and again to our touchstone, our sacred ground, whether we think of it as being religious or not. Then when we have our continuing conversations and debates about the reach of government and the authority of conscience, we will not abandon all tradition for progress or all progress for tradition. Instead, we will remember to understand church and state in context as we keep the ship of state anchored in what makes all of the conversations possible in the first place, always remembering that the dichotomy that counts is not religious vs. secular or absolute vs. relative—but is liberty and equal dignity vs. dominance. If we always return to our sacred ground, we can apply its principles to the shifting circumstances of our own time and of the future without unmooring the whole project from what gives us our core identity. This is what we largely have accomplished over time. We should do no less today.

NOTES

1. U.S. Const., Amend. 1.
2. See, e.g., *Church of Holy Trinity v. U.S.*, 143 U.S. 457 (1892); *Everson v. Board of Education* (1947); *Marsh v. Chambers*, 463 U.S. 783 (1983); *Wallace v. Jaffree*, 472 U.S. 38 (1985) (J. Rehnquist, dissenting).
3. Roger Williams, "Mr. Cotton's Letter Lately Printed, Examined and Answered," *The Complete Writings of Roger Williams*, vol. 1, p. 108 (1644).
4. John Adams, "To the Officers of the First Brigade of the Third Division of the Militia of Massachusetts," 11 October 1789, *The Works of John Adams, Second President of the United States with a life of the author, notes and illustrations*, compiled by Charles Francis Adams, 10 vols., vol. 9 (Boston: Charles C. Little & James Brown, 1850–1856), 228–229. (Hereafter *Adams Works*.)
5. At the time of the founding the word "secular" did not have the meaning it has today in common usage: non-religious. Instead, secular referenced "this-worldly" matters. Having been derived from Latin word "*saeculum*," which means literally "time" or "age," the word "secular" means "of this time," in other words of this world, as distinguished from matters of eternity. Consequently, it would have been possible to speak of religious matters that are secular, that is, focused on

this world in the here and now. Furthermore, the word "religion" also did not have the meaning it has today, which includes the institutions of religion, that is "objective systematic entities," for example, churches. Rather, "religion" meant personal piety and relationship with God or, at most, a system of beliefs, practices, and values. For more on this, see Barbara A. McGraw, *Rediscovering America's Sacred Ground* (Albany: State University of New York Press, 2003), 185–188, discussing Wilfred Cantwell Smith's classic work *The Meaning and End of Religion* (1962; Minneapolis: Fortress Press, 1991).

6. Thomas Jefferson, *The Writings of Thomas Jefferson*, Albert E. Bergh, ed. (Washington, D.C.: The Thomas Jefferson Memorial Association of the United States, 1904), vol. 16, pp. 281–282.

7. James Madison, "To Thomas Jefferson," 24 October 1787, *The Writings of James Madison*, ed. Gaillard Hunt, 9 vols., vol. 5 (New York, London: G.P. Putnam's Sons, 1900–1903), 30–31.

8. Thomas Jefferson, "A Bill for Establishing Religious Freedom," submitted to the Virginia General Assembly 1779, enacted in an edited form in 1789, *The Complete Jefferson: Containing His Major Writings, Published and Unpublished, Except His Letters*, ed. Saul K. Padover (New York: Duell, Sloan & Pearce, 1943), 946. [Hereafter *The Complete Jefferson*.]

9. See generally, Pauline Marie Rosenau, *Post-Modernism and the Social Sciences: Insights, Inroads, and Intrusions* (Princeton: Princeton University Press, 1992).

10. Robert S. Ellwood and Barbara A. McGraw, *Many Peoples, Many Faiths: Women and Men in the World Religions*, 8th ed. (Upper Saddle River, NJ: Prentice-Hall, 2005), 31, 44–50.

11. Ibid., 17.

12. Gregory VII, in what has been called the "Gregorian Reform" (1075–1122), asserted ultimate authority over church and state. Harold J. Berman, *Law and Revolution: The Formation of the Western Legal Tradition* (Cambridge, MA and London: Harvard University Press, 1983), 87. This understanding has roots in early Christianity, however. Christianity began as one of the many religions practiced in ancient Rome. However, Christians believed that their God was not of place or state, but stood above as God of the whole world, the universe. As a consequence, Christians refused to place the emperor—who Rome held to be the divine head of Rome—above their God. This is a main reason they came to be persecuted there. Consequently, one could argue that the idea of a religion being separate from the state actually evolved out of early Christian religious beliefs. See John Dominic Crossan and Jonathan L. Reed, *In Search of Paul: How Jesus' Apostle Opposed Rome's Empire with God's Kingdom* (New York: HarperCollins Publishers, Inc., 2004).

13. John Neville Figgis, *The Divine Right of Kings* (1896; Cambridge, UK: Cambridge University Press, 1922), 45–49.

14. Berman, *Law and Revolution*, 145, quoting Gratian, *A Concordance of Discordant Canons* (1140): "[T]he law of princes ought not to prevail over natural law." Even the pope's power "was limited . . . by natural and positive divine law [that is,

divine law laid down in the Bible and in similar documents of revelation]." Ibid., 99. See also ibid., 214.

15. Figgis, *Divine Right of Kings*, 58.
16. Ibid., 50–51, 65.
17. Ibid., 45.
18. The "divine right of kings" involved a "widespread" belief, which consisted of "the following propositions: (1) Monarchy is a divinely ordained institution. (2) Hereditary right is indefeasible . . . The right acquired by birth cannot be forfeited . . . (3) Kings are accountable to God alone . . . (4) Non-resistance and passive obedience are enjoined by God." Figgis, *The Divine Right of Kings*, 5–6. Furthermore, European emperors and kings generally claimed authority over popes and bishops. As Harold J. Berman has said, "The emperor [e.g., Charlemagne or Henry IV] claimed to be the supreme spiritual leader of Christendom, whom no man could judge, but who himself judged all men . . . " Berman, *Law and Revolution*, 89.
19. Ibid., 60, 65.
20. Gratian, an immensely influential Bolognese monk, divided the canon laws into a hierarchy of categories, each lower category being subject to the categories above: divine law ("the will of God reflected in revelation, especially the revelation of Holy Scripture"); natural law (found in "divine revelation and in human reason and conscience"); ecclesiastical laws and enactments; the laws and enactment of princes (secular authorities); and customs. Berman, *Law and Revolution*, 143, citing Gratian, *A Concordance of Discordant Canons* (1140). From this hierarchical division the idea that temporal laws could be "unjust laws" emerged. *Cf.* Anton C. Pegis, ed., *Introduction to St. Thomas Aquinas* (New York: Modern Library, 1848), 530, 542, 622.
21. David Wootton, "Introduction," in *Political Writings of John Locke* (New York: Mentor, 1993), 65.
22. Ibid.
23. This conception of human beings was evidenced in the work of St. Anselm and memorialized by Gratian (see note 20 *supra*), later espoused by Aquinas, and further developed in the modern period as liberalism took hold. See Berman, *Law and Revolution*, 159; Francis Oakley, *Natural Law, Laws of Nature, Natural Rights: Continuity and Discontinuity in the History of Ideas* (New York, London: Continuum, 2005), 70–72.
24. "[T]he canon lawyers laid a legal foundation for . . . resistance." Berman, *Law and Revolution*, 214. "[W]hen he who is chosen to defend the good and hold the evil in check himself begins to cherish wickedness, to stand out against good men, to exercise most cruelly over his subjects the tyranny which he was bound to combat; is it not clear that he justly forfeits the dignity conceded to him and the people stand free of his rule and subjection, since it is evident that he was the first to violate the compact on account of which he was made the ruler?" McIlwain, *Growth of Political Thought*, 209–210, quoting Manegold of Lautenbach (died c. 1103).
25. See, e.g., *Magna Carta* (1215); *Petition of Right* (1628); *Bill of Rights* (1689).
26. John Locke, *A Letter Concerning Toleration*, trans. William Popple (1685,

published 1689), *Political Writings of John Locke*, ed. David Wootton (London: Mentor, 1993), 397. [Hereafter *Letter Concerning Toleration*.]

27. "[S]he [truth] is the proper and sufficient antagonist to error, and has nothing to fear from the conflict unless by human interposition [she is] disarmed of her natural weapons, free argument and debate; errors ceasing to be dangerous when it is permitted freely to contradict them." Thomas Jefferson, "A Bill for Establishing Religious Freedom," 1779, *The Complete Jefferson*, 947.

28. John Locke, *Of Civil Government, Two Treatises of Government, The Works of John Locke*, 9 vols. vol. 4, Ch. II, ¶ 6, p. 341; Ch. XIII, ¶¶ 151–152, pp. 427–428 [Hereafter *Second Treatise*]; Locke, *Reasonableness of Christianity*, ed. George W. Ewing (Washington, D.C.: Regnery Gateway, 1965), ¶ 252, p. 192–193.

29. Locke, *Second Treatise*, Ch. II, ¶ 13, p. 345–346; Ch. III, ¶¶ 20–21, pp. 349–350.

30. Locke, *Second Treatise*, Ch. III, ¶ 16, p. 347.

31. Ibid.

32. Locke, *Letter Concerning Toleration*, 390.

33. Locke, *Second Treatise*, Ch. II, ¶ 13, p. 345–346; Ch. III, ¶¶ 20–21, pp. 349–350.

34. Locke, *Second Treatise*, Ch. VIII, ¶¶ 95–122, p. 394–411; Ch. XIV, ¶ 168, pp. 438–439.

35. Locke, *Letter Concerning Toleration*, 393.

36. "[E]veryone's sin is charged upon himself only." Locke, *Reasonableness of Christianity*, ¶ 4, p. 4; Locke, *Second Treatise*, generally.

37. Locke, *Of Government, Two Treatises of Government, The Works of John Locke*, 9 vols, vol. 4, Ch. IX, ¶ 86, p. 279. [Hereafter *First Treatise* and *Works*.]

38. Barbara A. McGraw, *Rediscovering America's Sacred Ground* (Albany: State University of New York Press, 2003), 26, citing Locke, *A Second Vindication of the Reasonableness of Christianity, Works*, 357; Locke *Reasonableness of Christianity*, ¶ 155, p. 114; Locke, *Essay on Human Understanding, Works*, Book IV. Ch. XIX, ¶ 4, vol. II, p. 273; Locke *First Treatise*, ¶ 86, p. 279; Locke, ¶¶ 39–40, pp. 24–26. See also Locke, *Reasonableness of Christianity*, ¶ 238, pp. 165–166; ¶ 241, pp. 169–172; ¶ 243, pp. 178, 180.

39. Locke, *Letter Concerning Toleration*, 431.

40. Locke, *Second Treatise*, generally.

41. Locke, *Letter Concerning Toleration*, 420–421.

42. Ibid., 401, 409, 417. "True religion consists in the inward persuasion of the mind." Ibid., 394. "[Tolerance is] the chief characteristical mark of the true church." Ibid., 390.

43. However, Locke's toleration did not extend to atheists nor to those who are intolerant. Locke, *Letter Concerning Toleration*, 426.

44. Ibid., 390.

45. Ibid., 420.

46. Ibid., 412, 420, 431.

47. Ibid., 431.
48. Ibid., 416.
49. Ibid., 400, 417, 431.
50. Ibid., 431.
51. Ibid., 402, 420.
52. Locke, *Essay on Human Understanding, Works,* vol. 2, Book IV, Ch. XIX, ¶ 4, p. 273.
53. Locke, *Letter Concerning Toleration,* 401.
54. Thomas Jefferson "copied long passages from Locke's *Letter Concerning Toleration* in his commonplace notebook, and used many of Locke's ideas and phrases in his own writing on the need for religious freedom." Charles B. Sanford, *Thomas Jefferson and His Library: A Study of His Literary Interests and of the Religious Attitudes Revealed by Relevant Titles in His Library* (Hamden, CT: Archon Books, 1977), 121. "[The colonists] thought themselves at full liberty . . . to establish such sort of government as they thought proper, and to form a new state as full to all intents and purposes as if they had been in a state of nature, and were making their first entrance into civil society. Bernard Schwartz, "Commentary" in *The Bill of Rights: A Documentary History,* ed. Bernard Schwartz (New York, Toronto, London, Sydney: Chelsea House Publishers, 1971) [hereafter *Documentary History*], 179, quoting a 1764 statement by Thomas Hutchinson (then Lieutenant Governor of Massachusetts). The colonists' writings clearly showed a debt to the writings of John Locke. See also, e.g., Samuel Adams, "The Rights of the Colonists and a List of Infringements and Violations of Rights" in *Documentary History*, 200–211.
55. See Harry S. Stout, "George Whitefield in Three Countries," *Evangelicalism: Comparative Studies of Popular Protestantism . . . . 1700–1900,* eds. Mark A. Noll, et al. (New York, Oxford: Oxford University Press, 1994), generally. See also John Boles, *The Great Revival, 1787–1805: The Origins of the Southern Evangelical Mind* (Lexington: University Press of Kentucky, 1972), 40.
56. Ibid., 63, 69.
57. James H. Hutson, *Religion and the Founding of the American Republic* (Washington, D.C.: Library of Congress, 1998), 39–42.
58. See, e.g., John Toland, *Christianity Not Mysterious* (London, 1696). Instead, those founders generally thought to be deists believed that God has a hand in history. McGraw, *Rediscovering America's Sacred Ground,* 70–71, quoting various founders.
59. Sanford, *Thomas Jefferson and His Library,* 150, citing Henry Stephens Randall, *The Life of Thomas Jefferson,* 3 vols., vol. 3 (New York: Derby & Jackson, 1858), 407–410, quoting Jefferson's grandson. Benjamin Franklin indicated that he had a belief in God and that God plays a role in human affairs when he said: "I have lived, Sir, a long time; and the longer I live, the more convincing proofs I see of this Truth—*that God governs in the Affairs of Men.* And if a Sparrow cannot fall to the Ground without his Notice, is it probable that an Empire can rise with his Aid?" Benjamin Franklin, "Motion for Prayers in the Convention," 28 June 1787, *Benjamin Franklin Writings,* ed. J.A. Leo Lemay (New York: The Library of

America, 1987), 1138–1139 (emphasis in original). Similarly, John Adams declared his belief in the intervention of God into human affairs when, in his proclamation for a national day of fasting, he stated: "[There is] the governing providence of a Supreme Being and of the accountableness of men to Him as the searcher of hearts and the righteous distributor of rewards and punishments . . . " eds. Paul H. Smith, et al., *Letters of Delegates to Congress 1774–1789*, 25 vols. (Washington, D.C.: Government Printing Offices, 1876–1998), 311–312.

60. See, e.g., James Winthrop, "Letter of Agrippa," 1788, *Documentary History*, 517; Thomas Jefferson, "A Bill for Establishing Religious Freedom," 1779, *The Complete Jefferson*, 947.

61. *Declaration of Independence* (1776).

62. Nathon O. Hatch, *The Sacred Cause of Liberty: Republican Thought and the Millennium in Revolutionary New England* (New Haven & London: Yale University Press, 1977), 11–13, 16–17. See also Hutson, *Religion and the Founding of the American Republic*, 39–42.

63. McGraw, *Rediscovering America's Sacred Ground*, 65.

64. Declaration of Independence (1776).

65. U.S. Const., Preamble.

66. Declaration of Independence (1776)

67. Thomas Paine, *Common Sense* (1776).

68. John Adams, *Adams Works*, vol. 4, p. 230; Massachusetts Constitution (1780), art. 30.

69. See, e.g., Montesquieu, *The Spirit of the Laws* (1748).

70. George Washington, "To the Hebrew Congregation," 18 August 1790, *The Papers of George Washington*, Presidential Series, ed. Dorothy Twohig, et al. 7 vols., vol. 6 (Charlottesville, VA: University Press of Virginia, 1987–2000), 284–285.

71. *Documentary History*, 201.

72. Richard Henry Lee, "To James Madison," 26 November 1784, eds. Robert A. Rutland, et al. *The Papers of James Madison*, 17 vols., vol. 8 (Chicago and London: University of Chicago Press; Charlottesville: University Press of Virginia, 1961–1999), 149.

73. Thomas Jefferson, "Notes on Religion," October 1776, *The Complete Jefferson*, 945.

74. Thomas Jefferson, Autobiography, *The Complete Jefferson*, 1147.

75. Thomas Jefferson, "Notes on Religion," October 1776, *The Complete Jefferson*, 945.

76. Richard Henry Lee, "Observations Leading to a Fair Examination of the System of Government," Letter IV, 12 October 1787, *Letters from a Federal Farmer*, 28.

77. Thomas Jefferson, "A Bill for Establishing Religious Freedom," *The Complete Jefferson*, 947.

78. John Adams, "To Thomas Jefferson," 28 June 1813, *Adams Works*, vol. 10, pp. 45–46.

79. John Dickenson, *Letters of Fabius*, 1788, *Documentary History*, 546.

Introduction: Church and State in Context • 37

80. See Mark Douglas McGarvie, *One Nation Under Law: America's Early National Struggles to Separate Church and State* (DeKalb: Northern Illinois Press, 2004).

81. "The constitutional amendments proposed by Madison were the logical culmination of what had gone before in both English and American constitutional history. In particular, the federal Bill of Rights was based directly on upon the great Charters of English liberty, which begin with the *Magna Carta* [1215]." Bernard Schwartz, "Commentary," in *Documentary History*, 3.

82. See, e.g., "The Declaration of Rights of the Stamp Act Congress" (1765): "[I]t is inseparably essential to the freedom of a people, and the undoubted rights of Englishmen, that no taxes should be imposed on them, but with their consent . . . " See also, e.g., Samuel Adams, "The Rights of the Colonists and a List of Infringements and Violations of Rights" in *Documentary History*, 202: "The absolute rights of Englishmen and all freemen, in or out of civil society, are principally personal security, personal liberty, and private property."

83. See generally, Alain Cabantous, *Blasphemy: Impious Speech in the West from the Seventeenth to the Nineteenth Century*, trans. Eric Rauth (New York: Columbia University Press, 2002); George Nokes, *A History of the Crime of Blasphemy* (London: Sweet & Maxwell, 1928); David Lawton, *Blasphemy* (Hemel Hempstead: Harvester, 1993), Leonard Levy, *Blasphemy: Verbal Offence Against the Sacred, from Moses to Salman Rushdie* (Chapel Hill: University of North Carolina Press, 1995).

84. There were many challenges to blasphemy laws on constitutional grounds well into the nineteenth century and even a few into the twentieth century. See, e.g., *The People v. Ruggles* (1811). It has been reported that the last blasphemy case resulting in jailing the defendant was in *Commonwealth of Massachusetts v. Kneeland* (1838). Leonard Levy, *Blasphemy in Massachusetts: Freedom of Conscience and the Abner Kneeland Case—a Documentary Record* (New York: Da Capo, 1973). In *Joseph Burstyn, Inc. v. Wilson*, 343 U.S. 495 (1952), the U.S. Supreme Court held that a New York State statute "authoriz[ing] denial of a license on a censor's conclusion that a film is 'sacrilegious'" was held to be "void as a prior restraint on freedom speech and of the press under the First Amendment." Nearly two decades later, in *State v. West* (1970), the Maryland Court of Appeals overturned the defendant's 1968 blasphemy conviction on the basis that the law violated the First Amendment, 263 A.2d 602 (Md. App., 1970). That case involved the last conviction for blasphemy in the United States. See Leonard W. Levy, *Blasphemy: Verbal Offense*. Interestingly, blasphemy codes remain on the law books in some states to this day, even though they no longer are enforced. See, e.g., Massachusetts General Law, Chapter 272, Section 36; http://mass.gov/legis/ laws/mgl/272-36.htm (accessed July 20, 2007).

85. William Blackstone, *Commentaries on the Laws of England* (Oxford: Clarendon Press, 1769).

86. Blackstone, vol. 4, p. 59.

87. *Updegraph v. The Commonwealth,* 11 Serg. & R. 393, 394 (1824), quoted

in David Barton, *The Myth of Separation: What is the Correct Relationship between Church and State?* (Aledo, TX: WallBuilder Press, 1992), 50.

88. *Updegraph v. The Commonwealth*, 11 Serg. & R. 393, 406–407, quoted in Barton, *Myth of Separation*, 55.

89. Ibid., 54.

90. *Documentary History*, 277.

91. Nine of the thirteen original colonies gave tax aid to their "established" churches prior to and at the time of the founding. John K. Wilson, "Religion Under the State Constitutions, 1776–1800," *Journal of Church and State* 32, no. 4 (1990): 754.

92. For example, Pennsylvania required the following oath before one could serve in that state's house of representatives: "I do believe in one God, the creator and governor of the universe, the rewarder of the good and the punisher of the wicked. And I do acknowledge the Scriptures of the Old and New Testaments to be given by Divine inspiration." *Documentary History,* 273. Similarly, the South Carolina Constitution (1778), which expressly established the Protestant Christian religion, required members of the state senate and house of representatives to be "all of the Protestant religion." Ibid., 326. The only states that did not have religious tests at the time of the founding were Virginia and New York. However, by 1792, religious tests were prohibited in Georgia, Delaware, Vermont, Tennessee. Wilson, "Religion Under State Constitutions," 765.

93. See, e.g., notes 94–96 *infra* and accompanying text.

94. Noah Webster, *History of the United States* (New Haven: Durrie & Peck, 1832), 300, ¶ 578, quoted in Barton, *Myth of Separation*, 125 (emphasis added).

95. John Adams, "To Thomas Jefferson," 28 June 1813, *Adams Works*, vol. 10, pp. 45–46 (emphasis added).

96. John Quincy Adams, *The Writings of John Quincy Adams*, ed. Worthington C. Ford (New York: The Macmillan Company, 1914), vol. 4, p. 215, quoted in Barton, *Myth of Separation*, 125 (emphasis added).

97. Edwin S. Gaustad and Leigh E. Schmidt, *The Religious History of America: The Heart of the American Story from Colonial Times to Today* revised ed. (San Francisco: HarperSanFrancisco), 123; Leonard W. Levy, *The Establishment Clause, Religion and the First Amendment*, 2nd ed. (Chapel Hill and London: The University of North Carolina Press, 1994), 146–147.

98. Wilson, "Religion Under State Constitutions," 753–763.

99. See note 84 *supra* and accompanying text.

100. Baron, *Myth of Separation*, passim.

101. The resolution of the issue of slavery and efforts after the Civil War to provide equal protection of the laws and due process rights to everyone regardless of race, among other things, resulted in the Fourteenth Amendment to the U.S. Constitution. Later, the U.S. Supreme Court held that the First Amendment and the other rights of the Bill of Rights were applicable to the states through the Fourteenth Amendment via the "incorporation doctrine." See e.g. *Cantwell v. Connecticut,* 310 U.S. 296 (1940) and *Everson v. Board of Education*, 330 U.S. 1 (1947).

102. Quoted in Gaustad and Schmidt, *Religious History of America*, 184.

103. George D. Armstrong, *The Christian Doctrine of Slavery* (New York: Scribner, 1857), 131–148. In *Religion in American History: A Reader*, ed. Jon Butler and Harry S. Stout (New York, Oxford: Oxford University Press, 1998), 236.

104. Thomas Bacon, *Two Sermons, Preached to a Congregation of Black Slaves, at the Parish Church of S[aint] P[eter's], in the Province of Maryland* (London, 1749), 7–38. In *Religion in American History*, ed. Jon Butler and Harry S. Stout (New York: Oxford University Press, 1998), 74–87. [Edited to modernize punctuation, capitalization, and spelling.]

105. Quoted in Gaustad and Schmidt, *Religious History of America*, 191.

106. Armstrong, *Christian Doctrine of Slavery*. In Butler and Stout, *Religion in American History*, 236.

107. McGraw, *Rediscovering America's Sacred Ground*, 91–105.

108. Declaration of Independence (1776).

109. McGraw, *Rediscovering America's Sacred Ground*, 55.

110. The commonly referred to public/private divide obscures the "public" function of the conscientious public forum. See ibid., 50–54.

111. Ibid., 125.

112. Thomas Jefferson, "Notes on Religion," October 1776, *The Complete Jefferson*, 946.

113. Locke, *Letter Concerning Toleration*, 409, 417; Jefferson, "A Bill for Establishing Religious Freedom." In *The Complete Jefferson*, 946. See also McGraw, *Rediscovering America's Sacred Ground*, 31–32.

114. James Madison, "Speech in the Virginia Ratifying Convention," 20 June 1788. *The Papers of James Madison*, edited by Robert A. Rutland et al., 17 vols., vol. 11, p. 163.

115. McGraw, *Rediscovering America's Sacred Ground*, 98.

FURTHER READING

For more on this author's views on the ideological grounding of the United States and the states, including church-state relations and the role of religion in public life, see Barbara A. McGraw, *Rediscovering America's Sacred Ground: Public Religion and Pursuit of the Good in a Pluralistic America* (Albany: State University of New York Press, 2003). For an interesting polemic that presents a view that opposes the one in this introductory chapter and this author's other work, see David Barton's *The Myth of Separation: What is the Correct Relationship between Church and State?* (Aledo, TX: WallBuilder Press, 1992). To explore further some of the historical themes presented in the beginning of this introductory chapter, study Harold J. Berman's historical analysis of the West's legal tradition in his highly-regarded *Law and Revolution: The Formation of the Western Legal Tradition* (Cambridge and London: Harvard University Press, 1983), which locates that legal tradition's roots in the papal revolution, as well as the revolution of jurisprudence arising out of feudal and royal systems. For a challenging account of the development of the political philosophy of John Locke, see John Marshall's *John Locke: Resistance, Religion, and Responsibility* (Cambridge: Cambridge University Press, 1994). For thorough accounts of the ideological origins of the United States, see Bernard Bailyn's *The Ideological Origins of the American Revolution*, enlarged ed. (1967 Cambridge, MA and London: The Belknap Press of Harvard University Press, 1992), which argues that republicanism was the most significant influence, and Huyler, Jerome's *Locke in America: The Moral Philosophy of the Founding Era* (Lawrence: University of Kansas Press, 1995), which argues that the nation's ideological origins, including republicanism, are found in the fundamentals of John Locke's liberalism. For an explanation and critique of the current debate between philosophers of democratic liberalism and theological traditionalism, see Jeffrey Stout's *Democracy and Tradition* (Princeton: Princeton University Press, 2004), which argues that democracy is not opposed to tradition, but is itself a tradition, which when understood as such makes possible finding common ground. For a thorough analysis of U.S. Supreme Court jurisprudence on issues involving the role of religion in public life and the degree to which church-state separation has evolved since the nation's founding, see James Hitchcock's *The Supreme Court and Religion in American Life: Volume II From "Higher Law" to "Sectarian Scruples"* (Princeton and Oxford: Princeton University Press, 2004), the second in a two volume series. For an interesting study of Revolutionary Era political thought at the state level, see Mark W. Kruman's *Between Authority and Liberty: State Constitution Making in Revolutionary America* (Chapel Hill and London: The University of North Carolina Press, 1997), which argues that power, even in the hands of elected state legislative representatives, was distrusted and therefore limited. For a worthy discussion of how Contracts Clause, Art. I, U.S. Constitution jurisprudence illuminates U.S. church-state jurisprudence generally, see Mark Douglas McGarvie, *One Nation Under Law: America's Early National Struggles to Separate Church and State* (DeKalb: Northern Illinois University Press, 2004).

1

Historical Perspectives on Church and State

Richard Bowser and Robin Muse

Religion, as most recognize, is an exceedingly potent force in virtually every society. In its authentic forms, it supplies answers to great questions regarding the meaning of life. As such it shapes and molds individuals. It commits them to thoughts and actions that profoundly affect their lives and their life together as a community. Religion is not only an active force, but also a resisting force.[1] It supplies the vision that permits folks who are of little cultural regard to stand against the most compelling of people and institutions. From Peter and later Paul before the Sanhedrin to Fannie Lou Hamer before Lyndon Johnson and Hubert Humphrey,[2] religious believers have stood against those in power, resisting the attempt to press upon them the society's answer to the questions of the meaning of life.

How should government treat the religious beliefs and the religious institutions of a society? Should it seek to affirm some beliefs and suppress others? If so on what basis does it make that choice? Should government, because of the difficulty of selection seek to affirm all? There is good reason to conclude that it cannot. In light of that impossibility, should government seek to affirm no religious beliefs or values at all? Such a position seems to deny the reality of the influence of such ideas in shaping visions of the common good that are shared by the governed. Should government affirm that which seems to be common to all? Some have suggested that such an approach only enshrines as governmentally approved a religion that few if any espouse. Should government affirm only those ideas and norms that appear to have been harvested from non-religious or secular seed? That only raises the philosophical question, is secularism only another religion because it purports to give an answer to questions regarding the meaning of life?

In the United States, these deeply important questions not only have a political dimension, they have a constitutional dimension because the opening sentence of the First Amendment to our Constitutional document provides the following: *"Congress shall make no law respecting the establishment of religion or prohibiting the free exercise thereof."* The Religion Clauses,[3] first made applicable to the federal government and then through the Fourteenth Amendment made applicable to the states,[4] are the principle points of constitutional reference in these matters.[5]

The interpretation and application of this sentence has not been easy. The words and phrases themselves have an enigmatic quality about them.[6] Why would the drafters chose to use the word "respecting?" What was in view when they used the word "establishment?" By "religion" did they mean Christian denomination, Christian and non-Christian theism, or one's "ultimate concern?" Partly as a result of the lack of precision with the words and partly as a result of a dispute about constitutional interpretation generally,[7] the Supreme Court has struggled to find coherent and consistent models of interpretation and application for the clauses. In fact, it has been suggested by some that the clauses operate in tension with each other, so much so that to advance the purpose of one clause is sometimes understood to mitigate the value sought to be advanced by the other. Before considering the competing models of interpretation, it will be helpful to consider what animated the framing generation's inclusion of the Religion Clauses in the First Amendment.[8]

The framers of the First Amendment would have been familiar with the establishment of religion. The Church of England was the established religion of the British Empire. Nine of the thirteen colonies had established churches at the time of the Revolution and approximately one-half of the states continued to have some form of established church when the First Amendment was ratified.[9] While establishment of religion was not monolithic in all details,[10] it generally included the government's control over what could be taught and who could teach it. With that control came a prohibition of teaching other doctrine. Such establishment generally would have included a prominent position for church leaders in the political structure of the government. For example, bishops in the Anglican Church sat in the House of Lords. This type of establishment would have also required the citizens to attend church and to support through taxes the work and ministry of the church.[11]

With this as their history, the founding generation supported the disestablishment of religion in the U.S. government. While the disestablishment announced in the First Amendment applied only to the federal government and worked only to retain the status quo with regard to the federal government and religion,[12] the conviction regarding religious liberty that disestablishment represents applied much more broadly. There were, as there are today, a number of sources for a commitment to religious freedom. Some grounded their commitment to religious liberty in their theological convictions; others found the source in political utility. Each different starting point, as well as their collective operation, provided a perspective that not only shaped the perceived contours of religious liberty at the time, but also set a course for its development for years to come. Considering the various sources for a commitment to religious liberty also helps to fight against the tendency to reductionism—a tendency to see the shaping of religious liberty through a single lens or according to a single metaphor, for example, as a wall of separation. The situation at the time of the Constitution ratification is much too complex for that.

While there was a full spectrum of views of religion and society at the end of the eighteenth century, it is helpful to consider at least four views that were represented within the political and theological communities of that day: (1) Puritan; (2) Evangelical; (3) Enlightenment; and (4) Civic Republican.[13]

PURITAN VIEWS

It may seem odd to consider Puritan views regarding religious liberty. Most individuals would assume that the Puritans in the colonies, having escaped the religious persecution of Europe, gave little thought to the subject of religious freedom, having now the freedom to establish a "city on the hill," a theocratic order. That picture, while not without some justification, is a caricature. The Puritans gave great thought to everything. The relationship between church and state was no exception. They considered the church and the state separate, but still covenantal, communities. Each was under the authority of God and each was to exercise that authority according to its calling.[14] The church was called to preach the word, administer the sacraments and care for the poor. The state held the power of the sword, the power to punish evil, to reward the good, to cultivate virtue and provide civil peace. While the institutions of church and state were understood to be separate, each was also understood to be an instrument of God's authority. In short, God reigned, or ought to reign, in both kingdoms. As such, there was considerable cooperation between the church and government. For example, the state provided aid to churches in the form of public property donated for the churches' use. The government's criminal law also provided support to the church—requiring church attendance and prohibiting the profaning of the Sabbath.[15]

Reciprocally, the church provided support to the state. Church properties were used for public purposes such as town meetings and educational instruction. Furthermore, the church, through its officials, encouraged support for the government. They preached that because the state was God-ordained, it deserved the obedience of the church members. Members were encouraged to be active participants, according to biblical principles, in political matters—something of which the parishioners were reminded at each annual "election day" sermon.[16]

EVANGELICAL VIEWS

The Evangelical tradition (or Pietistic Separatists) in the United States shared a considerable amount of the Calvinist theological commitments of the Puritans, but they drew different conclusions regarding the role of religion in society and the role of the state in religious affairs. These individuals, the chief proponent of which was Isaac Backus,[17] were not part of the religious insiders of the Anglican middle colonies or the Congregational northern colonies. But not only were they political outsiders, they were outsiders in large part because of their conviction regarding what God required of all men and women. Following the examples and instruction of Roger Williams and William Penn, the evangelicals of the late eighteenth century grounded the protection of liberty of conscience (a term common to the era) in their understanding of true religion—a voluntary obedience to the revealed will of God. For the good of true religion individually and corporately (the church), they considered it necessary to separate religion from the state. The state, for them as it was for Roger Williams more than a century before, was and always would be a wilderness that would overrun and destroy the garden of true religion if a wall separating the two was ever cracked.[18]

Not only should every individual's conscience be at liberty to choose whom and how to worship, but every religious body should be likewise treated. The church should be free from state control. There should be no state interference with the church's doctrine, discipline or government. And also like Williams before, the Evangelicals concluded the church should be free of the state's benevolence toward it, because those religious bodies that took the state's benefits would inevitably become a servant of the state and would no longer fulfill the calling to which God had called it.[19] They saw little need to develop a political theory. If they would have to choose one, they would no doubt have borrowed the contract theory of Locke. But they were "content with a state that created a climate conducive to the cultivation of a plurality of religions and accommodated all religious believers and religious bodies without conditions and controls."[20]

ENLIGHTENMENT VIEWS

Those within the Enlightenment tradition, men like Franklin, Paine, Jefferson, and Madison, had little interest in providing a theologically informed political theory. However, in shaping separation, and with it some form of religious freedom, they complemented well the theologically grounded views of the Evangelical separatists.[21] It was after all Jefferson who in 1802 availed himself of the wall of separation metaphor that Roger Williams had used more than a century earlier.[22] Whereas the religiously informed separatists had sought to free true religion from the corruptive power of the state, the Enlightenment separatists sought to free the state from the corruptive power of organized religion.[23] As such, most advocated that the state should give no special aid or support to religion. Those encouragements from the state that were common in Congregational New England or Anglican Virginia were to be resisted. There should be no more tax exemptions or subsidies for churches. State law should not be explicitly grounded in religious doctrine. Religious officials should not be used for public service. There should be no chaplains and no more opening of legislative sessions with prayer.[24]

Interestingly, the theory of the Enlightenment-guided activists did not match their practice. No doubt the political reality of governing a religious people and the novelty of having religion absent from public life moderated their theoretical agenda. It was Franklin who suggested that the Constitutional Convention open each day with prayer. Madison, as president, issued three proclamations recommending public humiliation and prayer and one recommending a day of thanksgiving.[25] Jefferson supported state legislation that punished disturbers of religious worship and Sabbath breakers. He also supported a state bill that appointed days of public prayer and fasting.[26]

CIVIC REPUBLICAN VIEWS

The "Civic Republicans," or as some have labeled them "political centrists,"[27] were a "group of politicians, preachers and pamphleteers who strove to cultivate a set of common values and beliefs for a new nation."[28] The label of Civic Republicans seems most fitting. It conveys well the notion that these men, like Washington, Adams, Ellsworth, and Marshall, were not simply attempting to find a common political ground between the other theologically and ideologically driven groups. Instead, these men seemed to sincerely believe that the best course for the new republic was for it to encourage private and public virtue, and the best way to accomplish that was to ground that virtue in the common religious convictions of the American people. While supporting the notion of the liberty of conscience for all and opposing religious influence that would rise to the level of a theocracy, these individuals sought "state support and accommodation for religious institutions, for they were regarded as allies and agents of good government."[29] Therefore, they supported tax exemptions for churches and tax support for religious schools and military chaplains and the offering of prayers at the opening of sessions of government, be they legislative, executive or judicial.[30]

The Civic Republicans seemingly cared little about the specific theological nuances of denominations. The theology that they supported was a morally accented theism that focused extensively on virtues such as honesty, diligence, self-negating love and patriotism. It also saw America as having a unique place in God's providential plan and therefore as a nation that had received and which would continue to receive God's unique blessing.[31] Its sacred texts were the Bible and the Constitution. Its "clergy were public-spirited ministers and religiously devout politicians."[32] Franklin called it "Publick Religion." The notion continues to persist. The twenty-first century term is "civil religion."[33]

CORE VALUES OF THE RELIGION CLAUSES

While the views of these groups in certain places differ significantly, there are some common themes that can serve as values to be secured by the Religion Clauses and therefore also as guides to their interpretation and application. Chief among them are separation, equality, and religious choice.[34]

Separation

All of the views discussed agreed that the there should at least be no formal integration of church and state. Some grounded that notion in the theological doctrine of two kingdoms. Others saw it as the only way to address concerns about intermeddling that would result in the ruin of one or the other institution. Regardless of the source, the history and the Religion Clauses themselves support the proposition that church and state should be formally separate entities. Formal separation is, however, not a matter of much dispute in the twenty-first century. The questions presented in this era involve the extent to which religion and religious influences should be permitted to have any influence on matters that modern day governments address. In short, the question is whether the value of separation demands the secularization of public political life.[35]

Equality

Incident to the value of separation is the value of equality. If there shall be no institutional unity of church and state, then such disestablishment implies that no single religious vision should be preferred over others. That is the non-controversial application of the equality principle.[36] The principle, in the context of the Establishment Clause, can, however, be applied in two much more controversial ways. First, some have argued that equality demands that non-religion be treated equally with religion so that government cannot prefer the theist to the atheist. Such a position accents the views of the Enlightenment Separatists, largely to the exclusion of the views held by the other segments of the founding generation and pushes in the direction of the secularization that was mentioned above.

The second controversial application of the equality principle is really the flip side of the first—non-religion cannot be favored over religion. In other words, government cannot take religion into account as it provides benefits or presses forward its purposes. It cannot deny its benefits or make participation in its programs unavailable to those who would use the benefit for a religious purpose (e.g., attending a religious institution on a governmentally supplied scholarship) or address a goal of a governmental program from a religious perspective (e.g., faith-based initiatives). As can be imagined, the Supreme Court has struggled as it has sought to bring to bear this equality principle in circumstances of particular cases.

Religious Freedom Non-Coercion

Some have argued that the truly core value of the Religion Clauses is religious liberty or choice and that the other values of separation and equality are actually instrumental to achieving that primary goal of religious freedom. As such, under this view, it would be permitted to sacrifice separation and equality if religious choice is advanced.[37] But religious liberty or choice is not necessarily a self-defining term. Instead, it can be understood to have a spectrum of meanings. On the one hand, it is possible to conceive of religious liberty in some sense in the context of an established church if the government does not directly coerce one to believe or act in a manner inconsistent with the believer's conscience. On the other hand, a broader definition of religious liberty would mandate that government, in addition to not using forms of direct coercion, should not use forms that indirectly coerce the believer or forms that would communicate that the individual is a political insider or outsider based on the believer's doctrine or practice. Such a definition of religious liberty would prohibit government from sponsoring religious practices or religious displays that have the effect of communicating to non-adherents that they are not full participants in the political community.

THE SUPREME COURT'S TREATMENT OF THE ESTABLISHMENT CLAUSE: A PERSPECTIVAL ANALYSIS

The views outlined and the values discussed have shaped the Supreme Court's treatment of the Establishment Clause. The debate centers around the perspectives of three groups: those in favor of strictly separating church and state, those willing to accommodate religious expression in the marketplace, and those who view government's proper role regarding religion as one of neutrality. These three competing perspectives will be identified as follows: strict separation, accommodation, and neutrality. Each category will be defined and explored through the lens of Supreme Court case law. While a multitude of Supreme Court cases could be explored under each category, only two cases will be used to illustrate the category.

Strict Separation

Strict separationists argue that the Establishment Clause requires complete separation of church and state. Government is a secular entity; religion is a private matter for every citizen to observe freely. Professor Erwin Chemerinsky summarizes the separationists' concern regarding governmental coercion: "When religion becomes part of government . . . there is inevitable coercion to participate in that faith. . . . Moreover, government involvement with religion is inherently divisive in a country with so many different religions and many people who claim no religion at all."[38]

Strict separationists find support in a number of Supreme Court cases. *Everson v. Board of Education* (1947) was the first Supreme Court case to affirm Thomas Jefferson's theory of the "wall of separation."[39] *Engel v. Vitale* (1962) also upheld the strict separation doctrine.[40]

In *Everson v. Board of Education*, the Supreme Court affirmed a New Jersey statute authorizing school districts to reimburse parents of children who attended any accredited school (public or private) for their children's public transportation to and from school.[41] While the Court ultimately affirmed the statute's constitutionality, the Court's analysis contradicted such a holding by insisting that a strict separation between church and state must be maintained in federal and state governments.

The Court incorporated the First Amendment into the Fourteenth Amendment, thereby making the First Amendment applicable to the states.[42] The Court affirmed Jefferson's words and ruled federal and state governments must keep "high and impregnable" the "wall between church and state."[43] The Court stated, "We could not approve the slightest breach."[44]

New Jersey did not breach the wall of separation when it enacted the statute authorizing school districts to direct school children's transportation to and from school.[45] The statute permitted the Town of Ewing to reimburse parents whose children attended public schools or Catholic parochial schools.[46] The appellant, a Ewing tax-payer, filed suit and argued the school district violated the Establishment Clause and used tax-payer funds to support Catholic education.[47]

In determining a violation did not occur, the Court went to great lengths to identify the First Amendment's purpose and its mandate against state-sponsored religion. The Court provided a brief history of the development of the First Amendment and noted a majority of America's settlers fled Europe to escape religious discrimination and governmental coercion of religion.[48] For centuries before and "contemporaneous to" America's founding, European nations were "filled with turmoil, civil strife, and persecutions, generated in large part by established sects determined to maintain their absolute political and religious supremacy."[49] To avoid "turmoil, civil strife, and persecutions" over religion, the First Amendment was created. Its purpose was to prevent federal and state governments from creating a state-sponsored church.[50]

While the Court ultimately detailed the need for a strict separation between church and state to avoid governmental coercion of religion, it identified New Jersey's statutory reimbursement as a public benefit similar to fire and police protection: "parents might be reluctant to permit their children to attend schools which the state had cut off from such general government services as ordinary police and fire protection, connections for sewage disposal, public highways and sidewalks."[51] According to the Court, the Town of Ewing contributed no direct financial support to the Catholic schools. The legislation merely provided children with a way to get to and from accredited schools.[52] Because the statute, as applied, did not result in government giving aid to the Catholic Church, the Court ruled the statute was constitutional.[53]

Strict separationists point to Justice Jackson's and Justice Rutledge's lengthy dissenting opinions for confirmation that the wall of separation must remain higher than *Everson* envisioned. Justice Jackson criticized the majority for acknowledging the wall of separation between church and state while "yielding support to [church and state] commingling in educational matters."[54] Because the statute only reimbursed parents whose children attended public schools or Catholic schools, it discriminated against families whose children attended private secular schools or private religious schools of other faiths.[55] Justice Jackson also argued the subsidy directly supported the Catholic Church, and the possible ramifications were great: "If the state may aid these religious schools, it may therefore regulate them. Many groups have sought aid from tax funds only to find that it carried political controls with it."[56]

Justice Rutledge agreed and affirmed James Madison's role in creating the First Amendment. Madison was committed to keeping church and state separate. He was opposed to state aid by taxation of a religious institution and stated, "If it were lawful to impose a small tax for religion, the admission would pave the way for oppressive levies."[57] Justice Rutledge argued the Establishment Clause prohibits any public funds from supporting any religious exercise.[58]

For the New Jersey statute to be constitutional, Justice Rutledge suggested state aid could have only been given to students who attended state schools.[59] He concluded by stating, "Now as in Madison's day" the principle of separation must keep the spheres of church and state as separate "as the First Amendment drew them."[60]

In 1962, fifteen years after its decision in *Everson*, the Supreme Court reaffirmed its separationist position. In *Engel v. Vitale*, the Court considered the constitutionality of a New York statute authorizing public schools to permit students to recite a standard prayer at the beginning of each school day.[61] The prayer stated, "Almighty God, we acknowledge our dependence upon Thee, and we beg Thy blessings upon us, our parents, our teachers, and our Country."[62]

The parents of ten students brought an action against the school district challenging the constitutionality of the statute.[63] The parents argued that the New York public school system violated the Establishment Clause by directing students to participate in a religious activity.[64] The Supreme Court agreed.[65] The nature of the prayer was religious, and the government had composed and endorsed the activity.[66] The statute "breach[ed] the wall of separation between church and state."[67]

The Court emphasized the need for church and state to remain separate in light of the historical reasons that "our early colonists [left] England

and [sought] religious freedom in America."[68] Religious groups lacking the political power necessary to affect governmental decisions regarding church and state matters have historically faced political discrimination.[69] The First Amendment was created to "guarantee that neither the power nor the prestige of Federal Government would be used to control, support, or influence the kinds of prayer the American people can say."[70] Because religion is personal, sacred, and holy, to permit a civil magistrate to direct its meaning and application could pervert it with political power and coercion and contradict the purposes of the Establishment Clause.[71]

While the public school prayer did not amount to a total endorsement of one religion, the Court recognized the historical dangers of governmental encroachment of religion and held that the statute was unconstitutional.[72] The Court concluded by quoting James Madison: "Who does not see that the same authority which can establish Christianity, in exclusion of all other Religions, may establish with the same ease any particular sect of Christians, in exclusion of all other sects?"[73]

Justice Stewart dissented and argued against such a strict interpretation of the Establishment Clause.[74] Because the nondenominational prayer did not interfere with the free exercise of religion, government did not establish a religion and therefore did not violate the Establishment Clause.[75] Rather, government provided school children the opportunity to share in the "spiritual heritage of our nation."[76]

Justice Stewart criticized the Court for adopting the metaphor "wall of separation" which is "nowhere to be found in the Constitution."[77] He reminded the Court that each of the Court's sessions begins with an invocation: "God save the United States and this Honorable Court."[78] Also, both the Senate and the House of Representatives begin daily sessions with prayer.[79] As Justice Stewart noted, "countless similar examples could be listed" that evidence the nation's spiritual awareness.[80] The New York public schools did not establish an "official religion;" they provided students the constitutional right to express that awareness by reciting a voluntary prayer.[81]

Accommodation

Those who are in favor of government accommodating religion view Jefferson's "wall of separation" as an analogy made to protect the church from the state's interference. Rather than focus on governmental coercion, accommodationists view the Establishment Clause as merely prohibiting a state-run church and requiring equal treatment among religious and nonreligious activities. Accommodationists argue government has a duty to accommodate the religious convictions of its citizens. The Supreme Court's decisions following *Everson* and *Engel* lend support to these ideas.

In a number of those cases, the Court moved away from strictly separating church and state and toward accommodating religious beliefs. Michael W. McConnell, a federal judge on the United States Court of Appeals for the Tenth Circuit, addresses this trend and writes, "The hallmark of accommodation is that the individual or group decides for itself whether to engage in a religious practice, or what practice to engage in, on grounds independent of the governmental action."[82] The analysis becomes whether the Establishment Clause permits the accommodation.[83]

In *County of Allegheny v. American Civil Liberties Union Greater Pittsburgh Chapter* (1989), the Court considered the constitutionality of two holiday displays located on public property in Pittsburgh.[84] The displays included a crèche on the county court house steps and a Chanukah menorah located outside a city building situated next to a Christmas tree and a sign saluting liberty.[85] The Court ruled the crèche display violated the Establishment Clause while the menorah display was constitutional.[86]

The Court applied the non-endorsement test to determine the constitutionality of the displays.[87] The test considers whether the governmental practice has the purpose or effect of endorsing religion.[88] As the Court stated, "Whether the word is 'endorsement,' 'favoritism,' or 'promotion,' the essential principle remains the same. The Establishment Clause, at the very least, prohibits government from appearing to take a position on questions of religious belief."[89]

Regarding the menorah, the Court found Allegheny County had not endorsed the religious perspective, and the display was therefore constitutional.[90] The deciding factor was the display's combination of the menorah, the Christmas tree and the sign.[91] A "reasonable observer" of the display would not interpret the symbols as governmental endorsement of religion.[92] Rather, an observer would recognize the display as "conveying the city's secular recognition of different traditions for celebrating the winter-holiday season."[93]

The county's crèche display was struck down as a violation of the Establishment Clause.[94] A Catholic organization donated the display to the county.[95] The display included a nativity scene with an angel proclaiming, "Gloria in Excelsis Deo."[96] The display was surrounded on three sides by a fence.[97] Two small evergreen trees with red bows were placed beside the fence's end posts. The display was located on the grand staircase of the county courthouse.[98]

The Court evaluated the crèche display in light of its earlier decision in *Lynch v. Donnelly* (1984): "[T]he effect of a crèche display turns on its setting."[99] In *Lynch*, the Court held a crèche display in Rhode Island did not have the effect of endorsing religion because it stood next to multiple holiday figures and objects.[100]

The Allegheny crèche display stood alone on the steps of the grand stairway.[101] The evergreen trees were not secular objects to detract from the central message: "It is as if the county had allowed the Holy Name Society to display a cross on the Grand Staircase at Easter, and the county had surrounded the cross with Easter lilies."[102] The Court ruled Allegheny County unconstitutionally endorsed the Christian message: "Glory to God for the birth of Jesus Christ."[103]

Four dissenters argued against the majority's use of the non-endorsement test and for application of the non-coercion test.[104] The non-coercion test considers whether government coerces individuals to take part in religious activities: "Non-coercive government action within the realm of flexible accommodation or passive acknowledgment of existing symbols does not violate the Establishment Clause unless it benefits religion in a way more direct and more substantial than practices that are accepted in our national heritage."[105]

Under that test, the dissenters argued city officials in both the crèche case and the menorah case sought only to "celebrate the season" by acknowledging the secular and religious nature of Chanukah and Christmas.[106] Justice Kennedy reasoned that while the Religion Clauses do not mandate governments to recognize these holidays, this country's "strong tradition of government accommodation and acknowledgment permits government to do so."[107] The facts in both cases did not indicate coercion on the part of government.[108] Citizens were not compelled to take part in religious activities.[109] Neither the city nor the county used tax funds to pay for the displays.[110] Observers who disagreed with the spiritual meanings behind the symbols were free to turn away from the displays.[111] Because there was no risk of coercion, both displays should have been found to be constitutional.[112]

In 2005, the Court reaffirmed its willingness to accommodate religion in *Cutter v. Wilkinson*.[113] Justice Ginsburg delivered the unanimous opinion of the Court.[114] The petitioners, current and former detainees at Ohio prisons, alleged that prison officials failed to accommodate their religions in accordance with the Religious Land Use and Institutionalized Persons Act of 2000 (RLUIPA).[115]

RLUIPA provides, "'No government shall impose a substantial burden on the religious exercise of a person residing in or confined to an institution' unless the burden furthers 'a compelling governmental interest,' and does so by 'the least restrictive means.'"[116] In response to the petitioners' allegations, the prison officials challenged the constitutionality of the statute and argued that the statute advanced religion in violation of the Establishment Clause.[117] The Court disagreed with the prison officials and held RLUIPA did not "exceed the limits of permissible government accommodation of religious practices."[118]

The Court discussed the legislative history behind RLUIPA and the necessity to accommodate institutionalized persons of religious faiths who are dependent upon government's permission to exercise their religions.[119] The Court justified the statute's purpose and use.[120] RLUIPA does not "elevate accommodation of religious observances over an institution's need to maintain order and safety."[121] The statute does not differentiate between different faiths and affords persons of all faiths protection against discrimination by prison officials.[122] In affirming RLUIPA's constitutionality, the Court summarized the statute's effect: "It confers no privileged status on any particular religious sect, and singles out no bona fide faith for disadvantageous treatment."[123]

Neutrality

Proponents of the neutrality doctrine argue that "the state may favor religion with public funds while remaining squarely within the bounds of the Establishment Clause, as long as the state favors all religions equally without betraying a preference for any particular religion or religions to the detriment of others."[124] They insist that the Court should revoke its use of the "wall of separation" metaphor and the principles of separation that the metaphor suggests.[125] Professor Frank Guluizza argues that the Court's application of the strict separation doctrine has resulted in hostility toward religion: "all the [C]ourt has managed to do is to confuse the concepts of separation and neutrality, and needlessly engender opposition to religion, generally, when it was probably necessary only to disestablish the Christian church from its previously preferred relationship with the state."[126]

Once disestablishment occurred, the Court should have jettisoned the separation doctrine and adopted a position of neutrality among issues involving church and state.[127] To effectuate a workable neutrality doctrine, Guluizza proposes that, "government must be neutral in its relationship between competing religions, churches, [and] beliefs."[128]

The Court has alluded to this doctrine repeatedly. In *Lemon v. Kurtzman* (1971), the petitioners challenged the constitutionality of Pennsylvania and Rhode Island statutes providing governmental aid to religiously affiliated schools.[129] The Pennsylvania statute authorized the reimbursement for nonpublic schoolteachers' salaries and costs of instructional materials for secular subjects.[130] The Rhode Island statute provided nonpublic schoolteachers a supplement of fifteen percent of their yearly salaries.[131] Both statutes were held to have violated the Establishment Clause.[132]

The Court conceded a strict separation between church and state is impossible because government and religious organizations will inevitably maintain some relationship.[133] The Court articulated a neutrality doctrine and created a three-part Establishment Clause test.[134] For a statute to be constitutional: "first, the statute must have a secular legislative purpose; second, its principal or primary effect must be one that neither advances nor inhibits religion; finally, the statute must not foster an excessive government entanglement with religion."[135]

With regard to the first prong of the test, the Court held the statutes had secular purposes—to enhance secular education.[136] The Court bypassed analysis of the second prong. Under the third prong, the statutes resulted in "excessive entanglement between government and religion."[137] The character and purposes of the institutions that benefited, the nature of the state aid, and the resulting relationship between the religiously affiliated schools and government "foster[ed] an impermissible degree of entanglement."[138]

The Court emphasized the need for government not to become entangled with religious matters and to remain neutral due to the disastrous potential for political divisiveness regarding religious practices.[139] To avoid entanglement, "Under our system, the choice has been made that government is to be entirely excluded from the affairs of the church. The Constitution decrees that religion must be a private matter for the individual."[140]

The move towards neutrality continued in *Rosenberger v. Rector & Visitors of the University of Virginia* (1995). The Court ruled a public university funding program could not constitutionally deny funding to a Christian campus newspaper when funding was made available to all campus newspapers.[141] The university violated the Establishment Clause by discriminating against religious publications rather than dealing with all publications in a neutral manner.[142]

The university withheld funding to student newspapers that "primarily promote[d] or manifest[ed] a particular belief in or about a deity or an ultimate reality."[143] The petitioners sought funding for their religious newspaper, Wide Awake Productions.[144] The newspaper's purpose was to "to facilitate discussion which fosters an atmosphere of sensitivity to and tolerance of Christian viewpoints" and "to provide a unifying focus for Christians of multicultural backgrounds."[145] As the Court noted, "The first issue had articles about racism, crisis pregnancy, stress, prayer, C. S. Lewis's ideas about evil and free will, and reviews of religious music."[146] The university denied the request for funding due to the paper's religious nature.[147]

The Court considered "whether the Establishment Clause compels a state university to exclude an otherwise eligible student publication from participation in the student activities fund, solely on the basis of its religious viewpoint, where such exclusion would violate the Speech and Press Clauses if the viewpoint of the publication were nonreligious."[148] Justice Kennedy noted the need for government neutrality regarding religion: "A central lesson of our decisions is that a significant factor in upholding governmental programs in the face of Establishment Clause attack is their neutrality towards religion."[149]

Concerns regarding government's role in advancing religion were misplaced.[150] The university's funding program promoted diverse student thought.[151] The program did not promote or advance religion.[152] The program valued the difference between government-sponsored speech and private speech.[153] The Court addressed the concern that Wide Awake's religious affiliation would be endorsed by the University and held it was not a plausible fear.[154] The state was not endorsing the speech, and it had not coerced the speech.[155] The Court ruled the denying of funds to religious groups "would risk fostering a pervasive bias or hostility to religion, which could undermine the very neutrality the Establishment Clause requires."[156]

While Supreme Court precedent regarding the relationship between church and state has varied in analysis and application, the common theme throughout church state jurisprudence remains: every citizen ought to worship freely without fear of governmental coercion. Religion will remain a potent force in American society. As John Witte notes, "It involves the responses of the human heart, soul, mind, conscience, intuition, and reason to revelation, to transcendent values, to what Rudolf Otto once called the 'idea of the holy.'"[157] To ensure the individual's quest to engage in this sacred pursuit, the Supreme Court must continue to affirm "this bold constitutional experiment in granting religious liberty to all."[158]

NOTES

1. Stephen L. Carter, "Liberal Hegemony and Religious Resistance: An Essay on Legal Theory," in *Christian Perspectives on Legal Thought*, ed. Michael W. McConnell, et al. (New Haven: Yale University Press, 2000), 25–53.

2. Acts 5:23 and Carter, "Liberal Hegemony."

3. Some argue that it is best to understand this phrase as a single Religion Clause. Others have treated it as two clauses, the Establishment Clause followed by the Free Exercise Clause. While there are very good reasons for treating the two as one, because this chapter will focus primarily on the first half of the clause we will treat the phrase as consisting of two clauses and will focus on the Establishment Clause.

4. The constitutional term for this is "incorporation." The Bill of Rights were understood to be applicable only to the federal government. *Barron v. Mayor and City Council of Baltimore*, 32 U.S. 243 (1833). They are now largely understood, with minor exceptions, to be made applicable to the states, having been incorporated in the Fourteenth Amendment's language of "due process." For a good introduction to this concept see Erwin Chemerinsky, *Constitutional Law: Principles and Policies* 3rd ed. (New York: Aspen, 2006), 491–507.

5. This is not intended to imply that the only constitutional text to consider is the Religion Clause. There are other provisions of the U.S. Constitution that may shape the outcome of particular disputes. For example, Article VI of the Constitution provides in part that "no religious test shall ever be required as a Qualification to any Office or public Trust under the United States." In addition, the constitutions of the fifty states provide a constitutional source of protection for the religious liberty of individuals within each respective state.

6. Former Chief Justice Warren Burger once observed that the clauses were "not the most precisely drawn portions of the Constitution." *Walz v. Tax Commission of City of New York*, 397 U.S. 664, 668 (1970).

7. For differing views of constitutional interpretation that exist on the Supreme Court, see Antonin Scalia, *A Matter of Interpretation*, ed. Amy Gutmann (Princeton: Princeton University Press, 1997) and Stephen Breyer, *Active Liberty: Interpreting Our Democratic Constitution* (New York: Knopf, 2005).

8. The First Amendment, along with eleven other amendments, were authored by the First Constitutional Congress and sent to the states for their approval in September 1789. Ten of those first twelve amendments—commonly referred to as the Bill of Rights—received the required three-fourths approval by the states when Virginia ratified them in December 1791. For a brief, but helpful, chronology of the Constitution, see Barnes and Noble, *The Constitution of the United States* (New York: Barnes & Noble Books, 1995), 121–127.

9. Michael W. McConnell, "Establishment and Disestablishment at the Founding, Part I: Establishment of Religion," *William & Mary Law Review* 44 (2003): 2105, 2107.

10. McConnell, "Establishment and Disestablishment." McConnell's excellent historical work is most helpful to understanding three things: (1) establishment was in some sense normal to the founding generation; (2) most members of the founding generation believed that some type of religious conviction was necessary for public virtue; (3) if establishment was to no longer be normative, the founding generation had to figure out what would take its place if public virtue was to be maintained and the republic was to succeed.

11. Michael W. McConnell, John H. Garvey, and Thomas C. Berg, *Religion and the Constitution* (New York: Aspen, 2002), 15–17.

12. McConnell, "Establishment and Disestablishment," 2108.

13. This four-category approach is the one offered by John Witte. John Witte, "Essential Rights and Liberties of Religion," *Notre Dame Law Review* 71 (1996): 371, 377–388. See also Arlin Adams and Charles Emmerich, *A Nation Dedicated*

to Religious Liberty (Philadelphia: University of Pennsylvania, 1990) for an analysis using three categories: (1) Enlightenment Separationists; (2) Political Centrists; and (3) Pietistic Separationists. Witte's approach seems superior, because it takes account of the large influence exerted by those whose thoughts on religion and society were still shaped by their Puritan thought and experience.

14. Witte, "Essential Rights," 377–381.

15. Ibid.

16. Ibid.

17. Adams and Emmerich, *A Nation Dedicated to Religious Liberty*, 29.

18. Mark D. Howe, *The Garden and the Wilderness: Religion and Government in American Constitutional History* (Chicago: University of Chicago Press, 1965).

19. Witte, "Essential Rights," 382–383.

20. Ibid., 383.

21. Ibid., 384.

22. Adams and Emmerich, *A Nation Dedicated to Religious Liberty*, 22.

23. Ibid.

24. Witte, "Essential Rights," 383–385.

25. Adams and Emmerich, *A Nation Dedicated to Religious Liberty*, 25.

26. Witte, "Essential Rights," 385.

27. Adams and Emmerich, *A Nation Dedicated to Religious Liberty*, 26–28.

28. Witte, "Essential Rights," 385.

29. Ibid., 386.

30. Ibid., 387.

31. For a full account of America's inclination to see itself as divinely appointed for God's purpose, see Ernest Lee Tuvenson, *Redeemer Nation* (Chicago: University of Chicago Press, 1968).

32. Witte, "Essential Rights," 386.

33. Robert Bellah has written extensively about the contemporary contours of this notion. The Supreme Court addressed the subject directly in *Lee v. Weisman*, 505 U.S. 577 (1992) and refused to permit the "establishment" of this civil religion.

34. Thomas C. Berg, *The State and Religion*, 2nd. ed. (St. Paul: Thompson-West, 2004) 15. For additional justifications see William P. Marshall, "Truth and the Religion Clauses," *DePaul Law Review* 43 (1994), 243. In addition to the ones commonly offered, Marshall catalogues such justifications as eliminating special suffering, reducing the risk of civil disobedience and promoting self identity. He also argues that the search for truth ought to guide the interpretation of the clause.

35. Berg, *The State and Religion*, 18.

36. Ibid., 19.

37. Ibid., 21.

38. Erwin Chemerinsky, "The Establishment Clause," *Constitutional Law Principles and Policies* (New York: Aspen Law & Business, 2002), 1150.

39. *Everson v. Board of Education*, 330 U.S. 1 (1947).

40. *Engel v. Vitale*, 370 U.S. 421, 422 (1962).

41. *Everson*, 330 U.S. at 15.
42. Ibid.
43. Ibid. at 18.
44. Ibid.
45. Ibid.
46. Ibid. at 3.
47. Ibid.
48. Ibid. at 8–9.
49. Ibid.
50. Ibid. at 16.
51. Ibid. at 17–18.
52. Ibid.
53. Ibid. at 18.
54. Ibid. at 19.
55. Ibid. at 20.
56. Ibid. at 28.
57. Ibid. at 40.
58. Ibid. at 41.
59. Ibid. at 60.
60. Ibid. at 63.
61. *Engel*, 370 U.S. at 422.
62. Ibid.
63. Ibid. at 423.
64. Ibid. at 424.
65. Ibid.
66. Ibid.
67. Ibid. at 425.
68. Ibid.
69. Ibid. at 427.
70. Ibid. at 429.
71. Ibid. at 432.
72. Ibid. at 436.
73. Ibid.
74. Ibid. at 445.
75. Ibid.
76. Ibid.
77. Ibid. at 446.
78. Ibid.
79. Ibid.
80. Ibid.
81. Ibid.
82. Michael W. McConnell, "Accommodation of Religion: An Update and a Response to the Critics," *George Washington Law Review* 60 (1992): 685, 688.
83. Ibid. at 687.

84. *County of Allegheny v. American Civil Liberties Union Greater Pittsburgh Chapter*, 492 U.S. 573 (1989).
85. Ibid. at 578.
86. Ibid.
87. Ibid. at 592.
88. Ibid.
89. Ibid. at 593–594.
90. Ibid. at 620.
91. Ibid. at 615.
92. Ibid. at 620.
93. Ibid.
94. Ibid. at 602.
95. Ibid. at 580.
96. Ibid.
97. Ibid.
98. Ibid.
99. Ibid. at 598.
100. *Lynch v. Donnelly*, 465 U.S. 668 (1984).
101. *Allegheny*, 492 U.S. at 598.
102. Ibid. at 599.
103. Ibid. at 601.
104. Ibid. at 662–663 (J. Kennedy, dissenting).
105. Ibid.
106. Ibid. at 663.
107. Ibid. at 664.
108. Ibid.
109. Ibid.
110. Ibid.
111. Ibid.
112. Ibid.
113. *Cutter v. Wilkinson*, 544 U.S. 709 (2005).
114. Ibid.
115. Ibid.
116. Ibid. at 712.
117. Ibid. at 713.
118. Ibid. at 714.
119. Ibid. at 720–721.
120. Ibid. at 722–724.
121. Ibid. at 722.
122. Ibid. at 723.
123. Ibid.
124. Richard Albert, "Religion in the New Republic," *Lousiana Law Review* 67 (2006) 1, 42.
125. Frank Guluizza, *Over the Wall* (Albany: State University of New York Press, 2000), 117.

126. Ibid., 118.
127. Ibid.
128. Ibid., 123.
129. *Lemon v. Kurtzman*, 403 U.S. 602, 606 (1971).
130. Ibid. at 606–607.
131. Ibid. at 607.
132. Ibid.
133. Ibid. at 614.
134. Ibid. at 612–613.
135. Ibid.
136. Ibid. at 613.
137. Ibid. at 614.
138. Ibid. at 615.
139. Ibid. at 623.
140. Ibid. at 624.
141. *Rosenberger v. Rector & Visitors of the University of Virginia*, 515 U.S. 819, 846 (1995).
142. Ibid.
143. Ibid. at 823.
144. Ibid. at 825.
145. Ibid. at 825–826.
146. Ibid. at 826.
147. Ibid. at 827.
148. Ibid. at 837.
149. Ibid.
150. Ibid. at 840.
151. Ibid.
152. Ibid.
153. Ibid. at 841.
154. Ibid.
155. Ibid. at 841–842.
156. Ibid. at 845–846.
157. John Witte, *Religion and the American Constitutional Experiment* (Boulder: Westview Press, 2000), 230.
158. Ibid.

FURTHER READING

Mark D. Howe's *The Garden and the Wilderness: Religion and Government in American Constitutional History* is a classic analysis of the religious and secular ideas that served as foundations for the political doctrine of separation. Howe's analysis is updated and focused on William Penn's religious freedom experiment in Pennsylvania in Arlin Adams and Charles Emmerich's *A Nation Dedicated to Religious Liberty*. For a broad but good introduction to the constitutional and political issues surrounding religious liberty, see Thomas C. Berg's *The State and Religion*. For an analysis on how the doctrine of strict separation can be hostile to religion, see *Over the Wall* by Frank Guluizza. John Witte's "Essential Rights and Liberties of Religion," in *Notre Dame Law Review* 77 (1996), is an excellent summary of the political and theological influences in the founding generation that shaped the crafting and understanding of the Religion Clauses of the First Amendment. For the most thorough and detailed treatment of the history of establishment of religion that would have been known to the founding generation see Michael W. McConnell, "Establishment and Disestablishment at the Founding, Part I: Establishment of Religion," *William & Mary Law Review* 44 (2003): 2105.

Religion, Rhetoric, and Ritual in the U.S. Government

Ann W. Duncan

In America today, witnesses in courts of law and newly elected officials swear oaths on the Bible, ending with "so help me God." Legislative and judicial bodies begin their sessions with prayers led by government-paid chaplains. U.S. currency bears the motto "In God We Trust." In a country that prides itself on the separation of church and state, the Supreme Court has upheld these practices and others that, at first glance, appear to be an establishment of religion. Why are these seeming violations of the Establishment Clause allowed to continue? Is this blurring of the line between politics and religion a danger to or a logical outgrowth of the separation of church and state?

To understand this complex situation, one must differentiate between historical fact and practiced reality. Despite the celebrated American distinction of religious freedom and anti-establishment principles, religious symbols, ideals and even explicit religious language find their way into the history and central documents of the nation's institutions and the rhetoric of the nation's governmental leaders. While an advocate of strict separation might point to religious language in the Constitution or early American speeches as historic relics, religious language can also be found in governmental practice today. While the Supreme Court has debated some examples such as "under God" in the Pledge of Allegiance and the payment of congressional chaplains with taxpayer money, other examples have been consciously untouched by the highest court in the country. This apparent selective attention to cases involving intersections of religion and politics raises questions not only as to Supreme Court criteria in choosing cases but also why the Court and the public at large feel comfortable with selective blurring of the separation of church and state.

Attempting to explain this phenomenon, Constitutional historian Leonard Levy has observed that the Supreme Court has exercised "good judgment" in avoiding some of these Establishment Clause cases. Levy argues that many of these issues, if brought to trial, would be found to violate the clause. However, Levy continues, "the Court has enough cunning to avoid rendering such judgments. Public opinion and historical custom dictate a prudent abstention."[1] Such a conclusion raises serious questions as to the nature of the separation of church and state that many Americans take for granted and the extent to which our modern nation differs from the early nation in which explicitly religious language was more widely acceptable. Why, when some issues of establishment are so hotly contested, are some of these more obvious uses of religion in government largely maintained and, in some cases, ignored? What is the utility of such convictions and how might they affect the status of church and state issues in America? Do these religious references amount to a "*de facto* establishment" of religion?[2]

By examining theoretical understandings of the religious element of American politics and some of the particular case studies of public use of religion in government settings, we will explore these questions in an attempt to understand better those many shades of grey in the separation of church and state. Beginning with an overview of theoretical ideas explaining this phenomenon of civil religion, this chapter will present a chronological development of these more amorphous issues involving the intersection of religion and politics, detailing relevant theological and political developments and court cases along the way. Through a thematic retelling of American political and religious development, we will discover that these unique enigmas in the land of separation have long been seen as the characteristics of America that give its policies meaning and purpose and define the distinctive American identity.

AMERICAN CIVIL RELIGION AND THE POWER OF RHETORIC

While many see the United States as a land of clear separation of church and state, from another perspective, the United States of America may appear to be a nation of contradictions and paradox. Numerous scholars of sociology, political science, and religious history have attempted to describe this unique relationship between religion and politics. Underscoring the high level of religious sentiment and practice in America, G.K. Chesterton called America "a nation with the soul of a church."[3] Similarly, sociologist Robert Bellah argues, "the separation of church and state has not denied the political realm a religious dimension."[4] While this may seem a paradox to some, to others it points to the existence of a civil religion.[5] According to Will Herberg, in civil religion, "national life is apotheosized, national values are religionized, national heroes are divinized, and national history is experienced as a . . . redemptive history."[6] The civil religion thus functions to allow for an interaction with the gods that strengthens and heightens one's feelings about themselves and their society—to allow for greater unity against common enemies and a concern for public morality.[7] This tendency to "harmonize the earth with Heaven" led Alexis de Tocqueville to label religion as primary among America's political institutions.[8]

According to its proponents, American civil religion manifests not only in the rhetoric of American leaders and the ideology of the country but also in its sacraments and symbols. The flag and Statue of Liberty are sacred, as are certain historical documents such as the Declaration of Independence and the Constitution. By sanctifying these elements of American history, Americans create a type of myth about the origins and purpose of the country that is expressed in a particular and, sometimes, religious language.[9] Through this language and myth, the civil religion serves as a source of identity, nationalism and integration of religious and national goals and beliefs, gives purpose to political action, and provides a compass for moral deliberation.

Indeed, from the beginning of the United States' history, the political leaders have used language that could be construed as religious. In his First Inaugural Address, George Washington expressed these ideals by suggesting, "no people can be bound to acknowledge and adore the Invisible Hand which conducts the affairs of men more than those of the United States."[10] This acknowledgment of an "Invisible Hand" that leads Americans to their destiny can be seen throughout presidential speeches up to the present. In his Second Inaugural Address, George W. Bush referred to "the Author of Liberty" and concluded with a simple, "May God bless you, and may He watch over the United States of America."[11]

With their religious tone, these words of our first and most recent president center on the divine as an entity with a special relationship to America and a strong role in the future of the country. But who is this "God" and from what religion does he come? Existing in a country that advocates the separation of church and state, the American civil religion conceives of a God neutral to all religions and, in some way, generic and universal enough to allow all religious individuals direct appeal. Describing the American God, Bellah writes that he "is not only rather 'unitarian,' he is also on the austere side, much more related to order, law and right than to salvation and love."[12] While this generic type of God can certainly be said to appeal to a broad spectrum of humanity, the growing diversity of religious beliefs within the country raises questions as to the acceptability of such religious language in a country espousing a separation between church and state.

Reference to God by governmental leaders often arises from more than simple personal devotion. According to Bellah, the idea of a country as God's chosen land has two rhetorical uses: it can be used to exert dogmatic influence over the "pagans" and "infidels" by claiming superior knowledge and right to power, and it can be used to express the desire to set an example throughout the world. In this latter view, America not only has a certain superiority and status arising from this chosenness but also a duty to share its wealth and wisdom with the unenlightened and uninspired.[13] Thus, not only does the civil religion in some ways legitimate references to God in governmental ritual and ceremony, but it also emerges in political rhetoric—particularly rhetoric concerning foreign policy. Bellah's schema for understanding the purpose of this civil religion underscores the role of the president as the paramount individual who emphasizes the preeminence of American ideals and a sense of divine duty to aid the world.

In this way, the American civil religion most clearly manifests in the rhetoric of the nation's leaders. As Robert Alley argues, this civil religion "has a history but no predictable future except as a function of the presidential will."[14] While such a statement certainly excludes some important manifestations of the civil religion such as articulations by other political leaders and language in the mottos and rituals of governmental practice, Alley makes an important point. It is the president who stirs the emotions of the people. It is he who rallies them to a cause, and thus the language often emerges most clearly in times of war and crisis. The impassioned language of the president at times of national crisis largely determines the opinions and emotions of the people and shapes the way Americans view their involvement in the world. Moreover, as an individual, the president is able to use religious language as personal expression in a way that religious legislation or policy cannot.

However, the role of the president has changed throughout American history. In their study of civil religious language and the presidency, Richard Pierard and Robert Linder argue that the state of modern media and the ease and speed with which Americans have access to the words and image of the president have affected their perceptions of the president's role. In modern times, "individual citizens have perceived their destinies to be bound up with that of their president . . . All of this quasi-religious political devotion and emotion is then channeled through many religious and political tributaries into the ocean of the presidency. This office is the single object of their flow."[15] A continuity in emphasis can be traced from Washington to our current president.

Though civil religious language often appears in speech, it also appears in less obvious ways. Other rituals, ceremonies and even monuments in governmental practice and on governmental properties express similar sentiments about the special mission and history of the nation and its undeniably religious roots. As the following historical overview will show, justifications for prayers before legislative sessions, the display of religious monuments and documents in governmental buildings and even national days of prayer and thanksgiving have been advocated and maintained through appeal to the ideals of civil religion. This historical overview will use scholarly perspectives, legal cases, and political and religious trends to demonstrate not only an adaptability of this civil religion to the needs and demographics of the time but also a constancy in the language and ideals of the American government.

INSPIRATION AND SEPARATION: COLONIAL AMERICA AND THE NEW REPUBLIC

This brief overview of theories of American civil religion provides a framework for understanding the non-legislated remnants of religion found in governmental practice and the theoretical roots of those concrete practices that have maintained reference to God throughout American history. We will now move from the theoretical to the historical and track the developments and changes in the use of religious language in governmental practice and rhetoric. Many scholars have located the beginning of civil religion in the earliest European settlements in America. In his study of what he terms the "American jeremiad," Sacvan Bercovitch points to the early Puritans as the first civil religion practitioners in America. As he writes, "Theirs was a peculiar mission, they explained, for they were a 'peculiar people,' a company of Christians not only called but chosen, and chosen not only for heaven but as instruments of a sacred historical design."[16] Arguing against characterizations by Perry Miller and others, Bercovitch describes this jeremiad as "corrective, not destructive," emphasizing that God's punishment for wrongdoing was certain but that "their punishments confirmed this promise."[17] With both an assurance of divine providence and an assurance of divine retribution if the nation fell short of its responsibility, the civil religion took on a restrained tone.

Yet many early Americans did not see this idea of divine judgment as a call for humility so much as a call to great things. John Winthrop, governor of the Massachusetts Bay Colony, expressed his idea of the ideal Puritan community in terms of a covenant philosophy. Speaking to his fellow immigrants as they traveled by boat to America, he famously remarked, "we shall be as a city upon a hill, the eyes of all people are upon us."[18] He then articulated the punishment that would await them if they failed in their duties. The conflation of civic and religious power was not problematic for these religious reformers in light of their firm belief that God's kingdom would come soon and all would be righted.[19]

Yet the Puritan perspective was not monolithic. For those who came to America seeking religious freedom, differentiation between religious and political power was crucial. It was these individuals who spurred the later movement for separation. Indeed, scholars such as Patricia Bonomi and Jon Butler argue that these plentiful and diverse religious groups necessitate as much attention, if not more, than the Puritans. As a result of this dramatic diversity combined with a common depth of religiosity, a new situation emerged. Between 1680 and 1760, a new manifestation of the state church formed in America.[20] Though the ideas of covenant and their role as a chosen people remained in religious rhetoric, the increasing diversity of American religion changed the state church and Puritan ideals were largely replaced by "Christian republicanism and Christian common sense."[21]

This transition was gradual. As the colonies began to multiply, a governing body became necessary to maintain order. The Continental Congress faced the task of reconciling and honoring the various usages of religious language and types of government in the colonies. Meeting from 1774 until the beginnings of our current Congressional system in 1789, this body had the difficult task of maintaining order over diverse and sometimes conflicting states while allowing these states the sovereignty they fervently demanded. Moreover, this Congress helped facilitate, negotiate, and conclude the War for Independence with Great Britain. In attempting both to leave religious matters to the states and also to lead the country effectively through this difficult time period, some recourse to Divine Providence and religious observance led to a complex and multifaceted approach to the relationship between church and state.

Like our present government, the Continental Congress sought both to prohibit the establishment of religion and to maintain religious liberty. For this Congress, these ideals were separate and not necessarily mutually dependent. The conflation of groups coming to America seeking a land without establishment to allow for their religious freedom and those groups who sought religious freedom in order to establish their own religion made such a distinction vitally important. Much of the attraction of the young country was the ability to establish one's own church-centered colony without outside influence or regulation. This did not necessarily mean the toleration of others and, indeed, often led to persecution of others to maintain the ideal.[22]

The move from establishment to disestablishment was partially a reaction to changed understandings of religion. The individualism and democratizing of American Christianity as a result of the Great Awakening of the 1730s and 1740s marked a growing emphasis on individual religious experience and a more democratic religious community. Prominent theologians such as Jonathan Edwards advanced a post-millennialist theology that advocated social and religious action to improve the world in order to hasten Christ's second coming.[23] Such a pro-active attitude toward Christianity fit well with ideas of the responsibility and active role for the United States on the world stage. As a result of these trends, Puritan ideals of hierarchy and strict rule declined and, in turn, so too did the belief in establishment.[24] This disestablishment increased as evangelicalism flourished and groups desired the freedom to express and forward their ideas.[25]

The years leading up to the Revolutionary War were marked by change in American religious life and the articulation of religious ideals that directly influenced the understanding of political action and the nation. After the Great Awakening, a profusion of denominational factionalism led many to bring their religious convictions to the political arena.[26] As a result, "In eighteenth-century America—in city, village, and countryside—the idiom of religion penetrated all discourse, underlay all thought, marked all observances, gave meaning to every public and private crisis."[27] Such factionalism would turn to unity under the American nation as the Revolutionary War drew near.

Politically, many colonists felt compelled to recommend caution in the face of the daunting enemy of Britain. Religiously, many felt compelled to call for action to bring down tyranny. In a pattern seen again during the two world wars, Americans wrestled with weighing religious and political ideals and eventually united both in a unified and virulent war effort. Indeed, as the war began, it was often clergy members who rallied the country into nationalist fervor. As Bonomi writes, "By turning colonial resistance into a righteous cause, and by crying the message to all ranks in all parts of the colonies, ministers did the work of secular radicalism and did it better: they resolved doubts, overcame inertia, fired the heart, and exalted the soul."[28]

This interaction between religious practice and political activity continued within the official bodies of colonial America, particularly the Continental Congress. The Congress frequently debated traditionally religious concepts such as "sin, repentance, humiliation, divine service, morality, fasting, prayer, mourning, public worship, funerals, chaplains, and 'true' religion" and never hesitated to use biblical quotations and allusions in its decisions.[29] The Congress formally utilized religion in such ceremonies as group prayer and sermons during gathered sessions, and on September 5, 1774, the Congress regulated prayer in legislative sessions through the appointment of a chaplain, a practice not questioned by the Supreme Court until the second half of the twentieth century.[30] Another practice inaugurated at this time, a day of humiliation and prayer, started on July 20, 1775, and was continued on into the early republic.[31]

Also common during this era were religious tests for public office, the requirements varying throughout the colonies. Of the original seven colonies, one required a Protestant affirmation, and three others mandated some form of Christian identity. Even as many states adopted new state constitutions in the years following independence, most kept these religious tests intact. Massachusetts, South Carolina and others justified exclusion of clergy from public office through an appeal to the desire to ensure clergy were rightly focused on their higher callings. However, anti-Catholic sentiments sometimes were expressed through specific legislation such as the 1777 provision by New York to prohibit "priests of any denomination whatsoever" from running for office.[32] Such provisions were also motivated by anticlericalism though, surprisingly, not because of a desire for separation.[33] Any appeals to the principle of separation—though in a negative way—came only from opponents to the provisions, such as Noah Webster, who wanted clergy involvement to increase their positive impact on society. On this view, separation would limit this necessary influence.[34] Thomas Jefferson's "Statute for Establishing Religious Freedom" of 1786 eliminated the practice of religious tests in Virginia.[35] As more states were formed in the late eighteenth century, many adopted religious tests and maintained them into the nineteenth and twentieth centuries.[36] It was not until 1961 that the Supreme Court weighed in on the matter and settled its constitutionality once and for all by disallowing the practice.

As some of these early examples show, the clean separation we imagine in the founding of the nation was not so clean. Religious language and laws permeated many aspects of colonial and early-republic America. Thus, while some historians place the beginning of this civil religion in the nineteenth century and the Civil War, others such as Catherine Albanese have argued that this American civil religion was firmly in place by the Revolutionary War. Albanese writes that the continued importance of the Revolutionary War as the founding of the nation and Washington as the preeminent founder provides unity and strength to Americans even to this day; in other words, this early civil religion influenced both its own time and the present day.[37]

Others have argued that the Revolution was largely a secular event. For example, Jon Butler notes that though religious language appears in the Declaration of Independence, the God referred to is a deist god of nature that is distinct from the Christian God worshiped by so many Americans. In this way, "the Declaration of Independence provides clear-cut evidence of the secondary role that religion and Christianity played in creating the revolutionary struggle."[38] Yet Butler also sees the time between the Revolution and the end of the century as a period of rearticulation of Christian views through Christian interpretations of the Revolution and the future American government, critiques of nonreligious individuals, and the proliferation of "distinctively American" new religious groups.[39]

Whatever one's historical perspective might be on the nature of the Revolution, the presence of religious language is undeniable. In many ways, this was the legacy of a century ripe with religious enthusiasm and mired in a deep and passionately believed millennialism. The perhaps natural fear of upcoming war and the difficulties involved in creating a new nation were replaced in the mid-1770s by hope and joy at coming changes.[40] In this way, the country began to use millennialism as a means of connecting their present status and their ideal of the Kingdom of God.[41] Past worries about the coming end time were replaced by an optimistic view towards a bright future and a belief that Americans had a unique role in bringing about the Kingdom of God on earth.

Such language found its way into the official proclamations of the Congress. In its Declaration of the Causes and Necessity for Taking up Arms, adopted on July 6, 1775, the Continental Congress repeatedly mentioned the influence of the "Divine Author," "Divine Favour" and "Providence" as preparing the country for battle and guiding it through the war. The declaration ended with the following invocation: "With an humble Confidence in the Mercies of the supreme and impartial Judge and Ruler of the Universe, we most devoutly implore his Divine Goodness to protect us happily through this great Conflict, to dispose our Adversaries to reconciliation on reasonable Terms, and thereby to relieve the Empire from the Calamities of civil war."[42] Indeed, as the war loomed large, ministers and politicians alike began to use the language of the antichrist to describe the enemy, a trend that would emerge again in later American wars.[43] As the war raged on and the difficulties of its aftermath began to emerge, "the theme of retributive judgment began to compete with that of impending millennial glory" and divisions began to grow again between differing denominational divisions.[44]

In the early years of the nation, the founders struggled to find the appropriate relationship between religion and politics in the diverse nation. In 1782, the initial national motto, *E Pluribus Unum,* or "One from many," reflected the unification of colonies into one country. This was a rather secular motto in comparison to the later motto, "In God We Trust," and was approved by Congress on June 10, 1782, and put onto coins in 1795. This motto celebrated the achievement of unity following the contentious colonial period. Yet with this unity came continued debate over the relationship between religion and government in the young nation.

The country's founders debated the question of religious tests for public office during the drafting of the U.S. and state constitutions. In his efforts to rid the government of untoward religious influence, Thomas Jefferson stipulated in the Virginia Constitution adopted in June 1776 that "all Ministers of the Gospel of every Denomination be incapable of being elected Members of either House of Assembly, or the Privy Council."[45] The Constitution of the United States later declared that "no religious test shall ever be required as a qualification to any office or public trust under the United States."[46] James Madison expressed concern with the exclusions of Jefferson's Virginia Constitution and asked whether this would "violate a fundamental principle of liberty by punishing a religious profession with the privation of a civil right."[47] Even at this early date, what seemed a danger of establishment for one seemed a violation of free exercise for another.

As Jefferson, Madison, and, perhaps most importantly, Washington arose as the nation's first leaders, the myth of the founding fathers began to develop. In their survey of civil religion and the presidency, Pierard and Linder describe this development and the conscious linking of these leaders with biblical figures. In the popular imagination, "Washington had become the Moses-liberator figure, Jefferson the prophet, and Lincoln [who would later serve as] the theologian of the national faith."[48] Washington himself often used biblical language of covenant in describing the nature of America. Articulating the idea of America as a chosen nation of God, he repeatedly asked for divine protection and favor for the country in his public discourses. In his annual message to Congress in 1794, Washington proclaimed, "Let us unite . . . in imploring the Supreme Ruler of nations, to spread his holy protection over these united States: to turn the machinations of the wicked to the confirming of our constitution: to enable us at all times to root out internal sedition, and put invasion to flight: to perpetuate and to verify the anticipations of this government begin a safe guard to human rights."[49] Indeed, it was Washington who, when taking his oath of office on April 30, 1789, added, "I swear, so help me God" to the oath, thus beginning a practice that would be continued to this day.[50] In his

Inaugural Address, Washington made it his "first official act" to emphasize "fervent supplications to that Almighty Being who rules over the universe, who presides in the councils of nations, and whose providential aids can supply every human defect."[51]

Throughout his presidency, Washington continued to infuse the new American political system with religious language and ceremony. It was during his presidency that the first official Thanksgiving Day was proclaimed. On February 19, 1789, Washington asked that all Americans "meet together and render their sincere and hearty thanks to the Great Ruler of Nations, for the manifold and signal mercies which distinguish our lot as a Nation [and] Humbly and fervently . . . beseech the kind Author of these blessings graciously to prolong them to us—to imprint on our hearts a deep and solemn sense of our obligations to him for them."[52] Similarly, Washington recognized this ruling force in American history and destiny in his Farewell Address to the nation, delivered on September 19, 1796. In the midst of a lengthy exhortation on proper government and American identity, Washington touched on this theme of providence. He enjoined all Americans to "observe good faith and justice towards all nations; cultivate peace and harmony with all" and then described the justification for such a role on the world stage:

Religion and morality enjoin this conduct; and can it be, that good policy does not equally enjoin it? It will be worthy of a free, enlightened, and (at no distant period) a great Nation, an exalted justice and benevolence. Who can doubt that in the course of time and things, the fruits of such a plan would richly repay any temporary advantages which might be lost by a steady adherence to it? Can it be that Providence has not connected the permanent felicity of a Nation with its virtue? The experiment, at least, is recommended by every sentiment which ennobles human nature.[53]

As the man seen by many as the founder of the nation and the purest example of American leadership and identity, Washington's rhetoric established a pattern followed by most subsequent presidents. His emphasis on codifying and explicitly articulating civil religious ideals about the mission and divine providence inherent in American action set the stage for the continued use of such language as the government developed and matured.

Yet there were challenges along the way. Thomas Jefferson and later Andrew Jackson expressed discomfort with the use of Thanksgiving and fast days by the president. Going beyond distinctions drawn in the Constitution, Jackson refused to call a fast day in the midst of the 1832 cholera epidemic by arguing that he could not do so without "transcending the limits prescribed by the constitution for the President; and without feeling that I might in some degree disturb the security which religion now enjoys in this country, in its complete separation from the political concerns of government."[54] Such concerns continued in regard to other issues throughout the first century of the presidency but were never so clearly vocalized as by Thomas Jefferson.

As a key player in the initial discussions of the nature of American democracy and the founding documents, Jefferson expressed a mixed perspective in his writings and public speeches as president. In his single published book, *Notes on the State of Virginia*, Thomas Jefferson wrote about the extent to which government should influence the practice of religion. He concluded, "The legitimate powers of government extend to such acts only as are injurous to others. But it does me no injury for my neighbor to say there are twenty gods, or no gods. It neither picks my pocket nor breaks my leg."[55] Yet despite his unease at explicit religious language, as president, Jefferson both maintained this belief in separation and continued to appeal to the divine. In his First Inaugural Address, Jefferson proclaimed, "may that Infinite Power which rules the destinies of the universe lead our councils to what is best, and give them a favorable issue for your peace and prosperity."[56] He continued this theme in his Second Inaugural:

I shall need, too, the favor of that Being in whose hands we are, who led our forefathers, as Israel of old, from their native land, and planted them in a country flowing with all the necessaries and comforts of life; who has covered our infancy with his providence, and our riper years with his wisdom and power; and to whose goodness I ask you to join with me in supplications, that he will so enlighten the minds of your servants, guide their councils, and prosper their measures, that whatsoever they do, shall result in your good, and shall secure to you the peace, friendship, and approbation of all nations.[57]

With his strong stand for religious freedom and political detachment from religious establishment, Jefferson's use of such rhetoric suggests that this religiosity or civil religion extended beyond the personal convictions of a president to a certain mode of discourse and way of understanding the nation's identity that would continue to develop into the next century. The civil religion thus developed less as a product of the particular beliefs of the nation's founder and more from timeless concepts about American identity.

As the nineteenth century began, the dust had largely settled from the Revolutionary War and government formation, but war tested the young country again with the War of 1812. During that war, President James Madison, a champion of religious liberty and church and state separation, declared a day of Thanksgiving, continuing the tradition established by

Washington. In his proclamation, Madison announced the joint resolution by Congress to declare a day "to be observed by the people of the United States with religious solemnity, as a day of Public Humiliation and Prayer and whereas in times of public calamity, such as that of the war . . . that the hearts of all should be touched with the same, and the eyes of all be turned to that Almighty Power, in whose hand are the welfare and the destiny of nations."[58]

Fueled by the religious enthusiasm generated by the Second Great Awakening and growing confidence in American strength and mission, ideas of millennialism and chosenness began to reemerge. In his monumental work, *Democracy in America*, Alexis de Tocqueville recorded his observation of 1830s Americans, remarking that "Americans so completely confuse Christianity and freedom in their minds that it is almost impossible to have them conceive of the one without the other . . . Thus it is that in the United States religious zeal constantly warms itself at the hearth of patriotism."[59] In his study *America's God*, Mark Noll describes these messianic tones in American political and religious speech as being "rooted in English ideas of national chosenness, Puritan assumptions about covenant with God, and the convictions of a wide range of Revolutionary and post-Revolutionary leaders (deists, the orthodox, sectarians) who believed that God had especially blessed the United States."[60] Though the founders themselves were not evangelicals, the religious enthusiasm of the early nineteenth century gave fuel to this fire.

As a result of these ideas, the concept of Manifest Destiny also began to emerge during the 1840s as the country expanded westward. Though the idea had preexisted its American expression by one hundred years, this political philosophy combined these religious ideals of millennialism and the hope and duty inherent therein with an increased desire to enlarge and fortify the country.[61] This confidence in God's unique concern for America combined with a proactive sense of mission and activism would come to a crossroads with the Civil War, in which two warring sides appealed to the same ideals and authority.

DIVIDED PROVIDENCE: THE CIVIL WAR AS TURNING POINT

Though countless books have been written on the subject of the American Civil War, it is only recently that scholars have begun to examine the religious elements of the war in any depth. Considering the themes of divine mission, providence and divine favor articulated and developed in early America, a battle between two segments of the American population inevitably unsettled these long-held notions about the nation. In many ways, the success of the Revolution and massive expansion and industrial growth in the early 1800s led to a widely held confidence in America's status as a chosen people with divine guidance. The Civil War problematized this understanding in a fundamental way. During the Revolutionary War, Americans could easily articulate an understanding of the war as between the God-inspired American freedom fighters and the oppressive British forces; yet when the battle became a fight between Americans, the questions of providence and divine guidance became muddled.

Scholars differ in their conclusions as to the importance of the Civil War for American Christianity and the American civil religion. Charting the theological developments in the American churches at this time, Mark Noll has argued that the Civil War marked a time of theological crisis within Christianity not only regarding the Christian position on slavery but also about the issue of providence.[62] Nowhere is this tension more evident than in Lincoln's Second Inaugural Address, a speech that historian Harry Stout calls, together with the Gettysburg Address, one of "America's greatest sermons."[63]

At this point in the Civil War, many Americans expected a particular type of speech that celebrated American ideals or provided justification for the Union cause. However, Lincoln refused to give a clear statement of divine providence but spoke of an active God who did not side with either of the warring factions. Instead, this God stood in judgment as his people falsely invoked his name and committed violence against one another. As Ronald White writes, Lincoln delivered discomfort and uncertainty instead of justification and encouragement and thus "offered the Second Inaugural as the prism through which he strained to see the light of God in the darkest hour of the nation's history."[64]

Such a unique view of providence certainly shocked many but also reflected the particular circumstances of the Civil War. Ultimately, Lincoln complicated the practice of associating God's providence with a particular cause. As he noted, both sides call to the same God and invoke the same principles and moral strength and, hence, both cannot be right:

Both read the same Bible and pray to the same God, and each invokes His aid against the other. It may seem strange that any men should dare to ask a just God's assistance in wringing their bread from the sweat of other men's faces, but let us judge not, that we be not judged. The prayers of both could not be answered. That of neither has been answered fully. The Almighty has his own purposes. Woe unto the world because of offenses; for it must needs be that offenses come, but woe to that man by whom the offense cometh.[65]

Appeals to God, Lincoln argued, could not be made so un-self-consciously, indiscriminately or unrepentantly.

Broadening the focus to include political and governmental actions as well as theological ones, Harry Stout has called the Civil War "the incarnation of a national American civil religion."[66] Stout points to the increasing importance of the flag and other national symbols as well as indicating the beginning of true patriotism or nationalism in the young United States of America.[67] Indeed, it was during the Civil War that Lincoln proclaimed a national day of Thanksgiving as "a time to reflect on the sacred destiny of America."[68] While we have seen that such declarations had earlier appearances, this one had a particular meaning in light of Lincoln's somewhat chiding and cautioning civil religion.

It was also during the war that the phrase "In God We Trust" found its place on American currency. Borrowing from the last stanza of Francis Scott Key's *Star Spangled Banner*, an Act of Congress in April 1864 authorized the placement of this phrase on a two-cent coin. A further act in March 1865 and the Coinage Act of 1873 authorized "the motto IN GOD WE TRUST to be inscribed on such coins as shall admit of such motto."[69] This move marked another aspect of Lincoln's careful approach to religion and politics. As Stout writes, "although unwilling to proclaim America a Christian nation on the grounds of the separation of church and state, and aware of the Confederacy's boasted Christianity, Lincoln agreed to a compromise that would strengthen the links between Christianity and America's civil religion, while keeping each distinct."[70] The change in currency was thus a means of appeasing those looking for a more explicit indication of the Christian roots of the country while heading off the worries of those against a Christian nation. This motto was originally billed as a means of expressing the sentiment, articulated in a letter from Secretary of the Treasury Salmon P. Chase to the Director of the Mint at Philadelphia on November 20, 1861, that "No nation can be strong except in the strength of God, or safe except in His defense. The trust of our people in God should be declared on our national coins. You will cause a device to be prepared without unnecessary delay with a motto expressing in the fewest and tersest words possible this national recognition."[71]

The unsettling of American providentialism combined with the increased religiosity common in times of stress, upheaval, and violence made the Civil War a turning point in the American civil religion. Yet, as the subsequent world wars show, such polarizing and distinctly religious language only returned to the American political lexicon as the power of Lincoln's words and the horror of a war between brothers turned to more romanticized views of the war. After the turbulent antebellum periods and the racial struggles inherent in the end of slavery, the American society faced a new challenge. Growing diversity as a result of immigration and increasing religiously-motivated activism set the stage for the tumultuous twentieth century.

REDEFINING AMERICA: CHALLENGES OF DIVERSITY

Beginning in the 1890s, many Christian communities began to fuse religion and politics in an early configuration of the modern faith-based activism now debated in our courts. The Social Gospel movement involved a concrete means of turning Christian doctrine into actual political and social action. By embracing a post-millennial outlook that maintained the improvability of the world and an optimistic view of human nature and potential, this movement spurred the creation of numerous voluntary societies that explicitly shunned any idea that religion should remain in the private realm. To Social Gospelers like Washington Gladden and Walter Rauschenbusch, a Christian American had certain responsibilities to act morally and to reform society in such a way as to eliminate social problems. For example, in his treatise *Applied Christianity*, Gladden explained that though Christianity and the wealth that came to many from industrialization are not incompatible, wealth "puts the possessor under heavy obligations to multitudes less fortunate."[72] Gladden then proceeded to give a detailed account of the myriad ways in which Christianity and American social and political improvement went hand-in-hand, including the proper actions of a Christian employer and the proper utilization of the Bible for moral education in public schools.

Despite continued concern among Protestant Americans about the growing influence of Catholicism as a result of increased immigration, parallel social movements were occurring within the Catholic population. Many recent immigrants struggled to balance assimilation into Protestant America with maintenance of Catholic identity and struggled to find a way to express Catholic morality in their new communities. Spurred on by the general spirit of faith-motivated social activism prevalent around the turn of the century and inspired by Pope Leo XIII's encyclical on social and labor concerns, *Rerum Novarum*, Catholics moved into action. Pioneers such as John Ryan made dramatic progress in labor and poverty issues.[73]

On a more sinister side, the increasing immigration and concurrent social problems of poverty and illiteracy caused some to articulate an exclusionary ideology. Josiah Strong's 1885 book, *Our Country*, expresses Manifest Destiny in terms of race. Strong's arguments were based on a belief in the vital importance of that particular moment in history for the rest of human existence on earth. He began his book with the claim that "dependence of the world's future on this generation in America is not only credible, but in the highest degree probable."[74] After describing the perils of immigration, increased racial and religious diversity, including the rise in Roman Catholicism and Mormonism, Strong describes the importance of Anglo-Saxon, Protestant Christianity for the nation's future. Calling for "the evangelization of the world,"[75] Strong wrote with a sense of urgency: "Notwithstanding the great perils which threaten it, I cannot think our civilization will perish; but I believe it is fully in the hands of the Christians of the United States, during the next ten or fifteen years, to hasten or retard the coming of Christ's kingdom in the world by hundreds, and perhaps thousands of years. We of this generation and nation occupy the Gibraltar of the ages which commands the world's future."[76]

Politically, the increased diversity and growing strength of America following the Industrial Revolution led to a more robust and aggressive political ideology. President McKinley continued to use the Manifest Destiny language of the 1840s in the 1890s to allow for involvement in other affairs. As was evident in the Spanish-American War, this led people to believe "it was 'inevitable' that America would carry the message of Christian civilization to the benighted and barbaric peoples in the 'uncivilized' quarters of the world."[77] This type of interventionist and involved political practice foreshadowed the move from isolationism to involvement in World War I.

During this period of increasing world power and religious diversity, President Theodore Roosevelt did not hesitate to continue the religious rhetoric now firmly established as custom in inaugural addresses. In his Inaugural Address of 1905, Roosevelt began by expressing "gratitude to the Giver of Good who has blessed us with the conditions which have enabled us to achieve so large a measure of well being and of happiness." He continued by reminding Americans that "Much has been given us, and much will rightfully be expected from us. We have duties to others and duties to ourselves; and we can shirk neither."[78] Yet his most interesting contribution to the development of governmental religiosity comes in the 1907 controversy over the motto "In God We Trust."

In November of 1907, Roosevelt attempted to remove the motto from the new penny. Though Roosevelt was unsuccessful and Congress restored its placement in July of 1908, Roosevelt's reasoning for the proposed change might seem surprising to modern readers who might object to such a motto for its religious character. Roosevelt articulated his reasons for removing the logo in a letter to Roland C. Dryer on November 11, 1907. As Roosevelt wrote,

To use it in any kindred manner, not only does not good but does positive harm, and is in effect irreverence which comes dangerously close to sacrilege. A beautiful and solemn sentence such as the one in question should be treated and uttered only with that fine reverence which necessarily implies a certain exaltation of spirit. Any use which tends to cheapen it, and, above all, any use which tends to secure its being treated in a spirit of levity, is from every standpoint profoundly to be regretted. It is a motto which it is indeed well to have inscribed on our great national monuments, in our temples of justice, in our legislative halls, and in buildings such as those at West Point and Annapolis—in short, wherever it will tend to arise and inspire a lofty emotion in those who look thereon.[79]

In America, Roosevelt argued, this test of emotion was not met. Nevertheless, the Congress decided to maintain the motto as a symbol of the religious foundations of the nation and the continued involvement of God in its history.

RHETORIC AND PUBLIC OPINION: THE CIVIL RELIGION AND THE WORLD WARS

At the beginning of the twentieth century, the living generations had for the most part not experienced war on a wide scale. They lived with both an extremely glorified and extremely removed view of war. They felt it was something unforeseeable in this time of peace, a phenomenon of legends, not reality. Though many had lost family and friends in the Civil War, this war had been romanticized by many into a necessary growing pain for the young country and the inauguration of a time of unity and peace.[80] This idea was carried through to the pre–World War I era as peace efforts and social reforms reached a peak. Churches and inter-church organizations throughout the world felt comfortable in this peace and were able to state, publicly and enthusiastically, their commitments to peace and social reform. To establish and maintain this view, several organizations were created during this time such as the Federal Council of Churches' Commission on Peace and Arbitration in 1911.[81]

When the first declarations of war were made overseas in 1914, America faced an unsettling jolt out of its comfortable isolationism. Reflecting their idealism and aversion to war, Americans were not only shocked that war was a reality but also shocked that their European peers were participating in this tragedy. Moreover, Americans were convinced that no matter how backsliding and unreasonable Europe could be, the United States would never enter into such a conflict.[82] People across the world felt this would certainly be a short war and, thus, American involvement was not necessary. However, America did eventually enter the war. America's entry into the First World War was late and, even at that point, uncertain. America had no true enemies in the conflict and had previously been most concerned with maintaining free trade with both the Entente and Axis powers. The unrestricted submarine warfare of Germany was the only truly offensive act against the United States and even that was not enough for many to justify involvement in this largely European war. For these reasons and more, the beginning of the war prompted much weariness and concern among Americans.

However, over the course of the First World War, American public opinion underwent a dramatic change. The pacifist ideologies before the war had been whole-heartedly supported by Christians and non-Christians alike, the politicians, and the clergy. The prevailing sentiment supported a largely noninterventionist country that worked to reform its own society while having only a conciliatory and peace-making role in the war. However, once American involvement was deemed necessary, political and religious leaders were able to turn public opinion around completely through propaganda and a deft use of civil religious and even Christian language. The same ideals that led to a pacifist ideology before were transformed into a zealous frenzy of support led by Christians. World War I is perhaps the most dramatic example in history of how the American civil religion can alter the minds of the public. The man most responsible for this transformation is the president during this war, Woodrow Wilson.

Wilson's religious views were largely based on a covenant theology at the center of the American civil religion. In the words of Pierard and Linder, he argued that "the world was a battlefield of good and evil, and one must not compromise principles in the struggle. God's law was the constitution for the world and the Bible the guide for a person's life. Hard work was a fulfillment of one's duty to God and would result in divine favor."[83] In the realm of foreign policy, Wilson also exhibited a sort of missionary approach that he shared with his Secretary of State, William Jennings Bryan. Their political decisions reflected the "desire to promote justice and international peace and give all peoples the blessing of democracy and Christianity, even if that meant interference in the internal affairs of other nations."[84] Though this view was not new to American political rhetoric, it was somewhat novel during this time as the country was only slowly moving to the interventionist philosophy of politics that is so familiar today. Wilson was reluctant at first to pursue an active foreign policy, but over the course of the war he utilized covenant ideology and missionary theology to justify the eventual American involvement.

Wilson articulated a role for the United States as mediator in the conflict through the early years of the war. At an address to the Associated Press in April 1915, Wilson remarked, "We are the mediating Nation of the world

... We are trustees for what I venture to say is the greatest heritage that any nation ever had, the love of justice and righteousness and human liberty."[85] Wilson, as a representative of America and democracy, was not attempting to forward America but "the cause of humanity itself."[86]

Though public opinion was mixed and somewhat reluctant to support a concerted war effort, with the unrestricted submarine warfare of the Germans, the infamous Zimmerman telegram, and other offenses, America entered the arena. Since the war was already well underway, the American government faced the need for rapid mobilization of armies and resources as well as public support. Expressing the competing sentiments of many Americans, Wilson remarked on February 2, 1916, in Kansas City, Missouri, "Madness has entered into everything, and that serene flag which we have thrown to the breeze upon so many occasions as the beckoning finger of hope to those who believe in the rights of mankind will itself be stained with the blood of battle, and staggering here and there among its foes will lead men to wonder where the star of America has gone and why America has allowed herself to be embroiled when she might have carried that standard serenely forward to the redemption of the affairs of mankind."[87] In this sense, the war was a tragic necessity. Americans had to support it, not because it was glamorous but because it was their duty.

Under the guise of the Committee on Public Information (CPI), Wilson enacted extreme propaganda to curb American reluctance to enter the war. The Committee produced posters, ads, films, and other such material that worked to demonize the enemy and to celebrate freedom and democracy. John Blum argues that the Committee forwarded two main ideas, "One, the postulate of the President, that Americans fought only for freedom and democracy; the other ... that the Germans, 'Huns' all, were creatures of the devil attempting by the deliberate, lustful perpetration of atrocities, to conquer the war."[88]

In reaction to such propaganda efforts and similar efforts at mobilization by Christian congregations, discussions of the war began to take on a religious tone. This was particularly true in demonizing the German nation. Propaganda frequently portrayed Germans and the Kaiser himself as the Devil, and this language translated to religious situations as well. Some clergy went so far as to call the war a crusade: "It is God who has summoned us to this war. It is his war we are fighting.... This conflict is indeed a crusade. The greatest in history—the holiest. It is in the profoundest and truest sense a Holy War ... Yes, it is Christ, the King of Righteousness, who calls us to grapple in deadly strife with this unholy and blasphemous power [Germany]."[89] Echoing similar language, Wilson described the ways in which American soldiers were perceived by those they encountered overseas: "They were recognized as crusaders, and as their thousands swelled to millions, their strength was seen to mean salvation."[90]

Such virulent patriotism reached a peak during this war and was followed by a time of self-examination and reflection for American churches and the nation as a whole. In the aftermath of the war, Americans were forced to examine not only the efficacy of American involvement in the war but also their own reactions and emotions. Those Americans who found Wilson's energetic attempts to spread American values and democracy through the world inappropriate or excessive were satisfied by the more tempered vision of Franklin D. Roosevelt.

Religious communities began to express pacifist philosophies and regret for their explicit patriotism during the war. Many participated in postwar pacts, leagues and councils such as the 1935 National Peace Conference and the 1936 Emergency Peace Campaign.[91] By the dawn of World War II, the majority of Christian denominations had proclaimed some sort of pacifism. Echoing these sentiments, Roosevelt promised "to throw the full weight of the United States into the cause of peace. In spite of spreading wars I think that we have every right and every reason to maintain as a national policy the fundamental moralities, the teachings of religion and the continuation of efforts to restore peace—because some day though the time may be distant, we can be of even greater help to a crippled humanity."[92] Though the political position of the nation and this Christian pacifism were then aligned, as the war progressed, the two became at odds.

As the war developed, it became clear that the only road to peace, for Roosevelt, was the success of democracy over the evil and repressive regimes elsewhere in the world. Even in the face of increased public pacifism in the inter-war years, Roosevelt was able to use this emphasis on democracy and the American ideals (which include Christianity), to garner support for the war effort. On Selective Service Registration Day, Roosevelt used this idea to justify the first draft ever conducted during peacetime in America. To those who were registering, Roosevelt emphasized the importance of their role in the war effort: "We of today, with God's help, can bequeath to Americans of tomorrow a nation in which the ways of liberty and justice will survive and be secure. Such a nation must be devoted to the cause of peace. And it is for that cause that America arms itself."[93]

During the war years, as Hitler's atrocities became public, Americans united behind the war effort and Roosevelt's use of quasi-religious language to justify combat and rally support continued. In a move later echoed by George W. Bush in speeches on terrorism, Roosevelt linked Hitler with evil, Nazism with tyranny. In 1942, Roosevelt spoke to Congress about the Allied Powers' role in the world and concluded that the Axis Powers "know that victory for us means victory for religion. And they could not tolerate that. The world is too small to provide adequate 'living room' for both Hitler and God."[94] In this way, World War II exemplified this American tendency to map religious language onto political realities as a means of securing national identity and political and ideological goals, as well as of continuing America's influence in the world.

DEFINING AMERICAN IDENTITY: THE SUPREME COURT WEIGHS IN ON THE LIMITS OF ESTABLISHMENT

Despite continued remorse over war and the atomic bombs, the defeat of Germany and Japan in the Second World War and the intimate involvement of most Americans in the war effort led to its romanticization and a continued sentiment that the United States of America should serve a leadership role in a world in crisis. As the 1940s drew to a close and the continued threat of communism loomed large, the American civil religion entered yet another phase. This phase was characterized by a decisive Supreme Court case directly addressing the establishment of religion, the entrance of subtle religious references into the public lexicon, increasing religious diversity, and the threat of non-religious communism.

Interestingly, it was soon after the Second World War that the Supreme Court directly addressed the issue of establishment in 1947's *Everson v. Board of Education of the Township of Ewing et al*. Examining a case involving governmental financial support for bussing to Catholic schools, the Court decided that such funding did not constitute a violation of the Establishment Clause. Though this practice did benefit a religious organization, the funding was also available for other types of schools. The majority opinion cited the First Amendment, the long struggle for religious liberty in early America and James Madison's "Memorial and Remonstrance" to underscore the importance of avoiding establishment. However, this opinion concluded that to deny the funding would mean to discriminate against religion. In the majority opinion, Justice Black interpreted the First Amendment as mandating "the state to be a neutral in its relations with groups of religious believers and non-believers; it does not require the state to be their adversary. State power is no more to be used so as to handicap religions than it is to favor them."[95]

This landmark decision would shape the profusion of later cases to arise out of the particular circumstances of the 1950s and 1960s, particularly in its stipulation that government should not be hostile to religion. This concern for maintenance of a religious culture but avoidance of establishment was a sign of the times. The harmony resulting from the complete mobilization of the country in war had helped to soften some of the lines dividing the nativists and immigrants of the late nineteenth century and helped to usher in a more unified vision of American identity. Perhaps most illustrative of this change is Will Herberg's oft-cited book, *Protestant-Catholic-Jew*. Exhibiting an evolution in American identity from the days of Josiah Strong but also a rather limited perspective in light of modern diversity, Herberg sought to paint a positive picture of the new, religiously diverse America. He argued that "both the religiousness and the secularism of the American people derive from very much the same sources." Catholicism, Protestantism and Judaism share a scripture, an Abrahamic heritage, the same God and similar morality.[96] Above all, and in marked contrast to Communism, "the primary religious affirmation of the American people, in harmony with the American Way of Life, is that religion is a 'good thing,' a supremely 'good thing,' for the individual and the community."[97] Americans, Herberg argued, can find unity in this belief in the general importance of faith without needing to reconcile the inevitable doctrinal differences among them.

Just as the Protestant American leaders began to recognize Catholicism and Judaism as acceptable and morally rigorous belief systems, so too did Catholics move toward a more pluralistic view of the country. John Courtney Murray, who had previously come under fire from Catholics at home and abroad for essays in the 1940s advocating religious liberty in America and beyond, began "to urge Catholics to strike a more temperate balance between Catholic principles and public consensus" and often spoke in forums concerning American pluralism.[98] Murray's most extensive treatment of this subject came in his 1960 book, *We Hold These Truths: Catholic Reflections on the American Proposition*, in which he simultaneously lauded religious freedom while also warning against replacing traditional religion with an over-developed faith in American ideals such as religious liberty.[99] Anticipating and later influencing the statement on religious liberty articulated by Vatican II, Murray underscored the vital importance of religious freedom to the American democratic system and, indeed, to the Catholic religion. In this way, he recognized pluralism in religious beliefs and growing conflict between differing groups while advocating a continued separation of church and state as a means of maintaining these differences while allowing for cooperation. For Murray, because "pluralism was the native condition of American society," this trend should not be fought against but embraced with a commitment to dialogue over warfare.[100]

President Dwight D. Eisenhower often articulated a similar sentiment. In terms of presidential politics, some scholars have viewed Eisenhower as a central figure in the trajectory of civil religious language. Hutcheson argues that "If Washington, Jefferson, and Madison were the formulators of

America's civil religion, then, and Lincoln was its major theologian, Eisenhower was its prime exemplar in modern times."[101] Indeed, responding to concerns regarding "atheistic communism" and the rise of McCarthyism, the Commander-in-Chief frequently referenced religion in many ways. Eisenhower's First Inaugural Address, January 20, 1952, began with a prayer written the morning of the Inaugural by the president himself. Through this "private prayer" Eisenhower asked for divine assistance and guidance, "beseeching that Thou will make full and complete our dedication to the service of the people in this throng, and their fellow citizens everywhere."[102]

Continuing in this vein, it was during Eisenhower's presidency that the phrase, "In God We Trust" became the national motto, on July 30, 1956. Though it was in use on currency since the 1860s, Eisenhower made the move to solidify the importance of this motto as a clear indicator of the religious ideals that shaped the lives of many Americans and which lay at the foundation of the country's identity. By 1966, the motto appeared on all paper money. It was also during the 1950s that other references to God appeared in the government such as "so help me God" added to the end of court oaths and "under God" added to the Pledge of Allegiance in schools. In many ways, this was a direct response to the fear of "Atheistic Communism" and a reaffirmation of American Judeo-Christian principles of divine dependence as the basis for government and civil society.

During his administration, Eisenhower also established a staff position in the White House to coordinate religious affairs and continually stressed the conflict between religion and communism.[103] A clear indicator of this increased religiosity in the White House was the institution of the National Prayer Breakfast, officially begun in 1953 by a group then known as the International Christian Leadership and now known generally as "the Fellowship," a Christian organization based in Washington, D.C. While invitations and official correspondence suggest a direct sponsorship by the Congress or president, the Fellowship funds and organizes the event while also avoiding publicity and recognition.[104] The general purpose of such meetings is understood to be "a genuine concern to minister to the spiritual needs of people in places of leadership," and the speakers at such meetings tend to articulate rather general religious sentiments.[105] These events have been low on publicity, and the press is discouraged to attend. Following the general prayer meeting, the Fellowship holds leadership forums or workshops for smaller groups and, in this context, forwards a more explicitly religious agenda.

Though such interaction between the government and Christian organizations has not lead to court challenges or legislative changes, it has elicited condemnation from strict separationists and those outside of Christianity.

Indeed, numerous court cases were tried over the next several decades deciding matters of establishment and where the tricky line of separation should lie. The civil rights movement raised questions as to the inclusiveness of the American civil religion in terms of race. Many began to ask whether racial discrimination suggested an unequal application of American principles of freedom and opportunity.

With the 1960s came increased religious diversity as many Americans became exposed to Eastern religions for the first time and changes such as Vatican II and the various political and social revolutions changed understandings of appropriate morality. With the election of the first Catholic president, Americans adopted broader understanding of the presidency. Yet, much remained continuous. Like Eisenhower before him, John F. Kennedy, Jr., continued the language of an American dependence on a broadly conceived Judeo-Christian God. Moreover, Kennedy demonstrated an intensely personal and private religious life apart from but in cooperation with his public role as president.[106] Kennedy appealed to this sense of public faith in his Inaugural Address:

Finally, whether you are citizens of America or citizens of the world, ask of us the same high standards of strength and sacrifice which we ask of you. With a good conscience our only sure reward, with history the final judge of our deeds, let us go forth to lead the land we love, asking His blessing and His help, but knowing that here on earth God's work must truly be our own.[107]

Yet, despite these continuities, the changing religious landscape and liberal understanding of morality led to the questioning of many long-held practices in government and schools.

Just as the 1960s marked unrest in the social and political realm at large, so too was there unrest over issues of church and state. During this period, numerous Supreme Court cases addressed applications of the establishment question raised in *Everson V. Board* in the late 1940s. In 1961, *Torcaso v. Watkins* dealt with the issue of religious tests first debated by the founding fathers. Striking down a Maryland decision to deny employment to a notary public based on his refusal to express belief in God, the Court again cited concerns over both religious establishment and freedom of belief. Referring to the historical debate and Article VI of the Constitution and Bill of Rights, the majority opinion by Justice Black sought to "reaffirm that neither a State nor the Federal Government can constitutionally force a person 'to profess a belief or disbelief in any religion.' Neither can constitutionally pass laws or impose requirements which aid all religions as against nonbelievers and neither can aid those religions based on a belief in the existence of God as against those religions founded on different beliefs."[108] Interestingly this case concluded that even something as neutral as belief in God, though devoid of any particular doctrinal specifics, preferences belief above unbelief. This has interesting implications for the morality of the American civil religion that, as we saw above, most often manifests in such seemingly innocuous references to a generic "God."

Addressing appeals to God in a different setting, the Court decided in the 1962 case, *Engel v. Vitale*, that daily classroom prayers in public schools were a clear violation of the Establishment Clause. Justice Black again gave the majority opinion writing "there can, of course, be no doubt that New York's program of daily classroom invocation of God's blessings as prescribed in the Regents' prayer is a religious activity. It is a solemn avowal of divine faith and supplication for the blessings of the Almighty." Then reaffirming the importance of religion in the history of mankind, Black wrote, "It is neither sacrilegious nor antireligious to say that each separate government in this country should stay out of the business of writing or sanctioning official prayers and leave that purely religious function to the people themselves and to those the people choose to look to for religious guidance."[109] The Court would not address similar prayers in congressional meetings until a later date. The difference in conclusions suggests the centrality of age and impressionability in the *Engel* case.

Though the Supreme Court has declined to hear appeals of the 1970s cases regarding the constitutionality of the national motto, "In God We Trust" (which, incidentally, hangs on the wall of the Court), several lower court cases are worth mention. In 1970's *Aronow v. United States*, the United States Court of Appeals for the Ninth Circuit found that this motto has only a "patriotic or ceremonial character" and thus does not constitute an establishment of religion.[110] This decision was upheld in the 1979 case brought by the founder of the American Atheists to challenge use of the motto, *Madalyn Murray O'Hair et al. v. W. Michael Blumenthal, Secretary of Treasury, et. al.* The United States Court of Appeals for the Fifth Circuit referred to the 1970 case in affirming that "the primary purpose of the slogan was secular," a conclusion echoed in later Supreme Court decisions on public monuments of the Ten Commandments.[111]

In 1973, a U.S. Appeals Court decided to allow the erection of a monument to the Ten Commandments at a courthouse in *Anderson v. Salt Lake City Corp.* In addition to the Decalogue, the monument contained various other symbols and references to Abrahamic faiths and U.S. history. The Court concluded that "the monolith is primarily secular, and not religious in character; that neither its purpose or effect tends to establish religious belief."[112] Though the court recommended an additional sign marking the secular and historical importance of this monument over its specifically religious content, the court maintained the significance as one of heritage and culture. The Supreme Court declined to review this ruling.

With the election of Jimmy Carter came a change in presidential application of religious language and continued change in the political climate. Unlike Kennedy, Carter's religion was both a personal and public matter and his explicit religiosity in public statements rubbed some people the wrong way in light of the increasingly religiously diverse society. Going beyond general reference to God or providence, Carter directly quoted the Bible in his Inaugural Address: "He hath showed thee, O'man, what is good; and what doth the Lord require of thee, but to do justly, and to love mercy, and to walk humbly with thy God." He then spoke of "a new beginning, a new dedication within our Government, and a new spirit among us all," presumably based on this guidance from God.[113] Such a spirit apparently failed to unite all Americans as several new cases came before the U.S. Appeals and Supreme Courts addressing perceived violations of the Establishment Clause. The variety of conclusions reached in these cases suggests a diversity of opinion in the public and within the courts and the complexity of the American civil religion.

Reviving an issue first debated in the eighteenth century, the 1978 Supreme Court ruling *McDaniel v. Paty* addressed seemingly conflicting claims to the Free Exercise and Establishment Clauses. In this case, the Supreme Court reversed a Tennessee statute that disallowed clergy from holding public office. Though Tennessee has not historically been alone in such a law, most states had hitherto removed this law from their books. Seven judges agreed with the majority opinion though for slightly different reasons. However, each judge emphasized the importance of free exercise and the idea of neutrality rather than hostility to or support of a particular religious practice. The ruling in *Torcaso v. Watkins* "does not govern," Burger's opinion stated. As he continued, since the disqualification is based on McDaniel's status as a clergyman, and since the law "is directed primarily at status, acts, and conduct it is unlike the requirement in *Torcaso*, which focused on *belief.* Hence, the Free Exercise Clause's absolute prohibition of infringements on the 'freedom to believe' is inapposite here." However, Burger continued, the Tennessee ruling is to be struck down because the Tennessee government failed to demonstrate that this minister would necessarily violate the Establishment Clause through untoward influence. Appealing to the earliest debates of this issue, Burger wrote, "However widely that view may have been held in the 18th century by many, including enlightened statesmen of that day, the American experience provides no persuasive support for the fear that clergymen in public office will be less careful of anti-establishment interests or less faithful to their oaths of civil office than their unordained counterparts."[114]

Soon thereafter, another establishment case came before a U.S. Appeals Court based upon events leading up to Pope John Paul II's October 1979 visit to Philadelphia. In the 1980 case *Gilfillan et al. v. City of Philadelphia*, the Court found the expenditure of $200,000 by the city to erect a special platform on which the Pope would deliver the Mass and give a sermon to be unconstitutional.[115] The Court ruled this to be a violation of the Establishment Clause because the city had violated all three requirements of the Lemon Test of 1971's *Lemon v. Kurtzman* by acting for a religious purpose, advancing religion, and promoting "impermissible entanglement."[116] The local Archdiocese reimbursed the city for the expenditures and the Supreme Court denied a rehearing in May 1981.

Using similar justification for disallowing another public religious display, the Supreme Court addressed the issue of display of the Ten Commandments in Kentucky public schools in *Stone v. Graham* in 1980. The court reversed a lower court decision allowing such display and claiming a secular application by arguing that the display of these documents could not have a "secular legislative purpose."[117] Again, appealing to the Lemon test, the court appealed to similar reasoning as the *Gilfillan* case. Interestingly, the court later found that such a display could have a primarily secular purpose outside of the classroom as shown below, again indicating a difference between settings involving children and those involving adults.

During the Reagan presidency, the relationship between religion and politics took an interesting turn. After Carter, Reagan stood as a sign of the changing nature of presidential politics and religion, as this very religious but very private president kept his practice and faith from public view while lending support to the growing Religious Right.[118] In his Inaugural Speech, Reagan spoke of "the American sound" and how Americans "raise our voices to the God who is Author of this most tender music." He then continued with the wish that, "He continue to hold us close as we fill the world with our sound, sound in unity, affection, and love; one people under God, dedicated to the dream of freedom that He has placed in the human heart, called upon now to pass that dream on to a waiting and hoping world."[119] Two years into his presidency, Reagan proclaimed 1983 "the Year of the Bible in the United States," recognizing its influence in the founding and governance of the country and encouraging "all citizens, each in his or her own way, to reexamine and rediscover its priceless and timeless message."[120] Interestingly, his presidency marked the emergence of both stronger and more visible religious political movement but also more awareness and opposition from those outside the movement.

In 1982, the U.S. Court of Appeals, Eleventh Circuit heard the case of the *ACLU v. Rabun County*, a case concerning the erection of a cross on an 85 foot structure in Black Rock Mountain State Park in Georgia. The local Chamber of Commerce was to pay for the upkeep of the cross and planned to dedicate it on Easter Sunday, 1979, saying in a press release that "the cross is a symbol of Christianity for millions of people in this great nation and the world."[121] Soon thereafter, the American Civil Liberties Union (ACLU) demanded the removal of the cross and the court battle began. Ultimately, the Appeals Court found the installation and maintenance of the cross to be a violation of the Establishment Clause of the First Amendment. The decision was made in large part due to the "noneconomic injury" suffered by those utilizing the state park that were unwittingly forced to have a particular religious experience through the unavoidable presence of the cross. Moreover, the installation of the cross violated all three of the criteria for establishment listed in the Lemon Test—it had no secular purpose, had a primary purpose of advancing religion, and suggested an inappropriate entanglement of government and religion.

In a remarkable case that underscored and perhaps affirmed theories of civil religion in America, the Supreme Court acted in 1983 to continue the use of prayer in governmental session. In *Marsh v. Chambers*, the Supreme Court overturned a Nebraska ruling that held that the paying of a chaplain to say a prayer at the beginning of the Nebraska legislative sessions was a violation of the Establishment Clause though the prayer itself was not. The majority opinion, written by Chief Justice Burger, recognized the Nebraska court's finding that such payment violated all elements of the Lemon Test but argued instead that the use of chaplains and prayer in legislative sessions "is deeply embedded in the history and tradition of this country."[122] The fact that such a practice has continued alongside the policies of disestablishment and religious freedom suggests it must remain and is not problematic. However, Burger was careful to articulate that he was not only arguing from historical consistency but from the idea that the founders clearly understood such practice to be consistent with these other principles of separation of church and state.

In an interesting turn in light of the 1982 lower court case, *ACLU v. Rabun County*, the Supreme Court upheld the constitutionality of a public crèche in *Lynch v. Donnelly*. Though four justices dissented, Burger's majority opinion held that since the crèche was part of a city Christmas display and included non-religious holiday elements as well, it did not have an explicitly religious purpose. The court thereby reversed two lower court decisions by pointing to the role of religion in U.S. history and such practices as Thanksgiving, the use of the national motto, and the fact that

Christian holidays are national holidays. In essence, Burger wrote, "the crèche in the display depicts the historical origins of this traditional event [the Christmas holiday season] long recognized as a National Holiday." As he continued, "the display engenders a friendly community spirit of goodwill" in much the same way as prayers before congressional sessions are immediately followed by heated debates over taxes and national defense.[123]

These cases demonstrate both the complexity of the separation of church and state and the increased contentiousness surrounding these issues in modern times. As religious diversity increases, many of the hitherto unquestioned religious elements of the United States government will likely be further questioned in the courts. However, the American civil religion born with the country and most eloquently described by Robert Bellah in 1969 continues strongly to shape our national rhetoric and ritual. In 2000, George W. Bush articulated the principles of this civil religion in his First Inaugural Address. He proclaimed, "We are not this story's author, who fills time and eternity with His purpose. Yet His purpose is achieved in our duty, and our duty is fulfilled in service to one another. Never tiring, never yielding, never finishing, we renew that purpose today; to make our country more just and generous; to affirm the dignity of our lives and every life. This work continues. This story goes on. And an angel still rides in the whirlwind and directs this storm."[124]

This whirlwind reached fever-pitch during the events of September 11, 2001, when America faced the realization that not all the world agreed with the policies and control of American foreign policy. With the effects of the terrorist attacks so devastating and shocking to Americans, it did not take long for President Bush to cast the event in religious tones. In a move reminiscent of the demonization of Germans during the World Wars, Bush quickly set up dramatic dualisms between America and its enemies. In his remarks on the South Lawn on September 16, 2001, Bush characterized the terrorists as "barbaric," as "evil-doers," and proclaimed that Americans had a duty "to hunt down, to find, to smoke [the terrorist organizations] out of their holes." This language makes the enemy simultaneous evil and animal-like and culminated in Bush's characterization of the War on Terror as a "crusade."[125]

These continuities continue in the courts as well. The 2005 case of *Van Orden v. Perry* argued the constitutionality of a public display of the Ten Commandments on the state capital grounds in Texas.[126] The monument was a gift from a private organization in 1961 and, in addition to the text, the monument was inscribed with symbols of Jewish faith, Christ, the American flag and other patriotic symbols and a plaque recognizing the donors of the gift. The Court agreed with the state's contention that such a monument did not advocate religion explicitly but recognized the importance of religion in the nation's and the state's history. According to the Court, appeal to religion in the context of common heritage continues to be acceptable.

In the same year, another case was decided with different results. In *McCreary County v. ACLU*, the Court argued that a display of a simple posting of the Ten Commandments and a passage from Exodus in two Kentucky county courthouses was unconstitutional in that such a monument had a religious purpose.[127] Without the additional symbols and historical focus of the *Van Orden v. Perry* monument, the court felt such a posting violated the establishment clause. Interestingly, in their dissent, Scalia, Rehnquist, and Thomas argued that the postings were constitutional in that they recognized a basic belief in God common to all Abrahamic faiths as expressed elsewhere in American government. Referring to presidential use of the phrase, "God Bless America" and presidential calls for public days of fasting and prayer, Scalia concluded that a denial of the religious basis of the country was a false belief in the neutrality of the government to religion in general. While one can argue whether these practices should be used as evidence or should be questioned themselves, this chapter has shown this continuity to be undeniable.

PRESENT AND FUTURE DEVELOPMENTS

On the 50th Anniversary of the national motto, "In God We Trust," George W. Bush called on all Americans to "remember with thanksgiving God's mercies throughout our history" and to "recognize a divine plan that stands above all human plans and continue to seek His will."[128] In so doing, Bush articulated the same appeal to a common religious heritage expressed by those on the Supreme Court who have advocated maintenance of religious language in government. The intent of this chapter has been both to provide an explanation for the development and reality of this peculiar role of religious language in American governmental practice and also to show the continuity and evolution of this reality to the present day. Just as debates have raged throughout American history over the appropriateness of such a reality, so too does the debate continue today. In addition to the more specific issues argued in the Supreme Court and political forums such as abortion, stem-cell research, and prayer in schools, political theorists and other figures have weighed in on the likely future intersections between religion and government.

Taking a negative stand towards these manifestations of civil religion, Gary Wills has argued that the Supreme Court should continue to remove religion from the government, including ceremony and proclamations hitherto untouched by legislative rulings.[129] On this view, references to God are inherently and entirely inappropriate in a diverse nation and should be eliminated. At issue here are two key concerns: the first being a desire to stay true to the founders' intention to avoid establishment of religion, and the second being a growing awareness of the increasing incompatibility between the seemingly innocuous civil religion and the variety of new faiths gaining prominence in the United States of America and abroad. Interestingly, these two issues are intimately and somewhat paradoxically related. As Os Guiness wrote in 1990, "modern pluralism stands squarely as both the child of, and the challenger to, religious liberty."[130]

Whether one agrees with the use of religious language in governmental rhetoric and ritual or not, it is also important to examine the extent to which this situation is likely to change. Hutcheson has articulated a consistency in the figure of the president and writes, "As long as moral questions continue to be asked, religious answers will be sought. American society's experiments with values divorced from religion have not been encouraging. Despite the complex reasoning of secular ethicists, Americans by and large remain convinced that morality and religion are inseparable. And as long as that remains the case, religion is likely to play a continuing role in the presidency, and the presidency in religion."[131] Describing this connection in a more general manner, Jeff Stout has recently written that "democracy . . . is misconceived when taken to be a desert landscape hostile to whatever life-giving waters of culture and tradition might still flow through it. Democracy is better construed as the name appropriate to the currents themselves in this particular time and place."[132] Perhaps it is inherent to democracy to use culture, religion, and tradition to revitalize its systems and inspire its citizens. The challenge of the twenty-first century will be to reconfigure the American civil religion in such a way as to appeal to the broad spectrum of religious and non-religious individuals now within its borders. Whether this can happen without sacrificing the vitality and mobilizing power of the civil religion remains to be seen.

NOTES

1. Leonard W. Levy, *The Establishment Clause: Religion and the First Amendment* (New York: Macmillan Publishing Company, 1986), 126–127.

2. Mark DeWolfe Howe, *The Garden and the Wilderness: Religion and Government in American Constitutional History* (Chicago: University of Chicago Press, 1965), 11.

3. Sidney E. Mead, "The Nation with the Soul of a Church," in *American Civil*

Religion, ed. Russell E. Richey and Donald G. Jones (New York: Harper and Row Publishers, 1974), 45.

4. Robert N. Bellah, "Civil Religion in America," *Daedalus* 96, no. 1 (Winter 1967), 3.

5. The term "civil religion" has received its most sustained and well-known treatment by Robert Bellah in his *Daedalus* article, "Civil Religion in America," and subsequent books, such as *The Broken Covenant: Civil Religion in a Time of Trial*. The term itself has had earlier articulations, most notably in Jean-Jacques Rousseau's *The Social Contract*, Book IV, Chapter 8.

6. Will Herberg, "America's Civil Religion: What it is and Whence it Comes," in Richey and Jones, 78.

7. Jürgen Moltmann, "Christian Theology and Political Religion," in *Civil Religion and Political Theology*, ed. Leroy S. Rouner (Notre Dame: University of Notre Dame Press, 1986), 47.

8. Alexis de Tocqueville, *Democracy in America*, Harvey C. Mansfield and Delba Winthrop, trans. (Chicago: University of Chicago Press, 2000), 275.

9. For a discussion of the history of this rhetoric, see Sacvan Bercovitch, *The American Jeremiad* (Madison: The University of Wisconsin Press, 1978), xi. Bercovitch describes this type of language as the "American jeremiad," which he defines as "a mode of public exhortation that originated in the European pulpit, was transformed in both form and content by the New England Puritans, persisted through the eighteenth century, and helped sustain a national dream through two hundred years of turbulence and change."

10. Arthur Schlesinger, Jr. and Fred L. Israel, eds., *The Chief Executive: Inaugural Addresses of the Presidents of the United States* (New York: Crown Publishers, Inc., 1965), 3.

11. George W. Bush, "Second Inaugural Address, January 20, 2005," http://www.whitehouse.gov/inaugural/

12. Bellah, "Civil Religion in America," 7.

13. Robert N. Bellah, *The Broken Covenant: American Civil Religion in a Time of Trial, 2nd Edition* (Chicago: The University of Chicago Press, 1992), 38–39.

14. Robert S. Alley, *So Help Me God: Religion and the Presidency, Wilson to Nixon* (Richmond, VA: John Knox Press, 1972), 24.

15. Richard V. Pierard and Robert D. Linder, *Civil Religion and the Presidency* (Grand Rapids, MI: Academie Books, 1988), 19.

16. Bercovitch, 7–8.

17. Ibid.

18. John Winthrop, "A Model of Christian Charity," in *The American Puritans: Their Prose and Poetry*, ed. Perry Miller (Garden City, NY: Anchor Books, 1956), 83.

19. Thomas J. Curry, *The First Freedoms: Church and State in America to the Passage of the First Amendment* (New York: Oxford University Press, 1986), 5.

20. Jon Butler, *Awash in a Sea of Faith: Christianizing the American People* (Cambridge, MA: Harvard University Press, 1990), 128.

21. Mark A. Noll, *America's God: From Jonathan Edwards to Abraham Lincoln* (New York: Oxford University Press, 2002), 32.

22. Derek H. Davis, *Religion and the Continental Congress, 1774–1789: Contributions to Original Intent* (New York: Oxford University Press, 2000), 27–28.

23. Millennial Christianity focuses on the Second Coming of Jesus and the realization of the Kingdom of God and can be further distinguished as pre- or post-millennialist. Pre-millennialists believe that the Kingdom of God cannot be realized here on earth and that Jesus must first come before the Kingdom will come to be. Thus, there are limits as to how much society can be improved by human means. For post-millennialists, the improvements made to society by humans serve to hasten Jesus' Second Coming. Once Christians establish this ideal world on earth, the Kingdom of God will be realized and Jesus will arrive. Thus, these Christians (other examples include the Social Gospelers and Nativists of the late-19th and early-20th centuries) see a need to improve societal conditions and work for the good in this lifetime.

24. Davis, 48. For a discussion of this democratizing element of American Christianity, see Nathan O. Hatch, *The Democratization of American Christianity* (New Haven: Yale University Press, 1989).

25. Noll, *America's God*, 174.

26. Patricia U. Bonomi, *Under the Cope of Heaven: Religion, Society, and Politics in Colonial America* (New York: Oxford University Press, 1986), 186.

27. Bonomi, 3.

28. Ibid., 216.

29. Davis, 65.

30. Ibid., 66.

31. Ibid., 84.

32. Philip Hamburger, *Separation of Church and State* (Cambridge: Harvard University Press, 2002), 81.

33. Hamburger, 83.

34. Ibid., 86.

35. John F. Wilson, "Religion under the State Constitutions, 1776–1800," *Journal of Church and State* 32 (Autumn 1990): 764.

36. Davis, 35.

37. Catherine L. Albanese, *Sons of the Fathers: The Civil Religion of the American Revolution* (Philadelphia: Temple University Press, 1976), 222.

38. Butler, 196.

39. Ibid., 212.

40. Ruth H. Bloch, *Visionary Republic: Millennial Themes in American Thought, 1756–1800* (New York: Cambridge University Press, 1985), 78.

41. Ibid., xiii.

42. "Declaration of the Causes and Necessity for Taking Up Arms: The Declaration as Adopted by Congress, July 6, 1775," *Jefferson & Madison on Separation of Church and State: Writings on Religion and Secularism*, ed. Lenni Brenner (Fort Lee, NJ: Baricade Books, 2004), 20.

43. Bloch, 56.
44. Ibid., 106.
45. "The Virginia Constitution as Adopted: June 29, 1776," Brenner, 23.
46. Constitution of the United States of America, Article VI.
47. "James Madison, Observations on Jefferson's Draught of a Constitution for Virginia [ca. October 15, 1788]," Brenner, 99.
48. Pierard and Linder, 51.
49. George Washington, State of the Union Address to Congress, November 19, 1794, available from the Library of Congress at http://memory.loc.gov/ammem/gwhtml/gwhome.html
50. Hutcheson, 37.
51. "George Washington: First Inaugural Address in the City of New York, April 30, 1789," *I Do Solemnly Swear: The Inaugural Addresses of the Presidents of the United States, 1789–2001* (Philadelphia: Chelsea House Publishers, 2001), 2–3.
52. "Proclamation for a Day of Thanksgiving by the President of the United States of America," containing a facsimile of his Public Accounts, kept during the Revolutionary War, and some of the most interesting documents connected with his military command and civil administration, 4th ed. (Washington, D.C.: Franklin Knight, 1844), 84.
53. "Washington's Legacy: or, Farewell Address to the People of the United States," *Monuments of Washington's Patriotism* (Washington, D.C.: Franklin Knight, 1844), 88.
54. Quoted in Hamburger, 186.
55. Thomas Jefferson, *Notes on the State of Virginia* (New York: W.W. Norton & Company, 1972), 159.
56. "Thomas Jefferson: First Inaugural Address, March 4, 1801," *I Do Solemnly Swear*, 19.
57. "Thomas Jefferson: Second Inaugural Address, March 4, 1805," *I Do Solemnly Swear*, 25.
58. "James Madison, A Proclamation of Thanksgiving, July 23, 1813," Brenner, 207.
59. De Tocqueville, 281.
60. Noll, *America's God*, 15.
61. Ernest Lee Tuveson, *Redeemer Nation: The Idea of America's Millennial Role* (Chicago: University of Chicago Press, 1968), 125.
62. Mark A. Noll, *The Civil War as a Theological Crisis* (Chapel Hill: The University of North Carolina Press), 2006, see especially Chapter 5, pages 75–94.
63. Harry S. Stout, *Upon the Altar of the Nation: A Moral History of the Civil War* (New York: Viking Press, 2006), 427.
64. Ronald D. White, Jr., "Lincoln's Sermon on the Mount: The Second Inaugural," in *Religion and the American Civil War*, ed. Randall M. Miller, Harry S. Stout and Charles Reagan Wilson (New York: Oxford University Press, 1998), 223.

65. Abraham Lincoln, "Second Inaugural Address, March 4, 1865," *I Do Solemnly Swear*, 156.

66. Stout, 459.

67. Ibid., 28.

68. Ibid., 271.

69. "Fact Sheets: Currency & Coins, History of 'In God We Trust,'" http://www.ustreas.gov/education/fact-sheets/currency/in-god-we-trust.shtml

70. Stout, 373.

71. Quoted in "History of 'In God We Trust,'" Fact Sheets: Currency & Coins, http://www.ustreas.gov/education/fact-sheets/currency/in-god-we-trust.shtml

72. Washington Gladden, *Applied Christianity: Moral Aspects of Social Questions* (Boston: Houghton, Mifflin and Company, 1886), 37.

73. For a detailed examination of the evolution of Catholicism in America with a focus on the relation of Catholic life to American democracy and changing attitudes of non-Catholics, see John T. McGreevy's *Catholicism and American Freedom: A History* (New York: W.W. Norton & Company, 2003). On social and labor issues at the turn of the twentieth century, see especially Chapter Five "The Social Question."

74. Rev. Josiah Strong, D.D., *Our Country: Its Possible Future and Its Present Crisis* (New York: The Baker & Taylor Co., 1891), 15.

75. Ibid., 209.

76. Ibid., 227.

77. Pierard and Linder, 134.

78. Theodore Roosevelt, "Inaugural Address, March 4, 1905," *I Do Solemnly Swear*, 230.

79. "Cheapening 'In God We Trust,' To Roland C. Dryer, Washington, November 11, 1907," *Theodore Roosevelt: Letters and Speeches*, Louis Auchincloss, ed. (New York: The Library of America, 2004), 537.

80. George Marsden, *Religion and American Culture* (Washington, D.C.: Harcourt Brace Janovich, Publishers, 1990), 175.

81. Ibid., 175.

82. Ray Abrams, *Preachers Present Arms* (New York: Round Table Press, Inc., 1933), 15.

83. Pierard and Linder, 146.

84. Ibid., 142.

85. Woodrow Wilson, "Address at a Meeting of the Associated Press, New York, April 20, 1915," in *President Wilson's State Papers and Addresses*, ed. Albert Shaw (New York: George H. Doran Company, 1917), 110–113.

86. Woodrow Wilson, "Address to the Daughters of the American Revolution, Washington, October 11, 1915," Shaw, 125.

87. Woodrow Wilson, "At Kansas City, MO, Feb. 2, 1916," Shaw, 208.

88. John Morton Blum, *Woodrow Wilson and the Politics of Morality* (Boston: Little, Brown and Company, 1956), 142.

89. George Ridout, *The Cross and the Flag* (Louisville, KY: Pentecostal Publishing Company, 1919), 55.

90. Conrad Cherry, *God's New Israel: Religious Interpretations of American Destiny* (Englewood Cliffs, NJ: Prentice-Hall, Inc., 1971), 286.

91. Gerald L. Sittser, *A Cautious Patriotism: The American Churches and the Second World War* (Chapel Hill: The University of North Carolina Press, 1997), 22–23.

92. Franklin D. Roosevelt, "Radio Address on Outbreak of the European War, September 3, 1939," in *The Roosevelt Reader: Selected Speeches, Messages, Press Conferences and Letters of Franklin D. Roosevelt*, ed. Basil Rauch (New York: Rinehart and Co., Inc., 1957), 225.

93. Franklin D. Roosevelt, "Radio Address on Selective Service Registration Day, October 16, 1940," Rauch, 258.

94. Quoted in Cherry, 297.

95. *Everson v. Board of Education of the Township of Ewing et al.* 330 U.S. 1 (1947).

96. Will Herberg. *Protestant-Catholic-Jew: An Essay in American Religious Sociology* (Chicago: The University of Chicago Press, 1955 [1983]), 3.

97. Ibid., 84.

98. McGreevy, 212.

99. John Courtney Murray, S.J. *We Hold These Truths: Catholic Reflections on the American Proposition* (New York: Sheed and Ward, 1960), 56.

100. Murray, x.

101. Hutcheson, 51.

102. Dwight D. Eisenhower, "First Inaugural Address, January 20, 1953," *I Do Solemnly Swear*, 325.

103. Pierard and Linder, 205.

104. For a treatment of the secretive elements of this event based on interviews with Fellowship members, see D. Michael Lindsay, "Is the National Prayer Breakfast Surrounded by a 'Christian Mafia'? Religious Publicity and Secrecy Within the Corridors of Power," *Journal of the American Academy of Religion* 74, no. 2 (March 2006): 390–419.

105. Richard V. Pierard, "On Praying with the President," *Christian Century* 99, no. 8 (March 10, 1982), 262–264.

106. Hutcheson, 55.

107. John F. Kennedy, "Inaugural Address, January 20, 1961," *I Do Solemnly Swear*, 344.

108. *Torcaso v. Watkins, Clerk*, 367 U.S. 488 (1961).

109. *Engel et al. v. Vitale et al.*, 370 U.S. 421 (1962).

110. *Aronow v. United States*, 432 F.2d 242 (9th Cir. 1970).

111. *Madalyn Murray O'Hair et al. v. W. Michael Blumenthal, Secretary of Treasury et al.* 588 F.2d 1144 (5th Cir. 1979).

112. *Alma F. Anderson, Diana Barclay, Betty Jean B. Neilson and Parker M. Neilson, Plaintiffs-Appellees, vs. Salt Lake City Corporation and Salt Lake County, Defendants-Appellands*, 475 F.2d 29 (10th Cir. 1973).

113. Jimmy Carter, "Inaugural Address, January 20, 1977," *I Do Solemnly Swear*, 372.

114. *McDaniel v. Paty et al.* 435 U.S. 618 (1978).

115. *Gilfillan v. Philadelphia*, 637 F.2d 924 (3rd Cir. 1980).

116. The so-called "Lemon Test" derives from the Supreme Court decision *Lemon v. Kurtzman*, 403 U.S. 602, 612–613 (1971). In his opinion, Chief Justice Burger stated that a statute must have a primarily secular legislative purpose with any religious purpose being incidental; the statute must not, as its primary purpose, advance or hinder religion; finally, the statute cannot lead to "an excessive government entanglement with religion."

117. *Stone v. Graham,* 449 U.S. 39 (1980).

118. Richard G. Hutcheson, Jr. *God in the White House: How Religion has Changed the Modern Presidency* (New York: MacMillan Publishing Company, 1988), 5–6.

119. Ronald Reagan, "Second Inaugural Address, January 21, 1985," *I Do Solemnly Swear*, 395.

120. Ronald Reagan, Proclamation 5018, February 3, 1983, available at http://www.reagan.utexas.edu/archives/speeches/1983/20383b.htm

121. *ACLU of Georgia v. The Rabun County Chamber of Commerce*, 678 F.2d 1379 (11th Cir. 1982).

122. *Marsh, Nebraska State Treasurer et al. v. Chambers*, 463 U.S. 783 (1983).

123. *Lynch v. Donnelly*, 465 U.S. 668 (1984).

124. George W. Bush, "First Inaugural Address, January 20, 2001," *I Do Solemnly Swear*, 427.

125. President George W. Bush, "Remarks by the President Upon Arrival," the South Lawn of the White House, September 16, 2001.

126. *Thomas Van Orden, Petitioner v. Rick Perry, in his official capacity as Governor of Texas and Chairman, State Preservation Board et al*, 545 U.S. 677 (2005).

127. *McCreary County, Kentucky et al., Petitioners v. American Civil Liberties Union of Kentucky et al.*, 545 U.S. 844 (2005).

128. George W. Bush, "50th Anniversary of Our National Motto, 'In God We Trust,' 2006: A Proclamation by the President of the United States of America," http://www.whitehouse.gov/news/releases/2006/07/2006727–12.html

129. Gary Wills, *Under God: Religion and American Politics* (New York: Simon and Schuster, 1990), 383.

130. James Davison Hunter and Os Guiness, eds., *Articles of Faith, Articles of Peace: The Religious Liberty Clauses and the American Public Philosophy* (Washington, D.C.: The Brookings Institution, 1990), 8.

131. Hutcheson, 235.

132. Jeffrey Stout, *Democracy and Tradition* (Princeton: Princeton University Press, 2004), 308.

FURTHER READING

On the topic of American Civil Religion, Robert Bellah's *Daedalus* article, "Civil Religion in America," and his book, *The Broken Covenant: Civil Religion in a Time of Trial*, map out the basic tenets of this "religion" and the ways in which religious language and myths have been engrafted into the foundations of the country. Though perhaps somewhat dated, Bellah's work remains the classic articulation of this concept. For a discussion of the rhetoric of civil religion throughout American history—its origins, development and characteristics—see Sacvan Bercovitch's *The American Jeremiad* or Ernest Tuveson's *Redeemer Nation: The Idea of America's Millennial Role*. For a discussion of how this civil religion relates to the figure of the president, I recommend Pierard and Linder's *Civil Religion and the Presidency*, which provides an historical overview of the distinctive applications of these principles of civil religion by various presidents and the historical context and personal beliefs that shaped each presidency. Moving beyond the theoretical to the historical, several studies are particularly helpful for demonstrating the above themes in particular historical contexts. For a fascinating portrait of the relation between religion and politics before the Revolution, see Patricia Bonomi's *Under the Cope of Heaven: Religion, Society, and Politics in Colonial America* or Jon Butler's *Awash in a Sea of Faith*. For an overview of the early American to Civil War time period and the role of evangelical religion in fashioning public religion, see Mark Noll's *America's God: From Jonathan Edwards to Abraham Lincoln*. For a detailed look at the role of religion in the rhetoric, motivations and political maneuverings of the Civil War, see Harry Stout's *On the Altar of the Nation: A Moral History of the Civil War*.

3

Public Expression of Faith by Political Leaders

W. Jason Wallace

In recent American history, politicians have been both celebrated and chastised for their enthusiastic use of religious rhetoric in the pursuit and maintenance of public office. Although conservatives—specifically, conservative Republicans affiliated with the Religious Right—are considered the primary practitioners of faith-based politics, examples of public expressions of religious convictions can be found across most of the political spectrum.

Religious testimonials abounded in both parties in the months leading up to the 2000 presidential campaign. In December 1999, when Republican presidential candidates gathered in Iowa for an early debate, they were asked by a panelist to name their favorite philosopher. GOP frontrunner and then governor of Texas, George W. Bush earned the admiration of some and the derision of others when he replied "Christ, because he changed my heart." Later, in the heat of the election year, and inspired by the tenth annual "March for Jesus" in Austin, Bush declared June 10, 2000, to be "Jesus Day" in the state of Texas. Democratic presidential candidate, then vice-president Al Gore, garnered equal attention when he told the *Washington Post* in July of 1999 that, when faced with tough decisions, he always asked himself a simple question—"What would Jesus do?" In December of the same year, he explained to a national television audience that he was "born-again" and that he did not like "making people who do believe in God feel like they're being put down."[1]

The man who preceded Gore as the Democratic presidential nominee, President Bill Clinton, also made frequent references to his personal religious beliefs. In 1994 he told a television reporter that "I don't think I could do my job as President, much less continue to try to grow as a person in the absence of my faith in God and my attempt to learn more about what it should be."[2] At his acceptance speech for the Democratic presidential nomination in 1992 Clinton, describing his vision for America, utilized a powerful biblical concept when he called his plan a "new covenant" between the people and their government. Though designed to expose what he believed to be inadequacies in the previous two administrations, Clinton's use of biblical rhetoric was not unlike that which Ronald Reagan had employed in his election eve speech twelve years earlier when, borrowing liberally from the Gospel of Matthew, he inspired Republican imaginations with the notion that they would be the party who kept faith with God and preserved for future generations the "shining city on a hill."

A quick glance at the modern presidency reveals that leaders of both political parties have, for a variety of reasons, indulged in public expressions of faith, and that, at least rhetorically speaking, there is little difference between a Republican president who declares "our nation is chosen by God and commissioned by history to be the model to the world of justice and inclusion and diversity without division," and a Democratic president who admonishes that "God can change us and make us strong at the broken places."[3] Of course, presidents and presidential candidates are not the only leaders who talk openly about their beliefs. Elected and non-elected officials at the local, state, and national levels frequently convey their religious convictions to the public as well. From seemingly innocuous and ill-defined references to "faith" and the "divine," to more serious attempts at providing religious rationales for the country's legal system, many contemporary American political figures have embraced the notion that faith commitments somehow belong in the public square.

Although not limited to the United States, the practice of "public confession" has over time become conspicuously connected with American political life, eliciting both inspiration and frustration from a citizenry who are by and large divided over the degree to which public expressions of faith should be tolerated. Cynics contend that politicians who advertise their beliefs are engaging in nothing less than Machiavellian propaganda, but some believers counter that this practice is a welcome indication of a leader's moral compass. One of the difficulties surrounding public expressions of faith by political figures is that there are no legal prohibitions against a politician conveying his or her personal religious convictions. Still, despite the lack of a positive prohibition, some Americans are uncomfortable with the practice and they view it, in principle, as a repudiation of the separation of church and state. The debate over the "public face" of American religion is indeed a pressing contemporary concern, but antecedents of the current discussion can be found in the religious and political heritage of America's colonial beginnings and can be traced through the course of the country's history.

RELIGIOUS RHETORIC AND PURITAN POLITICAL ANTECEDENTS

For most historians, the prominent place of religion in American public life began not with the earliest colonials to settle the New World, the Catholics of New Spain who arrived in the sixteenth century, but rather with the Protestants of New England who caught up with the overseas adventures of the Spanish a century later. Although Catholicism remained important throughout the colonial experience, it was Protestantism of the New England variety that provided both the vocabulary and the ideological constructs that would come to shape the religious rhetoric of so many public figures throughout American history. Central to New England Protestantism were the Puritans, or those who dissented from the established liturgical practices of the Church of England as they were forged under the reign of Elizabeth I and promulgated during the rule of the Stuart monarchs in the seventeenth century.[4]

Puritan dissent from the Church of England was neither arbitrary nor characterized by undisciplined enthusiasm for controversy. The disagreement with the established church was fundamentally a disagreement over how the Bible was to be interpreted and applied both to the church and the private life of the believer. What initially separated the Anglicans from the Puritans was a question of the scope and limits of Scripture with regard to regulating what should be normative for the Christian life. Both accepted the authority of Scripture, but Anglicans insisted that priority in biblical interpretation must be given to those matters considered necessary and essential for salvation and God's plan of redemption. They contended that there were many difficult and ambiguous passages in the Scriptures that would always present interpretive problems, but the Bible was nevertheless clear when it came to the indispensable matters of Christianity. Hence, for the established Church of England a degree of latitude was allowed in theological controversies considered superfluous to the primary message of salvation.

Puritans, by contrast, argued that there was nothing in the Bible that could be considered incidental to God's redemptive purposes. To be sure,

Christ was the unifying center through which both the Old and New Testaments were to be interpreted, but all of Scripture was necessary for understanding and living the Christian life, and therefore all of Scripture could be used to regulate any subject about which it spoke.[5] What gave formidable substance to the Puritan approach to Scripture was their formulation of the idea of the "covenant" as a controlling theme of biblical interpretation. Although not unique to the Puritans, covenant theology (or federal theology as it is sometimes called) reached a systematic clarity in their thought, and through Puritanism covenant theology entered the American colonial context.[6]

Covenant theology insists that the normal biblical pattern by which God established a relationship with fallen humanity was through a series of gracious compacts whereby divine favor was extended to his chosen, or elect, people. Attached to these compacts were certain expectations of obedience. If God's people obeyed his commandments they would be blessed, and if God's people disobeyed they would be cursed. This pattern unfolds in the biblical narrative through the Old Testament story of Israel, and it reaches its apex in the New Testament revelation of Christ and the establishment of the church.

The Puritans were divided over the extent to which Jesus transformed the requirements of human obedience necessary to continue in divine favor; however, there was general agreement on several important points: God had providentially provided mercy for the elect; the elect were in turn to respond with faith and obedience; and the proper response of faith and obedience entailed both personal and corporate responsibilities. On the one hand, the Puritan conception of the covenant was intensely individual, experiential, and private, yet on the other hand covenantal faithfulness included public activities—those social and political tasks necessary for the right ordering of a commonwealth. In England, the Puritan model of a society dedicated to the purposes of God would not flower until the interregnum of Oliver Cromwell and the Rump Parliament, but in New England, living as "providentially chosen people" would provide both solace and solidarity in a frightening wilderness far from home. The Puritan idea of "choseness," however, would also have lingering and complicated implications for later American conceptualizations of the proper relationship between church and state.

From its inception, the political project of New England was characterized by the language of covenantal theology, as the public officials of the early colonies intentionally used religious categories to justify and explain the proper purposes of civil government. Although their doctrinal laxity, their working class background, and their formal separation from the

Church of England distinguished the Pilgrims who settled the Pymouth Colony in 1620 from the more orderly and intellectual Puritans who later founded the Massachusetts Bay Colony, the Christian social vision of the Pilgrims was nevertheless in accord with Puritan political thought.

The forty-one male passengers who signed the Mayflower Compact agreed in their initial attempt at formal self-government that their undertaking was for "the glory of God, and advancement of the Christian faith," and they did "solemnly and mutually in the presence of God, and one another, covenant and combine [themselves] together into a civil body politic."[7] William Bradford, the author of the Mayflower Compact and the governor of the Plymouth colony for almost 35 continuous years, recorded in his book *Of Plymouth Plantation* that the primary reason the small group ventured to America was due to the "great hope and inward zeal they had of laying some good foundation, or at least to make some way thereunto, for the propagating and advancing the gospel of the kingdom of Christ in those remote parts of the world."[8] The Pilgrims were undoubtedly committed to the idea of a Christian society premised, even if loosely, on the notion of covenantal political-theology. However, the colony was slow to grow and they never flourished like their neighbor to the north, the Massachusetts Bay Colony.

The majority, but not all, of the first 400 settlers who would form the Massachusetts Bay Colony were Puritans. Although some joined the new colonial venture simply in the hope that they could turn a profit and afford themselves a measure of economic security unavailable to them in England, these enterprising capitalists did not represent the greater part of the undertaking. In 1630, the leadership of the new community explicitly set forth that, even though trade was indeed a partial motivation for their emigration, they were, nevertheless, attempting to form a Christian commonwealth guided by Puritan theological and political principles.

While still aboard the flagship *Arbella*, John Winthrop, the first governor of the colony, outlined the theocratic vision for the settlement in his famous sermon, *A Model of Christian Charity*. After exhorting the colonists to conduct themselves according to "the law of grace or the Gospel" so that they "might be all knit more nearly together in the bond of brotherly affection," he explained that the law of love that was to regulate their social behavior should be understood in terms of the covenantal pattern of blessings for obedience and curses for disobedience. If "the unity of the spirit in the bond of peace" was maintained, urged Winthrop, then "the Lord will be our God and delight to dwell among us, as His own people . . . We shall find that the God of Israel is among us . . . For we must consider that we shall be as a city upon a hill. The eyes of all the people are upon us."

"If," however, "we should deal falsely with our God in this work we have undertaken," he warned, the error of disobedience will "cause Him to withdraw His present help from us, we shall be made a story and a by-word through the world." Winthrop concluded his sermon with a direct quote from Deuteronomy 30 in which Moses says farewell to the Israelites and admonishes them that the Lord's promise of either blessings or curses depends solely on their observance of the law.[9]

Winthrop's message to the colonists was clear. The political and social project of New England was to be understood primarily in theological terms. In particular, public or communal relationships were to be ordered according to the Puritan belief that just as God related to Israel by establishing conditions that had to be met so that they might flourish, so too did God relate to "spiritual Israel," the true and faithful church. In effect, for the Puritans, the sacred history of Scripture had not ended, but continued in the mission of the "true" church, and in particular continued in the social experiment of New England.[10] Here, the purposes of the church and the purposes of politics were fused into the common cause of promoting the divine will.

What is important to note is that public figures like Bradford and Winthrop were not using religion merely as an appendage to political activity; rather, for them, religion, specifically Christianity, was the foundation of political activity. Their social vision was first and foremost a biblical interpretation of how life should be ordered as the true remnant, the elect people of God who allowed no rigid distinctions between the sacred and the mundane. When, in 1645, Winthrop was accused of exceeding his authority as a magistrate, he successfully defended himself by reminding his detractors that all lawful authority "has the image of God eminently stamped on it," and that contempt for those who legitimately hold public office "has been vindicated with examples of divine vengeance." A good servant, he argued, is one who governs to the best of his ability "by the rules of God's laws," maintaining the covenant oath that binds him both to God and to the people.[11]

Puritan theology held that Israel, not Athens or Rome, represented the political ideal of antiquity that believers should seek to emulate. In this regard, the Puritans shared some measure of continuity with the medieval political theology of the Catholic Church.[12] But the Puritan experiment was unique in the history of church-state relations in that theirs was indeed an "errand in the wilderness," a society largely set free from the burden of European history, and yet at the same time sincerely committed to reinventing a new kind of Christian culture with a positive sense of mission. Aspects of this Puritan sense of mission would slowly permeate the collective identity of both the colonies and the young republic, and in particular it would affect public expression of faith for later generations of Americans in two important ways.

First, the language of Scripture, especially the Old Testament, would easily translate into an American colonial—and eventually national—context that conceived of itself, even if metaphorically, as a covenanted "New Israel" set apart for a special purpose in human history. Second, the Puritan conviction that God was at work in history and that they were providentially chosen to be an example to the world of what a Christian society should look like imbued the American experience with a sense of higher purpose and significance that was readily adopted for political purposes as the United States grew into first its national and then its international identity. Tellingly, however, the theological presuppositions that informed the ways in which the Puritans expressed their faith would slowly be transformed and eventually discarded to meet the demands of an increasingly pluralistic society struggling to understand the practical implications of democracy.

POLITICS, RELIGION, AND THE EARLY REPUBLIC

Even in the early years of the New England experiment, the Puritan way never achieved complete unanimity. Dissenters such as Anne Hutchinson, Roger Williams, and Thomas Hooker emerged within a few years of the founding of the Massachusetts Bay Colony to challenge both the theology and politics of the young Puritan community. Over time Puritan solidarity fragmented and the sense of destiny that accompanied the second and third generations of New Englanders fluctuated with their political fortunes at home and abroad.

Outside of New England, colonists were having even more complicated experiences with religion and public life. By the 1700s, religious diversity was the rule in New York as Dutch Calvinists, Anglicans, Lutherans, German Reformed, Catholics, and Jews swelled Manhattan and the Hudson River Valley. Further south in the middle colonies of New Jersey, Pennsylvania, and Delaware, Quakers, Mennonites, Amish, and various sects of Pietists shared space with Lutherans, Presbyterians, Baptists, and Puritans who had left New England in search of even holier commonwealths. Maryland was founded as a haven for Catholics in 1632, and in 1649 the Catholic-controlled Maryland Assembly adopted an Act of Toleration welcoming all Christian faiths to the colony. Religious tolerance in Maryland, however, would ebb and flow throughout the seventeenth century according to whichever theological community held power.[13] In the southern colonies,

Anglicanism was in general the largest denomination until the English Act of Toleration was passed after the Glorious Revolution of 1689. As a result Protestant dissenters, primarily Baptists and Presbyterians, gradually began to occupy Virginia, the Carolinas, and Georgia.

Both inside and outside of New England seeds of religious pluralism were being sown, but the growth of denominationalism and sectarianism did not undermine the public place of religion in the colonies. Between 1720 and 1750 the revivals of the First Great Awakening rekindled the hopes for providential designs on America, and they provided a kind of ideological unity to the disparate religious landscape that would in time bolster the new nation. In particular revivalist preachers like Solomon Stoddard, George Whitfield, and Jonathan Edwards encouraged the expectation that the millennial Kingdom of Christ would emerge through the earnest efforts of committed Christians.[14] Frequently, the hope of Christ's future reign on earth was associated with the idea that young America would play an important role in God's ultimate plan for extending redemption to the world.

Even Jonathan Edwards, the most skeptical of all the Great Awakening leaders with regard to America's special place in redemptive history, confessed that since "the old continent has crucified Christ . . . 'tis probable that, in some measure to balance these things, the most glorious renovation of the world shall originate from the new continent."[15] By the middle decades of the eighteenth century, many Americans were convinced that the future success of the colonies depended upon the spiritual sincerity and moral fortitude of "converted" Protestants who had come to experience the power of God in very personal ways. This new spiritual personalism marked an important shift in American religious thought as more and more Protestants came to emphasize the emotional and subjective aspects of their faith over and against confessionalism and doctrinal assent.

The turn toward experiential religion in the eighteenth century was accompanied by equally dramatic changes in the relationship between religion and politics. From the late 1600s to the early 1800s, new trends in science and philosophy reshaped the intellectual landscape of both Europe and America by reordering, if not completely overturning, traditional assumptions about God, the natural world, and human nature. In this period, known as the Enlightenment, or the Age of Reason, writers and philosophers such as John Locke, David Hume, Montesquieu, Voltaire, Rousseau, and Immanuel Kant revolutionized human reflection about both God and nature. The consequences of Enlightenment thought were manifold, but particularly affected were conventional notions about the place of religious convictions in public life.

Although there is no single result that captures the impact of the Enlightenment on religious thought, in general terms the period witnessed a shift away from supernatural theism toward more rational or natural explanations of God's dealings with humanity. For some religion was dismissed as irrelevant, but for others it was only much more circumscribed than it had been in the Middle Ages and the Early Modern periods. Typically, supernatural events supported by the church such as miracles and divine revelation were rejected in favor of beliefs discovered by human reason and observation of the natural world, and this rational process in turn uncovered natural religious truths—truths that could be universally accepted because they were valid at all times and in all places, or because they had been imprinted into human consciousness by a god who was otherwise quite impersonal.

"Natural religion," or "natural theology," challenged the received confessional positions of both Catholics and Protestants, and it opened-up the possibility of safeguarding moral behavior without recourse to a particular sectarian interpretation of the Bible. Moreover, in the wake of the religious wars that ravaged Europe during the sixteenth and seventeenth centuries, as well as the rise of monarchical absolutism, Enlightenment approaches to religion led to new ways of thinking about how moral justifications for political activity could be retained without committing the state to a particular theological position.[16]

Taken together, the exigencies of religious pluralism, the millennial hopes of the Great Awakening, and the new intellectual currents emerging from Enlightenment thought changed the way public leaders expressed their faith during the American Revolution and the formative years of the early republic. Certain Puritan concepts were retained, but they were largely divorced from the ideal of an organic Christian society that viewed the Bible as a comprehensive guide to all of life. The dogmatic constructions of covenant theology that had been so essential to the Puritan experiment carried sectarian baggage that was in many ways irrelevant to the political purposes of the late 1700s. Yet the belief that government was entrusted with a "sacred purpose" remained viable to a population conditioned by religious awakening and in the main committed to a broadly conceived cultural Protestantism. No doubt religion still mattered, but for many political leaders it slowly began to matter as much for its social utility as its theological implications. "Providence" was still at work, but the idea lacked the well-defined biblical meaning it had carried for earlier generations of creedal Calvinists; the Bible still had something important to say about God and human nature, but not in terms of rigid dogma; theology was still significant, but primarily for its ethical imperatives rather than for its claims of supernatural authority.

As American Christianity—specifically, American Protestantism—evolved, so too did public expressions of faith by political leaders. On the one hand, public references to religion provided a moral, if not metaphysical, rationale for the American experiment. On the other hand, most political leaders carefully refrained from making dogmatic statements about their faith or referencing any particular confessional system as a guide to the "truth" of Christianity. Religion remained important, but its importance increasingly stemmed more from its usefulness to republican values rather than from its spiritual veracity. Nowhere is this shift more evident than in the political rhetoric of the Founding Fathers.

When Thomas Jefferson penned the Declaration of Independence in June 1776 he studiously avoided any references to Christianity, Jesus, or even God, and the contrast with the Puritan rhetoric of William Bradford and John Witherspoon is striking. Instead of quoting the Bible or referencing an exacting theological system to provide moral grounds for the colonial rebellion against England, Jefferson, and a committee of four others, chose the language of natural religion. People, they urged, are at times entitled to political revolt because "the Laws of Nature and Nature's God" guarantee certain rights. A "Creator" has made these rights possible, and "the Supreme Judge of the World" will, they hope, vindicate the intentions of the colonials to exercise their right to form free and independent states.

The document concludes that the signatories will rely on "protection of divine Providence" to secure their work. Notice there is no theological specificity to this language—no clarification or refinement of what exactly the Founders meant by "Creator," "Supreme Judge," or "Providence." The words no doubt invoked a measure of reverence or respect for the idea of the divine, and they clearly endowed the impending rebellion with a kind of sacral character, but still the religious language of the Declaration of Independence is neither confessional nor is it an expression of praise.

Jefferson's choice of words for the founding document of the United States presents an interesting paradox (one that exists to the present day) in the history of public expressions of faith by political leaders. Although the Founding Fathers understood that religion was important to the future of their political experiment—most argued that the moral authority of Christianity was indeed superior to other religions—they nevertheless made no attempt to secure Christianity as the official or established religion of the new nation, nor did they publicly address the details of the Christian message. In fact, many of the Founders expressed deep appreciation for the moral sentiments of Christianity while at the same time remaining indifferent to the theological claims of any one denomination.

Jefferson's personal beliefs about Jesus and Christianity fluctuated over the course of his life, and it is well known that he twice edited the New

Testament to remove what he considered to be the irrational content. His approach to religion was ultimately practical, and like other Founders he tolerated public expressions of Christianity only to the degree that they served the positive social benefit of cultivating virtue in a free populace. As with many of his contemporaries, Jefferson seemed to hold simultaneous and contradictory opinions about Christianity, and his private correspondence on the subject often differed from his public pronouncements.

He could fume that "Millions of innocent men, women and children, since the introduction of Christianity, have been burnt, tortured, fined and imprisoned," and also speculate, "Can the liberties of a nation be thought secure, when we have removed their only firm basis, a conviction in the minds of the people that these liberties are of the gift of God?"[17] He could dispute privately with a friend that "Christianity neither is, nor ever was a part of the common law," and yet publicly declare in his Second Inaugural Address that he will need "the favor of that Being in whose hands we are, who led our fathers, as Israel of old, from their native land and planted them in a country flowing with all the necessaries and comforts of life."[18] He could argue that "of all the systems of morality, ancient or modern, which have come under my observation, none appear to me so pure as that of Jesus," and yet lament that although many of Jesus' sayings were "of the most lovely benevolence," unfortunately many others were "of so much ignorance, so much absurdity, so much untruth, charlatanism and imposture as to pronounce it impossible that such contradictions came from the same human being."[19] Even in his latter years Jefferson maintained that Calvinism was demonic, that the virgin birth of Jesus was a fable similar to the emergence of Minerva from the head of Jupiter, and that atheists could be just as moral as Christians. But he also held that Jesus was "the most venerated reformer of human errors," and that freedom of thought would one day restore his "primitive and genuine" teachings.[20]

When Thomas Jefferson ran for president in 1800, his opinions about religion pushed many Protestant detractors decidedly into the camp of his Federalist opponent John Adams. In truth, however, Adams was little more interested in orthodox Christianity than Jefferson, and like Jefferson he too conveyed ambivalence in his appraisal of the place of religion in public life. When he helped pen the Massachusetts constitution in 1780, Adams declared it was the "duty of all men in society . . . to worship the Supreme Being, the great Creator and Preserver of the universe." Likewise, soon after he became vice president in 1789, he wrote that "our constitution was made only for a moral and religious people. It is wholly inadequate to the government of any other."[21] In a letter to Thomas Jefferson written in 1813 he said that "the general Principles of Christianity" were the principles that guided the Founding Fathers in their pursuit of independence from England.

Adams did not elaborate how the Founding Fathers understood the details of those "general principles," nor did he explain what the "general principles" actually were. Like Jefferson, Adams was content to use generic religious language in order to retain the moral capital of Christianity without ceding any particular doctrinal stance. Elsewhere, he decried the fact that "millions of fables, tales, and legends have blended with both Jewish and Christian revelation," making them "the most bloody religion[s] that ever existed," and he insisted that since the Reformation there never "existed a Protestant or dissenting sect who would tolerate a free inquiry."[22] As president, the most significant statement John Adams made concerning the religious character of the young country came when he signed the Treaty of Tripoli in 1796, which was brokered to end Muslim piracy in the Mediterranean Sea and to extend friendship to the coastal countries of North Africa. The treaty stated that "the United States is not, in any sense, founded on the Christian religion," and that "the United States is not a Christian nation any more than it is a Jewish or a Mohammedan nation."

The pattern of at once endorsing the ethical precepts of Christianity while avoiding assent to any specific creedal system can be found in the rhetoric of most of the Founding Fathers. Benjamin Franklin said that he thought religion suffered when orthodoxy was regarded more than virtue, and he urged that virtuous acts were much more important than personal religious beliefs.[23] Although he considered "the system of morals" taught by Jesus to be "the best the world ever saw or is likely to see," he also "found Christian dogma unintelligible" and he avoided going to church.[24]

Just before the outbreak of the revolution James Madison told a friend that "religious bondage shackles and debilitates the mind and unfits it for every noble enterprise, every expanded prospect." Yet, in the heat of the colonial revolt he acknowledged before the Virginia General Assembly in 1778 that the political institutions of the new nation depended upon a moral citizenry conditioned "according to the Ten Commandments of God." Later, before the same body, he advocated for the separation of church and state in his famous *Memorial and Remonstrance Against Religious Assessments*, in which he argued that when the state recognizes an established religion, it erects "a spiritual tyranny on the ruins of civil authority." Madison saw the need for public morality, but he remained a lifelong defender of the separation of religion from the purposes of government.[25]

The first president, George Washington, concurred. When clergy complained to him that the Constitution failed to mention Jesus Christ, he responded that the path of true piety required little political direction. He later reassured the Baptists of Virginia that everyone "ought to be protected in worshipping the Deity according the dictates of his own conscience."[26] Moreover, he repeatedly denounced religious controversies and disputations as antithetical to the "enlightened and liberal" purposes of the new nation and dangerous to the peace of society.[27]

Still, Washington was a practical leader who understood that religion could have a stabilizing effect on the moral disposition of the nation. Thus, in his farewell address at the end of his second term as president he declared that "of all the dispositions and habits, which lead to political prosperity, religion and morality are indispensable supports," and that "reason and experience both forbid us to expect, that national morality can prevail in exclusion of religious principle." Washington, using language common to so many other Founders, concluded his time in public service by consciously avoiding references to specific religious teachings or doctrines in favor of the importance of religion in general to the social well-being of the republic.

RELIGION AND POLITICS IN A FREE REPUBLIC: THE CHALLENGES OF THE NINETEENTH CENTURY

The Founding Fathers left the country a peculiar legacy with regard to the public expression of faith by political leaders. Virtue and morality were important to the nation, and indeed the ethical precepts of Christianity provided a code of personal behavior that could benefit all citizens. But if Christianity, or any religion for that matter, was to be useful to the republic, it had to be carefully contained. If disputes over nuanced theological positions or doctrinal convictions were to spill into public life, then the social order risked fragmentation and disarray. If, however, Americans could find a common core of religious teachings shared by everyone, then religion offered a powerful tool for unifying a diverse population. Public figures in the nineteenth and twentieth centuries would have to navigate this situation very carefully.

For much of the nineteenth century, most Protestant Americans had little trouble adjusting to the absence of an established religion as they found common cause in trans-denominational crusades designed to alleviate social-ills deemed dangerous to the country. Inspired by the revivalism of the Second Great Awakening (1800–1830s), numerous voluntary moral reform movements actively campaigned for causes such as temperance, maintenance of Sabbath laws, distribution of religious tracts and Bibles, and Protestant control of public education.[28] These activities secured vast networks of local organizations dedicated to transforming society, and they provided religious reformers a way to make their faith relevant for public life without violating the Founders' directive that moral usages of Christianity were appropriate so long as doctrinal or sectarian disputes could be avoided. Politically speaking, the Whig Party, much more than the Democratic Party, capitalized on the energy of revivalism and reform, and they more than the Democrats kept the moral sentiments of Christianity firmly in the public imagination.

Whigs believed themselves to be direct descendants of the Federalists, and in large measure they were the nineteenth-century standard bearers of conservative social ideals. They did not recoil at the thought of the church influencing moral legislation; they tended to support an industrial aristocracy grounded in Protestant values; they had an extreme dislike for the legacy of Thomas Jefferson, and they absolutely abhorred the populist Andrew Jackson. Whigs enjoyed enthusiastic support among those sympathetic with the notion that government action should be used to secure religious and moral improvement. Indeed, religion as a restraining social influence was believed to provide the perfect compliment to the liberating effects of political and economic freedom that characterized the young nation.

In 1840 the Whigs ran William Henry Harrison as their presidential candidate, and party publicists were careful to portray him as a "sincere Christian" and "a good Sunday School . . . church going man."[29] By contrast, his opponent, Democratic incumbent Martin Van Buren, was characterized as "undisciplined in ethics, morality, and religion," and his party was accused of conspiring to "expunge the whole Decalogue from our morals" and of seeking "the overthrow of the church . . . and the destruction of the ministers of religion."[30] The Whig tactic worked, and after Harrison defeated Van Buren, in disinterested language reminiscent of the Founders he declared that he had "a profound reverence for the Christian religion," and he expressed gratitude to "that good Being who has blessed us by the gifts of civil and religious freedom."[31]

The Whig party was short-lived, but their legacy of using Christian moral rhetoric for political purposes lasts until the present day. In the 1850s, the Whigs split over the two most pressing social issues of the mid-nineteenth century, slavery and Catholicism, and the division in the party over these questions reflected larger fractures developing within American culture. Catholics had faced seasons of intolerance and bigotry since the colonial period, but in the middle decades of the nineteenth century anti-Catholicism reached a new level of intensity. Between 1828 and 1844 over 500,000 immigrants, mostly Catholics, swelled the nation's northern cities, and both devout and nominal Protestants reacted by demanding legislation that would require the foreign-born to shed whatever real or perceived Old

World loyalties they retained in favor of republican values. For many Americans, the mediating institution between the immigrant and Americanization would be a public school system governed by generic Protestant principles and dedicated to ensuring a homogenous moral consensus.

Political leaders were quick to enter the fray over education and Americanization, and more often than not religious presuppositions guided their arguments either for or against the benefits of public schools. One of the leading advocates of the common school movement was Horace Mann, the secretary of the Massachusetts State Board of Education from 1836 to 1848, and member of the U.S. House of Representatives from 1848 to 1852. A former Calvinist turned Unitarian who had experience as an educator, as well as a lawyer and a state senator, Mann brought to the position of secretary of education a vision of how religion divorced from sectarianism could be used in public or "common" schools to build a consensus of good citizenship.

He developed his argument around three themes. First, he believed in the "absolute right of every human being that comes into the world to an education." Second, based on the conviction that people had a right to an education, he argued that it was the "correlative duty of every government to see that the means of that education are provided for all."[32] Finally, Mann suggested schools could use religion to teach people how to be good only if religious principles were extracted from denominational propaganda. He reasoned that religious education was not to be used to persuade a child to "join this or that denomination, when he arrives at the age of discretion." Instead, religious training could be used in schools to help the child "judge for himself, according to the dictates of his own reason and conscience, what his religious obligations are, and whither they lead."[33] To this end, Mann suggested that the best way to cultivate virtue in school children was to read them the "ethical" teachings of the Bible without commenting on the difficult points of doctrine that may surround any one interpretation. Mann's proposals found both supporters and detractors, but significantly his vision for using public education as a means of inculcating character development was premised on the belief that the moral essence of religion could be discerned and taught apart from denominational concerns.

The anti-Catholic, anti-immigrant furor that helped to fuel the common school movement in the 1830s and 1840s culminated in the formation of the Know Nothing Party in early 1850s. Also known as the American Party, the Know Nothings had supporters in every region of the country, and their political representatives in both local and federal assemblies employed pro-Protestant religious rhetoric to bolster their contention that America was not to be governed by Catholics or anyone who held European sympathies. Harangues against the iniquities of the Middle Ages and the papacy peppered Know Nothing political speeches and party literature. Moreover, they promoted proscriptive legislation that would severely limit the influence of Catholics and immigrants on American public life. The Philadelphia Platform, a statement of party principles adopted by the National Council of the American Party in 1855, asserted that Christianity "is considered an element of our political system," and "the Holy Bible is at once the source of Christianity, and the depository and fountain of all civil and religious freedom."

Congressman Lewis D. Campbell of Ohio, a Whig who switched to the American Party, typified Know Nothing rhetoric in his blustering attacks against Catholics on the campaign trail. "My partialities run with the Protestants," he declared before a Washington audience in 1856, "because in youth I was trained in that faith, and in manhood learned from the history of the past that the Protestant church has always been the church of Freedom." He added that Americans intend no union of church and state, and "if there be any Catholic in this country who is not satisfied with this sort of religious liberty I tell him the sooner he 'packs up his duds' and goes back [to Europe] the better."[34] Another Congressman, Joseph Chandler, a Catholic convert from Philadelphia, tried to persuade his colleagues in the House of Representatives that the pope no longer exercised political power as he had in the Middle Ages, and questions of Catholic loyalty to the United States should not be a topic of discussion in Congress. These public arguments over Catholic political loyalties exposed an inherited cultural assumption that although the United States had no established religion, it nevertheless retained a Protestant character that was to be upheld, if not by consensus, then, for some at least, by law.

The idea that the nation retained a certain Protestant character, even if ill-defined, provided a measure of social cohesiveness in the early decades of the nation's history. However, this proposal remained valid only to the extent that both religious denominations and political parties could agree on broad ethical imperatives that steered far away from contentious theological or social issues that exposed fault lines in generic public Protestantism. One issue that could not be avoided in the nineteenth century was the question of free versus slave labor, and entrenched disagreement over the matter manifested not only geographically and politically between the North and the South but theologically as well. Political and ecclesiastical leaders on both sides of the slavery debate were quick to use religion to justify their arguments, and their heated rhetoric portended the bloody calamity of the Civil War.

Eleven years before the war began, John C. Calhoun, the accomplished senator from South Carolina, recognized that the prelude to disunion could be seen in the divisions occurring in the denominations over the question of slavery. In his last major address before the Senate he told his colleagues that although there were many "chords" that held the Union together, the strongest bond was of a "spiritual and ecclesiastical nature," that is "the unity of the great religious denominations." Unfortunately, the sturdy ties of the denominations "were not able to resist the explosive effect of slavery agitation," and, as a consequence, Calhoun believed the Protestant consensus was slowly coming apart. "If the agitation goes on," he warned, "the same force, acting with increased intensity . . . will finally snap every chord, when nothing will be left to hold the States together except force."[35]

Daniel Webster, the equally distinguished Senator from Massachusetts, agreed with Calhoun. On March 7, 1850, three days after Calhoun's speech, Webster admonished his colleagues that questions like slavery are best left to the political process because once "discussed in religious assemblies of the clergy and laity," passions inevitably subvert good judgment to the point where "every thing is absolute; absolutely wrong, or absolutely right." People impassioned by religious sentiment cannot negotiate, said Webster, because "they are apt, too, to think that nothing is good but what is perfect, and that there are no compromises or modifications to be made in consideration of difference of opinion or in deference to other men's judgment."[36]

Webster and Calhoun proved prescient, but still political figures on both sides of the controversy continued to use religious rhetoric unabated in an effort to make sense of their respective positions. With the outbreak of the war, and as the carnage of battle took its toll, both Northern and Southern politicians described the meaning of it all in religious terms. Jefferson Davis, the president of the Confederacy, echoing the arguments of politicians and ministers throughout the South, passionately maintained a year into the war that slavery "was established by decree of Almighty God . . . it is sanctioned in the Bible, in both Testaments, from Genesis to Revelation . . . it has existed in all ages, has been found among the people of the highest civilization, and in nations of the highest proficiency in the arts."[37] In 1863, after the dramatic defeats of Gettysburg and Vicksburg, he borrowed the old Puritan covenantal theological categories of faithfulness and disobedience to explain the reversal of South's fortunes. Early success had made the South self-confidant, but now southerners were being chastised because they had forgotten their reliance upon God.[38]

Davis's counterpart in the North, Abraham Lincoln, was equally adamant that there had to be some kind of divine purpose behind the conflict, and in speeches that continue to inspire and haunt the American imagination he portrayed the goals of safeguarding the Union and ending slavery as almost redemptive causes. In fact it was Lincoln, perhaps more so than any other political figure in the nation's history, who used abstract religious rhetoric to try and give transcendent meaning to the purpose of the Union. After the Second Battle of Bull Run in August 1862, he mused that God willed the war for sacred reasons; further, although both sides claimed to act in accordance with the will of God, one side had to be wrong because "God cannot be for and against the same thing at the same time." Though he was never a member of a particular denomination, and at times in his life demonstrated outright skepticism, as president he maintained that a unified country needed a unifying religious sentiment. For Lincoln this sentiment involved carefully portraying the preservation of the nation, albeit a nation "reborn" in its commitment to liberal democracy, as a goal worthy of divine blessing.

With his election to the presidency, southern secession became a reality, and he tried to reassure in his First Inaugural Address that "Christianity, and a firm reliance on Him who has never yet forsaken this favored land," would help guide the country through the impending crisis. After the war began, he passed an executive resolution ordering that members of the military observe the Sabbath so that their cause might not be "imperiled by the profanation of the day or the name of the Most High."[39] When Northern prospects looked grim in the first two years of the struggle, he, like Jefferson Davis, explained the setbacks using language reminiscent of the Puritans. "We have forgotten God," said Lincoln in a call for Northerners to fast and repent, "we have vainly imagined, in the deceitfulness of our hearts, that all these blessings were produced by some superior wisdom and virtue of our own. Intoxicated with unbroken success, we have become too self-sufficient to feel the necessity of redeeming and preserving grace, too proud to pray to the God that made us."[40] Later, the day after the Union triumph at the Battle of Gettysburg, a more optimistic Lincoln allegedly told General Dan Sickles that he never dreaded the outcome of the battle because in prayer he had asked God for victory and told God that "this was His war, and our cause His cause."

That same summer he called for another national day of prayer, and in a rare reference to the third person of the Trinity by a public figure, he invited the people of the United States "to invoke the influence of His Holy Spirit to guide the counsels of the government with wisdom adequate to so great a national emergency," so that the nation might be led to "repentance and submission to the Divine will."[41] With encouragement from the Lincoln administration, Congress authorized the coinage of two-cent coins upon which the motto "In God We Trust" first appeared in April

1864. A year later on March 4, 1865, Abraham Lincoln delivered his Second Inaugural Address just weeks before his own assassination. Here, he framed the war between the North and South in overt theological terms, quoting from *Psalm 19* and *Matthew 18* to emphasize that American slavery was an offence against God which was being providentially purged at a cost of great sacrifice. A month later Lincoln was dead, and many would interpret his death as final price that had to be paid to save the Union. His former law partner, William H. Herndon, wrote in one of the earliest biographies of the president that "Lincoln was God's chosen one" and that the trials of his life had made him "the noblest and loveliest character since Jesus Christ."[42]

PUBLIC EXPRESSIONS OF FAITH IN THE TWENTIETH CENTURY

The Civil War, and specifically Lincoln's use of religious rhetoric in the cause of the Union, inspired a reinvigorated missiological zeal for the meaning of democracy in the modern world. After 1865, as America grew into a competitive industrial nation-state, at least the ideal of "freedom" if not the complete reality gained a consecrated significance not seen since the American Revolution, and the religious nationalism captured in the speeches of Abraham Lincoln continued in the oratory of political figures from all regions of the country. A major shift from the nineteenth to the twentieth century, however, was America's growing presence as a world power that could contend with European nations for military and economic superiority.

Where domestic quarrels divided Americans in the nineteenth century, increasingly international conflicts tended to unite them in the twentieth century. As the United States slowly assumed a dominant role on the world stage, political leaders again invoked God to sanction the meaning of democracy in almost spiritual terms. At the same time, twentieth-century political figures followed the pattern of their predecessors in public life by ignoring nuanced theological disputes in favor of rhetoric that supported a broad ethical consensus that could appeal to all Americans.

In 1915, President Woodrow Wilson continued the politician's habit of employing nonspecific religious language for moral causes while studiously avoiding any detailed denominational controversies in an address before the Federal Council of Churches—an ecumenical Protestant movement committed to progressive social reform. True Christianity, said Wilson, was not simply to be regarded as a "body of conceptions regarding God and man," but was also to be involved in the affairs of the world as well. "The church," he noted, "is the only embodiment of the things that are entirely unselfish—the principles of self-sacrifice and devotion," and as such it was "put into this world, not only to serve the individual soul, but to serve society also."[43]

For Wilson and many other elected officials who cut their political teeth in the Progressive Era, an important function of religion was to inspire public service, and after America entered World War I he encouraged participation in the cause overseas by associating public service with the spread of American democracy. On June 5, 1917, a day designated for national registration for the draft, he told a reunion of Confederate veterans that the Union had been preserved through the Civil War so that the United States could be "an instrument in the hands of God to see that liberty is made secure for mankind." Two weeks later he hosted a delegation from the Northern Presbyterian Church at the White House and explained to these ministers that "any great spiritual body" could support America's entrance into the European conflict because "if ever there was a war which was meant to supply new foundations for what is righteous, true and of good report, it is this war."[44]

Twenty-four years later, President Franklin Roosevelt used similar appeals in his State of the Union address one month after the Japanese attack on Pearl Harbor. With America's entrance into World War II the intentions of the United States and the aims of Nazi Germany were cast in terms of a stark dualism. The president urged that "victory for us means victory for religion. The world is too small to provide adequate living room for both Hitler and God." Roosevelt warned that the Nazis planned to enforce "their new, German pagan religion all over the world," and if this plan succeeded, "the Holy Bible and the cross of mercy would be displaced by 'Mein Kampf' and the swastika and the naked sword." He further reminded his audience that "inspired by a faith that goes back through all the years to the first chapter of Genesis," Americans "are striving to be true to that divine heritage" by defending democracy against the hostilities of Germany and Japan.[45]

In the post-war period, at the height of the Cold War and the anti-Communist suspicion of the McCarthy era, the idea of an absolute dualism between democracy and totalitarianism continued to influence public expressions of faith in the political arena. Partly in reaction to Communism, public officials increasingly characterized the United States as more committed to higher religious purposes than the country's ideological adversaries. Indeed, the 84th Congress passed a joint resolution to replace the existing motto, *E Pluribus Unum* (Out of many, One) with "In God we Trust." The new motto officially took the place of the original 180-year-old national motto when President Dwight D. Eisenhower signed the resolution into law on July 30, 1956.

By the 1950s, an entire generation of Americans had come of age witnessing both the abject poverty of the Great Depression and the devastating effects of a global war, and perhaps one consequence of such experiences was the prominence of public religiosity in the Eisenhower years. The president himself reflected the mood of the nation. On February 1, 1953, at the National Presbyterian Church in Washington, D.C., the newly inaugurated Eisenhower became the first president in history to be baptized while in office. He also took the unprecedented steps of offering his own prayer before his inaugural address, initiating the National Prayer Breakfast, and opening his cabinet meetings with prayer.

After hearing a sermon where the preacher noted that there was little difference between the American Pledge of Allegiance and other similar pledges, including that of Communist nations, Eisenhower concurred and spearheaded the movement to have the words "under God" added to the pledge. Approved by Congress and signed into law in June of 1954, Eisenhower celebrated the occasion by noting that "from this day forward, the millions of our school children will daily proclaim . . . the dedication of our nation and our people to the Almighty . . . In this way we are reaffirming the transcendence of religious faith in America's heritage and future; in this way we shall constantly strengthen those spiritual weapons which forever will be our country's most powerful resource."[46]

For all of his earnestness regarding the place of religious convictions in public life, a comment made while still president-elect in December 1952 indicates that Eisenhower, like most prominent twentieth century political leaders, viewed religion—at least in its public form—as a generic moral resource that served to secure the basic democratic premises of the American experiment. After meeting with Marshal Grigori Zhukov of the Soviet Army, Eisenhower revealed at a press conference that the two did not discuss religious issues because the he felt that efforts to talk about matters of faith with a Communist would be pointless. "Our form of government," he explained, "has no sense unless it is founded in a deeply felt religious faith, and I don't care what it is. With us of course it is the Judeo-Christian concept but it must be a religion that all men are created equal. So what was the use of me talking to Zhukov about that? Religion, he had been taught, was the opiate of the people."[47]

War and international conflict were not the only events provoking public expression of faith in the twentieth century. Like previous episodes in American history, Protestant suspicion of Catholic political loyalties characterized political usage of religion as well. On June 28, 1928, in Houston,

Texas, two weeks after the Republican Party chose Herbert Hoover as their candidate for the presidency, Franklin D. Roosevelt placed in nomination Governor Alfred E. Smith of New York as the Democratic Party's choice for the highest political office in the land. A Roman Catholic with an Irish lineage who openly opposed Prohibition, Smith instantly drew criticism from Protestant detractors. By the time he ran for president, Smith had served twelve years in the New York State Assembly, including a stint as speaker from 1913 to 1915, and he had completed two successful terms as governor of the Empire State. His political pedigree, however, did little to mollify fear that he might have divided allegiance between the Constitution and Rome.

One of the more colorful and antagonistic critics of Al Smith was the rabid anti-Catholic Senator from Alabama, J. Thomas Heflin. Heflin hailed from a small town in Northeast Alabama, and he had gradually worked his way up the party ranks, starting out as a mayor, then serving as a state legislator, a U.S. congressman, and since 1920, a U.S. Senator. He characterized the battle against Smith as nothing less than holy war, and the accusations he made against Catholics in general ranged from the hateful to the absurd. Catholics were labeled agents of the pope. The press who supported Smith was "Romanized." Jesuit priests were involved in a conspiracy to take over America's large cities. Jesuits and other Catholic leaders wanted to poison him, plunge the United States into foreign wars, and convert all Protestants through brainwashing and genocide.[48]

Those who agreed with Heflin's conspiracy theories relished in his rhetoric against Al Smith and the Catholic Church, and they empathized with his self-described sacrifice in the face of the vicious "Roman menace." On the Senate floor he declared for the record, "I have taken my stand for my country against the invisible government of the Pope of Rome, and I am going to uncover it in the United States in spite of what the Jesuits may do with dagger or poison . . . I defy these evil un-American forces of Rome. The people of my State are too high minded . . . [too] grounded in the principles of Martin Luther . . . to bow their knee to this veiled, insidious monster."[49]

Governor Smith tried to answer critics like Heflin by publicly declaring that although he worshipped "God according to the faith and practice of the Roman Catholic Church," he nevertheless believed "in absolute freedom of conscience for all men and equality in all churches," and he affirmed his support for the separation of church and state as well as his commitment to the "common brotherhood of man under the common fatherhood of God."[50] His defense echoed the public sentiments of most Protestant politicians, but it did little good in the election: he won only 87 of the 531 votes in the Electoral College. However, both his campaign and his insistence that Catholics, just as Protestants, could support a benign, non-dogmatic approach to the place of religion in public life anticipated John F. Kennedy's run for the presidency in 1960.

Like Smith, Kennedy also had to convince wary Protestant voters that his faith would not hinder his ability, if elected president, to uphold the Constitution of the United States. Even after he won primaries in Wisconsin and West Virginia, virtually securing the Democratic nomination for the presidency, the religion question would not go away. In September 1960, the Greater Houston Ministerial Association invited Kennedy to address the issue, and here, like Smith before him, he emphatically insisted that he did not speak for his church on public matters, nor did the church speak for him. Also, like many other political leaders, Kennedy upheld the hopeful notion that the United States will be a place where "religious intolerance will someday end," and where the various denominations and religions "will refrain from those attitudes of disdain and division which have so often marred their works in the past, and promote instead the American ideal of brotherhood." To reach this ideal, America had to strive to be a country where no "Catholic prelate would tell the president—should he be Catholic—how to act, and no Protestant minister would tell his parishioners for whom to vote; where no church or church school is granted any public funds or political preference, and where no man is denied public office merely because his religion differs from the President who might appoint him, or the people who might elect him."[51]

Kennedy's insistence that religion should be kept private when it came to matters of state succeeded in calming Protestant worries, and in 1960 he became the first Catholic president in United States' history. Ironically, however, the decade commenced by a presidency that insisted on distinguishing between what properly belongs in the realm of the public and what properly belongs in the realm of the private upended the notion that personal beliefs and interests either could be or should be neutralized in pursuit of the greater political good. It is interesting to note that one of the last successful appeals to the idea of a generic Protestant moral consensus came from the leadership of the African-American community in an attempt to convince the white majority that the country was not living-up to its pretence that "all men are created equal." Some of the most stirring rhetoric in American history can be found in the Civil Rights movement, where leaders frequently borrowed biblical language and imagery to underscore the need for racial justice and to demand equity before the law.

Martin Luther King, Jr. famously described what he believed to be the meaning of America in Christian terms, and in his powerful 1963 "I Have a Dream" speech he quoted the messianic dream found in the book of Isaiah to stress his hope that one day all "of God's children, black men and white men, Jews and Gentiles, Protestants and Catholics" would indeed be "free at last." But, as inspiring as King was in his ability to wed Christianity to American idealism, in fact he represented a rhetorical tradition that was increasingly fragmenting.

The late 1960s witnessed the birth of new emphases in American politics in which traditional conceptions of citizenship and national welfare were challenged in order that those people considered historically marginalized from making public policy might be empowered. Often referred to as multiculturalism, or identity politics, this dramatic shift in political life called into question the predominant influence commanded by white men from privileged social and economic backgrounds. Increasingly, considerations of ethnicity, class, and gender took precedence over broader conceptions of citizenship, and as the political landscape changed in the latter decades of the twentieth-century, so too did public expressions of faith by political leaders.

One historian has argued that the late 1960s and early 1970s officially mark the end of the Puritan era in American history, where the long-held notion that public morality could at least be nominally premised on abstract Protestant ethical imperatives ceased to hold sway over American political life.[52] Although the causes of this cultural transformation could long be debated, one result was that it fomented a reaction in conservative religious circles that is still being felt to this day. Shaken by the dramatic social upheavals of the Vietnam era, conservative Christians countered by mobilizing a concerted political effort to "return" America to the moral consensus they believed had been lost to the interests of secular elites who promoted a dangerous agenda both in the universities and in the government.

For a brief moment in 1976 these conservatives thought that they had found a politician who shared their perspective in the presidential candidacy of Governor Jimmy Carter of Georgia. Carter was a Southern Baptist who, in the middle of his campaign, casually mentioned to a *New York Times* that he was a "born again" Christian. The phrase became popular for the remainder of his run for the presidency, and Carter capitalized on the attention by frequently referring to the importance of his faith in his life. He even told *Playboy* magazine during the fall of the general election that, according to the precepts of Christ, he had committed adultery because he had lusted after women in his heart. Despite his public religiosity, Carter's record as president disappointed many conservatives; in particular, his waffling on the controversial question of abortion alienated many evangelical Christians who initially supported him.

Labeled the "culture war" in the early 1990s, the debate over the place of religious values in American public life has continued unabated through the administrations of presidents Ronald Reagan, George H.W. Bush, Bill Clinton, and George W. Bush. As the political fortunes of conservative Christians have waxed and waned over the last 30 years, however, the Religious Right has increasingly borrowed a page from the script of their multiculturalist antagonists by claiming that they, like other minorities, deserve a place at the table of public policy making. The 1980s proved a watershed decade for conservatives as organizations such as Jerry Falwell's Moral Majority and Pat Robertson's Christian Coalition rallied the evangelical vote by emphasizing their sense of cultural disaffectedness. A televangelist who founded the Christian Broadcasting Network in 1961, Robertson himself made headlines when, in 1988, he claimed God had told him to enter the presidential race. Robertson lost his bid for the presidency, but the impact of his, and other religious conservatives; efforts to control the Republican Party continues to shape the public dynamic between religion and politics on both sides of the aisle.

Though their agenda has met success in both local and national elections, conservative Christian political leaders have, at times, blurred the line between what reflects the received moral usages of religious rhetoric, and what constitutes a real violation of the separation of church and state. Indeed, the nature of the debate has evolved in recent years to include the extent to which symbolic expressions of faith by public officials can be tolerated.

On November 13, 2003, the Chief Justice of the Supreme Court of Alabama, Roy Moore, was removed from office because of his refusal to remove a 5,280-pound granite monument of the Ten Commandments from the central rotunda of the state judicial building. Standing three-feet wide by three-feet deep by four-feet tall and displaying quotes from the Declaration of Independence, the national anthem, and various Founding Fathers, Moore had the monument constructed and placed in the judicial building in the middle of the night on July 31, 2001. The monument was subsequently ruled a violation of the Establishment Clause and ordered removed by federal U.S. District Judge Myron Thompson. Moore refused on the grounds that the monument "reflects the sovereignty of God over the affairs of men," and that there was no violation of the separation of church and state because "the Judeo-Christian God reigned over both the church and the state in this country, and that both owed allegiance to that God."[53] By appealing to the "Judeo-Christian God" as well as insisting that God is somehow at work in a special way in the United States, Moore continued the rhetorical pattern of using loosely-defined Christian references to frame the theological underpinnings of America. According to the court, however, he went beyond past public expressions of faith when he used his office as a judge, as well as public property, to advertise his convictions.

CONCLUSION

Public usage of religious rhetoric by political leaders has been a part of the American experience since the country's colonial beginnings, and, at least in recent decades, it has become a source of controversy and division. While the practice has varied according to historical circumstance, there remain certain perennial characteristics to the way religion, specifically Christianity, has been appropriated by public officials in the United States. By and large, past public expressions of faith in America have stemmed from a Protestant theological disposition. In particular, they have orginated with the Puritan notion that Divine Providence secured in the American experiment a kind of sacred purpose unique among the nations. Fueled by revivalism in the eighteenth century, the notion of being "set apart" or "chosen by God" lingered in the American imagination long after Puritan solidarity collapsed and fragmented the New England theological landscape. With the coming of the American Revolution and the birth of the republic, however, the Protestant ethos established by the Puritans underwent a transformation that would have dramatic consequences for the future of religion in American public life.

After the Constitution of the United States was adopted by the various states, two important principles bequeathed by the Founding Fathers became part of the American identity: first, the country would have no established national religion; second, people would have the right to speak freely about religion. Under this arrangement, the confessional or dogmatic Protestantism of the early colonial period—that is, the Protestantism born out of the doctrinal controversies of the sixteenth and seventeenth centuries—slowly ceased to matter in a legal sense to American political life. No doubt within the denominational contexts (Presbyterian, Baptist, Methodist, etc.) the theological content of the faith remained important; however, in the United States, one's theological convictions would not be a prerequisite for citizenship, nor would creedal assent be necessary to participate in American civic life. Rather, in terms of its public importance, Christianity would be valued for its broad ethical imperatives and its ability to proffer a moral consensus for a free but otherwise disparate people. In other words, by the late eighteenth and early nineteenth centuries, owing in large part to the influence of both revivalistic conversionism and Enlightenment political thought, matters of faith became intensely personal.

The move toward the privatization of religious convictions did not, however, mean the absolute loss of Christian influence upon American culture, and as the religious climate of the nation changed, so too did public expressions of faith by political leaders. The moral and symbolic capital of Christianity, specifically Protestantism, remained and continued to be used by politicians even after nuanced doctrinal arguments became irrelevant to the legal construction of the American political project. Throughout the first half of the nineteenth century, as the responsibilities of democratic citizenship were increasingly viewed through the lens of Protestant social imperatives, sentimental notions of what it meant to be both an American and a Christian replaced the robust "public theologies" of earlier American life. These emotional ties were strong, and they provided a shared moral sensibility that united a number of social causes in the early decades of the republic. Still, they were not strong enough to keep at bay the profound political crises generated by the problems of slavery and immigration, and as these two issues divided the country, public expressions of faith were divided as well.

After the Civil War and well into the twentieth century, religion continued to matter for public life as long as theological disputes remained on the sideline of political discourse. As with previous generations, both the "idea" of God and the "social teachings" of Jesus were valuable to a democratic and free people, but arguments over doctrinal interpretation—such as the nature of atonement or the continuity between the two testaments of Scripture—were not. As the United States grew into a world power, the ideals and idealism of democracy assumed a hallowed place in the moral reasoning of many Americans, and in language that echoed both the Puritans and Abraham Lincoln, twentieth-century political leaders often described both the domestic and the global challenges facing the country in religious terms.[54] With the political and social upheavals of the 1960s and 1970s, however, the strained moral consensus forged out of the union of facile Protestant social sensibilities and democratic idealism collapsed.

Although a conservative cultural reaction continues to keep public expressions of faith at the fore of American politics, the exigencies of pluralism and multiculturalism and the legal difficulties surrounding the Establishment Clause complicate the place of religion in public life. Advocacy groups such as the American Civil Liberties Union and the People for the American Way insist that even though it is not legally forbidden, it is nevertheless bad precedent to interject personal beliefs into any aspect of politics, rhetorical or otherwise. Moreover, the limits of what the electorate will tolerate with regard to public expressions of faith outside the Christian tradition are yet to be fully realized. Although the year 2007 witnessed the first Muslim elected to Congress—Keith Ellison, who was sworn into office using a copy of Thomas Jefferson's Koran—as well as the first Mormon presidential candidate—former Governor of Massachusetts Mitt Romney—it is not clear how non-conventional religious expression will be received by a population that largely identifies itself as Christian.

Because many Americans value the cultural accord afforded by a common moral vision, the idea of a shared religious heritage carries substantial political cachet for those seeking public office. Even though this alleged religious heritage lacks specific doctrinal commitments, political leaders have successfully integrated it into their public rhetoric for over two centuries. Still, no matter how frequently God or religion is referenced by a politician, certain questions remain. If God matters to the public square, how does he matter? If religion is relevant to liberal democracy, how is it relevant? In the early years of the twenty-first century, answers to these questions still remain elusive; even so, the public usage of religious rhetoric by political leaders continues undiminished.

NOTES

1. Christopher Hanson, "God and Man on the Campaign Trail," *Columbia Journalism Review*, November/December 2000. Juan Stan, "Bush's Religious Language," *The Nation*, December 4, 2003. *Washington Post*, July 12, 1999, Section C, page 1; CBS News Interview by Lesley Stahl, *60 Minutes*, December 4, 2000.

2. ABC News Interview by Peggy Wehmeyer, *American Agenda*, March 22, 1994.

3. George W. Bush to the annual convention of B'nai B'rith International, quoted in the *New York Times*, September 3, 2000, Section 4, page 5; Bill Clinton before the 1998 National Prayer Breakfast, quoted in the *Washington Post*, September 13, 1998, Section C, page 7.

4. Dissatisfied with what were perceived as too many concessions to "Romanism," the Puritans wanted the Church of England to more closely resemble the reformed churches of the continent. Indeed, many essential theological positions of the English Puritans were refined during the Marian exile during which approximately 800 English Protestants fled to the Netherlands, Germany, Switzerland, and France to escape the Catholic counter-reaction to the English Reformation. The label "Puritan," a term of derision invented by their theological opponents, may apply to a number of late sixteenth-century Protestant churches committed in various ways to Reformed theology or Calvinism both on the European continent and in England. The English version, however, manifested around some very specific controversies involving opposition to the use of clerical vestments as well as opposition to the rituals and formulas of the *Book of Common Prayer*. In addition, many of the Puritans from southern England were Congregationalists (in Scotland they were Presbyterian) and hence they were antagonistic toward the Episcopal system of ecclesiastical government practiced by the established church.

5. Rowan Greer, *Anglican Approaches to Scripture* (New York: Crossroad, 2006), 9–15.

6. See Perry Miller, *Errand Into the Wilderness* (Cambridge, MA: Belknap Press of Harvard University Press, 1956, 1984).

7. William Bradford, "Of Plymouth Plantation," in *Anthology of American Literature*, ed. George McMichael, vol. 1, 4th ed. (New York: Macmillan Publishing Company, 1989), 44.

8. Ibid., 36.

9. John Winthrop, "A Model of Christian Charity," in *Anthology of American Literature*, 67–68.

10. See Sacvan Bercovitch, *The Puritan Origins of the American Self* (New Haven: Yale University Press, 1975), 36.

11. Winthrop, "Journal," in *Anthology of American Literature*, 75.

12. See Ernst H. Kantorowicz, *The King's Two Bodies: A Study in Mediaeval Political Theology* (Princeton: Princeton University Press, 1957).

13. Calvinists took control of Maryland in 1655, overturned the Act of Toleration, and banned Catholics from holding public office.

14. Darryl Hart, *A Secular Faith* (Chicago: Ivan R. Dee, 2006), 30.

15. Quoted in Gerald R. McDermott, *One Holy and Happy Society: The Political Theology of Jonathan Edwards* (University Park, PA: The Pennsylvania State University Press, 1992), 84.

16. On the Enlightenment and religion, see Henry F. May, *The Enlightenment in America* (New York: Oxford University Press, 1976), and Peter Gay, *The Enlightenment: An Interpretation* (New York: W. W. Norton & Company, 1996).

17. Thomas Jefferson, "Notes on the State of Virginia," in *Writings*, ed. Merrill D. Peterson (New York: Literary Classics of the United States, 1984), 286, 289.

18. Ibid., Thomas Jefferson, Letter to Thomas Cooper, February 10, 1814, 1325; and "Second Inaugural Address," March 4, 1805, 523.

19. Thomas Jefferson, Letter to William Canby, September 18, 1813; Thomas Jefferson, Letter to William Short, April 13, 1820, in *A Jefferson Profile*, ed. Saul K. Padover (New York: The John Day Company), 211, 311–312.

20. Thomas Jefferson, Letter to John Adams, April 11, 1823; Thomas Jefferson, Letter to Thomas Law, June 13, 1814; in *Writings*, 1466–1469, 1335–1339.

21. *The Works of John Adams, Second President of the United States; With A Life of the Author Notes and Illustrations of his Grandson Charles Francis Adams*. Vol. IX (Free Port, NY: Books For Libraries Press, first published 1850–1856, Reprinted 1969), 228–229.

22. John Adams, Letter to F. A. Van der Kamp, December 27, 1816; John Adams, Letter to John Taylor, 1814; quoted in Norman Cousins, *In God We Trust: The Religious Beliefs and Ideas of the American Founding Fathers* (New York: Harper, 1958), 108.

23. See Benjamin Franklin, *The Autobiography of Benjamin Franklin with Related Documents*, ed. Louis P. Masur (Boston: Bedford/St. Martins, 2003), 93–104.

24. First quote, Benjamin Franklin, Letter to Ezra Stiles, in Carl Van Doren,

Benjamin Franklin (New York: Viking Press, 1938), 777–778. Second quote, Victor J. Stenger, *Has Science Found God?* (Amherst, NY: Prometheus Books, 2003).

25. James Madison, *A Memorial and Remonstrance Against Religious Assessments,* addressed to the Virginia General Assemby, June 20, 1785.

26. George Washington, Letter to the United Baptist Chamber of Virginia, May 1789, in Anson Phelps Stokes, *Church and State in the United States,* Vol. 1. p. 495; George Washington, responding to a group of clergymen who complained that the Constitution lacked mention of Jesus Christ, in 1789, *Papers,* Presidential Series, 4:274,

27. George Washington, Letter to Edward Newenham, October 20, 1792; from George Seldes, ed., *The Great Quotations* (Secaucus, NJ: Citadel Press, 1983), 726; George Washington, Letter to Sir Edward Newenham, June 22, 1792.

28. For a helpful picture of how the idea of social regeneration in the nineteenth century compared and contrasted with the social implications of evangelicalism during and after the Second Great Awakening, see Edwin Scott Gaustad, *The Great Awakening in New England* (New York: Harper & Row, 1965), 1957; Rhys Isaac, *The Transformation of Virginia: 1740–1790* (Chapel Hill, NC: The University of North Carolina Press, 1982); and Nathan O. Hatch, *The Sacred Cause of Liberty: Republican Thought and the Millennium in Revolutionary New England* (New Haven: Yale University Press, 1977).

29. Quoted in Richard J. Carwardine, *Evangelicals and Politics in Antebellum America* (Knoxville: The University of Tennessee Press), 59.

30. Ibid., 65–66.

31. Inaugural Address, March 4, 1841, in *A Compilation of the Messages and Papers of the Presidents,* ed. James Richardson, vol. IV (New York: New York Bureau of National Literature, 1897), 1,875.

32. Horace Mann, in the Massachusetts Board of Education's *Tenth Annual Report* (1847), cited in Robert H. Bremmer, ed., *Children and Youth in America: A Documentary History Vol. I* (Cambridge, MA: Harvard University Press, 1971), 456.

33. Ibid. Also see Carl F. Kaestle, *Pillars of the Republic: Common Schools and American Society, 1780–1860* (New York: Hill and Wang, 1983), 77–103; and Lawrence A. Cremin, *American Education: The National Experience 1783–1876* (New York: Harper & Row, 1980), 133–137.

34. Lewis D. Campbell, "Americanism" speech delivered at the American Mass Meeting in Washington, D.C., February 29, 1856, published in the *American Organ.*

35. John C. Calhoun, "Speech on the General State of the Union," in *Union and Liberty: The Political Philosophy of John C. Calhoun,* ed. Ross M. Lence (Indianapolis: Liberty Fund, 1992), 586–588.

36. Daniel Webster, "The Constitution and the Union," *The Works of Daniel Webster,* vol. V. (Boston: Charles C. Little and James Brown, 1851), 331–332.

37. *Jefferson Davis,* Vol. 1, by Dunbar Rowland, pp. 286, 316–317.

38. Drew Gilpin Faust, *The Creation of Confederate Nationalism: Ideology and Identity in the Civil War South* (Baton Rouge: Louisiana State University Press, 1988), 33.

39. See Lucas E. Morel, *Lincoln's Sacred Effort: Defining Religion's Role in American Self-Government* (Lanham, MD: Lexington Books, 2000), 85.

40. Abraham Lincoln, "Proclamation Appointing a National Fast-Day, March 30, 1863," in *Complete Works of Abraham Lincoln*, eds. John G. Nicolay and John Hay, vol. VIII (New York: Francis D. Tandy Company, 1894), 236.

41. Abraham Lincoln, "Proclamation for Thanksgiving, July 15, 1863," in *Complete Works*, vol. IX, 33.

42. William Henry Herndon, *Abraham Lincoln: The True Story of a Great Life* (New York: D. Appleton, 1892).

43. Quoted in Richard M. Gamble, *The War for Righteousness: Progressive Christianity, the Great War, and the Rise of the Messianic Nation* (Wilmington, DE: ISI Books, 2003), 129.

44. Ibid.

45. *The State of the Union Messages of the Presidents, 1790–1966*, ed. Fred Israel, vol. III (New York: Chelsea House Publishers, 1967), 2863.

46. Speech regarding his addition of "under God" to the U.S. Pledge of Allegiance on June 14, 1954.

47. Quoted in William Imboden, "'One Cheer for Civil Religion'?," *Modern Reformation*, 13, no. 5 (September/October 2004).

48. Glenn Feldman, *Politics, Society, and the Klan* (Tuscaloosa: University of Alabama Press, 1999), 173.

49. Congressional Record, Senate extract, January 18, 1928, quoted in Feldman, *Politics, Society, and the Klan*, 173–174.

50. Hart, *Secular Faith*, 159.

51. Printed in the *New York Times*, September 13, 1960.

52. Sydney E. Ahlstrom, *A Religious History of the American People* (New Haven: Yale University Press, 1972), 1079.

53. *Glassroth v. Moore* (M.D. Ala. 2002).

54. In particular, the struggle against Communism and the struggle for Civil Rights were cast in religious terms.

FURTHER READING

The literature on the subject of public expressions of faith by political leaders is obviously vast and the following titles are meant to serve simply as a start. Works that offer helpful overviews as well as strong introductions to twentieth-century developments include A. James Reichely's *Religion in American Public Life*; Cushing Stout's *The New Heavens and the New Earth: Political Religion in America*, Russell Richey and Donald G. Jones' *Civil Religion*; John F. Wilson's *Public Religion in American Culture*, and Darryl Hart's *A Secular Faith*. Although the literature on the Puritans is enormous, the best introduction to Puritan theology and Puritan religious rhetoric remain Perry Miller's *Errand into the Wilderness*, Sacvan Bercovitch's *The American Jeremiad*, and Edmund Morgan's *The Puritan Dilemma*. The subject of the religion of the Founding Era and the early republic is also immense, but a good start would include Catharine L. Albanese's *Sons of the Fathers: The Civil Religion of the American Revolution* and Mark Noll's *America's God: From Jonathan Edwards to Abraham Lincoln*. On American Protestantism's democratic impulse in the nineteenth century, see Nathan O. Hatch's *The Democratization of American Christianity*, and on the subject of religious rhetoric and the Civil War consult Allen C. Guelzo's *Abraham Lincoln: Redeemer President* and Mitchell Snay's *Gospel of Disunion: Religion and Separatism in the Antebellum South*. Two good introductions to Catholic and Protestant tensions over the place of religion and American political rhetoric are Ray Allen Billington's *The Protestant Crusade* and John T. McGreevy's *Catholicism and American Freedom*.

4

The Internationalization of Church-State Issues

Zachary R. Calo

The law of church and state has traditionally referred, at least in American legal discourse, to First Amendment jurisprudence involving such issues as prayer in public schools, Sunday closing laws, public displays of religious imagery, and aid to parochial schools. Its particular concern has been the work of courts in interpreting the First Amendment's requirement that "Congress shall make no law respecting an establishment of religion, or prohibiting the free exercise thereof." First Amendment jurisprudence of this type remains the bread and butter of church-state law in America, as federal courts in recent years have considered the pros and cons of such issues as the "under God" clause in the Pledge of Allegiance, the teaching of intelligent design in public schools, and display of the Ten Commandments on government property. However, the twentieth-century human rights revolution, particularly in the area of religious liberties, has globalized the law of church and state and transformed the scope of debate about the relationship between religion, ethics, and government. The promulgation of the Universal Declaration of Human Rights in 1948, which established that "everyone has the right to freedom of thought, conscience and religion," ensured that church-state issues would no longer be within the exclusive province of the sovereign nation-state.[1]

The objective of this essay is to survey the landscape of church-state issues in light of the human rights revolution, recognizing that the international law of religious freedom has not yet had any explicit impact on First Amendment church-state jurisprudence in the United States.[2] U.S. courts continue to rule in this area without respect to international law. In fact, the issues at stake in the domestic law of church and state remain fundamentally different from those in the international arena. First Amendment cases typically involve a narrow set of facts interpreted in light of an established constitutional right to religious freedom; international debate, on the other hand, focuses on the existence, scope and content of the very right to religious freedom taken for granted in domestic constitutional law. References to church-state law in this essay should therefore be understood to refer not only to constitutional law but also to the broader relationship of religion, ethics, and government. In spite of these qualifications, it is nevertheless the case that domestic and international legal debates have become increasingly intertwined and that international law in the area of religious freedom has transformed the contours of American law and politics. A full discussion of church and state in America can no longer end with the First Amendment.

This chapter begins by detailing the emergence of international human rights law in the area of religious freedom. The discussion will focus on legal mechanisms established in the post–World War II period to protect the right to religious freedom. The chapter next examines two important areas in which international law and politics have shaped domestic law. First, it considers how the United States is using its foreign policy to promote religious freedom—what one commentator has referred to as "exporting the First Amendment."[3] Particular attention will be given to the International Religious Freedom Act of 1998, which created the Office of International Religious Freedom within the Department of State, a bipartisan commission on international religious freedom, and an ambassador at-large for religious freedom. This legislation established religious freedom as the official policy of the United States and committed the federal government to developing a foreign policy premised on the exportation of constitutional principles. The continuing debate over this legislation not only provides insights into the United States' contested relationship with the international human rights regime, but also into domestic church-state politics. The second topic considered is the burgeoning debate over the role of international law, particularly international human rights law, in shaping constitutional interpretation. International law has played an increasingly prominent role in constitutional jurisprudence, most notably in several recent Supreme Court decisions that invoke international law as persuasive authority. The importance of this legal development is enhanced because the cases have involved the death penalty, the rights of homosexuals, and other issues at the heart of contemporary moral and cultural debates.

The status of international law remains much debated by scholars, practitioners, and governments. Hovering in the background of these debates about religion, culture, and international law is thus a more foundational debate about the authority of international law, particularly with respect to domestic law. This is a complex and wide-ranging debate, much of which generally takes place among legal academics and which is beyond the necessary scope of this essay.[4] A leading textbook on international law, however, summarizes the debate as follows:

International law has had to justify its legitimacy and its reality. Its title to law has been challenged on the ground that, by hypothesis and definition, there can be no law governing sovereign states. Skeptics have argued that there can be no international law since there is no international legislature to make it, no international executive to enforce it, and no effective international judiciary to interpret and to develop it, or to resolve disputes about it. International law, it has been said, is not 'real law' since it is commonly disregarded, states obeying it only when they wish to, when it is in their interest to do so.[5]

Even the strongest and most sanguine defenders of international law and institutions accept that there are limitations to expanding international legal regimes. The greatest challenge for international law is that its authority depends ultimately on voluntary compliance by states, as there is no sovereign authority to enforce its provisions.

At the same time, defenders of international law emphasize that its norms shape the behavior of nation-states even in the absence of authorial enforcement mechanisms. Louis Henkin, one of the leading twentieth-century authorities on international law, argues, for instance, that "almost all nations observe almost all principles of international law and almost all of their obligations almost all of the time."[6] The reasons states act in this way are much debated. It is nevertheless clear that the vast web of laws, institutions, norms, and practices, particularly as developed in the post–World War II period, have legitimated international law and structured the way states act towards their citizens and other states. The "authority" of international law, it is true, remains fundamentally different from that of domestic law. Yet international law shapes the world in concrete ways, and the forces of globalization are now expanding the scope of international law's influence into areas of religious and cultural import that were formerly under the exclusive sway of domestic law.

RELIGIOUS FREEDOM IN INTERNATIONAL HUMAN RIGHTS LAW

The *Treaty of Westphalia* in 1648 ended the "Wars of Religion" and established protections for religious minorities. Yet at the same time as *Westphalia* set European society on the path towards religious freedom, it also birthed the sovereign nation-state, the political form that became the greatest threat to religious freedom. Daniel Philpott notes that "what Westphalia inaugurated was a system of sovereign states where a single authority resided supreme within a set of borders."[7] This system of sovereignty gave the state exclusive authority over its internal activities. The actions of a state toward its people were defined as a matter of purely domestic concern in which no external sovereign or authority could interfere. It took the Holocaust and the deaths of tens of millions at the hands of the state to weaken the stranglehold of Westphalian sovereignty and inaugurate the modern human rights movement. With the Universal Declaration of Human Rights came the symbolic end to absolute state sovereignty and the beginning of what Yale Law School Dean Harold Koh has termed "the globalization of freedom."[8]

At the heart of the modern human rights movement is the principle that certain fundamental norms are universal and inviolable. So central are these rights to the essential dignity of the human person that no political authority may deny them. Religious freedom has from the inception of the human rights movement been identified as such a right. In fact, religious freedom has long been deemed a foundational right upon which other rights rest, as attested by its designation as the "First Freedom." The right to free speech and association, the right of indigenous people to preserve their cultural practices, and the rights of parents to raise their children all rest upon a prior right to religious freedom.[9] If the right to religious freedom is impeded so too are these other rights.

Given its foundational importance, the right to religious freedom was clearly established in the founding documents of the human rights movement.[10] Both the United Nations Charter and the Universal Declaration of Human Rights name freedom of conscience and freedom of religion as basic rights. Article I of the United Nations Charter provides that a central aim of the organization is "promoting and encouraging respect of human rights . . . and fundamental freedoms . . . without distinction as to race, sex, language, or religion. . . ."[11] The Charter goes on to provide that the United Nations shall promote "universal respect for, and observance of, human rights and fundamental freedoms for all without distinction as to race, sex, language, or religion."[12] The lack of a more robust statement in support of religious freedom in the Charter reflects the influence of China and the Soviet Union in founding the United Nations.[13] The Universal Declaration of Human Rights (UDHR), promulgated December 10, 1948, is more explicit than the United Nations Declaration in establishing a right to religious freedom. The most important statement appears in Article 18, which provides that "everyone has the right to freedom of thought, conscience and religion; this right includes freedom to change his religion or belief, and freedom, either alone or in community with others and in public or private, to manifest his religion or belief in teaching, practice, worship and observance."[14] The breadth of this provision is notable. For one, the provision rejects a purely privatized account of religious belief and expression. It recognizes that religious belief is not a purely private matter but necessarily encompasses the whole of human life and community.[15] The UDHR also recognizes that freedom of religious belief is a meaningless right absent freedom to actualize beliefs in public and communal worship.[16] Finally, the UDHR recognizes the right to change religions, a particularly controversial provision that led a number of Islamic countries to abstain from voting.[17]

While the U.N. Charter and the UDHR both recognize a right to religious freedom, there was a lingering concern that these documents failed to provide adequate legal mechanisms for enforcing the right. The hope for establishing more robust legal protections was placed in future documents, most importantly in the International Covenant on Civil and Political Rights (ICCPR) and the International Covenant on Economic, Social, and Cultural Rights.[18] These two documents remain central pillars of the international human rights movement, and the ICCPR, adopted in 1966 and entered into force in 1976, remains the most important resource for advancing religious freedom. Article 18 of the ICCPR, which corresponds with and expands upon Article 18 of the UDHR, provides that:

1. Everyone shall have the right to freedom of thought, conscience and religion. This right shall include freedom to have or to adopt a religion or belief of his choice, and freedom, either individually or in community with others and in public or private, to manifest his religion or belief in worship, observance, practice and teaching.

2. No one shall be subject to coercion which would impair his freedom to have or to adopt a religion or belief of his choice.

3. Freedom to manifest one's religion or beliefs may be subject only to such limitations as are prescribed by law and are necessary to protect public safety, order, health, or morals or the fundamental rights and freedoms of others.

4. The States Parties to the present Covenant undertake to have respect for the liberty of parents and, when applicable, legal guardians to ensure the religious and moral education of their children in conformity with their own convictions.

Article 27 is also relevant. Applying principles earlier established in Article 18, Article 27 provides that "in those States in which ethnic, religious or linguistic minorities exist, persons belonging to such minorities shall not be denied the right, in community with the other members of their group, to enjoy their own culture, to profess and practice their own religion, or to use their own language." Finally, the ICCPR contains an optional protocol addressing what is widely recognized to be a major problem with the parent treaty: its lack of an effective enforcement mechanism.[19] An optional protocol is a treaty that accompanies and augments an existing human rights treaty. The Optional Protocol to the International Covenant on Civil and Political Rights allows individual citizens of signatory nations to appeal to the U.N. Committee on Human Rights when they believe rights established by the ICCPR have been violated and all domestic remedies have been exhausted.[20] This Optional Protocol effectively creates a private right of action under the ICCPR.

In part to address shortcomings in the protections afforded religion freedom in the UDHR and ICCPR, in 1981 the United Nations also issued the Declaration on the Elimination of All Forms of Intolerance and of Discrimination Based on Religion or Belief.[21] The stated purpose of the Declaration is "to adopt all necessary measures for the speedy elimination of [religious intolerance] in all its forms and manifestations."[22] Echoing principles set forth in previous United Nations documents, the 1981 Declaration declares in Article I that "everyone shall have the right to freedom of thought, conscience and religion" and that this right includes the freedom "to have a religion or whatever belief of his choice, and freedom, either individually or in community with others and in public or private, to manifest his religion or belief in worship, observance, practice and teaching." The Declaration also requires states to actively prevent and remove religious discrimination, to support the right of parents to raise their children in the faith of their choosing, and to worship, teach, and disseminate written materials. Discrimination on the basis of religion is decried as a violation of "fundamental freedoms" and an "affront to human dignity."[23]

This document was an important victory for the cause of religious freedom. Not only did it contain a broad definition of religious freedom, but it also is the only international human rights document concerned exclusively with religion and religious freedom. This victory, however, has been more symbolic than actual, for the 1981 Declaration has not been an effective vehicle for advancing human rights.[24] Twenty years of work at the United Nations produced only a declaration rather than a more-forceful covenant. A declaration carries only moral authority and is not a legally binding document that can be enforced against parties. Declarations, unlike covenants, do not establish monitoring committees or require signatory countries to provide annual reports. The 1981 Declaration therefore lacks any effective mechanism for enforcing the rights it establishes. In addition, the Declaration, like the ICCPR, fails to enunciate a right to convert or abandon religion altogether.[25] One commentator attributes this omission to the sizeable influence of Islamic states, many of which regard western conceptions of religious freedom as contrary to the tenets of Islam.[26] A "broad consensus of Muslim scholars" rejects the idea of full religious freedom as well as the proposition that Muslims have a "right" to convert.[27] For all its aspirations, the 1981 Declaration goes no further than previous human rights documents, and in certain respects it offers a more circumscribed definition of religious freedom than the UDHR and ICCPR.

The landscape of religious freedom has changed markedly in the twentieth century. It is now widely agreed that human persons possess a basic right to religious belief and practice and that this right is "firmly ensconced in international law."[28] Nevertheless, religious freedom remains of only marginal concern in the human rights movement and there is little momentum for expanding protections. In his recent book, *Can God & Caesar Coexist? Balancing Freedom and International Law*, Fr. Robert Drinan goes so far as to note that there has been an "absence of any real discussion on religious freedom at the world level."[29] This statement could be disputed, but Drinan is certainly correct to observe that religious freedom lags behind other causes. One commentator observes that "while many of the other protections accorded in UDHR have since been incorporated into binding covenants, the full panoply of religious protections have never attained more than 'declaratory' status."[30] In spite of the various statements affirming religious freedom—the U.N. Charter, the Universal Declaration of Human Rights, the International Covenant on Civil and Political Rights, and the Declaration on the Elimination of All Forms of Intolerance and of Discrimination Based on Religion or Belief—there is still not one effective enforcement mechanism.[31] The right to religious freedom remains a right on paper only. A recent analysis, in fact, concluded that international mechanisms for protecting religious liberty are largely a failure, given that the existing legal regime has done little to prevent numerous acts of genocide on the basis of religious identity.[32] In Rwanda, Sudan, and Bosnia, for instance, religiously-motivated genocide took place irrespective of international norms. One scholar has also noted that while almost every country signed the UDHR, at least eighty countries have engaged in documented acts of religious intolerance or persecution.[33] The International Religious Freedom Act reports in its findings that "more than one-half of the world's population lives under regimes that severely restrict or prohibit the freedom of their citizens to study, believe, observe, and freely practice the religious faith of their choice," while the most recent International Religious Freedom Report issued by the Department of State identifies a number of countries in which there is religious persecution and intolerance.[34]

The troubled state of religious freedom in international law can be attributed to a number of factors. One challenge involves defining "religion."[35] While the rights to life, speech, and political participation can be defined with relative precision, it is more difficult to clearly delineate what religious beliefs and actions ought to receive legal protection. At the most basic level is the question of when a set of beliefs becomes a religion. Does a religion require a community or can a religion exist with only one adherent? Does a religion require belief in a God or gods, or might a deeply held moral worldview qualify as a religion? The challenge of defining religion is not of merely theoretical concern but rather goes to the heart of what it means to protect religious freedom. The question of whether Scientology is considered a religion or a cult, for instance, determines whether European governments can permissibly ban it without violating international law.[36] The U.S. Supreme Court has addressed a number of cases that touch on this issue in the context of First Amendment jurisprudence and has established a fairly broad definition of religion.[37] The issues, however, become even more varied and complex under international law.

Another challenge has involved defining the scope and content of a right to religious freedom.[38] There is broad agreement that religious freedom ought to be protected but less agreement about what specifically are the rights worthy of protection. One problem arises when domestic law conflicts with international human rights law. The First Amendment protection of freedom of speech, for instance, places strict limits on the extent to which U.S. law can limit hate speech against religion.[39] Article 20(2) of the ICCPR, on the other hand, prohibits defamatory speech against adherents of a particular religion.[40] In this instance, the protection given religious freedom under international law is in conflict with U.S. constitutional law, thereby forcing the United States to include a reservation in its ratification of the ICCPR and to refuse to endorse this portion of the agreement. A reservation to a treaty allows a state to become a party without being bound to particular provisions of the treaty. In the case of the United States and the ICCPR, reservations arguably enhance international human rights law by fostering a higher level of state participation in an agreement. At the same time, many commentators believe that the purpose and effectiveness of a treaty is undermined when states condition their ratification on the rejection of certain provisions.

More serious problems arise over the right of governments to limit or curtail religious freedom on the grounds of public order and safety. It is widely recognized that states have a right to act on such grounds. Few would dispute, for instance, the right to prevent female genital mutilation and honor killings, even when done in the name of religious observance. The right of states to so act is set forth in Article 18 of the ICCPR, which provides that "freedom to manifest one's religion or beliefs may be subject only to such limitations as are prescribed by law and are necessary to protect public safety, order, health, or morals or the fundamental rights and freedoms of others." Commenting on this passage, Michael Perry of Emory University Law School notes, "So it is not as if there is no room, in a political community that accepts the right to freedom of religion, for the legislators to enact laws that they judge to be necessary to protect the community's morality."[41] The Tandem Project, a non-governmental organization founded to promote the 1981 U.N. Declaration on the Elimination of All Forms of Intolerance and of Discrimination Based on Religion or Belief, follows the language of ICCPR Article 18 in affirming "that States have a right to place limits on the manifestation of a religion or belief" on the grounds of law, safety, order, health, morals, and fundamental rights.[42] In practice, however, Article 18 can also serve as a shield for human rights violations committed in the name of state police power. Is China's policy of restricting foreign missionaries, for instance, a proper exercise of state police power, or is it a violation of religious freedom? Can a Muslim country limit the right of non-Muslims to publicly practice their faith? The "drafting loophole" in Article 18 has allowed countries to both affirm the UDHR while still engaging in what most would call religious discrimination.[43]

Finally, the issue of international religious freedom has become increasingly entangled in a contentious debate about the relationship between religion and politics in modernity. Boston University sociologist Peter Berger has famously quipped that America is a country of Indians ruled by Swedes, a reference to the disconnect between the pervasive religiosity of the American people as compared to the regnant secularism of the nation's elite. This same characterization could also be applied to the human rights movement, whose elite leaders and global bureaucrats often reject the religious views of the people they represent. Peter Berger noted on another occasion that human rights conventions and declarations "were not adopted by nations but by a small clique of lawyers, bureaucrats, and intellectuals who are highly westernized and most of who have absolutely nothing to do with the cultures in which most of their fellow nationals live."[44]

The effects of this disconnect have been revealed most vividly in the area of religion, which more than any other force exposes the cultural fault lines that define the modern world. A 2005 report issued by Human Rights Watch pointedly asked if there is "a schism between the human rights movement and religious communities." The answer given by this leading international human rights organization was clearly yes, as evidenced by debates over such "contentious issues" as reproductive rights, gay marriage, and blasphemy laws.[45] The report urged that efforts be made to bring about better relations but nevertheless emphasized that "the human rights movement should not sacrifice its most valued principles and objectives in order to protect its good relations with religious communities."[46] The ambivalence of many cultural elites towards religion leaves the cause of religious freedom marginalized within the broader human rights movement. Post-9/11 world affairs have only further marginalized religion by feeding the belief that radical religion is a greater political problem than religious persecution. As Daniel Philpott observes, there is a growing concern that "a religious and cultural backlash will weaken those institutions and practices whose limitations on sovereignty now enjoys a frail consensus—intervention, international judicial norms."[47] Promoting religious freedom, some argue, will unleash religion as a potent agent of political unrest that will undermine human rights more generally.

John Witte writes that that the modern human rights movement was an "attempt to harvest from the traditions of Christianity and Enlightenment the rudimentary elements of a new faith and a new law that would unite a badly broken world." Religious ideas and communities "participated actively as midwives in the birth of this modern rights revolution" but were then relegated to a lower priority.[48] The coming together of religious and secular human rights traditions was an important, and historically underappreciated, aspect of the twentieth-century human rights revolution. But the continued viability of this cooperative enterprise appears less certain. The struggle between religion and the human rights movement is more intense today than it was a half-century ago when the Universal Declaration of Human Rights was promulgated.[49] Religion indeed has the capacity to contribute to the vibrancy of the human rights movement. Some have even argued that the idea of human rights needs religion to maintain political vitality and intellectual coherence. Yet, because religion is such an explosive issue, the promotion of religious freedom also has the potential to "destroy an already fragile global consensus on human rights."[50]

EXPORTING RELIGIOUS FREEDOM: THE INTERNATIONAL RELIGIOUS FREEDOM ACT

Nearly all of the efforts to protect and promote international religious freedom have involved multilateral agreements. In 1998, however, Congress passed the International Religious Freedom Act (IRFA) and inaugurated a new approach to promoting international religious freedom by means of domestic foreign policy.[51] The text of IRFA begins with a claim about the importance of religious freedom to American democracy: "the right to freedom of religion undergirds the very origin and existence of the United States . . . From its birth to this day, the United States has prized this legacy of religious freedom and honored this heritage by standing for religious freedom and offering refuge for those suffering religious persecution."[52] Having established the centrality of religious freedom to the political ideals of the United States, IRFA proceeds to establish the importance of religious freedom to established international norms of justice: "Freedom of religious belief and practice is a universal human right and fundamental freedom articulated in numerous international instruments," including the Universal Declaration of Human Rights, the International Covenant on Civil and Political Rights, the Helsinki Accords, the Declaration on the Elimination of All Forms of Intolerance and Discrimination Based on Religion or Belief, the United Nations Charter, and the European Convention for the Protection of Human Rights and Fundamental Freedoms.[53] In light of religious freedom's importance both to American democracy and to international human rights, IRFA announces that the "policy of the United States" is now "to promote the right to freedom of religion" and "to oppose violations of religious freedom that are or have been engaged in or tolerated by the governments of foreign countries."[54] Though some critics have questioned whether the United States ought to privilege one human right over another, the claim developed in the opening section of the legislation is that religion is so central to the free society that it must receive special protection.

IRFA provides a number of mechanisms to advance religious freedom. First, it created the Office of International Religious Freedom within the Department of State and provided that the president shall appoint an ambassador at-large whose primary responsibility is "to advance the right of freedom of religion abroad, to denounce the violation of that right, and to recommend appropriate responses by the United States Government when this right is violated."[55] Second, the legislation requires the Secretary of State, with the assistance of the ambassador, to provide Congress with an Annual Report on International Religious Freedom.[56] The report must include a description of the status of religious freedom in each foreign country, an assessment of the nature and extent of violations of religious freedom in each country, and a description of the actions and policies of the United States in support of each foreign country engaging in or tolerating violations of religious freedom.[57] Third, IRFA establishes a Commission on International Religious Freedom that is responsible for reviewing the facts and circumstances of violations of religious freedom and making policy recommendations to the President, Secretary of State, and Congress with respect to matters involving international religious freedom.[58] Most significantly, IRFA sets forth a number of actions the President may take in response to violations of religious freedom. These actions include a private or official public démarche, a public condemnation, delay or cancellation of scientific or cultural exchanges, denial or cancellation of state visits, withdrawal or suspension of development or security assistance, requiring U.S. directors of international financial institutions to oppose or vote against loans primarily benefiting the foreign government, and prohibiting the U.S. government from procuring goods or services from the foreign government found to be in violation.[59]

Following two years of political debate, IRFA passed in both houses of Congress in October 1998. It took three attempts to pass the bill, and the version that did pass Congress was not as tough as earlier drafts that had included automatic sanctions and harsher penalties.[60] President Clinton signed the bill into law, although both he and the State Department had initially opposed it.[61] Religious organizations, on the other hand, were by and large supportive of the proposed legislation.[62] Allan Hertzke has described the emergence of an "unlikely alliance" in which "Evangelical, Catholic and mainline Protestant Christians found allies among Tibetan Buddhists, Iranian Bahai, Buddhists in Southeast Asia and China, and Muslim Uighars in western China."[63] Believing that existing international mechanisms were inadequate, this unlikely coalition persuaded Congress to pass IRFA.[64] American evangelicals played a particularly important role in this process.[65] Troubled by the plight of persecuted Christians abroad, evangelicals in the 1990s embraced the cause of religious freedom and pressured the American government to take a more active role in its prevention.[66] In a 2006 Pew Forum symposium on IRFA, Hertzke noted the importance of "church-based networks here in the United States, and, in particular, the activation of evangelical networks on behalf of the legislation."[67] The interest evangelicals showed in international religious freedom was particularly momentous given their historic focus on domestic political issues. The movement of evangelicals into this area pushed their moral concerns, as well as the nation's policy debate, in an international direction. With reference to conservative Christians, one commentator has in fact described IRFA as an attempt to "re-moralize" American foreign policy.[68]

Supporters of IRFA have been generally pleased with its execution. Reflecting two years after its passage, Elliot Abrams, then president of the Ethics and Public Policy Center, wrote that "[t]he State department has done a highly commendable job (with a few exceptions) in its first two annual reports of telling the tragic story of religious freedom around the globe."[69] Some supporters, however, have become less sanguine in their assessment, with internal dynamics at the State Department often blamed for IRFA's perceived failure to bring about political change commensurate with the legislation's stated ambitions. Thomas Farr, former director of the Department of State's Office of International Religious Freedom, took note of this problem in writing that the Department "treats religious freedom largely as a sequestered, humanitarian problem. The position of ambassador at-large, created by the act as 'principal adviser to the president and secretary,' is viewed at the State Department as a mere deputy in the human-rights bureau, itself perceived within the building as outside the diplomatic mainstream." "More than seven years into the implementation of the International Religious Freedom Act," Farr adds, "the United States' policy has failed to reduce worldwide religious persecution."[70] Farr made similar comments on another occasion, noting that "IRFA policy has in effect been pigeonholed at the State Department. Few senior U.S. officials believe advancing religious freedom could or should be used to encourage stable relationships between political and religious authorities in key countries."[71] At root, Farr's critique is not directed at the moral and political vision of IRFA but rather at a foreign policy establishment that endorses the "crippling assumption . . . that religious freedom entails the privatization of religion, the strict separation of religion from public life."[72] However, without greater support from the Executive Branch and the bureaucratic machinery at the State Department, IRFA might continue to disappoint its supporters.

While Farr is a friendly critic who supports the underlying objectives of IRFA, other commentators have directly attacked the legislation. One line of criticism has focused on the role of religious groups in passing IRFA. Several observers have argued that IRFA pandered to the interests of religious conservatives at the expense of pursuing more effective means of addressing human rights violations. William Martin of Rice University, for one, has dismissed the IRFA as a byproduct of the Christian Right's opposition to international organizations such as the United Nations, the European Union, and the Council on Foreign Relations.[73] Similar criticisms have been advanced by leaders within the human rights community. The executive director of Human Rights Watch criticized IRFA as a form of "special pleading" on behalf of certain victims, notably persecuted Christians.[74] John Shattuck, the former Assistant Secretary for Democracy, Human Rights, and Labor at the U.S. State Department, speaking at the Harvard Law School in 2002, similarly described IRFA as an effort "by the American Religious Right to advance a political agenda within the United States government that seeks to promote special religious interests overseas."[75] These critics have not questioned the existence of serious human rights violations perpetrated on the grounds of religion, but they have questioned whether religion ought to be given a privileged position.[76] One commentator has challenged IRFA on the grounds that it "creates an irrational hierarchy of human rights in U.S. foreign policy that makes the act vulnerable to politicization and abuse of the human rights agenda."[77] Other critics have argued that privileging religion creates practical difficulties in the execution of American foreign policy. "Will torture on the basis of religious belief now receive preferential treatment as a matter of U.S. foreign policy in comparison with, say, disappearances, torture, or suppression on the basis of racial, ethnic, political, cultural, or other factors?" asks one scholar.[78] "Can religious freedom," he adds, "ultimately be respected and ensured without corresponding protections for all other human rights?"[79]

Another criticism leveled at IRFA is that it endorses a narrowly "American or Western" conception of religious freedom.[80] It has been argued, in particular, that IRFA promotes "extreme individualism" as well as a privatized conception of the relationship between religion and the state.[81] David Smolin has thus concluded that IRFA attempts to "[export] our own confused First Amendment jurisprudence to other nations."[82] Another commentator claims that IRFA "views the international order as divided into two camps—liberal and illiberal."[83] Countries that fail to adopt an American version of religious freedom are classified as "illiberal" without respect to the particular nuances of their legal system. In response to such claims it can be noted that the rights protected by IRFA mirror those protected by Article 18 of the Universal Declaration of Human Rights. IRFA, in this respect, is no more overreaching than the Universal Declaration, which most countries have already endorsed. Of course, the real challenge for the United States involves determining whether a particular governmental action violates the right to religious freedom. It is in the course of making such prudential political judgments that controversy is likely to arise.[84]

Perhaps the most common critique of IRFA is that it bypasses existing international laws and institutions in favor of unilateral U.S. action. Rather than promoting religious freedom through international human rights law, IRFA establishes a competing legal instrument and assigns the United States sole responsibility for enforcement. Supporters of IRFA have defended this approach on the grounds that existing human rights laws are ineffective. Persecution on the basis of religion, it is noted, has grown in the half-century since the promulgation of the Universal Declaration of Human Rights. Critics, on the other hand, interpret IRFA as evidence of a deeply rooted American suspicion of internationalism. IRFA, writes one commentator, is "another example of unwarranted U.S. unilateralism."[85] Another commentator similarly describes IRFA as a "failure of international participation and cooperation," an example of "unilateral monitoring" and "self-help by a powerful state that undermines rather than improves, existing, albeit underdeveloped, multilateral enforcement mechanisms."[86] According to such critics, IRFA bolsters the already widespread belief that the United States freely ignores, and even seeks to undermine, the authority of international human rights law. Those advancing such arguments, however, generally bring to the debate presuppositions about the validity and efficacy of international law and institutions. The most dogged critics of IRFA's unilateralism have been academic commentators, political figures, and human rights advocates who support multilateral and international approaches to problems. These criticisms of IRFA are thus best viewed as part of a broader debate about the relationship between American foreign policy and the international human rights movement.[87] In short, IRFA created an opportunity for considering America's relationship to the global community and its governing institutions.

IMPORTING MORAL NORMS: HUMAN RIGHTS AND CONSTITUTIONAL INTERPRETATION

Few areas of law have escaped the influence of globalization. "Transnational" legal arrangements now exist in such diverse areas as labor law, criminal law, cyberlaw, public health, and refugee law.[88] Global lawmaking has transformed bodies of law that in the past were exclusively or at least primarily domestic in content. Globalization is also changing the face of constitutional law, as one of the most discussed and contested legal questions of the day is whether international and foreign law, particularly in the area of human rights, ought to inform constitutional interpretation.[89] Should international standards on torture, for instance, guide the Supreme Court's interpretation of the Eighth Amendment's "cruel and unusual punishment" provision? Should the Due Process Clause as applied to laws criminalizing homosexual activity be informed by foreign legal standards? To what extent should the Supreme Court's decision in *Bush v. Gore* be subjected to international standards of electoral fairness?

Intense questioning over the use of human rights law in constitutional interpretation during the recent confirmation hearings of Chief Justice John Roberts and Justice Samuel Alito demonstrated the legal and political importance of this issue in American public life.[90] It is not important because of implications for constitutional law, but also as a focal point for a broader political conversation about the relationship between domestic and international law and between American democracy and the global community.

Much of the commentary on this issue has come from legal scholars who have argued for the incorporation of human rights norms into American law by means of constitutional interpretation. The theory advancing this legal tactic is, at this point, ahead of its actual judicial implementation. Robert Lillich, for instance, writes favorably of "the possibility that a court will regard international human rights law as infusing United States constitutional and statutory standards with its normative content."[91] Another commentator speaks of "informing domestic constitutional standards by reference to international norms . . . such as the United Nations Charter, Universal Declaration of Human Rights, or the International Covenant on Social and Economic Rights."[92] ACLU President Nadine Strossen has argued that "international standards may provide guiding principles for interpreting federal and state constitutions and statutes" and serve as a tool "to expand, rather than to limit, protections of individual rights under domestic law."[93] Gordon Christenson has similarly proposed using international human rights norms to create higher levels of scrutiny in Equal Protection and Due Process Clause jurisprudence and "to use those open-ended provisions of the Bill of Rights as windows through which we may peer at the rich resources of fundamental rights or values beyond our own policy."[94] All of these proposals exhibit a basic commitment to bringing international norms to bear on the development of domestic constitutional law.

This development has not, however, been of interest to academics. A number of judges have publicly urged the use of international norms in constitutional interpretation. Supreme Court Justices Stephen Breyer and Justice Ruth Bader Ginsburg have both been very public in urging a greater reliance on international law. Harry Blackmun, writing in 1994 after his retirement from the Supreme Court, likewise expressed a desire to see judges rely more heavily on international law when interpreting the Constitution, and judges have increasingly demonstrated a willingness to do so.[95] The number of constitutional cases referencing foreign and human rights law remains small, and this tactic has not yet been employed in a First Amendment church-state case. This legal innovation, however, has had an impacted on a number of cases involving important cultural issues. Robert Delahunty and John Yoo critically observed in the *Harvard Journal of Law and Public Policy* that the use of international law has the potential to influence important questions in the United States, "including the rights of criminal defendants, the constitutionality of parental notification requirements for abortions . . . the extent of governmental leeway in religion cases, and the validity of various forms of capital punishment under the Eighth Amendment."[96] The potential influence of international law in such cultural debates will only increase as human rights law reaches into other spheres of society.

Death penalty cases have been most directly impacted by judicial reliance on international sources. In 1988, a plurality opinion in *Thompson v. Oklahoma* cited the views of "Western European" human rights agreements in holding the execution of a fifteen-year-old to be cruel and unusual.[97] The following year in *Stanford v. Kentucky*, a case involving the constitutionality of capital punishment for individuals who committed murders at ages sixteen and seventeen, Justice Brennan wrote in dissent that "[t]he views of organizations with expertise in relevant fields and the choices of governments elsewhere in the world also merit our attention as indicators whether a punishment is acceptable in a civilized society."[98] In *Atkins v. Virginia*, the Court also looked to international sources in holding it unconstitutional to execute a retarded man.[99] Yet, it was the Supreme Court's 2005 ruling in *Roper v. Simmons* holding that the Eighth Amendment prohibits the execution of offenders who were under eighteen years of age at the time the crime was committed that galvanized opinion about the use of international and foreign law in constitutional interpretation.[100] Justice Kennedy's opinion was most significant in its appeal to international sources. In arguing that execution of persons under the age of eighteen constitutes "cruel and unusual punishment" in violation of the Eighth Amendment, Kennedy cited Article 37 of the United Nations Convention on the Rights of the Child (which the United States has not ratified), the laws of the United Kingdom, and "the overwhelming weight of international opinion."[101] The extent of Kennedy's reliance on international authorities went beyond previous Supreme Court practice. One commentator summarizes the importance of Kennedy's *Roper* opinion as follows:

Justice Kennedy's Roper majority opinion puts paid to the conceit that this is all just a bit of fluff exaggerated into something sinister and conspiratorial by Federalist Society right-wing ideologues. Roper asserts far more, it turns out, than the prior use of foreign law in contemporary constitutional cases would have suggested. It blesses in the contemporary era a new doctrine of constitutional adjudication ... that is very far indeed from mere flirtation. It invites the deployment of a sweeping body of legal materials from outside U.S. domestic law into the process of interpreting the U.S. Constitution—and, moreover, invites it into American society's most difficult and contentious "values" questions.[102]

The *Roper* decision, and this line of death penalty cases more generally, pushed an important political and cultural battle into the international arena and provoked an outpouring of commentary on whether international law ought to be used more extensively in constitutional adjudication.

There has also been extensive interest in using international human rights law to advance constitutionally-based economic rights, such as a guaranteed minimum level of subsistence. Academics have been proposing this idea for at least two decades, although it has gained little attention outside the pages of law reviews.[103] The tradition of negative liberty, which concerns the limitations placed on actions of the state, remains too strongly embedded in American law for this concept to gain constitutional traction.[104] Nevertheless, literature on this topic further illustrates the strategy and goals developed by those seeking to advance the interpretive use of international human rights law.

While economic rights have never made domestic headway, international human rights law has repeatedly affirmed their centrality to a just society. Article 22 of the Universal Declaration of Human Rights declares that everyone has a right to "social security" and is "entitled to realization . . . of the economic, social and cultural rights indispensable for his dignity and the free development of his personality." Article 23 establishes a right to work, to join trade unions, to have protection against unemployment, and to receive just remuneration for work performed. Article 24 announces a right to rest and leisure and to "periodic holidays with pay." Finally, Article 25 states that "everyone has the right to a standard of living adequate for the health and well-being of himself and of his family, including food, clothing, housing and medical care and necessary social services, and the right to security in the event of unemployment, sickness, disability, widowhood, old age or other lack of livelihood in circumstances beyond his control." The International Covenant on Economic, Social, and Cultural Rights (ICESCR), whose provisions broadly mirror those in the Universal Declaration, is the most authoritative document in this area. Parties to the ICESCR recognize the right of workers to receive fair wages (Article 7), to form and join trade unions (Article 8), to receive "an adequate standard of living for himself and his family, including adequate food, clothing and housing, and to the continuous improvement of living conditions" (Article 11), and to free education including higher education (Article 13).

Given the perceived failure of the United States to address economic inequality and provide adequate social insurance, scholars have argued that a right to economic provision ought to be established by reading these international norms into the Constitution. One scholar has urged courts to interpret the Constitution's Due Process Clause in light of such international norms as "the rights to education and a minimum standard of living."[105] Nadine Strossen has proposed using the "international human rights trend" to undermine the "negative-rights defining aspect of the Supreme Courts judicial process" in economic rights cases.[106] Leading constitutional law scholar Erwin Chemerinsky, in an article endorsing the idea of a constitutional welfare rights, references this strategy of relying on international human rights law, "which does create a right to a minimum subsistence for all."[107] International sources provide an authoritative counterweight to the traditional American aversion to positive rights.

The Supreme Court's 2003 holding in *Lawrence v. Texas*, overturning a state law that criminalized sodomy on the grounds that it violated constitutional due process, thrust debates about the interpretive use of international law off the pages of law reviews and into more popular venues.[108] Particular attention was given to Justice Kennedy's reliance on international sources in the majority opinion, in which he referenced a decision by the European Court of Human Rights holding that laws prohibiting homosexual activity were invalid under the European Convention on Human Rights.[109] This ruling, Kennedy maintained, undermined the "sweeping" claim that "the history of Western civilization and ... Judeo-Christian moral and ethical standards" support legal and moral prohibitions on homosexual conduct.[110] Justice Scalia denounced this invocation of foreign law as "meaningless" and "dangerous" dicta.[111] Other conservative critics followed suit, denouncing the decision as a gross example of judicial activism.[112] These criticisms had been previously made in other contexts, but the important symbolic role of homosexuality in the contemporary culture wars heightened interest in the perceived encroachment by international law.

Certain aspects of the debate over international law's role in constitutional interpretation will remain the province of specialized legal scholarship. Yet the issues at stake are not merely scholarly. The attention given to this issue in more popular outlets such as newspapers, political journals, and even talk radio reveals the extent to which it has become part of the nation's political landscape. To look at this debate in exclusively, or even primarily, legal terms is thus to miss its import role in a broader debate about religion, culture, and ethics in an increasingly globalized world. As it now stands, international human rights norms have been invoked in only a few areas of religious and cultural dissension. However, driving the jurisprudential debate both at the scholarly and popular levels is the fear or hope that international law might be expanded beyond the death penalty and homosexuality to also influence constitutional decision-making in such contentious areas as church-state law, abortion, and end-of-life issues.

Progressives have been the most enthusiastic supports of expanding the interpretive role of international law. International human rights norms are often more in sync with progressive political sympathies than is domestic law. On the death penalty, economic rights, health care, women's rights, and war, international norms are perceived as "liberal" by American standards. Progressives are also less attached to schools of jurisprudence such as originalism that limit the freedom of judges to flexibly interpret the Constitution. Mark Tushnet of Harvard Law School, a leading progressive constitutional theorist, has written that "law, including constitutional law, is politics." As such, Tushnet concludes that "[n]othing generally distinguishes progressive constitutionalism from progressive policy prescriptions."[113] Under such a view of legal process, judges need not be bound by a formalistic interpretation of the Constitution. International human rights norms are nevertheless attractive in that they allow judges to ground their decisions in concrete legal norms. Taking note of this possibility, one scholar recently proposed that "[t]he most trenchant critique of this use of international materials is that it serves as mere cover for the expansion of selected rights favored by domestic advocacy groups, for reasons having nothing to do with anything international."[114]

Yet many supporters of interpreting the Constitution in this fashion unashamedly acknowledge their goal of promoting political and cultural change by pulling American law into conformity with the values of the international community. One commentator, for instance, has urged the U.S. Supreme Court to follow the "contemporary moral values" of the European Court of Human Rights when "determining what human rights are protected rights and who should protect them."[115] Another legal scholar has called on Americans to move beyond the belief that the Constitution "is the best possible constitution." In contrast, he praises "truly modern Constitutions . . . based on generally accepted international human rights norms" and urges the Supreme Court to "open itself to well reasoned foreign jurisprudential approaches."[116] Yet another scholar rejects American "Constitutional hegemony."[117] For its progressive advocates, the interpretive use of international human rights law has become a tool for bringing about political and cultural change that might not be feasible through the democratic process. In particular, international human rights norms serve as a counterweight to conservative, and often religiously-based, political values.

Conservative thinkers have dismissed the interpretive use of human rights law as an attempt to legitimate judicial activism. In 2004, a Republican-controlled U.S. House of Representatives Committee on the Judiciary Subcommittee on the Constitution held hearings on a resolution declaring "that judicial determinations regarding the meaning of the laws of the United States should not be based on judgments, laws, or pronouncements of foreign institutions unless such foreign judgments, laws, or pronouncements inform an understanding of the original meaning of the laws of the

United States."[118] Robert Bork has been a particularly strong critic of domestic internalization of international law. In his 2003 book, *Coercing Virtue: The Worldwide Rule of Judges*, Bork wrote, "International law is not law but politics . . . The problem is not merely the anti-Americanism that grips foreign elites and shapes law; it is also the American intellectual class, which is largely hostile to the United States and uses alleged international law to attack the morality of its own government and society. International law has become one more weapon in the domestic culture war."[119] Jack Goldsmith, an international law scholar at Harvard Law School, has similarly criticized arguments for expanding domestic reliance on international law on the grounds that "nations differ in their moral, political, legal, and cultural commitments . . . Where the human rights community demands that the United States make international human rights treaties a part of domestic law in a way that circumvents political control, it evinces an intolerance for pluralism of values and conditions, and a disrespect for local democratic processes."[120] Conservative legal thinkers, while not rejecting international law *in toto*, have rejected attempts to "give *decisional* effect to foreign materials" that lack any domestic legal authority.[121]

CONCLUSION

In a recent article that has attracted considerable attention, University of Texas School of Law Professor Sarah H. Cleveland argues that the "historical record establishes that our constitutional tradition is significantly more receptive to international norms than is understood in the current scholarly and judicial debate." She adds that "modern assumptions about the uniqueness of the American legal order" must be reconsidered.[122] Cleveland's historical claims will no doubt be further debated, but she is certainly correct to see a future in which legal and constitutional debates increasingly take place along international lines. Church-state issues have not been exempt from this globalizing trend. As this essay has detailed, the internationalization of church-state issues has taken many forms, the most significant of which has been the establishment of legal protections for religious freedom in international law. Closer to home, a host of political and cultural debates implicating the relationship between religion, ethics, and public life have been increasingly drawn into an international debate. This essay has considered two such instances, the International Religious Freedom Act of 1998 and the recent explosion of interest in using international human rights law as a tool in constitutional interpretation. New issues will certainly arise, for, as Harvard Law School's Gerald L. Neuman notes, "Some U.S. observers—and judges—insist that constitutional law should maintain its distance from the international human rights regime," even as the forces of internationalization make such separation ever more difficult.[123] The increased interdependence of legal institutions will prevent the return to an autonomous and insular legal regime, if indeed such a regime ever existed in America.[124]

These developments aside, international law remains deeply contested and debated. Among judges and academics, debate rages over the authority of international law, its proper scope, and its role in domestic jurisprudence. At a more popular level, politicians, pundits, and citizens debate the consequences of international law for sovereignty, justice, humanitarianism and human rights. In part because of the ever-expanding web of international laws and institutions, political and cultural debates have taken on an international dimension unimaginable not long ago. Americans, by and large, have accepted emerging global political realities and support greater interaction between the United States and international institutions. One leading study found, for instance, that "Most Americans want to pursue foreign policy goals chiefly through cooperative and multilateral means, with a large role for the United Nations."[125] The report adds that there is strong support for participation in international treaties and agreements. A substantial majority of Americans also support the United States assuming a greater role in international affairs, particularly as part of multilateral actions.[126]

Even as Americans have accepted some aspects of internationalization, they have remained suspicious of others. Large numbers of Americans, for instance, oppose U.S. cooperation with the United Nations.[127] A strong commitment to political sovereignty, encouraged by a continuing sense of exceptionalism, leaves many Americans suspicious of legal internationalization.[128] International law has proven to be most contentious when it becomes entangled with the domestic culture wars. Debates over family planning, population control, women's rights, children's rights, the death penalty, and the International Criminal Court have thrust the work of international institutions out of the bureaucratic shadows and into the mainstream of American political life. The deep religiosity of the American people, particularly in comparison to the regnant secularism of many global political elites, creates a divide between the moral views of many Americas and the norms enshrined in human rights law.[129] This moral conflict perpetuates American resistance to more fully embracing international law. Church-state issues have also been thrust into this global arena. Domestic debates about religious freedom have impacted international politics, and international laws have increasingly framed domestic debates about religion and culture. The analysis of church-state issues in America today must take account of developing global circumstances, and the nation's culture wars cannot be appraised without reference to these international dynamics.

NOTES

1. Universal Declaration of Human Rights, Article 18. For a history of the UDHR, see Mary Ann Glendon, *A World Made New: Eleanor Roosevelt and the Universal Declaration of Human Rights* (New York: Random House, 2001).

2. Both bodies of law took shape around the same time. The modern human rights movement was born with the promulgation of the Universal Declaration of Human Rights in 1948. Modern church-state jurisprudence began with the seminal case of *Everson v. Board of Education*, 330 U.S. 1 (1947). In a 5–4 ruling, the U.S. Supreme Court voted to uphold a New Jersey statute funding the transport of Catholic schoolchildren to parochial schools. In addition, this decision incorporated the First Amendment into the Fourteenth Amendment so it would henceforth apply to the states as well as the U.S. government.

3. Christy Cutbill McCormick, "Exporting the First Amendment," *Journal of International Legal Studies* 4 (Summer 1998): 283–334.

4. For an important and representative work of scholarship in this field, see Curtis A. Bradley and Jack L. Goldsmith, "Customary International Law as Federal Common Law: A Critique of the Modern Position," *Harvard Law Review* 110, no. 4 (February 1997): 815–876.

5. Lori Fisler Damrosch et al., *International Law: Cases and Materials* (4th ed.) (St. Paul, MN: West Group, 2001): 16.

6. Louis Henkin, *How Nations Behave: Law and Foreign Policy* (New York: Columbia University Press, 1979): 47l.

7. Daniel Philpott, "Religious Freedom and the Undoing of the Westphalian State," *Michigan Journal of International Law* 25 (Summer, 2004): 981.

8. Ibid., 986; Harold Hongju Koh, "The Globalization of Freedom," *Yale Journal of International Law* 26 (Summer 2001): 305–312.

9. Nathan A. Adams, "A Human Rights Imperative: Extending Religious Liberty Beyond the Border," *Cornell International Law Journal* 33:1 (2000): 23–25.

10. Robert F. Drinan, S.J., *Can God & Caesar Coexist: Balancing Religious Freedom and International Law* (New Haven: Yale University Press, 2004): 31.

11. UN Charter, Article 1(3).

12. UN Charter, Article 55(c).

13. Drinan, *Can God & Caesar Coexist*, 31.

14. Universal Declaration of Human Rights, Article 18.

15. "As international legal documents articulate it, religious freedom is a right enjoyed through worship, public expression of beliefs, education of children into such beliefs, the operation of houses of worship, schools, universities, seminaries, enjoyment of freedom from discrimination in employment and political access, and the liberty to take up, abandon, proclaim or dissent from one's religion. States threaten this right when they limit these practices through killing, imprisonment, torture, or otherwise discrimination against believers." Philpott, 991.

16. Courts in the United States have also considered the tension between religious belief and practice. The Supreme Court's decision in *Employment Division v.*

Smith, 494 U.S. 872 (1990), held that a law criminalizing use or possession of peyote did not violate the First Amendment right to the free exercise of religion, even though certain Native American religions consider the use of peyote to be an essential practice. In the majority opinion, Justice Scalia acknowledged that the free exercise of religion "often involves not only belief and profession but the performance of (or abstention from) physical acts: assembling with others for a worship service, participating in sacramental use of bread and wine, proselytizing, abstaining from certain foods or certain modes of transportation. It would be true, we think (though no case of ours has involved the point), that a state would be 'prohibiting the free exercise [of religion] if it sought to ban such acts or abstentions only when they are engaged in for religious reasons, or only because of the religious belief that they display." A majority of the Supreme Court, however, argued that a generally applicable criminal law prohibiting the use of peyote did not violate the First Amendment.

17. Drinan, 32.
18. Ibid., 34–35.
19. Ibid., 37; Adam M. Smith, "The Perplexities of Promoting Religious Freedom Through International Law: A Review of Robert Drinan's Can God and Caesar Coexist?" *North Carolina Journal of International Law and Commercial Regulation* 30 (Spring 2005): 742.
20. Article I of the Optional Protocol provides as follows: "A State Party to the Covenant that becomes a Party to the present Protocol recognizes the competence of the Committee to receive and consider communications from individuals subject to its jurisdiction who claim to be victims of a violation by that State Party of any of the rights set forth in the Covenant. No communication shall be received by the Committee if it concerns a State Party to the Covenant which is not a Party to the present Protocol."
21. For a further discussion of this Declaration in historical context see Derek H. Davis, "The Evolution of Religious Freedom as a Universal Human Right: Examining the Role of the 1981 United Nations Declaration on the Elimination of All Forms of Intolerance and of Discrimination Based on Religion and Belief," *Brigham Young Law Review* (2002): 217–236.
22. Preamble to the Declaration on the Elimination of All Forms of Intolerance and of Discrimination Based on Religion or Belief.
23. Ibid., Article 3.
24. Drinan, 40–41.
25. Smith, "The Perplexities of Promoting Religious Freedom Through International Law," 740–741.
26. Ibid., 741.
27. Philpott, 992.
28. Ibid.
29. Drinan, 13.
30. Adams, "A Human Rights Imperative," 3.
31. Drinan, 37–38, 41.

32. Adams, 16.

33. McCormick, "Exporting the First Amendment," 284.

34. 22 U.S.C. 6401(a)(4); http://www.state.gov/g/drl/rls/irf/

35. Smith, 4.

36. On Germany and Scientology, see McCormick, 309–310.

37. A court held in *Lee v. Crouse*, 284 F. Supp. 541 (D. Kan. 1967) that "Black Muslims," who combined orthodox Islam with a belief in racial segregation, constitued a religion. The case of *Malnak v. Yoge*, 592 F.2d 197 (Fed. Cir. 1979), held that Transcendental Meditation is a religion. Jonathan Weiss, writing in 1964, captured the challenge in observing that "to define the limits of religious expression may be impossible if philosophically desirable . . . any definition of religion would seem to violate religious freedom in that it would dictate to religions, present and future, what they must be." Jonathan Weiss, "Privilege, Posture and Protection: 'Religion in the Law,'" *Yale Law Journal* 73, no. 4 (March 1964): 604.

38. Smith, 747–748.

39. Drinan, 36.

40. International Covenant on Civil, Political, and Cultural Rights, Article 20(2) provides that "any advocacy of national, racial or religious hatred that constitutes incitement to discrimination, hostility or violence shall be prohibited by law."

41. Michael J. Perry, "A Right to Religious Freedom? The Universality of Human Rights, the Relativity of Culture," *Roger Williams Law Review* 10 (Spring 2005): 413.

42. See http://www.tandemproject.com/part2/article1/art1_3.htm

43. Smith, 2.

44. Quoted in Smolin, "Will International Human Rights be Used as a Tool of Cultural Genocide: The Interaction of Human Rights Norms, Religion, Culture, and Gender," *Journal of Law and Religion* 12, no. 1 (1995–1996): 170.

45. A number of countries have laws that criminalize blasphemy. A number of states including Afghanistan and Pakistan have laws that prohibit blaspheming against the Islamic faith. Some European countries including England, Germany, and Denmark also have blasphemy laws on the books although they are rarely enforced.

46. See http://hrw.org/wr2k5/religion/index.htm

47. Philpott, 993.

48. John Witte, Jr., "Law, Religion and Human Rights," *Columbia Human Rights Law Review* (Fall 1996): 5–6.

49. These tensions became particularly manifest, for instance, during the UN's 1995 Conference on Women, when conflicts arose over issues of family, gender, population control, and abortion. See Mary Ann Glendon, "What Happened at Beijing," *First Things* 59 (January 1996): 30–36; Mary Ann Glendon, "Foundations of Human Rights," *American Journal of Jurisprudence* 44 (1999): 1–10.

50. Philpott, 996.

51. Drinan, 62–85.

52. 22 U.S.C. 6401(a)(1).

53. 22 U.S.C. 6401(a)(2).
54. 22 U.S.C. 6401(b)(1); 22 U.S.C. 6441(a).
55. 22. U.S.C. 6411.
56. 22 U.S.C. 6412.
57. Ibid.
58. 22 U.S.C. 6432; 22 U.S.C. 6432.
59. 22 U.S.C. 6445(a).
60. McCormick, 323.
61. Ibid., 328.
62. Some more liberal religious organizations, such as the National Council of Churches, opposed the legislation. See Peter D. Danchin, "U.S. Unilateralism and the International Protection of Religious Freedom: The Multilateral Alternative," *Columbia Journal of International Law* 41:1 (2002): 100n.215.
63. Pew Forum on Religion and Public Life, Symposium on "Legislation International Religious Freedom," November 20, 2006. A transcript of the event is available at: http://pewresearch.org/pubs/105/legislating-international-religious-freedom. For a more extended discussion of this topic see Allen D. Hertzke, *Freeing God's Children: The Unlikely Alliance for Global Human Rights* (Lanham, MD: Rowman & Littlefield, 2004).
64. The statute is available at http://usinfo.state.gov/usa/infousa/laws/majorlaw/intlrel.htm
65. The connections between the emerging concern of evangelicals with religious freedom and the passage of the IRFA were strong. In a *Wall Street Journal* editorial credited with drawing attention to the issue of religious persecution abroad, Hudson Institute fellow Michael Horowtiz, though himself Jewish, argued that human rights for Christians ought be used to promote human rights more generally. McCormick, 285.
66. See http://www.eppc.org/publications/pubID.1795/pub_detail.asp
67. Pew Forum on Religion and Public Life, Symposium on "Legislation International Religious Freedom," November 20, 2006. A transcript of the event is available at http://pewresearch.org/pubs/105/legislating-international-religious-freedom
68. Jeffrey Goldberg, "Washington Discovers Christian Persecution," *New York Times Magazine* (December, 21 1997): 46.
69. "Candles in the Darkness: Religious freedom is a foreign policy beacon," *Washington Times* (December 31, 2000).
70. Thomas F. Farr, "The Diplomacy of Religious Freedom," *First Things* (May 2006): 12–15; Thomas F. Farr, "Religious Realism in Foreign Policy: Lessons from Vatican II," *The Review of Faith & International Affairs* (Winter 2005–2006): 28.
71. Farr, "Religious Realism in Foreign Policy," 28.
72. Ibid., 28–39.
73. William Martin, "The Christian Right and Foreign Policy," *Foreign Policy* 114 (Spring 1999): 78.
74. Philpott, 995.

75. John Shattuck, "Religion, Rights, and Terrorism," *Harvard Human Rights Journal* 16 (Spring 2003): 185.

76. Ibid.

77. Danchin, "U.S. Unilateralism and the International Protection of Religious Freedom," 41.

78. Ibid., 104.

79. Ibid.

80. Shattuck, 185.

81. Smolin, "Will International Human Rights be Used as a Tool of Cultural Genocide," 8.

82. David M. Smolin, "Exporting the First Amendment?" Evangelism, Proselytism, and the International Religious Freedom Act," *Cumberland Law Review* 31, no. 3 (2000–2001): 685.

83. Danchin, 42.

84. Even among countries that endorse religious freedom, there remains debate about what such a right requires. Proselytizing has been a particularly thorny issue in international human rights law, and Smolin asserts that the IRFA promotes a "laissez-faire attitude towards evangelism/ proselytism" consistent with American liberal principles. While the IRFA promotes a cause "that appears deceptively simple from an American perspective appears," Smolin adds, it involves "for much of the rest of the world . . . a delicate balancing of interests and careful line-drawing, which often can be resolved only on a case-by-case basis." Smolin, "Exporting the First Amendment?" 686.

85. Smith, 4.

86. Danchin, 41, 46, 73.

87. The United States, for example, has not ratified a number of significant human rights agreements, including the Convention on the Rights of the Child, the Convention on the Elimination of All Forms of Discrimination Against Women, and the International Covenant on Economic, Social, and Cultural Rights.

88. Koh, "The Globalization of Freedom," 306.

89. See generally, Roger P. Alford, "Misusing International Sources to Interpret the Constitution," *American Journal of International Law* 98 (January 2004): 57–69; Gerald L. Neuman, "The Uses of International Law in Constitutional Interpretation," *American Journal of International Law* 98 (January 2004): 83–90; Michael D. Ramsey, "International Materials and Domestic Rights: Reflections on *Atkins* and *Lawrence*," *American Journal of International Law* 98 (January 2004): 69–82.

90. See Ronald Dworkin, "Judge Roberts on Trial," *New York Review of Books* 52:16 (October 20, 2005): 14–17.

91. Richard B. Lillich, "Invoking International Human Rights Law in Domestic Courts," *University of Cincinnati Law Review* 54 (Spring 1985): 408.

92. Ann I. Park, "Human Rights and Basic Needs: Using International Human Rights Norms to Inform Constitutional Interpretation" *U.C.L.A. Law Review* 34 (April 1987): 1249.

93. Nadine Strossen, "Recent U.S. and International Judicial Protection of Individual Rights: A Comparative Legal Process Analysis and Proposed Synthesis," *Hastings Law Journal* 41 (April 1990): 805–806.

94. Gordon A. Christenson, "Using Human Rights Law to Inform Due Process and Equal Protection Analyses," *University of Cincinnati Law Review* 52 (1983): 4, 13.

95. Harry A. Blackmun, "The Supreme Court and the Law of Nations," *Yale Law Journal* 104 (October 1994): 45.

96. Robert J. Delahunty and John Yoo, "Against Foreign Law," *Harvard Journal of Law and Public Policy* 29 (2005): 296.

97. *Thompson v. Oklahoma*, 487 U.S. 815 (1988). Justice Scalia, writing in dissent, sharply challenged the majority's invocation of international sources. Scalia argued that: "That 40% of our States do not rule out capital punishment for 15-year-old felons is determinative of the question before us here, even if that position contradicts the uniform view of the rest of the world. We must never forget that it is a Constitution for the United States of America that we are expounding... But where there is not first a settled consensus among our own people, the views of other nations, however enlightened the Justices of this Court may think them to be, cannot be imposed upon Americans through the Constitution. In the present case, therefore, the fact that a majority of foreign nations would not impose capital punishment upon persons under 16 at the time of the crime is of no more relevance than the fact that a majority of them would not impose capital punishment at all, or have standards of due process quite different from our own." 487 U.S. at 869n.4.

98. *Stanford v. Kentucky*, 492 U.S. 361, 384 (1989).

99. *Atkins v. Virginia*, 536 U.S. 304 (2002).

100. *Roper v. Simmons*, 543 U.S. 551 (2005).

101. 543 U.S. at 576–578.

102. Kenneth Anderson, "Foreign Law and the U.S. Constitution," *Policy Review* 131 (June–July, 2005): 33–51.

103. In spite of the work of these academics, the idea has gained little judicial traction. There were, to be sure, some important legal victories for welfare rights. In *Goldberg v. Kelly*, 397 U.S. 254 (1970), the first of the so-called new property cases, the Court held that due process forbade the termination of welfare benefits without providing certain procedures, where state law had granted an entitlement to qualified persons. The Court also made favorable rulings in *Plyler v. Doe*, 457 U.S. 202 (1982), in which it struck down denial of public education to certain alien children, and *Shapiro v. Thompson*, 394 U.S. 618 (1969), in which it struck down a one-year residency requirement for receiving welfare benefits. But the Court refused to move beyond these procedural guarantees to recognizing the existence of economic rights not already established in statute. A host of decisions such as *Dandridge v. Williams*, 397 U.S. 471 (1970), and *San Antonio School District v. Rodriguez*, 411 U.S. 1 (1973), showed the limits of the Court's jurisprudence. This refusal to recognize economic rights reflects that deeply embedded assumption that the U.S. Constitution is a document of negative, not positive, rights. As Judge

Richard Poser wrote in *Bowers v. DeVito*, 686 F.2d 616, 618 (7th Cir. 1982), the Constitution "tells the state to let people alone; it does not require the federal government or the state to provide services, even so elementary a service as maintaining law and order." Chief Justice Rehnquist wrote similarly in *DeShaney v. Winnebago County Dept. of Social Services*, 489 U.S. 189 (1989), that the Due Process Clause "is phrased as a limitation on the state's power to act, not as a guarantee of certain minimum levels of safety and security." "To sum up," writes one commentator, "the Supreme Court has rejected socio-economic rights claims under both Substantive Due Process and Equal Protection doctrines." Mark S. Kende, "The South African Constitutional Courts' Embrace of Socio-Economic Rights: A Comparative Perspective, *Chapman Law Review* 6 (Spring 2003): 151.

104. The "negative rights-defining aspect of the Supreme Court's judicial process sets it apart from the international human rights trend." Strossen, "Recent U.S. and International Judicial Protection of Individual Rights," 875.

105. Connie de la Vega, "Protecting Economic, Social and Cultural Rights," *Whittier Law Review* 15 (1994): 476.

106. Strossen, 875.

107. Erwin Chemerinsky, "Under the Bridges of Paris: Economic Liberties Should Not Be Just for the Rich," *Chapman Law Review* 6 (Spring 2003): 40.

108. *Lawrence v. Texas*, 539 U.S. 558 (2003).

109. 539 U.S. at 573.

110. 539 U.S. at 572. Chief Justice Burger made this comment in *Bowers v. Hardwick*, 478 U.S. 186 (1986), in which the Supreme Court upheld a Georgia anti-sodomy law similar to the one at issue in *Lawrence*.

111. 539 U.S. at 598.

112. On the use of foreign law in *Lawrence*, see Rex D. Glensy, "Which Countries Count?: Lawrence v. Texas and the Selection of Foreign Persuasive Authority," *Virginia Journal of International Law* 45 (Winter 2005): 358–449.

113. Mark Tushnet, "What is Constitutional about Progressive Constitutionalism?" *Widener Law Symposium Journal* (Spring 1999): 19–20.

114. Michael D. Ramsey, "International Materials and Domestic Rights: Reflections on Atkins and Lawrence," *American Journal of International Law* 98 (January, 2004): 69.

115. Tania Schriwer, "Establishing an Affirmative Governmental Duty to Protect Children's Rights," *University of San Francisco Law Review* 34 (Winter 2000): 9.

116. Kende, "The South African Constitutional Courts' Embrace of Socio-Economic Rights," 160.

117. Peter J. Spiro, "Treaties, International Law, and Constitutional Rights," *Stanford Law Review* 55 (May 2003): 1999.

118. 108th Congress, 2d Session, H. Res. 568, March 17, 2004.

119. Robert H. Bork, *Coercing Virtue: The Worldwide Rule of Judges* (Washington, D.C.: The AEI Press, 2003): 21.

120. Jack Goldsmith, "Should International Human Rights Law Trump US Domestic Law?" *Chicago Journal of International Law* 1 (Spring 2000): 338.

121. Delahunty and Yoo, "Against Foreign Law," 296.

122. Sarah H. Cleveland, "Our International Constitution," *Yale Journal of International Law* 31 (Winter 2006): 124. See also Anne-Marie Slaughter, "A Global Community of Courts," *Harvard International Law Journal* 44 (Winter 2003): 191–219.

123. Gerald L. Neuman, "Human Rights and Constitutional Rights: Harmony and Dissonance," *Stanford Law Review* 55 (May 2003): 1864.

124. See Mark Tushnet, "The Possibilities of Comparative Constitutional Law," *Yale Law Journal* 108 (April 1999): 1225–1309.

125. See http://www.thechicagocouncil.org/UserFiles/File/GlobalViews06Final.pdf

126. See http://www.worldpublicopinion.org/pipa/articles/brunitedstatescanadara/256.php?nid=&id=&pnt=256&lb=brusc. A recent survey found also that a sizeable majority of Americans support greater United States and international involvement in addressing the Darfur situation. See http://www.worldpublicopinion.org/pipa/articles/brunitedstatescanadara/181.php?nid=&id=&pnt=181&lb=bthr

127. See http://www.worldpublicopinion.org/pipa/articles/brunitedstatescanadara/270.php?nid=&id=&pnt=270&lb=brusc

128. "The United States has often encouraged the development of transnational regimes" as a solution to political problems, but there is "no similar perception of failure in the United States and, therefore, no sense of a need to participate in the remedy." Paul W. Kahn, "American Exceptionalism, Popular Sovereignty, and the Rule of Law," in *American Exceptionalism and Human Rights*, ed. Michael Ignatieff (Princeton: Princeton University Press, 2005): 217.

129. The Pew Global Attitudes Project, http://pewglobal.org/reports/display.php?ReportID=167, found that the United States is unique among wealthy nations in its embrace of religion.

FURTHER READING

The most important source is to look to the relevant legal instruments including the Universal Declaration of Human Rights (1948), International Covenant on Civil and Political Rights (1960), and the United Nations Declaration on the Elimination of All Forms of Discrimination Based on Religion and Belief (1981). A historical perspective on the subject of religious freedom and international is found in Daniel Philpott's "Religious Freedom and the Undoing of the Westphalian State," *Michigan Journal of International Law* 25 (Summer, 2004): 981–999, while a helpful analysis of the most significant international document on religious freedom is Derek H. Davis, "The Evolution of Religious Freedom as a Universal Human Right: Examining the Role of the 1981 United Nations Declaration on the Elimination of All Forms of Intolerance and of Discrimination Based on Religion and Belief," *Brigham Young Law Review* (2002): 217–236. As former director of the Office of International Religious Freedom, Thomas Farr offers an inside account of the International Religious Freedom Act of 1998 in "The Diplomacy of Religious

Freedom," *First Things* (May 2006): 12–15. There are also a number of scholarly treatments of the history and structure of the IRFA, including Nathan A. Adams, "A Human Rights Imperative: Extending Religious Liberty Beyond the Border," *Cornell International Law Journal* 33, no. 1 (2000): 1–66, and Christy Cutbill McCormick, "Exporting the First Amendment," *Journal of International Legal Studies* 4 (Summer 1998): 283–334. The debate over international law and constitutional interpretation is still developing. For two critical assessments of the practice, consider Robert H. Bork, *Coercing Virtue: The Worldwide Rule of Judges* (Washington, D.C.: The AEI Press, 2003) and Robert J. Delahunty and John Yoo, "Against Foreign Law," *Harvard Journal of Law and Public Policy* 29 (2005): 291–330. For an article defending the use of international sources of constitutional interpretation that draws on historical sources see Sarah H. Cleveland, "Our International Constitution," *Yale Journal of International Law* 31 (Winter 2006): 1–126.

5

The Status of Faith-Based Initiatives in the Later Bush Administration

Douglas L. Koopman

As the two major-party candidates for president in 2000, Al Gore and George W. Bush both promoted a larger role for faith-based groups in the provision of social services funded by the federal government. Democrat Gore had publicly supported faith-based expansion in early 1999, before Republican Bush had done so. As the campaign intensified in late 2000, however, Gore downplayed his faith-based ideas for more populist and partisan appeals, while Bush made the initiatives the centerpiece of his "compassionate conservative" agenda. It was, at least on the surface, a compelling idea for Republicans. Policy wise, it was a logical next step for welfare reform that had increasingly relied on lower levels of government and outside agents to deliver social services. Politically, it helped identify Bush as both religiously sincere and ideologically moderate, a clear advantage in a closely divided election. Even in the tumult of the late election season, faith-based initiatives seemed to be the rare set of issues around which bipartisan consensus could form and legislative progress could be quickly made, whoever was ultimately elected president. But the nastiness of the 2000 election and its Florida aftermath doomed any chances of bipartisanship on much of anything, especially on issues that might touch upon race and religion, which the faith-based initiatives clearly do. As such, the politics of the faith-based issue and its establishment in the various branches and levels of government have become far more complex.

As it entered its last two years, the Bush administration had advanced its faith-based initiative about as far as it could through Congress and the federal bureaucracy. The legislative record was sparse—strong efforts the first year and sporadic attempts in the next five produced little new law. Small amounts of compassion capital funds were allowed. A few social service program authorizations and reauthorizations for the first time allowed intensely and overtly religious groups to apply for funds in programs that had been closed to them. In the bureaucracy, President Bush's initiatives had a great deal more success. Federal agencies, through newly established faith-based offices within them, conducted massive audits of programs and policies, looking for anti-religious discrimination practices. Audit results set an internal agenda for change and reform. Extensive outreach efforts by the central White House Office of Faith-Based and Community Initiatives (WHOFBCI) and its agency-based affiliates created publicity about the initiative, networking among faith-based groups and between them and federal officials, and braver and more demanding constituencies to which programming officials had to attend. By early 2007, the faith-based initiative was thus firmly entrenched within the federal bureaucracy.[1]

While the changes escaped heavy media attention and congressional involvement, they were not unnoticed by interest groups opposed to the administration's faith-based agenda. Adversaries wanted chances to challenge faith-friendly actions in court, but they needed to wait for the changes to manifest themselves in actual programs and activities. The American legal process is long and complex, and it works in favor of the initiator of the challenged action—in this case the Bush administration. Executive branch staff could revise regulations, promulgate procedures, and commence pro-faith-based outreach and program administration, while opponents had to wait for the new activities to result in real or perceived violations before they could start legal action. With so many faith-based administrative actions undertaken simultaneously, there were many instances where opponents could make legal challenges. Even a large number of cases, however, collectively have little material effect in the short term until their legal journeys end with definitive rulings.

As of early 2007, many faith-based challenges had been filed, but few had been settled.[2] Combined with the legal limbo of individual cases was the changed makeup of the U.S. Supreme Court. New Justices John Roberts and Samuel Alito replaced deceased Chief Justice William Rehnquist and retiring Justice Sandra Day O'Connor. O'Connor was the "swing" vote on so many religious cases that nearly all legal speculation (and, in fact, much of the legislative and administrative language of the Bush Administration's faith-based proposals) has been based upon the complex and individualized church-state views of Rehnquist Court decisions written or strongly influenced by O'Connor.[3] The views of Roberts and Alito on church-state issues, as on so many others, are largely unknown, although it seems quite possible the changed court will shift toward greater sympathy for religious influences in the public square. And if the new Roberts-led court is inclined to take an additional step and lay out clear and broadly applicable standards, the field of church-state legal precedent could shift quite drastically.[4]

Unsettled legal questions about the faith-based initiatives, combined with questions of their efficacy and political benefit, make it impossible to make confident estimates of their eventual success. The best one can do at this juncture is to provide some context: describe the initiatives as promoted by President Bush, comment on the root of their controversy, delve into some history of the relationship between church and state in providing government-supported social services, and clarify the main legal points of the past that future Supreme Court decisions will have to review and reconsider. The remainder of this article does this by providing some essential background to understanding today's faith-based debate, both in the broad political sense and in the narrower sense of issues within the federal court. The first essential is to understand the multiple initiatives under what really is a "faith-based initiatives" umbrella. The second essential is to see how the faith-based debate connects to a broader "culture war" that some see raging in American society and affecting partisan discourse. It is also critical to have some background in the long history of how religious traditions have interacted with government in providing social services, the third essential. After what is necessarily a brief summary of these first three essentials, this chapter reviews the most important foundational and recent federal court decisions, as well as those that seem certain to arise in the near future. While it is always difficult to predict Supreme Court decisions and the future course of policy, legal and bureaucratic trends both point in the same direction: a larger and more constitutionally-secure role for more types of faith-related groups to partner with government in providing social services.

ESSENTIAL 1: MANY INITIATIVES WITH ONE GOAL

President Bush's faith-based initiative has never been one single, simple idea. It is more accurate to describe his 2000 presidential campaign proposals and early legislative efforts as encompassing a wide set of initiatives clustered around three different areas with one far-reaching goal: to expand the variety of religiously affiliated social services that receive financial help from the federal government in carrying out government objectives.

One priority was an aggressive outreach plan to welcome smaller and community-based social service agencies (which are overwhelmingly connected to churches and religious organizations) to apply for funds to carry out government programs. Many claimed such groups were discriminated against in the application for federal dollars, structuring a bias against religion and reducing the effectiveness of government spending. This first goal of outreach could be done administratively and without much controversy, as it involves little more than welcoming additional groups into an application process that may or may not result in actual government support. The Bush administration has aggressively pursued outreach, with regular regional conferences sponsored by the WHOFBCI and other agency Faith-Based and Community Initiative (FBCI) offices touting the new "faith friendliness" of the federal bureaucracy.

A second priority area was to vastly expand tax incentives, particularly a charitable tax deduction for individuals not itemizing deductions on their tax returns. This new non-itemizers' deduction would potentially direct billions of additional dollars to faith-based organizations. This priority was badly damaged early on in the Bush Administration, partly through its own doing. Whereas the new president had proposed a major non-charitable tax incentive very early in 2001, by June it had been dropped out of the first, and what turned out to be the only, major tax reform proposal to become law. The president's desired tax breaks have, thus, never materialized.

The third priority was to codify in legislation the most faith-friendly interpretation of recently announced Supreme Court decisions on the Constitution's religion clauses, particularly the Establishment Clause. Ideally, these changes should have gone through the legislative process to establish them more firmly in law. But the White House's legislative strategy for these changes, too, failed in 2001 and was essentially abandoned by the end of 2002 as the faith-based initiative generated more opposition in Congress than nearly anyone anticipated. The administration has changed its strategy completely, and through its rulemaking power has quietly and unilaterally implemented its faith-friendly interpretation of these decisions.[5] Legal challenges to these interpretations are legion, but largely unsettled.

For many years these challenges will percolate through the judicial system. No one knows how and when they will be settled. An older stream of cases interpreting the First Amendment religion clauses severely restricted permissible financial interactions between government and religious entities, thereby tending to create a "no involvement" standard between the government and religion and close scrutiny of the particular religious entities receiving aid in any given case. But decisions in the late 1990s and since have been increasingly permissive in letting government and religion mix. In its later decisions, the Rehnquist Court seemed to be bordering on a "neutrality" standard in which the federal program in question is scrutinized, rather than the religion, or non-religion, of that program's implementing partner. In short, Establishment Clause interpretation is at the moment very unsettled and awaits new decisions of a significantly changed (and potentially even more changed) Supreme Court.

ESSENTIAL 2: A SMALL PIECE OF THE CULTURE WAR DEBATE

The fate of the faith-based initiatives is not a mere matter of dry legal interpretation, but also a matter of the heart. The public debate about faith-based initiatives has proven highly-charged, emotionally and ideologically. This is so because the initiatives challenge some bedrock assumptions of modern liberal democracy that are rarely re-examined in most political discourse.[6] Modern liberal democracy avers allegiance to making only rational arguments in the public square based on verifiable evidence on which all rational people can agree. Because these assumptions are often implicit rather than explicit, they bear brief mention here. The first assumption is that robust religion is dangerous in the public square. Religion, from this view, is an exclusivist, emotional, irrational means of thinking and arguing that has no place in an American public arena that is rational, and therefore tolerant. In this view, religious faith and religious people are tolerated politically *if* that faith has no public expression that offends persons of other religions or no religion: as such, a fairly cramped definition of toleration underlies the modern liberal public square. Jefferson's "wall of separation" language is used, in this view, to preemptively brand as illegitimate religious arguments in political debates. Because President Bush's faith-based initiatives give greater government sanction for robust and overtly religious people, groups, and reasoning in political debates and government operations, according to this view the initiatives must be opposed.

The second presumption against faith-based initiatives is the view that social services mixed with strong doses of religion are qualitatively inferior to secular social services, an unfair bias in the view of faith-based proponents. According to this second presumption, faith-intensive social services are almost certainly ineffective, unscientific, and unprofessional. Faith-based initiatives must be opposed so that the quality and accountability of social services funded by government does not decline. While little true effectiveness data has ever been compiled for traditional providers, faith-based opponents argue that the superior effectiveness of faith-intensive programs should be proved first, before they are allowed to compete for federal funds.[7]

These assumptions about dangerousness and effectiveness relate to religious legitimacy in modern American politics—religion's legitimacy in government-sponsored arenas and faith-based social services' legitimacy in seeking government support for helping it meet human needs. Reviewing the underlying philosophical predisposition of many faith-based opponents clarifies these connections. Quite opposite assumptions in faith-based proponents, and their increasing strength in today's politics, complete the picture. While it is beyond the scope of this chapter to address this conflict in detail, to avoid the clash of worldviews behind the key combatants is to miss much of what is at stake. Simply put, the faith-based initiative is connected to the broad and vehement "culture war" that seems to dominate America's elites in the present day.[8]

ESSENTIAL 3: A LONG HISTORY

An historical perspective, the third essential understanding behind today's debate, sets these current controversies in better context.[9] Religious organizations have operated human service programs throughout America's history. Caring for one's neighbor has been seen nearly always and everywhere as a religious act and obligation: American churches and religiously inspired voluntary organizations have always done so. When industrialization, mass immigration, and racial tension created far more complex problems in the late nineteenth century, religious groups responded with more complex and durable organizations to address these needs. These interventions were not neutral across faith traditions; in fact, one part of the fundamentalist/mainline split within Protestantism can be traced to the church's reaction to modernization. Moderate and liberal denominations tended to be more active and ecumenical in their welfare programs, responding to and in some ways reinforcing the "social gospel" movement of the latter nineteenth century that emphasized new themes of Jesus' humanity, morality, and social concern over traditional theological ideas about Jesus. For these more liberal elements, to truly follow and respect Jesus meant to be more active in meeting human needs and to de-emphasize Jesus' divinity and even the importance of religious belief. In reaction, more theologically traditional faiths put relatively more emphasis on doctrinal issues than ever, even in their social programs that were often explicit tools for evangelism and conversion to particular faith ideas.

But church activity alone, or nearly alone, was a losing battle, even when fundamentalist and mainline efforts are considered in total. In the early and mid-twentieth century, industrialization and economic depression increased the frequency and intensity of requests *from* religious organizations *to* government for help in human service tasks too large and complex to be addressed solely by private efforts. One hundred years ago, joint government-religious efforts to meet human needs would be described by observers as *government* entering the sphere of *religious* responsibility.

Whereas local and state governments moved into the field early on, the federal government did not formally get involved in welfare programs until the Great Depression of the 1930s. The 1935 Social Security Act established the federal Aid to Dependent Children program, which gave states matching federal funds to "assist, broaden and supervise existing mothers' aid programs." The middle decades of the twentieth century saw a marked expansion of government-funded social welfare programs, with thousands of workers and billions of dollars devoted to the cause. As government assistance grew, religious efforts were by no means reduced, although it might have seemed that way from historical records. The "new thing" was government, not religion, and it was the "new" that received official comment and, a few decades later, seemed the *status quo*.

The late 1950s brought the Civil Rights movement; the early 1960s, its maturation. The nation could not avoid knowing of severe poverty in the South, Appalachia, and industrial cities everywhere. Pressure built to bring relatively recent government social services to a broader and higher level, from the New Deal to the Great Society. President Johnson in his 1964 State of the Union address declared an "unconditional war on poverty." New federal social service programs such as Job Corps, Head Start, and Medicaid followed.

A constantly improving economic climate and growing spending by these and other federal programs reduced the poverty rate significantly throughout the remainder of the 1960s, and kept it fairly level through the mid-1970s. Much was accomplished beyond reducing the incidence of poverty; social problems among some target populations, especially the elderly, declined. Religious groups and government were often partners, formally and informally, in these Great Society efforts. But because the focus remained on the growing federal role, the longstanding role of churches and other religious organizations was largely overlooked in the literature and in public debates.

THE FUNDAMENTALIST/MAINLINE SPLIT IN INTERACTING WITH GOVERNMENT

Differences among religious groups in their interactions with the growing government were becoming more apparent. While the two camps both had extensive social services networks before the split and continued them afterward, views about collaborating with government diverged along the same lines.

Those religious organizations that did partner with government were mostly of the modernist stripe; those that did not were mostly more conservative. The politics of most of the modernist willing partners were liberal and their theology ecumenical and humanitarian. Politically, such groups were willing to be junior partners to the government in providing services supported by government dollars. Theologically, their ecumenism made them more willing to downplay the religious content of their programs to meet concerns of government administrators about sectarianism and coercion. They established non-sectarian and even non-religious governing boards, applied for and received 501(c)3 tax-exempt status, partnered with secular non-profits and all levels of government, and became more sophisticated organizationally and more directly involved politically. By the late twentieth century, many mainline Protestant, Catholic, Jewish, and ecumenical groups were long established, had decades of experience dealing with government programs, and, for better or worse, shared with the government itself whatever reputation social services had in the mind of voters.

Meanwhile, theologically conservative and evangelical groups continued to provide services that mixed social services with religious messages. Many of them became joint church efforts or para-church organizations and generally did not seek government funds. Thus, they did not arrange their management and staff to meet the expectations of government funders, look for employees with professional credentials, or separate the marks of faith from the acts of social service. These groups tended to be smaller, more independent from each other, and organizationally part of a church rather than "spun off" into separate entities. In a few cases, these intensely and overtly religious groups might have received government agency support. Public officials would sometimes ignore the religious content or affiliations of programs as long as social services were provided to targeted groups. But, generally, the conservatives operated smaller social service programs, independent of government support. Neither side much bothered the other, and certainly not in Washington, D.C.

1970s DISCONTENT WITH GOVERNMENT

Just as Great Society programs became established in the early 1970s, they became threatened by political and economic tensions. The energy crisis and Lyndon Johnson's dual wars on poverty and in Vietnam stalled the post-WWII economic boom, sharply limiting the natural rise in federal revenues that were partially spent on growing anti-poverty programs. High-paying manufacturing jobs started to be threatened from the rebuilt economies of Japan and Western Europe. As the peak events of the Civil Rights movement lost their immediate force, there was a growing indifference to the rights and social situation of minorities. Stories of waste in government social service programs accumulated, eroding public support. The progress against poverty and other negative social indicators had stalled, if not reversed, by the late 1970s.

In this new environment, there arose three distinct but related criticisms of federally supported social services, each of which came to fruition in arguments for President Bush's faith-based and community initiatives. First, some claimed that federal spending on social services was simply too high, given tight federal revenues and the unique obligations of the central government for national defense and international affairs. They argued that the federal government could simply not afford to fund social services; state and local governments and the nongovernmental sector would have to carry a larger burden. Second, critics charged that the federally directed War on Poverty was excessively detailed and restrictive. National control, through excessive regulation over budgets and credentialing (rather than performance), they said, stifled the adaptability, wisdom, and grassroots participation that locally-run programs provided. They argued that the federal government should pull back to release the energies of others. Third, it became common to argue that newly flat social indicators showed that the root cause of poverty was more moral than economic. Spending more money, at least in the same places with the same programs, simply would not do any good; deeper behavioral and attitudinal changes by the poor and needy were required.

1980s: STARTING THREE WAVES OF CHANGE

These criticisms had their effects on federal social service policy in the last quarter of the twentieth century. Change came in three successive waves, each with a slightly different emphasis. The first wave, under the Reagan administration in the early 1980s, was mostly a simple reduction in the federal share of social service spending. Domestic spending by the federal government did not really fall but more accurately leveled off, but the federal share of total welfare spending did decline. Whereas no additional aid to specifically religious service providers—direct or indirect—was urged, faith-based organizations were often touted as effective service providers that could take up any slack in services due to government cuts with private funds. In effect, in this first wave of change, intense and overt religious social service providers were touted as an alternative to, not a new partner with, government efforts.

The next wave, in the mid-1980s, emphasized increased state and local flexibility in social services. The federal government began to solicit from states and grant to them waivers of administrative rules so that they and their subdivisions could experiment and innovate. This federal deregulation of social services greatly increased the incidence of state and local governments contracting with and/or purchasing services from private, mostly non-profit, agencies. Devolution to states and localities meant these lower levels of government took management responsibility for social welfare, while private organizations were the real deliverers of social services. The private groups operated as a sort of government-by-proxy and were often required by state and local governments to abide by laws and regulations—including religion-related laws and regulations—as if they were direct government entities, or agents.

Today's faith-based debate is really the third wave of change, which began rather inauspiciously with the 1996 welfare reform law. That law ended the drive for real cuts in welfare funding; at the same time, it continued the logic of devolution and outsourcing in the second wave. Little noticed at the time, charitable choice language in the 1996 law prohibited the government from discriminating against religious providers in making contracting arrangements for the welfare programs reauthorized under this particular law. Charitable choice declared that it is constitutional to provide direct government support to at least the non-religious elements of social service programs provided by even quite intensely and vocally religious providers, including individual churches with service programs. It passed through largely unnoticed because of the much larger controversies in the new law, chief of which was President Clinton's expressed willingness to position himself and his party as more socially conservative and fiscally responsible.

President George W. Bush's outreach to faith-based and community providers aims to expand the number of potential providers that bid for government-funded social service contracts. Regulatory and statutory changes aim to open as many federally-funded programs as possible to bidding by faith-based groups. Partly after the example of innovative states and partly through its own faith-friendly perspective, the Bush administration wants the potential marketplace of providers to be less dominated by large government-directed, secular, and nominally religious providers, and more open to smaller, community-based, and more openly religious providers.

Initiative supporters claim that what they want is "a level playing field" on which all providers compete, and that the constitution allows for such a field. Opponents attack the potential disruption and dangerous competition these changes would bring and bring in constitutional arguments to keep the market small. While the Bush administration has promised no additional program funds in a more competitive market, it has argued that more people can be served, and that a broader provider marketplace will lead to more effective and efficient social services at any given spending level.

Philosophically, faith-based initiatives are the last of three reform waves and the logical conclusion to two quite different ideas, both of which are dominant in today's Republican Party. The first idea is at its root religious—a desire for a more secure role for a particular kind of faith, a conservative Protestant evangelical faith that during most of the twentieth century sought separation from government and society but now seeks their formal acknowledgement. The second idea is at its root economic—the push for a freer and more open market in delivering social service programs supported by the federal government. Pro-faith and pro-market views, similar to the social conservative and economic conservative wings of the Republican Party, worked together in the Bush administration to push through faith-friendly changes in the bureaucracy and set up high stakes challenges in the courts.

ESSENTIAL 4: CONSTITUTIONAL CONSIDERATIONS

Whether the pro-faith and pro-market forces ultimately triumph is dependent, ultimately, upon the federal courts. The First Amendment's Establishment Clause is the reference point for what religious freedom means in the United States. Many people came to the New World to escape religious persecution in their native land, as the newcomers had practiced a faith contrary to that officially established by the state. The Framers placed the Establishment Clause in the Constitution's First Amendment to prevent a repeat occurrence in their new nation. At the very least, the Establishment Clause was intended to prevent the federal government (and, later, through the Incorporation Doctrine, state and local governments) from supporting a particular religion through its laws and subsidies. Until the 1940s, the Establishment Clause had essentially been a dormant piece of the Constitution, at least with respect to state and local governmental action and, because the federal government had not involved itself much in welfare policy before mid-century, for federal policy toward social services as well.

A constitutional defense of the faith-based initiatives was easy to make as the Bush administration started, although the key grounds for the argument were not particularly long standing. Establishment Clause interpretation was moving slowly but clearly in an accommodationist direction for more than a decade before 2000.[10] Current Establishment Clause reasoning seems to be more favorable toward government/religious sector collaboration today, at least in the realm of government financial aid to religious institutions, which is the core of the initiatives' purpose.[11]

WHAT IS "ESTABLISHMENT" OF RELIGION?

The current scene is a reversal of what now appears to have been a short separationist season for the Court, running roughly from the 1940s to the 1980s. With its 1947 *Everson v. Board of Education* decision, the Supreme Court woke to Establishment Clause questions, usually in the context of public aid to Catholic parochial schools. In this period the Court was relatively stringent in barring the use of public funds to support educational enterprises in religious contexts. In so doing, it presumed religious schools to be "pervasively sectarian" institutions and thus disqualified from public aid because such aid would inevitably promote a particular religious—in most cases Catholic—teaching. The separationist season featured mind-numbing complexity for scholars wanting to decipher the Court's intent. *Everson* put the claim that the Establishment Clause had built a high "wall of separation" between church and state, borrowing a phrase from an 1802 personal letter by Thomas Jefferson to Danbury, Connecticut Baptists. "No establishment" meant to the *Everson* court more than not supporting a particular religion; it barred any state action that even touched upon religion generically. The language seemed overwrought even at the time, as the decision itself allowed a local New Jersey public school system to reimburse to parents the costs of using the public transit system to send their children to school, regardless of whether the school was government- or church-run. While *Everson* was kindly to religion in the facts of the case, its vivid, extra-constitutional, and increasingly anachronistic image of a wall imposed itself on later court decisions and public discussions.

WHAT IS "SEPARATION" OF CHURCH AND STATE?

In a series of rulings after *Everson*, the Court seemed to create two meanings of the term "separation," each of which it applied in different contexts and in apparently inconsistent ways. One meaning is *strict separation*—that law and government should not touch religion in any way. This definition is prevalent in cases, usually involving the education of youth, which prohibited organized prayer in public schools, prayer led by public school teachers or other public officials, and on-campus released-time or after-school programs for religious activities. At other times, the Court advanced another definition of separation, usually in cases outside of the education of youth, which could better be termed *neutrality* (or, sometimes, *accommodationist*) and whose major effect is to be far more indifferent to slight taints of religion. Neutrality means that it might be constitutional under some situations for religion generally to benefit from a law or government action. Some examples of neutrality rulings include allowing property tax exemptions for churches, or allowing the Bible to be read in public schools as long as it is taught as literature. The Court has invoked neutrality more frequently in recent years that it did early in the separation season. That does not mean, however, its rulings have become more predictable or fit a tight chronological pattern.

    The so-called *Lemon* test, derived from the 1971 *Lemon v. Kurtzman* decision, provides a means to examine, if not exactly explain, the Court's key Establishment Clause decisions. In *Lemon*, a majority of the Court held that government involvement in religion might be acceptable provided the program in question met three tests. First, the government must have a *secular purpose*, not a religious one, in whatever program or policy is challenged. Second, the government's program must *neither advance nor inhibit religion*, either a specific religion, or religion in general relative to non-religion. Third, the operation of the program must not create an *excessive entanglement* between government and religion. If the challenged government program or policy met all three criteria, it was constitutional. If it failed even one prong of the test, a Court strictly adhering to the *Lemon* test would strike it down.

    The *Lemon* test is relatively clear, yet the Court's application of the test in later cases is not. Courts rule on particular cases that have particular facts and circumstances. While courts usually take pains to articulate broader principles into which these unique cases supposedly fit, it is sometimes difficult to discern a consistent logic to court decisions in complex areas such as church/state relations. A review of rulings in specific Establishment Clause cases illustrates the point. The Supreme Court has said that Congress can hire chaplains who open with prayer each day it is in session, yet public school teachers cannot begin their classes with prayers or with even a moment of silence if prayer is listed as one of the options for students to spend that quiet time. Public school professionals can come to church-related schools to administer diagnostic hearing and eyesight tests to such students, but if they find a problem they must provide therapy off private school grounds. Children in church-related schools can ride a public school bus to and from their school, but not the same bus on a field trip. A public school district can lend a religious school its textbooks on U.S. history with a picture of Abraham Lincoln on its cover. It cannot, however, lend the same picture, by itself, to the same religious school.

Observers convinced there is *some* logic to these rulings suggest dividing them into three categories: one, rulings in cases about *vouchers*—government support to individuals who then use the funds on their own to indirectly support religion; two, those that are about *direct* government support for religious institutions; and, three, those that are about supporting clearly religious *activities*.[12]

Vouchers as Mostly Permissible

In the first category, the court has been willing to allow many things that support religion, if such support flows first to individuals who then choose to use those funds for religion-related services. *Everson*, in part, can be read as providing such justification. Most recently, *Zelman v. Simmons-Harris* (2002) reinforced and expanded the permissibility of vouchers. In general, the Court has stated its view that vouchers are to be thought of as grants to parents and children, not to the agencies themselves. Head Start vouchers can be given by parents to churches. Similar logic allows tuition tax credits and federal educational grants and loans for parents who send their children to religious colleges.

Direct Aid as Mostly Impermissible

The second category, direct support for programs operated by religious institutions, has less order. Sometimes the Court has allowed government to directly support religious institutions such as hospitals and religious liberal arts colleges. Other times it has not; for example, it rarely permits the direct support of religious elementary schools. If one forces some logic on these rulings, perhaps it can be stated that, for direct support programs, the younger the beneficiary of a questioned program and the more educational/ideational (as opposed to material/concrete) the assistance, the less likely it was to be allowed. For example, direct support to Christian elementary school instruction is probably not constitutional, but direct support for church-sponsored housing for the elderly probably is.

It seems that there may be two "sliding scales" of beneficiary independence and program content. Younger recipients are more likely to be influenced by religious messages that older persons can filter out, so programs for the young are treated more skeptically than those for adults. Intangible benefits such as education or counseling are more likely to carry religious content than more tangible benefits such as housing, health care, and clothing; so, as an illustration, schools are treated more skeptically than food banks.

Three recent accommodationist rulings show that these sliding scale government direct aid cases are in jeopardy. The 1988 *Bowen v. Kendrick* decision upheld a federal statute that allowed openly religious service providers to be direct grantees of a program aimed at teen pregnancy. In *Agostini v. Felton* (1997), the Court upheld a program that allowed public employees to provide remedial educational services on-site at religious schools, directly reversing a ruling made only twelve years earlier in *Aguilar* (1985). Finally, in *Mitchell v. Helms* (2000), the Court approved a federal statute that made funding to local educational agencies for library, media, and computer materials equally available to both public and private schools, including schools that were predominantly religious.

Clearly Religious Activities as Clearly Impermissible

In the category of directly supporting expression that is clearly religious, separationist standards seem to be holding more firmly. The Court has in the past rarely been willing to permit government support for clearly and directly religious activities such as posting the Ten Commandments in government buildings, allowing devotional Bible reading in public schools, or printing prayers at government expense. The rare exceptions are when the Court determines that the religious content of the activity in question has been so diluted that it is merely a cultural habit or public convenience.

THE PERVASIVE CONFUSION OF PERVASIVELY SECTARIAN

While vouchers seem acceptable, and direct support of religious activities clearly not, direct aid to religious groups is full of confusion. The third prong of the *Lemon* test, "excessive entanglement," effectively denied many intensely and overtly religious groups access to government funds. At the height of its separationist season, a Court majority would routinely examine closely the nature of the service agency itself in its rulings. If the institution was "pervasively sectarian"—a term the justices often used but never clearly defined—government funding would be denied. The Court reasoned that even if such intensely and vocally religious organizations *could* run a government-funded program in a sufficiently secular manner, the administering government agency would have to monitor the program in question so closely that such oversight would amount to excessive entanglement in religion.

Directly funded faith-based social services are in the thick of the pervasively sectarian confusion because the "faith elements" of these services are so varied. First, "faith-based" can refer to the *location* of the social service, such as a church, a religious school, or an office building owned by a religious organization. Government funds might, it is argued, support a religious location. While a religious location in itself has no effect on program content, the federal government in the past has sometimes prohibited aid on that basis only. Second, "faith-based" can also be tied to a social *agency* so that government funds could subsidize a religious group. Services may be provided by members of a religious order, for example, or by the hired clergy or staff of a local church. Even if the professional staff in contact with clients is chosen independent of religious affiliation, the management or governing board of a service agency may be restricted to members of a particular faith tradition. Some such providers have sometimes been categorically prohibited from receiving government funds. Third, *volunteer* "faith-based" aid can be involved in supporting an otherwise non-religious program. Volunteers assisting an agency may come chiefly or exclusively from faith groups; nuns may volunteer at a government-funded hospice, or church members may tutor in an after-school program for elementary students. Even if no direct government funds go to these volunteers (as they are unpaid), some programs have been deemed ineligible for government support on these grounds. There are simply so many dimensions of faith to consider it is hard to make rulings that seem clearly fair and consistent with precedent.

The Bush administration has brought some, but not perfect, consistency to the question. It has written that federal funds to faith-based groups cannot directly support activities such as prayer, scripture reading, and worship, and that the activities themselves need to be separate in place or time from federally-funded elements. But there remains some ambiguity about intensely religious social service treatments, and whether and to what extent one must or should separate the religious from the non-religious. For many programs eager to apply for federal funds, "faith" is an integral part of treatment. Clients in drug or alcohol recovery programs may be encouraged to make religious commitments to help them change their behavior. Prayer before meals may be required to receive food at a soup kitchen. Memorization of Bible passages about the use of money may be part of a financial management seminar. Only situations of this type, direct mixing of religious messages and social programs, appeared almost certainly unconstitutional to the Rehnquist/O'Connor court, with O'Connor's views holding sway. For some of the Court's members, however, even these programs should, in some circumstances at least, be eligible for direct government funds.

NOT SO FAST; NOT SO SIMPLE

There are other complications in predicting the future judicial approach to faith-based initiatives. First, even the most generous analysis seeking consistency in court rulings has to admit hard-to-defend cases. For example, Head Start, a highly popular federally supported educational program for pre-school age children, may be housed in churches and operated by church members. In this case, it appears that popular acceptance influences legal analysis. Second, actual practice does not always follow constitutional guidelines. There have always been relationships between government agencies and religious providers functioning at variance with court decisions. While some government administrators have unnecessarily prohibited certain organizational arrangements, others have knowingly allowed religious practices in funded programs. And even with good intent to follow legal rulings, the line between what the government may and may not support is not clear, even to personnel in the groups involved.

The three-pronged *Lemon* test guidelines started to become diluted soon after their first articulation. The "primary effect" and "excessive entanglement" prongs have collapsed into one test of whether or not a program served to promote religion. And while the Court continues to cite the language of pervasive sectarianism in determining which religious organizations might qualify for public monies, the principle itself seemed to be eroding as attention shifts to the neutrality of the program and away from the organizational details of its beneficiaries.

The Rehnquist/O'Connor court seemed on the verge of endorsing neutrality as its new starting point for Establishment Clause cases. But for O'Connor's unwillingness to completely give up the *Lemon* language, the full embrace of neutrality might already be here. With her departure from the Court, it may now be at hand.

THE FUTURE: WHAT KEY CASES TELL US ABOUT TOMORROW (MAYBE)

The trend in the Court's establishment thinking is most easily seen in a review of key cases decided after 2000, those already settled, and those, in early 2007, making their way to the top of the federal system.

Decided Cases: *Mitchell, Zelman,* and *Locke*

Mitchell v. Helms *(2000)*   In *Mitchell*, the Court upheld a supplementary education program that provided direct aid in the form of educational materials to public and private schools, both religious and non-religious, and expressly overruled two church-state cases from the 1970s. A plurality opinion of four justices (Kennedy, Scalia, Thomas, and Rehnquist) launched an open attack on the pervasively sectarian standard, characterizing it as "born of bigotry" for its roots in nineteenth-century anti-Catholicism. They called for abandoning the separationist practice of a searching inquiry into aid recipient organizations, and urged only an examination of the law in question. If laws were neutral toward religion and non-religion, that neutrality should be enough to pass constitutional muster.

Court-watchers sympathetic to faith-based programs claimed *Mitchell* heralded the end of pervasive sectarianism. While with *Mitchell*, constitutional jurisprudence continued to shift in favor of faith-based proponents, advocates were mistaken if they thought this meant a future free pass. The plurality in *Mitchell* had been unable to win a decisive fifth vote to bury the pervasively sectarian inquiry or firmly establish neutrality. Justice O'Connor wrote a concurrence, which Justice Breyer joined, that refused to accept facial neutrality of the law as the sole governing principle of aid to religious organizations. O'Connor and Breyer defended a searching inquiry into the nature of the aid and found, in the facts of *Mitchell*, particular types of aid and safeguards against its religious use that in this particular case passed a constitutional test. Thus, even after *Mitchell*, five justices then on the court would still consider public funding of religious organizations according to some standard more demanding than simple neutrality.

An out-of-court settlement in a direct funding case may hint at how much the Bush administration was willing to assume the Rehnquist/O'Connor Court's separation season was over. In May 2005 the Massachusetts ACLU sued the U.S. Department of Health and Human Services (*ACLU v. Leavitt*) over its direct money grants to a Massachusetts nonprofit, the Silver Right Thing (SRT), to fund its sexual abstinence program. The state ACLU claimed the program was too infused with religious content and advocacy, and its financial protections too weak, to be constitutional. Rather than contest this case in court, HHS reached an agreement with the ACLU, terminated its contract with SRT, and issued "safeguard" guidelines for use of its funds. A key element of these safeguards is to assert that religious content of youth sexual abstinence program materials cannot be government funded, partly because of the young age of the program's beneficiaries. By implication, the settlement states HHS's intent that it did not seek to provide direct financial support for the specifically religious elements of such programs, even if they are otherwise constitutional.[13]

Zelman v. Simmons-Harris *(2002)* The constitutionality of indirect government aid to religious providers, such as vouchers, became clearer in the summer of 2002 with the Supreme Court's much anticipated school voucher decision in *Zelman v. Simmons-Harris*. The case was a challenge to the Ohio Pilot Project Scholarship Program, which provided school tuition vouchers for students in the Cleveland city schools. The vouchers were distributed on the basis of financial need and could be spent at a number of schools. On its face, the program made no distinctions between, nor expressed a preference for or against, public or private schools. However, voucher recipients were limited to participating schools—those willing to accept the vouchers. The law let both public and private institutions accept vouchers. Most public schools refused to participate, and participating schools, and affected students, were overwhelmingly in religious education.

The Court upheld the program 5 to 4. The majority opinion rested squarely upon the principle of neutrality. As long as the voucher program was neutral with respect to religion, the Court said, it was not susceptible to an Establishment Clause challenge. Aid had gone to religious schools only indirectly, through parental choice and only as the result of their independent decisions, thus avoiding the danger of government endorsement of or support for religion. Even though the vast majority of the tuition aid ended up with religious schools, the majority concluded that the parental choice insulated the voucher program from government endorsement or approval. The program was neutral on its face, providing no incentive or encouragement to use vouchers at religious rather than secular schools.

Justice O'Connor added her voice to the four neutrality advocates in *Mitchell*. Her vote hinged on the "primary effect" prong of *Lemon* and the government's avoiding the appearance of religious "endorsement." To her, the absence of governmental endorsement depended on an affirmative answer to two questions: was the aid administered in a neutral fashion without consideration for the religious status of beneficiaries or service providers, and did beneficiaries have a genuine choice among religious and non-religious organizations? O'Connor determined that the Cleveland voucher program met both of these demands.

Zelman changed the faith-based landscape in ways both general and specific. Most broadly, it showed that the "wall of separation" vision of neutrality—no funding that would aid or support religion—was over for the Rehnquist/O'Connor court. It clearly stated that neutrality is not synonymous with separation but, rather, it is evenhandedness toward things religious and secular. Equal treatment of one religious entity toward other religious entities, and of these toward secular entities, is what is required. The specific implications of *Zelman* for voucher-based social service delivery programs were also clear. If vouchers were okay for schools, they almost certainly would pass this court's tests in other programs. The win for faith-based initiatives advocates was clear. Social service voucher programs that include religious service providers appeared to be constitutional, as long as the program is appropriately (i.e., neutrally) constructed. If a law is on its face neutral toward religious and secular social service providers, if vouchers are available to program recipients without reference to their religious preferences or beliefs or lack thereof, and if the program offers real choices—religious and non-religious—for beneficiaries, faith-based programs constructed along these lines are constitutionally sound.

No one could be completely confident, of course, that the Court would rule all voucher programs constitutional. Aid to schools has historically raised the highest establishment concerns, since it involves education of youth, the most closely scrutinized category in prior Court decisions. The case for the constitutionality of vouchers in most faith-based social service programs, hence, seems stronger than the question in *Zelman*, and highlighted that the type of aid, direct or indirect, is material to a case.

Locke v. Davey (2004) Many federal social service programs are in fact operated by state and local governments. Many states have what are generically called "Blaine Amendments"—constitutional amendments or statutory provisions that have a stricter, more separationist standard between church and state entities than the U.S. Constitution's First Amendment. In the late 1800s, partisanship was in part sectarian, as Republicans were overwhelmingly Protestant. Democrats, on the other hand, were more open to Catholics, partly because working class immigrants of the time originated in predominantly Catholic European nations like Italy and Ireland.

The amendments are named after James G. Blaine, a former Speaker of the U.S. House of Representatives and Republican presidential candidate, who in 1884 ran against Democrat Grover Cleveland and lost. He attributed his loss to overzealous supporters, some of whom accused the Democrats of being the party of "Rum, Romanism, and Rebellion." Blaine lost New York, which Republicans then usually won, and thus lost to Cleveland.[14]

Even though the Blaine amendments instituted by states in the late nineteenth century were partially borne out of the same anti-Catholic sentiment that the Court has associated with the "pervasively sectarian" standard, opponents of faith-based efforts have appealed to Blaine language to slow those programs down.

Locke v. Davey, decided by the Supreme Court in 2004, provided support for the federalism-based arguments of faith-based opponents. Ruling on a Washington state scholarship program that specifically excluded students intending to enter the formal pastorate, a majority of the Court said states could maintain their own policies of church-state separation even if those policies were more separationist than enunciated in the First Amendment.

As such, the many states with Blaine-like language are not automatically and universally required to hold to the First Amendment standards that the Rehnquist/O'Connor Court, or later Supreme Courts, might allow for federal programs. While the *Locke* decision's 7–2 margin implies that the Court's view will hold in the new Roberts/Alito Court, future Blaine-related challenges can be expected.

Pending Cases: *Americans United* and *Freedom from Religion*

Americans United v. Prison Fellowship Ministries *(pending in early 2007)* In February 2003, Americans United for Separation of Church and State took direct aim at a program greatly admired by President Bush: the InnerChange Freedom Initiative of Iowa, a program developed by Prison Fellowship Ministries, a longstanding evangelical ministry devoted to prison reform and prisoner rehabilitation. InnerChange had obtained a contract with the Iowa State Department of Corrections to operate a portion of its Newton correctional facility. The program was a pre-release anti-recidivism program intensively infused with religious content of the Christian variety, including Bible reading and instruction in religious precepts.

Americans United challenged this faith-infused program on several specific points, patterned after the criteria the swing voters on the Rehnquist Court hinted they would use in evaluating Establishment Clause cases. In June 2006, U.S. District Court Judge Robert Pratt issued a detailed opinion in favor of the group's challenge.[15] His declaration against the constitutionality of the program rested on several points. First, the state had artificially structured the contract proposal to ensure that InnerChange would win it, violating the neutrality requirement for constitutional state action. In fact, he said, InnerChange effectively operated as a "state actor" in this program, requiring it to abide by federal and state guidelines on church/state separation. Second, the judge employed the pervasively religious standard (which he applied in a relatively novel way—to a program and not an institution) to find that the program's religious elements were so prevalent and integrated into the whole program that none of it could be supported by the state. Third, he found that the program preferred evangelical Christian inmates as potential participants because of the nature of the InnerChange curriculum and the absence of alternatives that had other-religious, and non-religious, perspectives. Finally, he found that the *per diem* payment plan to InnerChange (instituted mid-stream by the state) did not constitute a voucher-like program of the sort upheld in *Zelman*.

As of early 2007, the case was on appeal to the 8th Circuit Court. Should this case reach the Supreme Court, it provides the opportunity to rewrite and clarify many of the key issues in Establishment Clause cases, should the Court's majority choose to write an expansive opinion on the issues involved.

Freedom from Religion Foundation *(argued February 2007)* A final key case pending in early 2007 does not deal directly with faith-based programs, but rather with the issue of taxpayer standing in court and whether and to what Establishment Clause challenges should singularly affect the standing issue.

As a general rule, individual taxpayers do not obtain standing in federal court if they seek to challenge federal agency actions, although they may contest acts of Congress. But it is unclear if particular standing claims in essential areas of the Constitution, such as the Establishment Clause, might be special cases where standing is easier to obtain. *Freedom from Religion Foundation (FFRF) v. Hein* (previously *v. Towey* and then *v. Grace*, for the previous WHOFBCI director and acting director) began in 2004 when FFRF complained that a variety of WHOFBCI activities, particularly its regional outreach and networking conferences, supported religion and therefore violated the Establishment Clause. The standing of FFRF, and several joining plaintiffs, to bring the claim rested on their status as taxpayers and the root of their claims in the Establishment Clause.

The federal district court dismissed the case in November 2004 on the grounds that the plaintiffs lacked standing, and did not address the substance of the complaints. On appeal, in January 2006 a panel of judges from the 7th Circuit partially reinstated FFRF's lawsuit in an opinion that supported a very broad view of taxpayer standing. In its ruling, the circuit court explicitly asked the Supreme Court to clarify standing issues related to Establishment Clause cases. The Court did take the case, and heard oral arguments in late February 2007. While a review of the oral arguments hint that granting standing in this case would be a surprising outcome, the Court could decide the issue narrowly or broadly.[16]

HIRING FREEDOM: THE MOUSE THAT ROARED (FOR A WHILE)

In the faith-based congressional debates of 2001, opponents cast about for an issue that might slow advocates' apparently strong legislative momentum. They stumbled upon a winner in raising alarms about the right, and supposed abuse, of government-funded religious organizations to make hiring decisions based on religious belief. Dire warnings of "publicly funded discrimination" proved an effective brake on faith-based bills in the House and Senate.

For religious groups intent on preserving their character, the right to hire individuals whose beliefs are in accordance with their religious identity or mission is critical. It is also, generally speaking, unlimited with regard to religious preferences of employees if a group does not directly receive federal government funds. The Bush initiative recognized the importance of hiring freedom, proposing in its 2001 legislation the same kind of hiring protections in the 1996 charitable choice statute, which specified that religious nonprofits would not have to forfeit their prerogatives to make personnel decisions based on the religious commitments of applicants.

Opponents charged that the protections were a guise for allowing overly zealous religious organizations to practice intolerance through discriminatory hiring practices. The charges gained traction in the media and public, and created a media firestorm like no other aspect of the faith-based proposal, sinking nearly all the faith-based legislative package.

The constitutional merits of the issue were considerably more pedestrian than the public uproar implied. The current state of constitutional doctrine protects religious providers' hiring autonomy as a general rule, with possible exceptions, as has been the case for decades. Churches and other religious groups have long enjoyed exempt status under the Civil Rights Act, which permits them to take religious affiliation or conviction into account in their hiring and personnel decisions. That exception was validated by the Supreme Court, unanimously, in *Corporation of the Presiding Bishop v. Amos* in 1987. The only twist is that the exemption, contained in Title VII of the Civil Rights Act, does not specifically include *publicly funded* faith-based service providers under its protection. Initiative opponents argued that public funding disqualified religious groups from that special status. They claimed that applying the religion-specific hiring exemption to situations involving federal contracts or grants was tantamount to government endorsing discriminatory hiring. Indeed, they employed the neutrality argument usually used by the other side. In this instance, faith-based foes contended it was illogical to treat a religious provider as a neutral dispenser of secular services for funding purposes on the one hand, while simultaneously giving it special allowance to hire religiously compatible workers and employees on the other hand.

Faith-based backers counter that maintaining hiring freedom is both essential and logical in following the Court's rulings. The more new rulings warm to formal neutrality overall as one expression of religious tolerance, the more likely is the formal grant of hiring autonomy to publicly funded religious groups. In addition, backers pointed out that publicly funded *secular* organizations may hire only those applicants who are aligned with their ideological or policy aims, and who can be counted on to carry them out.

All groups should be allowed to retain their ideological identity—religious or non-religious—when they carry out government supported social services. If not, the unequivocal message would be one of government bias against religious providers. *Lown v. Salvation Army,* decided in 2005 by a federal district court in New York, appears to have largely settled this issue in the favor of faith-based friends.[17] *Lown* challenged the Salvation Army's hiring selectivity, as well as the government's funding of the Army's programs and employees. Judge Sidney Stein dismissed the plaintiff's arguments about hiring selectivity: however, he did agree to examine elements of the challenged programs themselves. While hiring freedoms and restrictions remain politically volatile, it seems clear that the federal government can decide, either within a specific federal program or more broadly, whether and to what extent religiously-affiliated program providers may or may not take the religious views of their employees and potential employees into account. While the *Lown* case has not conclusively ended its judicial journey, Judge Stein's ruling is thorough, carefully reasoned, and attentive to all the relevant arguments. The political struggles over this point will continue, but the opinion has probably discouraged potential new litigants seeking to press the point.

CONCLUSION: ON THE VERGE OF . . . WHAT?

Attention only to the congressional controversies over President Bush's faith-based initiatives and how they were reported by the national media misses the most important and, for supporters, most encouraging developments related to the initiative. A dismal legislative record and little active public support for the initiative would, by itself, suggest its failure.

But the quietly built administrative record and the trend of judicial decisions suggest something quite different. By the last half of his second term, President Bush's faith-based initiatives had so settled themselves into administrative procedures at the federal and some state and local governmental levels that they will be hard to dislodge, even if the next president would seem inclined to do so. Judicially, faith-based proponents have enjoyed many advances already. More victories for their side are quite conceivable as key cases face the Supreme Court in 2007 and later. The revised Supreme Court roster under new Chief Justice John Roberts seems almost certainly to be at least as "faith-friendly" as the Rehnquist Court. Few would be surprised at, although some would fear, a series of Court decisions that would more fully embrace an accommodating, neutralist reading of the constitutional interplay between church and state. That would be a critical, if largely silent and incremental, revolution in federal judicial interpretation of the First Amendment religion clauses.

NOTES

1. For a comprehensive treatment of the issue's background and the first two years of the Bush Administration's efforts, see Amy E. Black, Douglas L. Koopman, and David K. Ryden, *Of Little Faith: The Politics of George W. Bush's Faith-Based Initiatives* (Washington, D.C.: Georgetown University Press, 2004). For a brief statement of current status and future prospects, see Stanley Carlson-Thies, "David Kuo's Temptations," October 14, 2006, Center for Public Justice, http://www.cpjustice.org/temptingfaith (accessed March 8, 2007).

2. Ira C. Lupu and Robert W. Tuttle, *The State of the Law 2006: Legal Developments Affecting Government Partnerships with Faith-Based Organizations* (Washington, D.C.: Roundtable on Religion and Social Policy, 2006).

3. Jeffrey Polet and David K. Ryden, "Religion, the Constitution, and Charitable Choice," in *Sanctioning Religion? Politics, Law, and Faith-Based Public Services*, ed. David K. Ryden and Jeffrey Polet (Boulder, CO: Lynne Rienner Publishers, 2005), 9–33.

4. Ira C. Lupu and Robert W. Tuttle, *The State of the Law 2005: Legal Developments Affecting Partnerships Between Government and Faith-Based Organizations* (Washington, D.C.: Roundtable on Religion and Social Policy, 2005), 19.

5. Amy E. Black and Douglas L. Koopman, "The Politics of Faith-Based Initiatives," in *Religion and the Bush Presidency*, ed. Mark J. Rozell and Gleaves Whitney (New York: Palgrave/Macmillan Press, 2007).

6. E. J. Dionne, Jr. and John DiIulio, Jr. "God and the American Experiment: An Introduction," in *What's God Got To Do With The American Experiment?* (Washington, D.C.: Brookings Institution, 2000), 1–13.

7. Recent books that provide evidence of faith-based efficacy in mostly sympathetic terms include Stephen V. Monsma's *Putting Faith in Partnerships: Welfare-to-Work in Four Cities* (Ann Arbor: University of Michigan Press, 2004) and Monsma with J. Christopher Soper, *Faith, Hope and Jobs: Welfare-to-Work in Los Angeles* (Washington, D.C.: Georgetown University Press, 2006). One with a more skeptical view is Sheila Suess Kennedy and Wolfgang Bielefeld, *Charitable Choice at Work: Evaluating Faith-Based Job Programs in the States* (Washington, D.C.: Georgetown University Press, 2006). The Roundtable on Religion and Social Policy, a project by the Rockefeller Institute of Government, State University of New York (with a wealth of Internet resources at http://www.religionandsocialpolicy.org) is probably the most authoritative social science source. In a review of sources it is difficult, however, to avoid the conclusion that seeking complete objectivity on the issue of faith-based efficacy is a fool's errand.

8. "Culture wars" is a term popularized by James Davison Hunter in his 1991 book, *Culture Wars: The Struggle to Define America* (New York: Basic Books). For a recent summary of the debate about how well the term did or does describe public discourse in America, see Hunter and Alan Wolfe, *Is There a Culture War?: A Dialogue on Values And American Public Life* (Washington, D.C.: Brookings Institution, 2006).

9. This portion of the paper is my own interpretation and summary of a variety

of sources, including Stephen V. Monsma, *When Sacred and Secular Mix: Religious Nonprofit Organizations and Public Money* (Lanham, MD: Rowman & Littlefield, 1996), Marvin Olasky, *The Tragedy of American Compassion* (Lanham, MD: Regnery Gateway, 1992), Theda Skocpol, "Religion, Civil Society, and the Social Provision in the U.S.," in *Who Will Provide: The Changing Role of Religion in American Welfare*, ed. Mary Jo Bane, Brent Coffin, and Ronald Thiemann (Boulder, CO: Westview Press, 2000), 21–50, and Robert Wineburg, *A Limited Partnership: The Politics of Religion, Welfare, and Social Service* (New York: Columbia University Press, 2001).

10. See Black, Koopman and Ryden, "Pervasive Confusion: The Federal Courts and Faith-Based Initiatives," in *Of Little Faith: The Politics of George W. Bush's Faith-Based Initiatives.*

11. Polet and Ryden, "Religion, the Constitution, and Charitable Choice."

12. This portion of the chapter is my own interpretation and summary of Carl Esbeck, "Religion and the First Amendment: Some Causes of the Recent Confusion," *William and Mary Law Review* 42:3 (2001), 883–918; Ryden and Polet, *Sanctioning Religion?*; and Mark D. Stern, "Charitable Choice: The Law as it is and May be," in *Can Charitable Choice Work?* ed. Andrew Walsh (Hartford, CT: The Leonard E. Greenberg Center for the Study of Religion in Public Life, 2001), 157–177.

13. Lupu and Tuttle, *State of the Law 2006*, 2–19.

14. Philip Hamburger, *Separation of Church and State* (Cambridge, MA: Harvard University Press, 2004).

15. *Americans United for the Separation of Church and State v. Prison Fellowship Ministries* (S.D. Iowa, 2006), http://www.iasd.uscourts.gov/iasd/opinions.nsf/ 55fa4cbb8063b06c862568620076059d/f0e6eb32c02 590a786257184006464d5/ $FILE/Americans%206–2-06.pdf (accessed March 9, 2007).

16. Anne Faris, *Supreme Court Hears Taxpayer Challenge to Faith-Based Initiative*, Roundtable on Religion and Social Policy, February 28, 2007, http://www.religion andsocialpolicy.org/news/ article.cfm?id=6106 (accessed March 8, 2007), and Linda Greenhouse, "Court Hears Arguments Linking Right to Sue and Spending on Religion," *New York Times*, March 1, 2007 A14.

17. Lupu and Tuttle, *Lown (and others) vs. The Salvation Army, Inc.: Commissioner, New York City Administration for Children's Services (and others)*, Roundtable on Religion and Social Policy, October 11, 2005, http://www.religionandsocialpolicy .org/legal/legal_update_display.cfm?id=38 (accessed March 8, 2007).

FURTHER READING

The faith-based story involves several different dimensions. Understanding it well requires some background in American welfare policy and the relevant constitutional law. One can get a reasonably comprehensive picture of welfare policy, although from very different perspectives, with Robert Wineburg's *A Limited Partnership: The Politics of Religion, Welfare, and Social Service* (New York: Columbia

University Press, 2001), Marvin Olasky's *The Tragedy of American Compassion* (Lanham, MD: Regnery Gateway, 1992), and, in an edited volume, Mary Jo Bane, Brent Coffin, and Ronald Thiemann (eds., *Who Will Provide: The Changing Role of Religion in American Welfare* [Boulder, CO: Westview Press, 2000]). One example where legal issues are addressed broadly is Philip Hamburger's *Separation of Church and State* (Cambridge, MA: Harvard University Press, 2004). Because the Supreme Court cases directly related to the faith-based initiative are of recent vintage and relatively few in number, relevant summaries of the legal issues can be found in more general works, such as David K. Ryden and Jeffrey Polet, eds., *Sanctioning Religion? Politics, Law, and Faith-Based Public Services* (Boulder, CO: Lynne Rienner Publishers, 2005) and in Amy Black, Douglas Koopman and David Ryden, *Of Little Faith: The Politics of George W. Bush's Faith-Based Initiatives* (Washington, D.C.: Georgetown University Press, 2004). The resources of the Roundtable on Religion and Social Policy, a project of the Nelson Rockefeller Institute of Government at the State University of New York, Albany (http://www.religionandsocialpolicy.org), are also invaluable, especially in regard to the legal issues.

6

Political Endorsements by Churches

Mary C. Segers

A perennial issue in church-state relations in the United States is the matter of political endorsements by churches. There are many ways that churches and religious organizations attempt to influence election results, whether by issuing voting instructions from the pulpit, distributing voter guides, inviting political candidates to take the pulpit, addressing issues in such a way that the clergyman's candidate preferences are clear, or by allowing favored political parties access to church directories for purposes of political mobilization. Some of these actions are legally permissible while others are prohibited by federal tax law. Churches cannot, for example, endorse or oppose political candidates for public office, but they can conduct nonpartisan voter registration drives. This chapter examines what is *legally* permissible in church electioneering; it also explores what is *morally* prudent for churches seeking to influence voter choices.

Regardless of what is legally allowable or morally appropriate, these actions by churches raise profound questions about religious freedom, church-state separation, and the relation between religion and politics in a pluralistic society committed to liberal democracy. On one hand, religious groups have a right to contribute to public debate about appropriate public policy. On the other hand, this is a religiously diverse society with a constitutional commitment to church-state separation. The tension between the two religion clauses of the First Amendment is evident here: the Free Exercise

Clause protects the rights of religious citizens to participate in public life, yet the Establishment Clause prohibits the setting up of a state church, government endorsement of a particular religion, or preferential treatment by government of one church over others. In reconciling the rights of clergy and religious believers with these constitutional constraints, the United States has developed norms and practices that define appropriate interventions by churches in the electoral political process.

LEGAL ISSUES AND HISTORICAL BACKGROUND

Since the birth of the federal income tax in 1913, churches have been exempt from taxation. The tax-exempt status of churches is a benefit conferred by the Internal Revenue Service on the condition that churches, temples and mosques do not, among other things, endorse or oppose political candidates. The status of religious organizations was clarified in section 501(c)(3) of the Internal Revenue Code of 1954. This provision of federal tax law applies to religious, social, educational, literary, and charitable nonprofit organizations and exempts them from federal taxation under certain conditions. The benefits of classification as a 501(c)(3) organization include exemption from paying income taxes. Moreover, tax law permits individual donors to deduct contributions to the organization from their income taxes.

However, the benefit of tax-exemption for 501(c)(3) organizations comes at some cost, namely, limitations on the ability of the religious or charitable organization to participate in the political process. There are two principal restrictions. Tax-exempt organizations, including churches, cannot engage in substantial efforts to influence legislation, and they cannot intervene in any political campaign activity.

Lobbying focuses on efforts to influence legislation; the IRS interprets this to include ballot measures such as referenda, initiatives, bond measures, and constitutional amendments. Lobbying also includes politicking for or against confirmation of Supreme Court and other presidential nominations; that is, it applies to appointive offices. IRS regulations stipulate that churches and charities cannot engage in "substantial" lobbying, a term which is vague and undefined. The federal government obviously does not want to confer the benefit of tax-exemption upon an organization whose primary activity is political lobbying for preferred legislation and appointments. At the same time, the government must respect the rights of churches and charities to attempt to influence public policy. In striking a balance, federal tax law stipulates that "churches may engage in lobbying activities only if they do not constitute a substantial part of their total activities, measured by time, effort and expenditure." According to tax lawyers, "the line between what is substantial and what is insubstantial lies somewhere between 5% and 15% of an organization's total activities."[1] In short, tax-exempt organizations can lobby, but within strict limits.

As for political campaign activities, the ban on church electioneering is more stringent. Section 501(c)(3) prohibits tax-exempt organizations from participating in or intervening in any political campaign on behalf of, or in opposition to, any candidate for public office. This ban applies to *all* section 501(c)(3) organizations, not just churches and religious organizations. It was introduced by Senator Lyndon B. Johnson during Senate floor debate on the 1954 version of the IRS tax code. While there is no legislative history providing a definitive account of why LBJ proposed this amendment to the tax code, the research of several scholars shows that his amendment was directed at right-wing, tax-exempt organizations which supported Dudley T. Dougherty, a conservative Texas Democrat who challenged Johnson's renomination and reelection to the Senate in 1954. As Davidson states, "The provision grew out of the anti-communist frenzy of the 1950s and was directed at right-wing organizations such as Facts Forum and the Committee for Constitutional Government. It was introduced by Lyndon Johnson as part of his effort to end McCarthyism, protect the loyalist wing of the Texas Democratic Party, and win reelection to the Senate in 1954."[2]

When Johnson introduced his amendment preventing all section 501(c)(3) tax-exempt organizations from endorsing political candidates, he was chiefly concerned about right-wing political groups. It is unlikely that religious organizations and churches were his targets. Nevertheless, "the electioneering ban applies to churches because they share the same tax-exempt status as the political groups Johnson was really after—not because of anything having to do with religion or churches per se."[3] Indeed, George Reedy, then Johnson's chief aide, stated that he was "confident that Johnson would never have sought restrictions on religious organizations, but that is only an opinion and I have no evidence."[4]

To summarize, federal tax law merely limits lobbying by churches and religious organizations but strictly prohibits political campaign activity. However, as we shall see, enforcement of the ban on electioneering is uneven. While the IRS has received numerous complaints about churches and charities violating tax law, only one church has lost its tax-exempt status as of this writing.

The IRS has penalized several religious organizations and other nonprofits by applying excise taxes, issuing warnings, and, in some cases, revoking tax-exempt status. In contrast to churches that are formally organized according to a faith tradition with creedal doctrines and an ordained clergy, religious organizations are associations formed for broadly defined religious purposes. For example, the Christian Coalition, founded in 1989 from the remnants of Pat Robertson's 1988 presidential campaign, is not a church but an advocacy and educational group known for its distribution of voter guides in churches at election time. In 1999, the Christian Coalition was denied tax-exempt status upon a showing that the voter guides were not neutral but rather were biased toward Republican candidates. Similarly, in 1964, the IRS revoked the tax-exempt status of Christian Echoes National Ministry, Inc., a non-profit corporation founded to establish and maintain religious radio and television broadcasts. Christian Echoes lost its tax exemption because "it had directly and indirectly intervened in political campaigns on behalf of candidates for public office."[5]

ENFORCEMENT OF THE BAN ON CHURCH ELECTIONEERING

The resurgence of conservative evangelicals in the United States in the last quarter of the twentieth century has led to increased political activism on the part of many religious groups. The emergence of controversial issues such as abortion, school prayer and gay marriage has also drawn religious groups into the political process. As churches have mobilized to influence public debate and public policy, their activities and strategies have triggered complaints to federal authorities about church electioneering. IRS Commissioner Mark W. Everson stated that after the 2004 elections, the agency received 170 allegations from the public of improper political activity by 501(c)(3) organizations. He said a panel of three IRS career civil servants reviewed the complaints and launched inquiries into 132 organizations, including about 60 churches. Most of these inquiries concluded with warning letters being sent to the non-profit organization; in some cases, organizations were ordered to pay fines.[6] As we shall see, some of these cases are still pending.

Marcus Owens, former director of the IRS division for tax-exempt organizations from 1990 to 2000, who is now a tax attorney in Washington, attributed the increase in complaints of improper political activity by churches and other non-profits to changes within the agency itself. He said that "the IRS is undertaking church examinations on far less compelling facts, on far more borderline cases, than it has historically." In his view, part of the problem is that "neither IRS guidelines nor court cases have made it clear what line a tax-exempt organization cannot cross, short of an explicit call to vote for, or against, a particular candidate or party." He also noted that "the IRS has given mid-level officials the authority to decide whether there is 'reasonable belief' that a church has violated the tax laws—a decision which used to be made by regional commissioners several rungs higher on the institutional ladder."[7] According to Owens, this relatively recent delegation of audit authority to agents on the front lines is a major reason for the increase in cases (from about 20 letters to churches per year in the 1990s to at least double that amount in 2004, 2005, and 2006).

In February 2006, the IRS said it had noticed a sharp increase in prohibited activities by charities and warned that it planned to reverse the trend. The agency issued a report on its "Political Activity Compliance Initiative," concluding that nearly three-quarters of 82 groups examined, including churches, "engaged in some level of prohibited political activity."[8] In the run-up to the 2006 mid-term elections, IRS Commissioner Mark Everson promised more intense scrutiny and robust enforcement of laws limiting churches and charities from involvement in political campaigns. Both the agency and an independent advocacy group, Americans United for Separation of Church and State, undertook educational efforts in 2006 to explain to clergy and religious groups what is permissible and impermissible participation in the electoral process.[9] A review of the literature indicates that there is much that religious groups can do without violating the federal law prohibiting political endorsements by churches.

The IRS states that intervention in a political campaign is unlawful. Impermissible activities include churches endorsing or opposing political candidates, churches donating money to political parties, clergy endorsements from the pulpit, hosting fundraising events in churches on behalf of political candidates, churches distributing campaign literature, and holding campaign rallies in churches. On the other hand, there are many permissible activities churches and religious organizations can conduct. Issue-based advocacy in churches is absolutely permitted.[10] Churches can conduct nonpartisan voter registration drives (in the interest of helping citizens perform their civic duty of voting in elections). Churches can hold educational forums to discuss issues, inviting all candidates for a position to the church social hall (even if all do not come). This is a permissible form of public education. Churches can transport voters to the polls so long as they do not tell voters whom to vote for. They can engage in other activities to encourage voter turnout. A pastor can stress the importance of voting and preach on the civic duty of being politically engaged. Finally, the IRS guidelines allow churches to publish voter guides as long as they avoid political bias.

Of course, there are gray areas. Fear of crossing the line from legal to illegal activity may make pastors overly cautious. But the IRS insists that enforcing federal law does not infringe on the First Amendment rights of churches. According to Commissioner Mark Everson, "Freedom of speech and religious liberty are essential elements of our democracy. But the Supreme Court has in essence held that tax exemption is a privilege, not a right, stating 'Congress has not violated [an organization's] First Amendment rights by declining to subsidize its First Amendment activities.'"[11]

Critics argue that houses of worship are being muzzled by the federal government and that churches' rights of free speech and religious liberty are being suppressed. Some members of Congress have introduced legislation to repeal the IRS language. Republican Congressman Walter B. Jones of North Carolina has repeatedly proposed bills to modify or eliminate the federal tax law ban on church electioneering. In the Senate, Republican Senator James Inhofe of Oklahoma introduced the Religious Freedom Act of 2006 to protect the free speech rights of churches.[12]

However, public opinion polls have consistently shown strong opposition to pulpit-based politicking. There is general recognition that allowing churches and clergy to endorse political candidates would have a very divisive effect within a congregation. This in turn could jeopardize a pastor's job, especially in congregations that choose their pastors. Others contend that issuing voting instructions from the pulpit simply is not part of the job description for church ministry (leadership); seminaries do not prepare clergy for this. Still others recognize the importance of maintaining church independence and autonomy, of not letting a house of worship become a cog in some candidate's political machine.

POLITICAL ENDORSEMENTS BY CHURCHES: TWO CASES

Two examples of IRS investigation of church politicking illustrate the complexity of compliance with federal tax law banning political endorsements by 501(c)(3) organizations. The case of the Church at Pierce Creek, near Binghamton, New York, is the only case thus far in which the IRS has revoked the tax-exempt status of a church solely because of its partisan politicking. Pierce Creek illustrates a relatively clear violation of the law. The case of All Saints Church in Pasadena, California—still pending—is an example of an unclear, ambiguous, and therefore contested violation of federal tax law. Federal privacy rules make it all but impossible to determine how IRS cases are resolved. We know about the Church at Pierce Creek from federal court records. We know about All Saints Church because the church has released on its website most of the records of its correspondence with the IRS.

The Church at Pierce Creek was a Christian church operated by Branch

Ministries, Inc., whose senior pastor was Daniel J. Little. Located in Vestal, New York, outside Binghamton, the church requested and received from the IRS a letter recognizing its tax-exempt status in 1983. On October 30, 1992, four days before the presidential election, the church placed full-page advertisements in *USA Today* and the *Washington Times*. Designed as an open letter to the Christian community, each ad bore the headline "Christians Beware: Do Not Put the Economy Ahead of the Ten Commandments." Each asserted that Arkansas Governor Bill Clinton's positions concerning abortion, homosexuality, and the distribution of condoms to teenagers in schools violated biblical precepts. The ads included biblical citations against such practices, and then asked: "How then can we vote for Bill Clinton?" The following appeared, in tiny type, at the bottom of each advertisement:

This advertisement was co-sponsored by the Church at Pierce Creek, Daniel J. Little, Senior Pastor, and by churches and concerned Christians nationwide. Tax-deductible donations for this advertisement gladly accepted. Make donations to: The Church at Pierce Creek. [mailing address].[13]

The ads did not go unnoticed. The next day a front-page article in the *New York Times* mentioned the ads; a later column by Anthony Lewis stated that the sponsors of the ad had almost certainly violated federal tax law.[14] The ads also came to the attention of the Regional Commissioner of the IRS, who notified the church on November 20, 1992, that he had authorized a church tax inquiry based on "a reasonable belief . . . that you may not be tax-exempt or that you may be liable for tax" due to political activities and expenditures. The church denied that it had engaged in any prohibited activity and declined to provide information requested by the IRS. Following two later unproductive meetings, the IRS revoked the church's tax-exempt status on January 19, 1995, citing the newspaper advertisements as prohibited intervention in a political campaign.

Pastor Little and the Church at Pierce Creek then sued in federal court, a decision that had the effect of suspending revocation of the church's tax-exemption until the district court reached its ruling. Attorneys for the church argued that the IRS had exceeded its statutory authority in revoking the tax-exemption, that the revocation violated its free speech and free exercise rights under the First Amendment and the Religious Freedom Restoration Act of 1993, and that the IRS had engaged in selective prosecution in violation of the Equal Protection Clause of the Fifth Amendment. Pointing to some 65 instances where Democratic candidates spoke in or campaigned at other churches, they noted that the IRS had not penalized those churches—proof, they argued, that the IRS selectively enforced the ban on intervention in a political campaign.

However, most of the 65 examples cited were substantially different from the case of the Church at Pierce Creek; they involved candidates giving speeches or churches sponsoring political debates or forums—all permissible activities under federal tax law. Government attorneys defended the IRS action regarding the Church, arguing that its anti-Clinton advertisements were an "egregious violation" of the campaign ban.[15] The IRS decided to revoke the church's tax-exempt status, they contended, because the church had run a partisan print advertisement in two national newspapers, that was fully attributable to the church, that opposed the election of a candidate, and that solicited tax-deductible donations to defray the cost of the advertisement.[16]

The district court judge ultimately accepted this argument, noting that the action taken by the Church at Pierce Creek was unique and that the IRS was justified in revoking the tax-exempt status of the church:

In the circumstances presented here—where a tax-exempt church bought an advertisement that stated its opposition to a particular candidate for public office, attributed the advertisement to the church and solicited tax-deductible contributions for the advertisement—the IRS was justified in revoking the tax-exempt status of the church ... In the absence of any showing that any other churches engaged in similar conduct and did not have their tax-exempt status revoked, plaintiffs have failed to establish discriminatory effect.[17]

Upon appeal, the Circuit Court of Appeals for the District of Columbia upheld the district court ruling. A unanimous three-judge panel held that the IRS acted within its statutory authority, that its revocation of tax-exempt status did not restrict the church's religious freedom, and that the government had not "violated the church's First Amendment rights by declining to subsidize its First Amendment activities." At the same time, Judge James Buckley, writing for the court, minimized the potentially negative tax consequences of the appeals court's ruling, noting that revocation was not permanent, that it did not necessarily make the church liable for the payment of taxes, and that it affected principally the tax-deductibility of donor contributions. Stating that the revocation was "likely to be more symbolic than substantial," Judge Buckley wrote, "As the IRS confirmed at oral argument, if the Church does not intervene in future political campaigns, it may hold itself out as a 501(c)(3) [tax-exempt] organization and receive all the benefits of that status ... Contributions will remain tax-deductible as long as donors are able to establish that the Church meets the requirements" of the tax code.[18]

While the case of the Church at Pierce Creek presents a fairly clear violation of federal tax law banning interventions in political campaigns, the case of All Saints Church in Pasadena illustrates a more ambiguous claim of such a violation. At issue here is whether a sermon given two days before the 2004 presidential election crossed the borderline between permissible preaching and impermissible endorsement of, or opposition to, a political candidate. This case is pending as of this writing. Moreover, All Saints Church has vigorously contested the IRS's allegation that it has violated the ban on church electioneering.[19]

The sermon in question, titled "If Jesus Debated Senator Kerry and President Bush," was given on October 31, 2004, by Rev. George Regas, guest preacher and former rector of All Saints Episcopal Church, which describes itself as a peace and justice church. Regas's sermon contained an explicit disclaimer, "I don't intend to tell you how to vote." He acknowledged that "good people of profound faith will be for either George Bush or John Kerry for reasons deeply rooted in their faith." At the same time, Regas felt obliged to preach about the connection between Christian values and public policy on the eve of an election: "I want to say as clearly as I can how I see Jesus impacting your vote and mine."

Regas addressed several issues: ending war and violence, and eliminating poverty. He imagined Jesus would say to Bush and Kerry: "War is itself the most extreme form of terrorism." He reminded members of the congregation that "the killing of innocent people to achieve some desired goal is morally repudiated by anyone claiming to follow [Jesus] as their savior and guide." He said that Jesus would confront both Senator Kerry and President Bush, saying, "The sin at the heart of this war against Iraq is your belief that an American life is of more value than an Iraqi life. That an American child is more precious than an Iraqi baby." He imagined Jesus addressing President Bush: "Mr. President, your doctrine of preemptive war is a failed doctrine. Forcibly changing the regime of an enemy that posed no imminent threat has led to disaster."

On the issue of poverty, Rev. Regas imagined that, "if Jesus debated President Bush and Senator Kerry, he would say to them: 'Why is so little mentioned about the poor?'" Jesus would say to Bush and Kerry: "Poverty is a central issue in this political campaign." Rev. Regas suggested that poverty is not a partisan issue but a religious issue. And he defined abortion as an issue of poverty: "Economic policy and abortion are not separate issues; they form one moral imperative." The former rector concluded his sermon with the following admonition: "When you go into the voting booth on Tuesday, take with you all that you know about Jesus, the peacemaker. Take all that Jesus means to you. Then vote your deepest values. Amen."

The IRS was alerted to this sermon by an article published in the *Los Angeles Times* the next day (November 1, 2004) titled "The Race for the

White House: Pulpits Ring with Election Messages."[20] The article described how six congregations across the country stressed the importance of the presidential election in their Sunday services, yet noted that "most church officials stopped short of endorsing President Bush or Senator John F. Kerry, mindful that such activism could endanger their congregation's tax-exempt status." The list of six congregations included All Saints Church in Pasadena, described as "a liberal Episcopal congregation of 3,500 members." Rev. Regas's sermon was characterized as "a searing indictment of the Bush administration's policies in Iraq." On June 9, 2005, the IRS sent a letter to All Saints Church initiating a church tax inquiry based on concerns raised by the *Los Angeles Times* newspaper article.

All Saints Church promptly hired Marcus Owens, a Washington tax attorney and former head of the IRS tax-exempt section, to represent the church in its correspondence with the agency. In an October 2005 letter to the IRS, Owens stated the church's position. Noting that Rev. Regas was a guest preacher, Owens wrote that "the Church does not believe the law requires it to preview or edit every guest's remarks—much less mandate that a preacher's sermons may not discuss moral values during the congregation's time of worship. It seems ludicrous to suggest that a pastor cannot preach about the value of promoting peace simply because the nation happens to be at war during an election season."

In November 2005, Senior Pastor Rev. Edwin Bacon informed the congregation of the IRS charge of campaign intervention resulting from Rev. Regas's sermon, and summarized the Church's initial response:

It is important for everyone to understand that the IRS's concerns are not supported by the facts. George Regas's sermon upheld the core values of this church as a Peace Church. We have been a self-identified Peace Church since a resolution was identified by the Vestry in 1987. The sermon in question explicitly stated, "I don't intend to tell you how to vote." We at All Saints, of course, will continue from a nonpartisan perspective to teach and proclaim with vigor the core values of Christianity as we stand in the prophetic tradition of Jesus the peacemaker. This is our responsibility as followers of Christ and as Americans who claim our freedom of speech and freedom of religion.

All Saints Church held several conference phone calls with the IRS in an effort to resolve the case. In its correspondence, the church questioned the agency's compliance with certain procedural safeguards in the IRS Code designed to protect churches against unnecessary audits. Owens, lead counsel for All Saints, noted that the IRS's initial inquiry "seemed to place more emphasis on a journalist's description of the Rev. George Regas's guest sermon than it did on analysis of the actual text of the sermon." The Church also challenged the IRS's view that the sermon constituted *implicit* intervention in the 2004 presidential election when the Rev. Regas *explicitly* stated at the outset of his sermon that he was not advising anyone how to vote. Throughout the controversy, All Saints Church emphasized its commitment to a longstanding policy of nonpartisanship in elections and compliance with the IRS rules against church intervention in political campaigns. Moreover, the church denied any wrongdoing in this case. When an IRS audit team offered the church a settlement in the fall of 2005, the church declined the offer. According to Owens, "They said if there was a confession of wrongdoing, they would not proceed to the exam stage. They would be willing not to revoke tax-exempt status if the church admitted intervening in an election."[21] But Rev. Edwin Bacon, current rector of the church, refused the offer "on the grounds that All Saints has done nothing wrong. Furthermore, over the years we have consistently worked within the IRS regulations—regulations we consider to be healthy for our democracy and which we believe protect the precious principles of freedom of speech and freedom of religion."[22]

All Saints clearly mounted a very aggressive campaign against the IRS charge that the church intervened in the 2004 presidential election. They hired expert counsel, challenged the IRS on procedural grounds, refused the offer of a settlement, and in 2006 refused to comply with two IRS summonses in order to force the matter into federal court (where they can challenge the IRS's right to issue the summonses). They also mobilized national support by publishing case documents on their website and by appearing on national media interview shows to publicize the case.[23] Despite the liberal character of All Saints, the Church received support from religious groups across the political spectrum, from the National Council of Churches to the National Association of Evangelicals.[24]

This case raises very important issues in the general area of religion and politics and in the particular area of federal prohibitions of interventions by churches and non-profits in political campaigns. In general, the federal ban on church electioneering does not prevent church organizations from addressing the moral aspects of public policy issues. But the All Saints controversy does raise issues of context and timing. A key question is: when, in the eyes of the IRS, does issue advocacy cross over into candidate support or opposition? This is admittedly a gray area where the IRS Commissioner must evaluate facts and circumstances in trying to separate issue advocacy from candidate endorsement. An examination of the church's position, based on the documents posted on the website, is instructive about both the difficulties of the IRS's prohibition of intervention in political campaigns and the deeper church-state issues at stake in this controversy.

All Saints Church has cited its long history, tradition and reputation for liberal social activism. During the Second World War, its rector spoke out against the internment of Japanese Americans. The Rev. George Regas, who headed the church for 28 years before retiring in 1995, was well known for opposing the Vietnam War, championing women clergy and supporting gays in the church. Appealing to the Biblical prophetic tradition, the church stated that it must bring the perspectives of the Christian faith to bear in addressing moral aspects of public policies. As the Rev. Edwin Bacon, the current rector, noted, "Our faith mandates that we speak out against unjust or inhumane policies. Christians and the Christian churches cannot remain neutral or silent in the face of injustice."

At the same time, church leaders have insisted that while All Saints is a social action church, it is not a politically partisan church. All Saints agrees with the IRS prohibition on church intervention in political campaigns and has a long-standing policy opposing partisan endorsements of candidates for public office. As Rev. Bacon wrote, "We have always been mindful of the IRS regulations against campaign intervention, respect those regulations, take steps to ensure compliance and have always been in compliance. We believe that All Saints has not engaged in campaign intervention on behalf of any particular candidate or party—not in October 2004 or at any other time."[25]

Furthermore, All Saints Church argued that the IRS actions in this case implicate First Amendment principles of religious freedom and freedom of speech and threaten core values and practices of the congregation. Owens explained that the Church "takes pride in a long history of active involvement in the community and a steadfast and theologically-based commitment to alleviating poverty and promoting equality, social justice and peace."[26] Church leaders defended the right and duty of the church to comment on public issues from a theological and moral perspective. They worried that the actions of the IRS in this case would have a potentially chilling impact on protected First Amendment rights.

The standard IRS response to this argument is to say that rights-talk is irrelevant because tax exemptions are not rights but benefits, conditional upon accepting the burdens of restricting involvement in partisan politics. But All Saints officials challenged this characterization of their case. As Rev. Bacon stated, "All Saints is energetically resisting the IRS's interpretation of the IRS regulations. The IRS is arguing that they can investigate a church based on a field officer's *subjective* determination that a preacher's sermon *implicitly* opposes or endorses candidates, regardless of the *explicit* statements of the preacher. This means that any sermon that states a church's core values, when proclaimed during an election season, can be subjectively deemed to be campaign intervention. If this IRS interpretation stands, that means that a preacher cannot speak boldly about the core values of his or her faith community without fear of governmental recrimination."[27] Hence the conclusion that perhaps the government's position has a potentially repressive effect on protected speech.

Finally, All Saints Church challenged directly the IRS's interpretation of its 501(c)(3) prohibition of intervention in political campaigns. Church officials questioned the meaning of the term *political*. Church leaders use the term broadly to mean how we apply values to public life, whereas the IRS tends to define the term narrowly to refer to campaigns and elections for public office. According to Rev. Bacon, "Faith in action is called politics. Spirituality without action is fruitless and social action without spirituality is heartless. We are boldly political without being partisan."[28] This distinction between political and partisan is a central element in the overall argument of All Saints Church. It clarifies their argument and their challenge to the IRS. As Bacon stated:

No church should be at risk of losing its tax-exempt status because its clergy express a congregation's core moral and theological values. There is a huge distinction to be made between political and partisan. Moral values form the foundation for much public political discourse and action. They can be presented in a non-partisan way. That distinction is threatened by the IRS position. Preaching that the war in Iraq is immoral and that poverty in America must be reduced are not partisan positions—they are core moral beliefs at All Saints. We, in fact, have no argument with the tax law as it stands, and we take great pains not to trespass over a wise boundary into partisan campaign intervention.[29]

MORAL ISSUES IN CHURCH ELECTIONEERING

The cases of All Saints Church and the Church at Pierce Creek are reminders that churches have constitutional rights to contribute to public debate and to address the moral dimensions of public policies, and that clergy have rights as private individuals to participate in the political process (they do not give up their civil rights at ordination). At the same time, church leaders must be careful in their public witness not to violate federal law banning electioneering by non-profits. These are the *legal* realities churches face in American public life. But churches, temples, and mosques face serious *moral* issues as well. These concern permissible, prudent conduct by churches and clergy as they seek to contribute to public debate on a variety of issues. Beyond legal restrictions on church politicking, it is necessary to consider moral dilemmas that arise for church leaders and congregants in cases where:

1. Church leaders criticize a political candidate for not being religiously orthodox, thereby implying that the candidate is unfit for public office. This might be considered indirect political endorsement.
2. Church leaders criticize a candidate for refusing to translate the church's moral teaching into public policy (on, for example, contraception, abortion, gay marriage, or stem-cell research). This raises basic questions about the relation between law and morals—between religious belief, public morality, and public policy.
3. Church officials announce that it would be "sinful" to vote for a candidate. This is tantamount to issuing voting instructions from the pulpit for doctrinal or religious reasons. (It is different from a clergyman stating simply that he favors or opposes candidate X in an election). As we shall see, these cases are not that uncommon in American politics. They raise moral questions about what it is right for clergy to do, rather than legal questions about what churches may do while retaining their tax-exemption.

To some extent, these actions by church leaders concern internal matters—issues of belief, conformity or nonconformity to doctrine, membership criteria and policies. Pastors may, for example, discipline or sanction church members for beliefs or practices regarded as false, wrong, or inappropriate. However, when a church member is simultaneously a candidate for public office, internal sanctions may have external effects. They may color the perception of a candidate by other citizens who are not church members. In effect, sanctions for religious reasons may be an indirect way that church officials can politically endorse or oppose a candidate for public office.

Churches and Identity Politics

Direct political endorsement by a clergyman is illustrated by the conduct of former Congressman Floyd Flake who, in February 2000, as pastor of a New York City church, invited Al Gore to speak to his congregation. Pointing to Gore, Rev. Flake said, "I don't do endorsements from across the pulpit because I never know who's out there watching the types of laws governing separation of church and state. But I will say to you this morning and you read it well: This should be the next president of the United States." Predictably, the IRS investigated, Flake conceded he had broken the law, and signed an agreement not to do it again.[30]

But clergy sometimes engage in what might be called indirect political endorsement. That is, church leaders criticize the religious orthodoxy of candidates who are church members, thereby implying that such candidates are untrustworthy, unreliable, and unfit for public office. Such negative criticism of, and implied opposition to, political candidates occurred in the 1984 vice-presidential campaign of Geraldine Ferraro and, most recently, in the 2004 presidential campaign of John Kerry. In both cases, church authorities suggested that these candidates were not authentically Catholic because their views on abortion policy did not accord with the policy views of church leaders. By challenging directly the religious orthodoxy of a candidate, church leaders implied indirectly that the candidate was generally unreliable, unreasonable, inconsistent, and morally suspect. There are other instances of church officials employing litmus tests of religious orthodoxy to influence elections, but these two cases are perhaps the most egregious examples of indirect political intervention by churches.

In the United States, politicians usually want to be seen by voters as loyal church-goers partly because this helps to confer legitimacy on their campaigns. Awareness of this gives church leaders some leverage over candidates who are also church members. For example, during the 2004 elections, former Senate majority leader Tom Daschle was told privately by his bishop in South Dakota to remove the word "Catholic" from his campaign literature because of his pro-choice position on abortion. From the perspective of his church, Daschle's unorthodox views on abortion policy called into question his ability to present himself publicly as a Catholic.[31] The treatment of Senator Daschle was mild, however, when compared with church officials' actions during the Ferraro and Kerry campaigns.

In 1984, Walter Mondale, Democratic candidate for president, made history by selecting as his vice-presidential running mate Geraldine Ferraro, the first woman ever to run on a major party ticket for high national office in the United States. While most Americans celebrated this important "first" in American politics, the leaders of Ferraro's church did not. In contrast to fellow citizens who welcomed this historic advance towards genuine political democracy, prominent Catholic bishops reacted to Ferraro's nomination with a concerted effort to undermine her candidacy because of her position regarding abortion policy.

Ferraro, a Democrat and a Catholic, was a three-term Congresswoman from New York who, though personally opposed to abortion, supported a woman's legal right to choose. While Ferraro accepted her church's teaching that abortion was wrong, she did not believe that she had a moral duty as a lawmaker to translate her church's teaching into civil law. She cited her experience as a prosecutor of rape and child abuse cases in the Queens County District Attorney's office in the mid-1970s, an experience which educated her to an awareness of the complexity of the abortion issue and bred in her a reluctance to use the coercive sanction of the law to exact from non-Catholics adherence to the demands of the church's moral theology.[32]

Ferraro was subjected to a barrage of attacks by Catholic bishops who questioned whether Catholic politicians could separate their personal convictions from their public stance on abortion. New York Archbishop John O'Connor charged Ferraro with misrepresenting church teaching on abortion. Insisting that he would never tell anyone to vote "for her or against her," O'Connor told reporters, "The only thing I know about her is that she has given the world to understand that Catholic teaching is divided on the subject of abortion. Geraldine Ferraro doesn't have a problem with me. If she has a problem, it's with the Pope."[33]

Such a direct attack by a Catholic bishop upon a candidate for high public office is exceptional in American politics. It seemed to signal a real effort to discredit Ferraro in the eyes of Catholic voters as a disobedient churchwoman, presuming to defy church leadership. Other bishops chimed in. Cardinal John Krol of Philadelphia sent a message to all parishes of his archdiocese, stating publicly that "every Catholic is obliged in conscience to oppose abortion both as a personal decision and as a policy in society."[34] After organizers invited Ferraro to lead Philadelphia's Columbus Day parade, Krol threatened to pull out all the Catholic schools and bands if Ferraro marched. She withdrew, thereby allowing Philadelphia parade organizers to avoid a confrontation with Krol.[35]

In New York, O'Connor refused to invite Ferraro to the important Al Smith Dinner, an annual archdiocesan fund-raising event and nonpartisan banquet that Mondale could not attend. Bishops from Hartford, Buffalo, Scranton, Boston, Stockton (California), and from the New England states made statements critical of Ferraro and sought out photo opportunities with the Republican candidates, Ronald Reagan and George H.W. Bush. Departing from their professed role of being nonpartisan regarding the presidential election, church leaders continued to question Ferraro's orthodoxy and fidelity to church teaching. The implication was clear. If she was not a good Catholic, it was unlikely that she would be a good vice-president.

Twenty years later, the 2004 campaign of John Kerry, Democratic nominee for president, triggered an even more determined effort by Catholic clergy to undermine a political candidate by questioning his Catholic identity. Some Roman Catholic bishops declared that it was sinful to vote for Senator John Kerry because he was "pro-abortion." Other bishops announced that Kerry would be denied Holy Communion if he set foot in their dioceses, implying that he was not really Catholic because of his pro-choice stance on abortion policy. The ensuing debate about the use of religious sanctions against political candidates came to be known as "the Communion Wars."

Kerry's policy positions on three issues prioritized by conservative bishops—abortion, stem cell research, and gay marriage—differed from the policy views recommended by church leaders. Kerry, a life-long Catholic, supported legal abortion as well as federal funding for abortion. He voted against the ban on "partial birth" abortion because it did not allow for abortion when the life and/or health of the woman was endangered. He said he would appoint only judges who support abortion rights to the U.S. Supreme Court. On same-sex marriage, Kerry said he did not favor gay marriage, but opposed a federal constitutional amendment banning it and said individual states should decide. He supported civil unions and said he would, if elected, ban job discrimination against gays and also would extend hate-crime protections to gays and lesbians. On embryonic stem cell research, Kerry supported federal funding of such research while providing strict ethical guidelines to prevent abuse.[36]

Kerry questioned the wisdom of simply translating Catholic doctrine into public policy in a religiously diverse society. At the same time, Kerry made an effort to explain his Catholicism to voters during the presidential debates. He emphasized how important his faith was during his service in Vietnam and insisted that his Catholic faith "affects everything I do and choose." He described Catholic values—a vision of the common good, a sense of interdependence and solidarity, respect for individual rights and duties, the obligation to love one's neighbor, the idea that "faith without works is dead." While saying that he could not simply translate specific tenets of Catholic doctrine into public law, he tried to convey how a Catholic worldview and sense of values could and would inform his conduct as president.

Unbeknownst to Kerry, however, the pro-life movement, led by the American Life League, announced in January 2003 a new campaign to draw attention to Catholic politicians who support abortion rights. The League targeted 12 Catholic office holders for defeat, including Tom Daschle, Barbara Mikulski, Ted Kennedy, Christopher Dodd, Tom Harkin, Susan Collins, Patty Murray, John Kerry, Nancy Pelosi, and others.[37] For the next 20 months, the American Life League, together with other pro-life groups, pressured the American bishops to penalize Catholic politicians who made policy judgments at odds with those of their church leaders. This lobbying effort apparently convinced a handful of American bishops to announce they would sanction nonconforming Catholics by denying sacraments to such politicians and by warning voters that it would be sinful to vote for such candidates (arguably, a thinly disguised form of political intervention in an election).

In January 2004, Bishop Raymond Burke ordered priests of the La Crosse,

Wisconsin, diocese to deny Communion to state and federal lawmakers (including Democratic Congressman David Obey) who openly support "procured abortion or euthanasia." Burke said sanctions were necessary "in order that the faithful in the diocese not be scandalized, thinking that it is acceptable for a devout Catholic to also be pro-abortion."[38] In February 2004, Burke, who had since become archbishop of St. Louis, admonished Senator Kerry not to take Communion if he attended Mass there. In May 2004, Bishop Michael Sheridan of Colorado Springs went further, writing in a pastoral letter that Catholic politicians who support abortion rights, stem-cell research, homosexual marriage and/or euthanasia—as well as the voters who back them—could not receive Communion until they have "confessed in the sacrament of Penance." In other words, voting for John Kerry was sinful.[39]

By late spring of 2004, the public statements of a minority—some 15 bishops out of 300 American prelates—made it appear that the Catholic Church in the United States backed the Republican candidate for president. Not surprisingly, Catholic lawmakers protested the actions of these bishops. On May 10, 2004, forty-eight Catholic members of the House of Representatives, including about a dozen pro-life Democrats, sent a strongly worded letter to Cardinal Theodore McCarrick of Washington, stating that denying sacraments to an individual on the basis of a voting record "would be counter-productive and would bring great harm to the church." Furthermore, they emphasized, "We do not believe that it is the obligation of legislators to prohibit all conduct which we may, as a matter of personal morality, believe is wrong. Likewise, as Catholics, we do not believe it is our role to legislate the teachings of the Catholic church . . . Because we represent all of our constituents, we must, at times, separate our public actions from our personal beliefs."[40]

It would be an understatement to say that these events triggered intense controversy among Catholic clergy and laity (as well as non-Catholics) over the role of Catholics in American public life. The debate went on through most of the 2004 election season. Public opinion polls showed widespread disapproval of the bishops' actions among Catholics, with 72 percent of Catholics saying that denying Communion to lawmakers who support abortion rights was inappropriate.[41] The bishops themselves were deeply divided over the wisdom of sanctioning Catholic politicians. Prelates in New Orleans, St. Louis, Newark, Denver, and Camden favored sanctions, while the archbishops of Chicago, Los Angeles, New York, and Washington opposed Communion bans. Cardinal McCarrick summarized the objections to sanctions: "We should not tell people how to vote or sanction voters. This is contrary to our teaching, may be a violation of civil law and is often counterproductive." As for the practice of denying Communion to Catholic politicians, McCarrick noted "significant concern . . . that the sacred nature of the Eucharist could be trivialized and might be turned into a partisan political battleground." He urged renewed efforts at dialogue and persuasion rather than penalties. He concluded by saying the bishops needed to be "political but not partisan" as they exercised their teaching, pastoral, and leadership roles in the church.[42]

Others argued that sanctions were tried in the past and did not work. Barring pro-choice Catholic politicians from speaking engagements in Catholic institutions and banning them from receiving Holy Communion were measures tried in the late 1980s and early 1990s that did little to reduce the incidence of abortion.[43] Moreover, in sanctioning Catholic lawmakers, conservative bishops were adopting a tactic that was coercive rather than persuasive; such a tactic was wholly inappropriate in a presidential election campaign. It was also counter-productive and self-defeating. As one commentator noted, "The imposition of sacramental penalties reinforces the notion of abortion as a religious issue, a sectarian Catholic issue, rather than a human rights and bioethical issue; this will only confirm the views of those who accuse the pro-life movement of imposing specifically religious tenets upon the American people."[44]

But the most telling criticism of this church practice of sanctioning politicians had to do with its obvious partisanship. The bishops were selective in applying sanctions. During the 2004 Republican National Convention, for example, three pro-choice politicians were featured speakers: New York Governor George Pataki, California Governor Arnold Schwarzenegger, and former New York City Mayor Rudolph Giuliani. Nothing was said by any bishop about these pro-choice Catholics. Yet Senator Kerry was singled out by some bishops and threatened with denial of the Eucharist because of his policy views. He was running for president; they (the three Republicans) were not. Undoubtedly, the possibility of a pro-choice Catholic president was alarming to the American Catholic hierarchy. Indirect political endorsement was a solution to their problem. While they could not oppose Kerry directly, they could challenge his Catholicity and thereby cast suspicion on his fitness for the White House.

The partisanship was there for all to see. Because of the action of a handful of bishops, the official church appeared to be taking sides in a nationwide presidential election. The bishops themselves, in their quadrennial election-year statement, "Faithful Citizenship," acknowledged the need to be:

- Principled, but not ideological.
- Political, but not partisan.
- Clear, but also civil.
- Engaged, but not used.

But the actions of a few bishops, in the intensely polarized, red-state-blue-state climate of the 2004 presidential election, appeared to be endorsing a Republican over a Democrat. Such partisanship by church leaders in a presidential election is inappropriate. As one Catholic editor wrote, "If the fear that had to be dispelled in 1960 when John Kennedy ran for president was that the pope would somehow dictate U.S. policy, the fear I have in the wake of the 2004 race is that the church, at least in the public's perception, will be so aligned with one party that it will be severely compromised."[45]

Political Endorsements by Churches: Conflating Law and Morals

The controversy in the 1984 and 2004 presidential campaigns illustrates a second major dilemma that arises frequently in discussions of political endorsements by churches, namely the relation between law and morals. The 48 Catholic congressional representatives who challenged their church leaders during the 2004 election alluded to this distinction between legality and morality in their statement that it is not "the obligation of legislators to prohibit all conduct which we may, as a matter of personal morality, believe is wrong." These lawmakers were on firm ground.

Both American legal tradition and Catholic jurisprudence recognize that, while law and morality are related, they are not coterminous. Not every sin needs be made a crime. Prudence is necessary, which means looking to the possible consequences of banning abortion or any other behavior one regards as immoral. Public officeholders have a duty to estimate, as best they can, the consequences of, for example, reinstating restrictive abortion law. Policymakers must calculate the *efficacy* of restrictive laws (whether citizens will obey them), the *enforceability* of such laws (whether police will enforce them selectively, uniformly, or not at all), and the *effects* of such laws (whether, on balance, the negative effects of reinstating restrictive laws will outweigh the positive benefits). Thus, even if a popular consensus develops in favor of restrictive abortion laws, lawmakers (Catholic and non-Catholic alike) are still obliged to judge whether the proposed policy will make sound law.

But the conservative bishops ignored the moral duties politicians have to make sound law and public policy. Instead they sanctioned lawmakers whose policy views did not reflect the bishops' political judgments. They conflated legality and morality by, for example, insisting that the distinction between being pro-choice and pro-abortion was meaningless.

Traditional legal and political theory recognizes that there are limits to the law as a method of social control. Lawmakers must consider whether the measures they enact will achieve their intended effect or result in a situation far worse than the original problem the law was supposed to remedy. Driving abortion underground by re-criminalizing it, for example, is not necessarily what pro-life citizens and lawmakers intend, but it may be an unintended consequence of passing such restrictive laws. These questions of sound lawmaking assume even greater significance in a pluralistic, religiously diverse society, such as the United States, which is constitutionally committed to religious freedom and church-state separation. American lawmakers must function in this context. Congressman David Obey (D-WI), one of three Catholic politicians denied Communion by Bishop Burke, emphasized this fact in his public response to Burke's sanction, saying that Burke's actions bordered on the unconstitutional:

Bishop Burke has a right to instruct me on matters of faith and morals in my private life and—like any other citizen—to try by persuasion, not dictation, to affect my vote on any public matter. But when he attempts to use his ecclesiastical position to dictate to American public officials how the power of law should be brought to bear against Americans who do not necessarily share our religious beliefs, on abortion or any other public issue, he crosses the line into unacceptable territory. The U.S. Constitution, which I have taken a sacred oath to defend, is designed to protect American citizens from just such authoritarian demands.[46]

In suggesting that Bishop Burke exceeded the limits of his episcopal authority, Representative Obey defended the constitutional right and duty of lawmakers to make sound public policy. His criticism of the bishop for overstepping church-state boundaries implied that church leaders should respect the expertise legislators and policymakers have in governmental affairs.

Political Endorsements by Churches: Issuing Voting Instructions

Finally, several examples from the 2004 presidential election campaign illustrate another dilemma regarding churches and American politics, namely, church leaders using sermons and statements to issue voting instructions. On at least two occasions, church officials announced or implied that it would be sinful to vote for a particular candidate. Bishop Michael Sheridan of Colorado Springs stated that Catholic politicians who support abortion rights, stem-cell research, and gay marriage—and the voters who support them—must first go to confession before receiving Communion. Why? Because voting for politicians like Kerry and Ferraro was sinful. There was no nuance to Sheridan's position, no suggestion that there might be other reasons to vote for a candidate like Kerry, reasons having to do with a comparison of the two major-party candidates' views on issues of economic justice, poverty, healthcare, war and peace, and government accountability.

The Reverend Chan Chandler, a young minister who led a Baptist congregation of about 100 people in Waynesville, North Carolina, from 2002 to 2005, was another clergyman whose actions implied that he thought voting for a particular candidate such as John Kerry was sinful. In May 2005, Chandler was forced to resign from his congregation for asking members to "repent or resign" if they had voted for Kerry in the 2004 race.[47] During his tenure as pastor, Chandler set out to make his congregation politically active and endorsed President Bush from the pulpit during the 2004 campaign. He also announced that anyone who planned to vote for Senator Kerry stood for abortion and homosexuality and could either "repent or resign." Nine members said they were expelled from the church. According to one commentator,

Pastor Chandler insisted he had been within his rights to deny those folks membership—and he was correct up to a point. Pastors have the right to set the parameters for church membership. But many members of Chandler's congregation decided they did not care for Chandler's decision to link church membership to political affiliation. Many left the church. Among them were several Republicans. They had not voted for Kerry but could not tolerate a pastor who refused to respect political differences. Eventually, Chandler had to resign from the pastorate. Chandler had obviously made his political views known, but at what cost? His church was splintered, and he lost his job.[48]

When clergy announce from the pulpit or through a pastoral letter that it would be "sinful" to vote for candidate X (thereby opposing candidate X and implicitly endorsing candidate Y), they are engaging in yet another form of indirect political endorsement. For Rev. Chandler and Bishop Sheridan, the act of voting was a civic decision which they felt competent to evaluate in religious terms ["sinful," "repent," "confess in the Sacrament of Penance"]. This seems misplaced, improper and inappropriate. In effect, they made a category mistake, using inappropriate reasoning and language to evaluate public policies and political choices.

In a liberal democracy, it is improper for clergy to tell congregants how to vote. It is also arrogant. As Lynn notes, "It's insulting for any religious leader to assume that his congregants are too stupid to know what to do unless taken by the hand and led into the voting booth."[49] Such condescension or paternalism also runs counter to the egalitarian assumptions underlying democratic government. As Rousseau noted, equal citizenship is essential to political participation in a democratic republic.

Yet, as our examples indicate, issuing voting instructions is often done by clergy despite IRS strictures against political endorsements. Clergy are, after all, in positions of authority within congregations, and the temptation to abuse that authority is always present. Factors such as ecclesiology and conceptions of ministry may heighten the probability of overstepping boundaries. For example, if a church is hierarchically structured—organized in top-down fashion with local clergy appointed by bishops rather than selected by congregations—there may be little pressure from parishioners for what might be called "democratic accountability." If clerics see themselves as teachers who have privileged access to revealed truth, they may come to think of themselves as having expertise in other (non-religious) areas and as competent to tell folks in the pews how to vote. Similarly, if bishops define themselves as teachers of doctrine (as they do in the Roman Catholic tradition), they may feel that they have a pastoral duty to guide parishioners at the ballot box.

Assumptions like these underlay Bishop Burke's defense of his denial of Communion to pro-choice politicians. He said sanctions were necessary "in order that the faithful in the diocese not be scandalized, thinking that it is acceptable for a devout Catholic to also be pro-abortion." Bishops and pastors may feel they must protect their flock of sheep from being led astray and that this necessitates issuing voting instructions. But such paternalistic conceptions of church polity and church ministry are not easily squared with democratic citizenship. Bishops and clergy may have teaching authority within their churches, but in secular society they and their congregants are citizen equals and no longer involved in a hierarchical relationship.

This is not to belittle the religious authority of bishops or to suggest that pastors should not address public policy issues from a faith-based moral perspective. But in a liberal democracy, church leaders and parishioners must be clear about what is appropriate when making voting decisions. This is especially true within hierarchically structured churches such as the Roman Catholic Church. Catholics regard their bishops and priests as officially appointed teachers of religious doctrine and accord their judgments a certain degree of respect and deference. Problems arise, however, when bishops and clergy use the pulpit to suggest which *political* judgments citizens should make. While lay Catholics owe their religious leaders respectful consideration, they do not and cannot, as citizens in a democracy, abdicate their responsibility to make their own prudent political judgments about candidates and issues. Clergy who ignore these political realities act to undermine principles of democratic governance and civic participation. In using the privileges and trappings of religious authority to influence political decision-making, clergy fail to show proper respect for the political autonomy of their parishioners, who are, after all, their political equals in a liberal democracy.

CONCLUSION

The issue of political endorsements by churches is a complex matter that raises fundamental questions about religious freedom and church-state relations in the United States. IRS rules against church interventions in political campaigns fall under the larger category of government regulation of political lobbying and electioneering by tax-exempt non-profit organizations. Although there has been an increase in alleged violations of IRS restrictions on church electioneering in the 2000 and 2004 presidential elections, only one church to date has lost its tax-exempt status solely because of its partisan politicking. Other churches have been warned about illegal activity, and a few have been fined. Challenges to the federal tax law such as the All Saints Church case will continue, given the increased involvement of churches and religious organizations in American politics and society.

While churches risk losing their tax-exempt status by intervening in political campaigns, there are many issue-advocacy and voter-education activities they can conduct legally during an election season. However, there are some types of election-related activities, such as electioneering, which are questionable from a moral perspective. These forms of indirect political endorsement include challenging the religious orthodoxy of a candidate, thereby implying unfitness for public office; oversimplifying public policy issues by conflating legality and morality; and telling congregants it is sinful to vote for a particular candidate. In a religiously diverse society committed constitutionally to religious liberty and church-state separation, it seems imprudent and inappropriate for churches to engage in such borderline activities that leave them open to accusations that they are meddling in politics and breaching the wall of separation.[50]

In defense of religious organizations, it should be noted that churches, like All Saints Church in Pasadena, distinguish between being political and being partisan and claim they can legitimately address contemporary issues of politics and policy. So it seems proper to restate the moral-political arguments for and against church politicking. First, churches play a prophetic role in American society, calling attention to evil and injustice and urging citizens and governments to remedy wrongs and inequities. Church leaders have a right and duty to fulfill this prophetic calling. The American tradition of religious liberty and the constitutional provisions of the First Amendment protect this prophetic witness of the churches. More importantly, God trumps Caesar, that is, fidelity to God takes precedence over allegiance to country. So churches have little choice in the matter and must "speak truth to power." As Rev. Bacon states, "Our faith mandates that we oppose injustice."[51]

Second, church autonomy is an important value in a liberal society. Churches cannot play a prophetic role if they are inordinately dependent upon and beholden to the state, the culture, and the larger society. They must be counter-cultural at the same time that they work to remedy injustice and build up civil society. To preserve church autonomy, religious leaders insist upon their right, as church officials, to define doctrine, interpret and apply church teaching, set the parameters of church membership, govern their congregations and lead their congregants. Churches are voluntary societies in Lockean liberal theory and should, within limits, be free from intrusive government regulation.

However, as this chapter illustrates, churches can occasionally intrude upon the rights of citizens to participate in the political process and to live freely in society. If churches stress freedom for religion to flourish, separationists struggle to defend government from religious dominance and citizens from occasional clerical coercion. Separationists are vigilant about church intervention ("meddling") in politics because they are aware of a history of sectarian strife in European and colonial American history, and because the United States today is a pluralistic society committed to religious freedom and non-establishment. They therefore caution against excessive lobbying and electioneering by churches. Their warnings include the following: First, such activities can be terribly divisive of congregations and religious communities; they can encourage bitter hatred rather than brotherly love. Second, such activities are misplaced; they focus on the wrong issue, on the religious identity/orthodoxy of candidates instead of their public policy views and leadership potential. They come close to violating the constitutional provision against religious tests for public office. Third, the political interventions of church leaders are sometimes imprudent and unwise. It is very difficult to translate church teachings into public law without careful attention to policy consequences. Clergy would be wise to avoid the kind of reductionism that comes from conflating law and morals on controversial issues. Fourth, attempts by church leaders to issue voting instructions can undermine democratic citizenship. Bishops and pastors can and should proclaim church teaching, but they must leave ballot box decisions to the political judgments of informed citizens. Sanctioning congregants for their political judgments is inappropriate in a democratic society. Clergy must recognize and respect the fact that citizens can in good faith disagree with the political judgments of church leaders.

It is easy to say that a balance must be struck between religious freedom and the rights of churches on the one hand and the claims of democracy on the other. Obviously, churches need not be democratic in their internal structure; theological ideas about church polity and ecclesiology vary widely, as evidenced by the existence in the United States of hierarchically structured bodies such as Mormonism and Roman Catholicism. But in the United States, these churches operate in a political democracy with an egalitarian ethos. The challenge is to negotiate perhaps inevitable tensions between authoritative religions and a democratic society.

What can churches do to avoid IRS scrutiny and the moral pitfalls outlined here? First, they can be prophetic in calling attention to social injustice; secular society will always need their prophetic witness. They can contribute a moral dimension to public discourse and address moral aspects of public policy. They can clearly proclaim values and moral principles while leaving to citizens the difficult task of applying those principles to particular cases. Secondly, they can continue to build up civil society through the many educational and social assistance programs they already conduct. Finally, with respect to political campaigns, churches can contribute thoughtful analyses of major issues—on the dignity of human life, the need to help our neighbors, the duty of stewardship of creation, the necessity of devising policies that will make society more just. Proclaiming fundamental values on these and other issues will keep our churches and clergy busy enough.

NOTES

1. Office of General Counsel, United States Conference of Catholic Bishops, "2007 Political Activity Guidelines for Catholic Organizations," January 15, 2007, 3, http://www.usccb.org/ogc/guidelines.shtml. Americans United for Separation of Church and State is one of the few educational and advocacy organizations that lost its tax-exempt status because of excessive lobbying.

2. James D. Davidson, "Why Churches Cannot Endorse or Oppose Political Candidates," *Review of Religious Research* 40, no. 1 (September 1998): 16. See also Deirdre Dessingue Halloran and Kevin M. Kearney, "Federal Tax Code Restrictions on Church Political Activity," 38 *Catholic Lawyer* 105 (1998). Accessed on January 3, 2007 at http://web.lexis-nexis.com.proxy.libraries.rutgers.edu/universe/document. See also Patrick L. Daniel, "More Honored in the Breach: A Historical Perspective of the Permeable IRS Prohibition on Campaigning by Churches," 42

Boston College Law Review 733 (2001). Accessed on January 2, 2007 at http://web.lexis-nexis.com/universe/document.

3. Davidson, "Why Churches Cannot Endorse or Oppose Political Candidates," 17.

4. Halloran and Kearney, 106.

5. See *Christian Echoes National Ministry, Inc. v. United States* 470 F.2d 849 (10th Cir., 1964). As for the Christian Coalition, see Thomas B. Edsall and Hanna Rosin, "IRS Denies Christian Coalition Tax-Exempt Status," *Washington Post,* June 11, 1999, A4. In 1999 the Christian Coalition countersued the IRS. In 2005 a settlement was reached that secured the Coalition's status as a 501(c)(4) lobbying and educational institution. See Alan Cooperman and Thomas B. Edsall, "Christian Coalition Shrinks as Debt Grows," *Washington Post,* April 10, 2006, A01. Finally, in 1993, the IRS revoked the tax-exempt status of Jerry Falwell's organization, the "Old Time Gospel Hour," for two years because it used its personnel and assets to raise money for a political action committee. At that time, Falwell's organization also paid $50,000 in taxes and agreed to change its organizational structure to prevent any further violations. See Halloran and Kearney, "Federal Tax Code Restrictions on Church Political Activity," 38 *Catholic Lawyer* 105 (1998). These examples should clarify the difference between a church and a religious organization.

6. Alan Cooperman, "IRS Reviews Church's Status," *Washington Post,* November 19, 2005, A3.

7. Ibid. See also the comments of Owens in Patricia Ward Biederman and Jason Felch, "Antiwar Sermon Brings IRS Warning," *Los Angeles Times,* November 7, 2005. Marcus Owens is the attorney representing All Saints Church in Pasadena, which is under investigation by the IRS for violating the law against intervening in political campaigns and elections. This case is nationally known because the church is contesting the charge. The above newspaper materials are available at the Church's website, www.allsaints-pas.org.

8. Rob Boston, "Churches, Politics and the IRS," *Church & State,* 59, no. 8 (September 2006), 6. See also Laurie Goodstein, "IRS Eyes Religious Groups as More Enter Election Fray," *New York Times,* September 18, 2006, A20; Gillian Flaccus, Associated Press, "IRS Church Probe May Reverberate in Political Season," *The Star-Ledger,* September 21, 2006, 10; Stephanie Strom, "Anti-Abortion Group Loses Tax Exemption," *New York Times,* September 15, 2006, A16. [*The Star-Ledger,* based in Newark, is the leading major newspaper in New Jersey.]

9. Rob Boston, "Project Fair Play," *Church & State,* 59, no. 8 (September 2006), 11–12.

10. However, the IRS cautions that an issue advocacy communication may constitute intervention in a political campaign through the use of code words, such as "conservative," "liberal," "pro-life," "pro-choice," "anti-choice," "anti-family," "Republican," "anti-environment," or "Democrat," coupled with a discussion of a candidacy or election, even if no candidate is specifically named. Labeling candidates and thereby indicating approval or disapproval of a candidate should be

avoided. See Office of General Counsel, United States Conference of Catholic Bishops, *2007 Political Activity Guidelines for Catholic Organizations*, January 15, 2007, 8. See also Halloran and Kearney, "Federal Tax Code Restrictions on Church Political Activity," 3–4.

11. Everson's remarks are cited in Rob Boston, "Churches, Politics and the IRS."

12. In the 109th Congress, both of these bills died with the end of the Congress in January 2007 (they were not reported out to the floor for a vote).

13. This description is taken from the three federal court rulings in this case: *Branch Ministries v. Richardson*, 970 F.Supp. 11 (D.D.C. 1997); *Branch Ministries v. Rossotti*, 40 F.Supp. 2d 15 (D.D.C. 1999); and *Branch Ministries v. Rossotti*, 211 F.2d 137 (D.C. Cir. 2000); 341 U.S. App. D.C. 166 (2000). Branch Ministries, Inc., operated the Church at Pierce Creek. The ad is also described in Barry Lynn, *Piety & Politics: The Right-Wing Assault on Religious Freedom* (New York: Harmony Books, 2006), pp. 148–149. Lynn suggests that the case was "carefully choreographed" by Religious Right activists as a test case challenging the law banning partisan endorsements. He bases this supposition on the fact that the Church at Pierce Creek was the congregational home of Randall Terry, founder of Operation Rescue, an anti-abortion organization, and also on the fact that the Church at Pierce Creek was defended in later court proceedings by the American Center for Law and Justice, a litigational interest group founded by Pat Robertson.

14. Peter Applebome, "Religious Right Intensifies Campaign for Bush," *New York Times*, October 31,1992, A1; Anthony Lewis, "Tax Exempt Politics?," *New York Times*, December 1, 1992, A15.

15. *Branch Ministries Inc. v. Richardson*, 970 F.Supp.11 (D.D.C. 1997).

16. Ibid., 40 F.Supp.2d 15 (D.D.C. 1999).

17. Ibid., 40 F.Supp.2d 15 (D.D.C. 1999).

18. Ibid., 211 F.3d 137 (D.C. Cir., 2000). Judge Buckley added that the Church could create a political action committee through another entity, a 501(c)(4) organization separately incorporated. "Such organizations are exempt from taxation; but unlike their section 501(c)(3) counterparts, contributions to them [by donors] are not deductible. Although a section 501(c)(4) organization is also subject to the ban on intervening in political campaigns, it may form a political action committee that would be free to participate in political campaigns." Such a separately funded PAC fund could receive contributions and make expenditures in a political campaign. While he held this out as an "alternative means of political communication for the Church," Judge Buckley stressed that the Church could not use its tax-free dollars to fund such a PAC. See *Branch Ministries v. Rossotti*, 211 F.3d 137 (D.C. Cir. (2000). Jay Sekulow, chief counsel for the American Center for Law and Justice, which represented the Church, expressed disappointment at the appeals court's decision, but was "encouraged that this court appears to provide a blueprint for churches to express their beliefs in a political context." See Jeremy Leaming, "Federal Appeals Panel Upholds IRS Decision to Strip Church of Tax-Exempt Status," *The Freedom Forum Online*, May 15, 2000, http://www.firstamendmentcenter.org/news.aspx?id-7169. Noteworthy in this case were the *amicus curiae* briefs

filed at the appeals court level. The Family Research Council and Landmark Legal Foundation supported Branch Ministries while Americans United for Separation of Church and State and People for the American Way filed briefs in support of the Internal Revenue Service.

19. A virtually complete record of the correspondence between the IRS and All Saints Church, plus the original sermon and related documents, is accessible on the church's website: www.allsaints-pas.org

20. Josh Getlin, "The Race for the White House: Pulpits Ring with Election Messages," *Los Angeles Times,* November 1, 2004.

21. Patricia Ward Biederman and Jason Felch, "Antiwar Sermon Brings IRS Warning," *Los Angeles Times,* November 7, 2005.

22. Rev. J. Edwin Bacon, Jr., Rector, All Saints Church, "The IRS Goes to Church," a sermon preached at All Saints Church, Pasadena, California, November 13, 2005. Accessible at www.allsaints-pas.org.

23. Media interviews included Rev. Ed Bacon's appearances on the *Lehrer Newshour* on PBS, February 3, 2006; National Public Radio's *All Things Considered,* December 16, 2005; and National Public Radio's *Weekend America,* March 4, 2006. Editorials supporting All Saints Church have appeared in the following newspapers: *New York Times,* November 22, 2005; *Chicago Sun-Times,* November 22, 2005; *Washington Times,* November 14, 2005; *Miami Herald,* November 11, 2005; *Dallas Morning News,* November 11, 2005; *Seattle Times,* December 2, 2005; *Pasadena Star News,* December 2, 2005; *St. Louis Post-Dispatch,* November 9, 2005; and *The Christian Century,* November 29, 2005.

24. Alan Cooperman, "IRS Reviews Church's Status," *Washington Post,* November 19, 2005, A03. See also Jason Felch and Patricia Ward Biederman, "Conservatives Also Irked by IRS Probe of Churches," *Los Angeles Times,* November 8, 2005, www.latimes.com/newes/local/la-me-irs8nov08.

25. Rector Ed Bacon and Senior Warden Bob Long, "Where We Are With the IRS: A Special Update for the Parish," appended to the *2006 Annual Report of All Saints Church,* October 8, 2006. See www.allsaints-pas.org.

26. Letter to IRS from Marcus Owens, October 11, 2005, 2.

27. Rev. Edwin Bacon, "The IRS Goes to Church," Sermon at All Saints Church, November 13, 2005, 2.

28. Ibid.

29. "All Saints Rector Thanks [Congressman] Schiff for Letter to IRS and Treasury," Press Release, November 16, 2005.

30. This example is from Barry W. Lynn, *Piety and Politics* (New York: Harmony Books, 2006), 155–156.

31. Bishop Robert Carlson of Sioux Falls, South Dakota, instructed Daschle to remove from his Congressional biography and campaign documents all references to his being Catholic. Briefs, "In Catholic Circles," *Conscience* (Summer 2003), 9.

32. Geraldine A. Ferraro with Linda Bird Francke, *Ferraro: My Story* (New York: Bantam Books, 1985), 215–218.

33. *New York Times,* September 9, 1984, p. 34. See also Mary C. Segers, "Fer-

raro, the Bishops, and the 1984 Election," in *Shaping New Vision: Gender and Values in American Culture*, ed. C.W. Atkinson, C.H. Buchanan, and M.R. Miles (Ann Arbor: UMI Research Press, 1987), 143–167. [The Harvard Women's Studies in Religion Series.]

34. Cardinal John Krol, "Protecting God's Precious Gift," A Message to be Read at All Parishes of the Archdiocese of Philadelphia, on Respect Life Sunday, October 7, 1984; reprinted in ed. Daughters of St. Paul, *Life, A Gift of God: U.S. Catholic Leaders Speak Out on Life Issues* (Boston: Daughters of St. Paul, St. Paul Editions, 1985), 53.

35. Ferraro, *Ferraro: My Story*, 231–232.

36. On these three issues prioritized by conservative Catholic bishops during the 2004 campaign, Kerry's policy position differed from that recommended by his church. The Catholic Church opposes abortion as the unjustified destruction of innocent human life and favors restricting abortion rights, if not completely delegalizing the practice. The church strongly opposes same-sex marriage as well as civil unions—while also opposing discrimination against gays and lesbians. The church supports adult stem cell research but opposes embryonic stem cell research because it involves the destruction of human life (living human embryos).

37. Joe Feuerherd, "Public Life, Public Dissent," *National Catholic Reporter* 39, no. 29 (23 May 2003), 3.

38. NCR Staff, "Bishop Denies Communion to Politicians Who Support Abortion and Euthanasia," *National Catholic Reporter* 40, no. 12 (23 January 2003), 5.

39. Bishop Michael G. Sheridan, "A Pastoral Letter to the Catholic Faithful of the Diocese of Colorado Springs on the Duties of Catholic Politicians and Voters," EWTN News Feature, May 14, 2004, www.EWTN.com. Accessible on http://www.freerepublic.com/focus/f-religion/1135851/posts. See also Associated Press, "Group Asks IRS to Revoke Catholic Diocese's Tax Exemption," May 28, 2004, http://www.firstamendmentcenter.org/news.aspx?id=13441&printer-friendsly=y

40. *New York Times*, May 20, 2004, A1. See also Andrew Walsh, "Kerry Eucharistes," *Religion in the News*, Vol. 7, No. 2 (Summer 2004), 4.

41. The PEW Research Center for the People and the Press, "Religion and the Presidential Vote," December 6, 2004. See http://people-press.org/commentary/display.php3?AnalysisID=103. A *Time* magazine poll of Catholic voters in May 2004 found that 75 percent disapproved of bishops using bans to discipline Catholic pro-choice politicians.

42. Jerry Filteau, "Cardinal McCarrick: No Simple Answers on Bishop-Politician Relations," *Catholic News Service*, June 23, 2004.

43. A noteworthy example of the use of church sanctions occurred in 1989. On November 15, three weeks before a special run-off election for the California State Senate, Bishop Leo Maher of San Diego prohibited Catholic State Assemblywoman Lucy Killea, a contender for a Senate seat that would tip the balance to a pro-choice majority, from receiving Holy Communion because of her pro-choice position on abortion. In the December 5 election, Killea defeated favored Republican opponent Carol Bentley, thereby shifting the California Senate to a pro-choice majority.

Bentley attributed her stunning defeat to Maher's intervention in the political process. She claimed the bishop's action made Killea an "international celebrity and martyr." *New York Times,* December 6, 1989, A12. See also Catholics For a Free Choice, "Episodes in Abortion Politics," in *Everything You Always Wanted to Know About the Catholic Vote* (Washington, D.C.: CFFC, 1996), 20.

44. Robert W. McElroy, "Prudence and Eucharistic Sanctions," *America* 1982, no. 3 (January 31, 2005), 8–10.

45. Tom Roberts, Editor's Note: "A Few Bishops Seduced by Politics," *National Catholic Reporter* 40, no. 43 (8 October 2004), 2. "Faithful Citizenship" is the quadrennial report discussing the issues of each presidential election issued by the United States Conference of Catholic Bishops.

46. Joe Feuerherd, "Rep. Obey Unlikely Target of Church Discipline," *National Catholic Reporter* 40, no. 15 (13 February 2004), 3.

47. "Church Shaken By Remarks," *New York Times,* May 16 2005, A1, A19. See also Associated Press, "N.C. Church Split Highlights Divide Over Pulpit Politics," May 19, 2005. Available at www.firstamendmentcenter.org/news.aspx?id=15283.

48. Barry Lynn, *Piety & Politics* (New York: Harmony Books, 2006), 161–162.

49. Ibid., 162.

50. It should be noted that the examples of inappropriate, imprudent political intervention described here all seem to involve church partisanship on the side of the Republican Party or GOP candidates. I have been unable to find examples of blatant church partisanship favoring the Democratic Party. In the context of recent American politics, the following factors may explain why church partisanship has tended to favor the GOP. First, the resurgence of conservative evangelicals led them to become a powerful presence within the Republican Party. By the mid-1990s, they had gained control of at least 30 state GOP party organizations. As a result of this mobilization and political effort, conservative evangelicals have become a major party of the base constituency of the Republican Party. Second, several factors have facilitated entry of Roman Catholics into national politics—from the election of President John F. Kennedy in 1960 to changes in church teaching at the Second Vatican Council to greater church involvement in secular society as a result of Vatican II. In American politics and society, the end of the Cold War and the emergence of "culture wars" over contraception, abortion, and gay marriage have had the effect of mobilizing conservatives among both evangelicals and Catholics. Both of these groups have sought to preserve their religious communities against what they perceive as a morally degenerating culture. As conservatives, they would perhaps inevitably gravitate to the Republican Party. Among American Catholics, however, the political interventions of their bishops in electoral campaigns have deeply divided the Catholic community.

51. The fact that both liberal and conservative religious groups strongly support the Rev. Ed Bacon and All Saints Church in their challenge to the IRS indicates wide agreement among American church leaders about their right and duty to contribute to public debate about policy issues. Where churches differ, of course,

is how they prioritize issues. While All Saints Church tends to stress the importance of poverty and peace, the Church at Pierce Creek emphasizes issues such as abortion and same-sex marriage. This simply confirms what we know—that the American religious landscape is as pluralistic as American society generally (as a whole).

FURTHER READING

Controversies about religion and politics in American society have generated some excellent work on church-state relations, including Robert Miller and Ronald Flowers, *Toward Benevolent Neutrality: Church, State, and the Supreme Court* (Waco, TX: Baylor University Press, 1997) and Stephen V. Monsma and J. Christopher Soper, *The Challenge of Pluralism: Church and State in Five Democracies* (Lanham, MD: Rowman & Littlefield, 1997). Monsma and Soper examine church-state arrangements in five liberal democracies (United States, United Kingdom, Netherlands, Germany and Australia), criticize the model of strict church-state separation in American society, and suggest that Americans might learn from other nations how to promote government neutrality towards religion and genuine religious freedom. Several articles examine the historical roots of the ban on church intervention in political campaigns; these include James D. Davidson, "Why Churches Cannot Endorse or Oppose Political Candidates," *Review of Religious Research,* Vol. 40, No. 1 (September 1998), pp. 16–33; Patrick L. O'Daniel, "More Honored in the Breach: A Historical Perspective of the Permeable IRS Prohibition on Campaigning by Churches," 42 *Boston College Law Review* 733 (July, 2001); and Deirdre Halloran and Kevin Kearney, "Federal Tax Code Restrictions on Church Political Activity," 38 *Catholic Lawyer* 105 (1998). For classic work on churches and taxation, see Dean M. Kelley, *Why Churches Should Not Pay Taxes* (New York: Harper & Row, 1977), and Paul J. Weber and Dennis Gilbert, *Private Churches and Public Money* (Westport, CT: Greenwood Press, 1981). Finally, a useful examination of opposing views about recent religion-and-politics controversies in the United States is the book by Mary C. Segers and Ted G. Jelen, *A Wall of Separation: Debating the Public Role of Religion* (Lanham, MD: Rowman & Littlefield, 1998). This volume also contains relevant historic documents such as the writings of Jefferson and Madison, speeches of John F. Kennedy and Mario M. Cuomo, and pivotal Supreme Court rulings on church-state issues.

7

The Relevance of State Constitutions to Issues of Government and Religion

David K. Ryden

> *The text and history of the Establishment Clause strongly suggest that it is a federalism provision intended to prevent Congress from interfering with state establishments. Thus . . . it makes little sense to incorporate the Establishment Clause . . . As a textual matter, [the Establishment Clause] probably prohibits Congress from establishing a national religion. Perhaps more importantly, the Clause made clear that Congress could not interfere with state establishments . . .*
>
> —Justice Thomas (concurring in *Elk Grove Unified School District v. Newdow*, 2005)[1]

Justice Thomas's comments in *Newdow* were more than the idle musings of an isolated dissenting judge. Rather, they anticipated what is likely to be a key line of debate in the years ahead in the realm of church/state relations—the applicability of state constitutional religion clauses to church/state issues, and the interplay between state and federal constitutions in this area. Indeed, Justice Thomas's contemplation of a federalism-infused church/state jurisprudence is gaining support, on the Court and off.

This important constitutional development is already evident in several recent judicial decisions. In *Locke v. Davey* (2004), the U.S. Supreme Court affirmed the state of Washington's decision to exclude from a state scholarship program otherwise qualified candidates who intended to apply the scholarship to pursuing religious or pastoral studies majors in college. While opining that Washington *could* have included such students in the program consistent with the Establishment Clause of the First Amendment, the majority recognized the state's corollary right to exclude people according to its state constitution and the traditions and practices that had arisen under that constitution. Art. I, §11 of Washington's state constitution prohibited public money from being "appropriated for or applied to any religious worship, exercise or instruction, or the support of any religious establishment."[2] The Court, by a 7–2 margin (ironically with Thomas dissenting), found that the specific provision of the state constitution had been authoritatively interpreted as "prohibiting even indirectly funding religious instruction that will prepare students for the ministry . . . "[3]

Thirty-seven states have comparable constitutional amendments that explicitly address religion; they typically are far more precise in barring state support of religion than is the federal Establishment Clause. These "mini-Blaine amendments"—named after senator and presidential candidate James Blaine and his ultimately unsuccessful late nineteenth century efforts to amend the U.S. Constitution—have largely been ignored, in the wake of the incorporation of the Establishment Clause to apply against state and local governments. As a result, federal and state courts alike have tended to rely almost exclusively upon the federal Establishment Clause to resolve conflicts arising out of church/state interaction. Unfortunately, this approach has spawned an Establishment Clause jurisprudence lacking either clarity or coherency.

As criticism of Establishment Clause doctrine has persisted, voices from across the political spectrum have seriously challenged the wisdom and historical accuracy of a uniform all-encompassing church/state law based exclusively on the First Amendment of the U.S. Constitution. This essay explores the growing movement to elevate state law as a formative dimension of church/state law and considers the practical consequences that might flow from an injection of principles of federalism—creating greater space for states to develop independent religion policy based upon state constitutions—into church/state jurisprudence. A confluence of factors—including the ongoing problems with current Establishment Clause jurisprudence, the rise of the faith-based social services initiative, and its spread to states and localities—suggest that the time is ripe for a potentially dramatic shift in church/state constitutional doctrine.

THE TEXTUAL GROUNDS FOR STATE RELIGION POLICY: STATE CONSTITUTIONS

The outlines of a federalism-centered approach to church/state law are already discernible, on a theoretical level if not in practice, in the existing texts of state constitutions. The specific substantive provisions of state constitutions offer distinctive approaches to the regulation of government/religion interaction. A sizeable majority of states' governing documents explicitly address the role of religion relative to government, and they do so in widely varied ways. A cataloguing of state constitutional religion provisions demonstrates their considerable range and diversity:

- Thirty-seven state constitutions contain provisions that preclude public expenditures for the benefit of religiously affiliated organizations.
- Eleven states have general non-Establishment Clauses that largely echo the Establishment Clause of the U.S. Constitution.[4]
- Twenty-seven states have "no preference" provisions that probably would be interpreted as being less stringent than the First Amendment.[5]
- Twenty-nine states have provisions that explicitly prohibit state funding for private and/or parochial schools.
- Ten states specify the kinds of aid that can or cannot be given to religious organizations, distinguishing between direct and indirect forms of aid. These provisions typically disapprove of direct spending on religious organizations but allow indirect aid, such as vouchers.

Finally, a handful of states ignore the church/state relationship altogether.[6]

In other words, the vast majority of states has constitutionally codified their values regarding the appropriate intersection of government and religion but have done so in markedly divergent ways.[7] Church/state interaction is heavily regulated at the state constitutional level, but that regulation varies in ways that fit with or correspond to the particular views and values of individual states. Hence, "some states adhere to a church-state policy of strict separation, others adhere to a position of neutrality, and still others show favoritism toward religion."[8]

THE ESTABLISHMENT CLAUSE AND THE TRUMPING OF FEDERALISM

The rich tapestry of church/state law embodied in the texts of state constitutions has gone virtually unrealized in practice. Instead, state-based constitutional values have been trumped by a pre-emptive and uniform reliance upon the Establishment Clause of the U.S. Constitution. That plank of the federal constitution had, until the middle of the twentieth century, been largely dormant, receiving little attention from litigants or courts. This period of dormancy ended with the U.S. Supreme Court's 1947 decision in *Everson v. Board of Education*.[9] Since then, the Establishment Clause has governed church/state interaction, not only on the federal level, but at the lower levels of government as well.

The First Amendment by its terms included only the federal government. It was Congress alone that was warned off laws respecting religion. Given this, how has the Establishment Clause become the last word on all church/state interaction across all levels of government? The answer lies in the process of incorporation, a doctrinal tool by which the Supreme Court has applied most of the rights of the Bill of Rights to states and localities via the Fourteenth Amendment and the "due process" and "privileges and immunities" it affords all citizens.

By 1947, the Court already had held a number of First Amendment rights to be incorporated through the Fourteenth Amendment to all governmental entities. Its incorporation of the Establishment Clause in *Everson* was another step in that direction, assuring that the Court's interpretations of that provision would likewise bind the actions of lower levels of government as well as Congress. *Everson* ushered in the modern era of church/state jurisprudence, in which the Court has consistently and actively regulated relations between religious actors and governmental actors from the local to the national level.

Consequently, the constitutional treatment of church/state relations has been identical for all governmental entities. The Supreme Court's interpretations of the Establishment Clause have been relied upon not just by federal judges; state courts have been complicit in yielding the delineation of church/state parameters to Supreme Court precedents and federal court interpretations of those precedent. When faced with church/state disputes, state courts overwhelmingly have fallen back on Supreme Court interpretations of the Establishment Clause rather than carving out an independent religion policy based upon their respective state constitutions. This uniform acceptance of the federal Establishment Clause's applicability to the states has effectively forestalled any reliance upon state constitutions and their textual treatment of religion. Thus has the potential for distinctive state constitutional treatment of religion that exists on paper failed to materialize in fact.

REVISITING THE FRAMING OF THE ESTABLISHMENT CLAUSE: JURISDICTIONAL OR SUBSTANTIVE?

The federalism movement in the context of church/state doctrine is grounded in a strong intellectual challenge to incorporation in light of the text and historical roots of the Establishment Clause. That challenge consists of a twofold attack on the Court's incorporation of the Establishment Clause in *Everson*. The first argument focuses on the original intent underlying the drafting of the Establishment Clause, the second on the questionable wisdom of incorporation in light of that original intent.

There are two competing views of the overriding objectives behind the drafting of the Establishment Clause. One is easily stated, since it has been the dominant principle upon which church/state doctrine has been founded for the past sixty years. It holds that the Establishment Clause reflected a basic commitment to the substantive value of disestablishment. This *substantive* view asserts that the Establishment Clause was meant to shape and govern the very nature and make-up of the relationship between government and religious institutions. It was adopted in *Everson* in 1947 and has been steadfastly adhered to ever since. Consequently, the long line of Establishment Clause cases since *Everson* has revolved around whether particular points of contact or interaction between government and religion are permissible under the First Amendment.

The federalism movement is grounded in an alternative understanding, one that contends that the substantive view is at best woefully incomplete, and at worst patently incorrect. Reflected in the pronouncements of Justice Thomas and advanced by a number of scholars, this *jurisdictional* view holds that the Establishment Clause was less about substantive values than it was about setting parameters for the jurisdictional authority over church/state matters. Justice Thomas, in his concurring opinion in *Newdow*, invoked this jurisdictional interpretation as he summarized the historical objectives of the framers of the Establishment Clause:

The text and history of the Establishment Clause strongly suggest that it is a federalism provision intended to prevent Congress from interfering with state establishments . . . it protects state establishments from federal interference but does not protect any individual right . . . (*Newdow*, 542 U.S. 1 [2004])

Thomas was relying upon an extensive body of scholarship that has been amassed regarding the intent underlying the Establishment Clause. Historical analyses provide substantial support for the claim that it was in large part, if not predominantly, a provision concerned with federalism.[10] That is, its aim was to maintain the regulation of church/state affairs as a preserve of the states rather than of the centralized government. This historical argument views the Establishment Clause at its core as a procedural and jurisdictional provision more than a substantive constitutional principle. In contrast to the contemporary substantive understanding of the Establishment Clause, the thrust of the clause was not to separate things religious from those governmental. It imposed no particular constitutional theory of church/state relations on the country, nor did it reflect any value or judgment one way or the other on government/religion interaction.

Rather, the Establishment Clause was "agnostic" on the issue of religious establishment in keeping with the absence of broader consensus across late eighteenth-century America on the overarching subject of church/state separation. The Establishment Clause confronted that lack of consensus by striking the only workable compromise; it procedurally removed the federal government from legislating or regulating the entire affair. Congress was without authority either to disestablish or establish. Instead, the clause left the "unfettered choice between establishment and disestablishment . . . to the states."[11] This "antidisestablishmentarian principle" was meant to prevent "Congress from abolishing state laws that were constitutionally deemed, or judicially deemed, to be religious establishments . . . [and to prevent] Congress from deciding for the nation what state laws excessively favor or disfavor any religion."[12]

Under this jurisdictional scheme, each state reserved the right to settle on whatever forms of religious establishment, if any, that it preferred.[13] By prohibiting Congress from interfering with local religion-related laws, the First Amendment ensured "what the Federalists had said was already implicit in the Constitution: that '[t]here is not a shadow of right in the general government to intermeddle with religion.'"[14]

This interpretation rings true in light of circumstances existing in the states at the time of the framing. State practices regarding religion were widespread and varied, with assorted degrees of toleration and religious establishment.[15] In stark contrast to these wide-ranging state policies, no federal policy on religion existed at all. Understanding the Establishment Clause as a federalism provision coincided with the view of the country as comprised of relatively autonomous states.[16] It made sense that such autonomy would extend to religion policy, especially since it was virtually absent on a nationwide scale.

The jurisdictional reading of the Establishment Clause also meshes with the understanding of the Bill of Rights as a whole, the overall purpose of which was to serve the dual goals of protecting personal rights *and* restricting federal power.[17] As Daniel Dreisbach asserts in his historical study of Jefferson's "wall of separation" metaphor, the enactment of the Bill of Rights served two objectives. One was to ensure that the federal government would not encroach upon the civil religious liberties of individuals, the second to protect states against the federal government's possible usurpation of states' jurisdiction over civil and religious liberties.[18]

Dreisbach's analysis suggests that Jefferson's "wall of separation" metaphor has miscast the First Amendment as primarily about church-state relations instead of church-federal relations.[19] The overall thrust of the Bill of Rights was to harness and constrain the power of the federal government. Added to the Constitution at the behest of anti-federalists, it limited the power and reach of the central government, not only in its application against individuals but also against states. While various amendments undeniably carved out substantive rights for protection, the Bill of Rights was a blend of substantive and structural, with the structural aimed at preserving states rights from a potentially domineering federal government.[20]

This duality was exemplified in the religion clauses. On one hand, the Free Exercise Clause safeguarded the individual right to religious freedom; on the other hand, the Establishment Clause restricted federal power to interfere with or subvert state action regarding that right.[21] From this vantage point, the two religion clauses do not exist in tension with each other; rather they fit together logically and coherently. Thus does the jurisdictional understanding of the Establishment Clause fit neatly with the specific text of the First Amendment and with the overarching theory of the Bill of Rights as a whole.[22]

In the end, the jurisdictional interpretation of the Establishment Clause is premised on principles of limited government and federalism. Congress was limited to its enumerated powers, which did not include religion policy. As such, it lacked authority over the subject of religion, which consequently was reserved as a matter of state and local policy.[23] From this perspective, the top-down, uniform church/state jurisprudence of the past sixty years is a historical aberration. At the very least, the Establishment Clause has a significant federalism dimension or component aimed at protecting states from federal meddling in the realm of religion.[24]

The original intent behind the Establishment Clause does not end the current debate over the authority of states to develop distinctive religion policies apart from federal constitutional law. If the post–Civil War Fourteenth Amendment was enacted with a specific intent to apply principles of separation to the states, that would override the jurisdictional intent underlying the Establishment Clause. One must then evaluate the propriety of the *Everson* Court's decision to incorporate the Establishment Clause.

WHY IT MATTERS: THE ILLOGIC OF ESTABLISHMENT CLAUSE INCORPORATION

The thrust of incorporation was to extend federal policies over states. To the extent the original clause was jurisdictional in part or in whole, it was intended to insulate states (and by extension existing state religion policies) from an overly intrusive federal government. And if the jurisdictional objective was to safeguard states' control from federal pre-eminence, that seemingly would render the Establishment Clause more resistant to or immune from incorporation. With respect to religion, incorporation would push uniform, nationwide disestablishment principles upon states in a manner directly contrary to the underlying jurisdictional nature of the Establishment Clause.

Understanding the Establishment Clause as a reflection of federalism raises the burden of proof for those arguing for full-scale incorporation via the Fourteenth Amendment. The Establishment Clause understood as a states rights provision renders it by its very nature resistant to incorporation, if not manifestly incorporation-proof, absent some compelling definitive evidence to the contrary. Hence incorporation presents a logical problem. How can the Court incorporate against the states a provision that the historical evidence indicates was designed at least in part to protect the states? If the Establishment Clause was intended to bar the federal government from interfering with state authority in the realm of religion, incorporation of that provision against the states turns it on its head. Incorporation achieves precisely the opposite result of that which was intended, eliminating state authority that the First Amendment was designed to ensure.[25]

Justice Thomas cited this contradiction in his *Newdow* opinion—"an incorporated Establishment Clause prohibits exactly what the Establishment Clause protected—state practices that pertain to 'an establishment of religion.'" Thus does it make "little sense to incorporate the Establishment Clause."[26] As Akhil Amar puts it, "to apply the [establishment] clause against a state government is precisely to eliminate its right to choose whether to establish a religion—a right explicitly confirmed by the Establishment Clause itself!"[27] It is impossible, therefore, for the Establishment Clause to be incorporated without "eviscerating its raison d'etre," namely its original federalist purpose.[28] The practical result of an incorporated Establishment Clause has been the reverse of what was intended. By nationalizing the legal jurisprudence regulating church/state relations, incorporation "[suspended] the federalism concerns implicit in the Religion Clauses."[29]

Opponents of incorporation also raise an ancillary objection; that the jurisdictional aims of the Establishment Clause differ from the usual justification for incorporation. Incorporation by way of the Fourteenth Amendment typically is rooted in the protection of individuals from deprivations of liberty. Incorporation was designed to promote and preserve fundamental dimensions of liberty. Thus the incorporation of free speech and press, religious exercise, and other individual liberty interests.

But the Establishment Clause was not an expression of individual liberty, but rather "a structural limit upon federal power and a reservation of authority to the states."[30] It lacked the explicit language of the expressive rights clauses (speech, press, petition, assembly, religious exercise) of the First Amendment, which on their face are purely, simply, and undeniably about rights. The Establishment Clause instead invokes bland, ambiguous language about laws "respecting the establishment of religion."[31] Again, the Establishment Clause seen as a jurisdictional provision presents fundamental problems for incorporation. It does not involve a liberty akin to those core liberties in the Bill of Rights at which Fourteenth Amendment incorporation was aimed. It lacks the compelling basis for incorporation that exists in other instances.

THE COURT, INCORPORATION, AND *EVERSON*

Nevertheless, incorporation still would be appropriate if there were evidence that the Fourteenth Amendment was intended to encompass the Establishment Clause. The original historical foundation for the Establishment Clause is relevant to the question of incorporation, but it is not irrefutable. The framers of the Fourteenth Amendment could have intended specifically to include disestablishment within the meaning of "due process" or "privileges and immunities."[32] If so, the Fourteenth Amendment would supersede the earlier intent of the Establishment Clause. But incorporation of the Establishment Clause should have required explicit, convincing proof that the framers of the Fourteenth Amendment so intended.[33]

Unfortunately, Justice Black's *Everson* opinion failed to come close to meeting that burden. *Everson* achieved incorporation largely by judicial sleight of hand, thus assuring that it would be the object of scholarly disparagement, if not outright derision, for decades to come. The decision to incorporate was made in an offhanded fashion, as if it were a given. Justice Black made virtually no effort to discern a historical or textual rational for incorporation; he simply asserted that "The First Amendment, as made applicable to the states by the Fourteenth, commands that a state 'shall make no law respecting an establishment of religion, or prohibiting the free exercise thereof . . .'" As Harvard law professor Mary Ann Glendon noted, it was striking "how little intellectual effort the Court devoted . . . to the enormously complex issues created by the effort to make the establishment language of the First Amendment binding on the states."[34]

Black and the other justices in *Everson* accepted without reflection or independent justification that the incorporation of other First Amendment rights warranted incorporation in this case.[35] They did little to anchor the incorporation decision in the text, framers' intent, or history of either the First or the Fourteenth Amendments. This cursory treatment of incorporation of the Establishment Clause to the states was "unreflective" and "deeply unsettling," demonstrating a "willful ahistoricity" on the part of the Court.[36]

Nor has much come to light since *Everson* that would suggest the Court might have been able to justify incorporation, had it been interested in doing so. On one hand, it seems likely that the framers of the Fourteenth Amendment had lost interest in preserving religious "establishments" in the states. Most states had voluntarily disestablished by the time of the passage of the Fourteenth Amendment. But this is not the same as concluding that the drafters of the amendment intended to go further and end all state involvement with religion. A majority of the states continued to practice governmental accommodation of religion in one form or another.[37] In sum, the historical evidence strongly supports the conclusion that "whatever else the Framers of the Fourteenth Amendment may have intended, they did not intend to incorporate the Establishment Clause."[38]

A RETURN TO FEDERALISM IN CHURCH/STATE JURISPRUDENCE: WHY NOW?

The movement to reshape church/state doctrine in the mold of federalism seems finally to have acquired sufficient momentum to actually impact the law. Critiques of a uniform, one-dimensional law centered on the federal Establishment Clause are by no means new. The incorporation of the Establishment Clause in *Everson* launched a steady drumbeat of criticism. In 1954, Joseph Snee published a thorough and highly critical historical analysis of *Everson*.[39] Since then, attacks have surfaced intermittently—questioning the historical basis for the decision to incorporate, criticizing the logic of that decision, and generally panning the overall incoherency of a top-down church/state jurisprudence. The weight of the commentary clearly has been on the side of those who viewed incorporation as a mistake; yet the frequent challenges gained little traction in actually influencing or altering church/state constitutional doctrine.

Given the persuasiveness of these arguments, it is striking how universally unsuccessful and immaterial to actual constitutional practice they proved to be. The criticisms of incorporation, coming in fits and spurts, never quite disappeared for good, nor did they ever quite find a friendly reception among judges who might actually work to make a change in the law.

So what is behind the most recent push for a melding of federalism and faith? And why is it resonating after decades of falling upon deaf ears? One reason is simply the weight and breadth of the scholarly critiques of the incorporation of the Establishment Clause. A growing number of critics of Establishment Clause jurisprudence are offering increasingly sophisticated and rigorous arguments attacking the basic unitary premise upon which the past sixty years of church/state law has rested.[40] These are not merely accommodationists seeking justification for a more religion-friendly constitution. Rather, they include highly reputable constitutional scholars, some of whom are neutral or even skeptics on the broader question of church/state interaction.

Moreover, it certainly has bolstered the critics of Establishment Clause incorporation to find a sympathetic ear on the Court itself. Justice Thomas has repeatedly criticized *Everson* and called for a church/state jurisprudence that would allow for differences at the state level. Thomas's opinions seem to have energized those who seek to soften or scale back the role of the Establishment Clause in state-level issues.

Likewise, recent changes in the personnel on the Court raise the possibility that a federalism-based shift in church/state jurisprudence is no longer merely an abstract proposition. Unless the Supreme Court is amenable to revisiting its sixty-year history of jurisprudence under a fully incorporated Establishment Clause, the intellectual arguments, no matter how strong, are unlikely to carry much weight. Although counting Supreme Court votes is always a tenuous exercise, the Court may now be inhabited by a critical mass (i.e., a majority) of justices open to more fundamental change in church/state jurisprudence. The Court has been closely divided in recent years on church/state issues, with most of the important cases being decided by a vote of either 5–4 (*Van Orden v. Perry* [2005]; *McCreary County v. ACLU* [2005]; *Zelman v. Simmons-Harris* [2002]) or 6–3 (*Good News Club v. Milford Central School* [2001]; *Santa Fe Independent School Dist. v. Doe* [2000]; *Mitchell v. Helms* [2000]).[41]

The cleavages on the Court were especially apparent in the *Mitchell v. Helms* case, when a plurality of four justices stated their willingness to abandon the (in)famous and much maligned *Lemon* test in favor of a standard of strict neutrality. That collective stance was readily understood to be more accepting of government/religious interaction than *Lemon* would allow. Yet a fifth vote in favor of that looser standard proved elusive, at least until now. The substitution of Justice Sam Alito for the ever-cautious, restrained, and noncommittal O'Connor could place a majority of justices in the accommodationist camp, though only time will tell. Whether that translates into anything more than tinkering with current church/state doctrine likewise will have to await the arrival of more cases on the Court's docket.

Meanwhile, others have favored a federalism-based approach to church/state relations for quite different reasons and in pursuit of quite different ends. Those urging the need to look to state constitutions to resolve church/state conflicts are not solely on the right. Those ultimately seeking a more separationist church/state jurisprudence have witnessed a Supreme Court that in recent decades has grown increasingly sympathetic to the accommodation of religious activities by government. From their vantage point, state constitutions may be the last hope for barring the government doors (and coffers) from intrusion by religious enterprises and interlopers.

In particular, the much-awaited voucher decision in *Zelman v. Harris* (2004) was thoroughly disheartening to strict separationists. The Court's imprimatur on vouchers and other indirect forms of governmental support for religious institutions was the culmination of a series of decisions that gradually but inexorably loosened the constraints on church/state interaction. *Zelman* confirmed the general unreliability of the Supreme Court on matters of church/state separation, elevating the importance of state constitutions as the final barrier against more extensive involvement by government in the matters of the church, and vice versa. In the wake of *Zelman*, strict separationists embraced state mini-Blaine amendments as a constitutional firewall against greater church/state interaction.

Clearly various proponents of distinctive state religion policies under state constitutions have radically divergent views of the church/state law that might arise from the application of state constitutional law. But the fact that conservatives and liberals alike are willing to look to state provisions as determinative has paved the way for what was once purely theoretical to now be practically possible.

FAITH-BASED SOCIAL SERVICE POLICY AND FEDERALISM-BASED LAW

Finally, and perhaps most significantly, a natural vehicle has arrived which could transport church/state law into a new federalism-based phase. That vehicle is the policy of government-subsidized, faith-based social service delivery that has flourished in the past half-dozen years or so. The faith-based initiative has elevated questions about the intent of the Establishment Clause and its incorporation from the merely academic realm into that of actual constitutional practice, with potentially far reaching implications.

As a signature piece of the incoming Bush administration's domestic agenda in 2001, the faith-based initiative was conceived of primarily as a federal policy. When faith-based legislative proposals in Congress sputtered and died, the Bush administration moved to an administrative strategy to implement faith-based social service policies through the federal bureaucracy. But, while the policy was initially implemented on the federal level, that is no longer the case. It has by now spread across state and local governments throughout the country; today the faith-based initiative is driving "an expansion of church-state collaborations at the state and local level that deviate from a unitary 'one-size fits all' model."[42] As such, the policy might well necessitate a reconstituted church/state jurisprudence that mirrors the diversity of the policy itself.

In the past five years, faith-based social service policy has mushroomed into a pervasive, far-reaching, multifaceted endeavor. It now encompasses virtually every imaginable social service that government provides and has been implemented in richly diverse and widely varied forms and settings. Government-based social services that are delivered via religiously identified organizations range from correctional and prison programs to drug and substance abuse treatments, from adoption and family services to job training and mentoring for the difficult-to-employ. They include marriage support counseling and after-school mentoring, housing and short-term shelter assistance, emergency food and soup kitchens, and virtually every other form of aid imaginable.

In short, the stamp of federalism is imprinted all over this policy. Though the Bush administration was the driving force impelling the faith-based initiative forward, the mushrooming policy now functions at all levels of government. The degree to which faith-based policy has seeped down to, and been absorbed by, states and localities is remarkable. Consider the following benchmarks of federalism in this context:[43]

- *State legislation.* Between 2003 and 2005, twenty-seven states passed legislation that impacted in some way partnerships between state governments and faith-based organizations (FBOs). Of these twenty-seven, only one state adopted a more restrictive approach to church/state interaction. In the other twenty-six, the legislation minimally acknowledged, and usually enhanced, the delivery of social services by FBOs.[44]
- *State administrative action.* Similarly, twenty-eight states took significant administrative action on faith-based matters between 2003 and 2005. These included, among other things, (1) establishing faith-based offices, councils, or liaisons, (2) hosting summits, expos, or other events with a faith-based focus, and (3) an-

nouncing coordinated efforts with faith-based actors to attack certain problems (the aftermath of Hurricane Katrina, for example).[45]
- *Pre-existing faith-based activity.* The above figures may actually understate the degree of the faith-based activity at the state level. A number of states took no new action in the past few years, legislatively or administratively, because "longstanding relationships between state agencies and faith-based organizations and service providers" already existed.[46]
- *State liaisons.* By 2005, at least 32 states had a designated individual or office that bore the official responsibility of serving as liaison to the faith community in that particular state.[47] Many mid-sized and large cities also created similar offices or liaisons at the municipal level to better connect with the faith-based sector of those communities.

These statistics are only the tip of the federalism iceberg that is the faith-based policy. As of December 2006, thirty-three governors had formal strategies for expanding the involvement of FBOs across the range of social services.[48] Eleven states in the past several years provided capacity-building or start-up grants to assist FBOs as novice service providers.[49] An equal number have changed their procedures for soliciting grant proposals to make them friendlier to FBOs. A number of states have modified their contract processes to encourage smaller, neighborhood-oriented service providers (including FBOs) to participate. Many states have encouraged contractors to sub-contract with religiously affiliated providers as well.

These figures capture a central emphasis of the faith-based initiative: the devolution of church/state policy down to lower levels of government. Faith-based policy increasingly bears the hallmarks of federalism, reflecting in administration and substance the diversity of the range of jurisdictions where it can be found. This is so significant because the faith-based initiative may inevitably drive a jurisprudence that acknowledges and allows for the vast differences in implementation that exist in the policy across, and even within, the states.

Both the increase in church/state interaction in the wake of faith-based initiatives and the diverse forms that it has taken heighten the constitutional stakes. I have suggested elsewhere that government/religious sector social service collaboration is likely to be the decisive battlefield upon which the legal and constitutional battles over church/state relations will be waged in the coming years.[50] The faith-based initiative already has triggered extensive litigation over various aspects of government/religious sector partnerships.[51] Most of those lawsuits involve state-administered programs rather than the federal faith-based initiative.

Faith-based social service policy is sure to continue to generate substantial legal conflict over the acceptable interplay between religion and government. As the legal disputes over faith-based programs raise questions over an increasingly broad range of policy particulars, the search for a consistent, comprehensible, and lucid church/state doctrine will be more daunting and formidable than ever. It seems a misplaced hope, in light of past problems, that a single, uniform top-down standard would be minimally sufficient to answer the array of legal conflicts sure to arise. If history is any guide, the constitutional demands of the faith-based policy will overwhelm federal courts opting to rely solely upon the First Amendment of the U.S. Constitution.

The nature and breadth of faith-based policy and its implementation point toward a federalist constitutional regulatory approach. The more faith-based policy embodies the elements of federalism in its enactment and administration, the more compelling is the case for legal and constitutional regulations that parallel that federalism. If faith-based policy is a thoroughly federalized policy, so too perhaps should be the mode of regulating the policy constitutionally. As such, the ever-expanding arena of faith-based social service delivery provides a natural policy environment within which to carry forward the evolution of church/state law to reflect a federally diverse constitutional regime.

THE POLICY APPEAL OF A DECENTRALIZING CHURCH/STATE DOCTRINE

The status quo might be acceptable if the doctrinal efforts in the church/state area were even modestly satisfactory. But the utter confusion and incoherency that has characterized the Supreme Court's Establishment Clause jurisprudence lend credence to the federalism-based critiques. What other doctrine area has been on the receiving end of more criticism and second-guessing than Establishment Clause jurisprudence? The Court's approach—largely detached from the governing text and its underlying aims—has yielded an undeniable mess. Nor is it likely to get better. The burgeoning church/state conflict that has been stirred up by the faith-based initiative is sure to prove even more challenging to the Court.

The Court's futile striving after a uniform stance on church/state issues has had deleterious consequences, both on the national psyche and on the caliber of constitutional jurisprudence. The quest for a single doctrinal standard in the absence of broader consensus as to the relationship between religion and politics has at various times left those on all sides feeling aggrieved and dissatisfied. The separationist line characterizing the 1960s and 1970s produced a sense that the very religiosity of a highly religious country was under attack from the law of the Constitution. Policies shielding government from the undue influence of religion felt like outright discrimination against religious people, a frustration rather than an embodiment of the popular will.[52] That sentiment has persisted even as the Court has grown more accommodationist. Meanwhile the Court's accommodationist turn has left strict separationists feeling threatened by a seeming loss of governmental neutrality toward things religious. Hence widespread dissatisfaction with church/state jurisprudence exists across the ideological spectrum.

Herein lies one of the main policy appeals of federalism, namely to accommodate "as many religious perspectives as possible without offending the rights of the majority."[53] While some commentators continue to promote a commitment to legal uniformity,[54] such uniformity is misplaced in the realm of church and state. The differing views on religion and politics may mean that anything close to consensus is beyond reach. Positions are too polarized, and the respective positions held with too much fervor, to coalesce or cohere around a single standard or approach.[55]

The perpetual discontent with church-state law suggests the need to return to core principles of constitutionalism grounded in constitutional rules, structures, and arrangements that are generally reflective of the will and character of the people being governed. Federalism makes room for differences across states and regions that persist even in contemporary America. States and regions of the country vary both in their religiosity and in the citizenry's comfort level with religion as a public influence. In some areas, there exists a deep desire to tap into heavily religious communities for the public good. In other areas, there may be great reluctance to do so. Those differences in religious identity and values support giving states greater latitude to determine for themselves strategies for navigating church/state strictures. Principled constitutionalism favors a doctrinal approach that respects and reflects those divergent values of the citizenry.

The deeply ingrained preference for constitutional uniformity in this context is misplaced. A one-size-suits-all regulatory approach to interaction between religious and governmental entities is an ill fit for the reality of America's highly diverse and multi-faceted religiosity. Constitutionalism properly understood as self-expression and self-rule demands a church/state jurisprudence that is attuned to the rich variations in religious identity and form in America.

Decentralized decision making on church/state issues also acknowledges that lower level governments are better equipped to discern and respond to the citizenry and to adapt their laws to conform to local conditions and preferences.[56] As decision-making moves closer to the people, it should increase the numbers of people who are satisfied with policy outcomes.[57] Put another way, the differences in religious character that defined America at the outset (and which compelled inclusion of the original federalist-motivated Establishment Clause) continue, albeit to a lesser extent. Those religious differences between people, states, and regions in turn warrant different treatment legally.

Here the philosophical advantages of federalism—as more reflective of where Americans are across the spectrum of church/state positions—converge with practical considerations regarding the clarity (or lack thereof) in the constitutional law. The appeal of a uniform nation-wide doctrine on church/state relations falls away in view of the Court's inability to arrive at a doctrine that is even minimally consistent or comprehensible.[58] It has struggled mightily to divine a reasonably coherent or logical Establishment Clause jurisprudence. People's trust in the law has been undermined as their ability to discern or understand it has been thoroughly undercut by the hair-splitting, logic defying work of the Court.[59] These failures are sufficient in themselves to warrant a recalibration of the modes of resolving church/state issues back toward the original meaning of the Constitution. The woes of church/state jurisprudence will not be cured by any specific theory or understanding of church/state policy. Rather the answer lies in "the same concept of federalism advocated by the Constitution's framers."[60]

Other textbook objectives underlying the federalist arrangement likewise apply. One such aim is to free up states and localities to serve as *laboratories of policy innovation and experimentation*. Certainly this applies in the church/state context and the faith-based initiative. On a policy level, states ought to be free to engage (or not to engage) the religious nonprofit sector and local churches in ways that are deemed most appropriate and effective for those particular states and communities. For example, in some rural areas the only providers of a particular service are religiously affiliated; that reality might compel some loosening of legal constraints. Heavily churched or deeply religious communities might integrate religious organizations in providing public services differently and to a greater extent than might other communities.

In the current debate over faith-based initiatives, many of the claims of peril to religious liberty on the one hand, and the assurances proffered on the other, are educated guesses at best and hyperbolic speculation at worst. On one hand, faith-based service providers' claims of greater effectiveness and efficiency are largely untested. Conversely, warnings of the possible dangers of excessive church/state cooperation are similarly speculative. Federalism would facilitate the testing of both sets of claims in the realm of practical politics and actual programs rather than in the abstract or at the hypothetical level. It makes sense to test the policy effectiveness of various faith-based practices at lower levels, and to do so with an eye on the impact on religious freedoms as well.

Finally, a federalist approach would have the added benefit of *isolating legal questions and conflicts*, unlike what has occurred with a uniform body of church/state law handed down from above.[61] Resolving legal challenges at the lower level would alleviate the pressure for a uniform standard that would answer all questions and conflicts. State legislatures and courts would not have to "produce decisions for the entire country and instead [could] concentrate their attention on a much more precise policy goal."[62] They would not face the daunting task of setting definitive constitutional parameters for all questions arising related to the faith-based initiative. The reach of a particular decision would extend only to that state. Thus would judges and legislators be better able to balance competing considerations in ways that best fit their residents.

A NEW CHURCH/STATE DYNAMIC: MODIFIED INCORPORATION

As previously noted, the scholarly objections to incorporation of the Establishment Clause have had little discernible impact on the constitutional practice surrounding church/state relations. One likely reason is the fear that softening the doctrine of incorporation would radically alter church/state relations in practice and threaten basic religious liberties. But is that fear justified? Would shrinking incorporation of the Establishment Clause dramatically change the nature of the relationship between religion and government in America? The answers to these questions may dictate whether calls to decentralize church/state boundaries are heeded amid the flurry of legal challenges stemming from faith-based public policy. It is worth attempting, therefore, to sketch what the future might look like under a devolved church/state law.

Though the crystal ball is cloudy, it is fairly safe to conclude that modifying the incorporation doctrine probably would not cause the full scale erosion of church/state separation that some fear and others desire. Religious liberty would continue to be preserved apart from the Establishment Clause—through state constitutions, the Free Exercise Clause, and the reality of religious pluralism in America.[63] It would unlikely trigger an era of widespread melding of religion and governance. Nevertheless, questions remain, the answers to which would shape the future of a de-incorporated Establishment Clause.

First, it is important to note that the freedom of religious exercise would continue to apply against all levels of government. Unlike the Establishment Clause, free exercise is a fundamental individual liberty within the "privileges and immunities" of the Fourteenth Amendment. It therefore would remain fully incorporated. While states might be freer under the pertinent state constitutional provision to seek more active engagement of the religious community or religious actors, protection of religious liberties would continue through the ongoing application of the Free Exercise Clause.[64] Free exercise considerations would have a significant impact on the details of church-state interactions, either prohibiting such efforts or at least ensuring that structural precautions were in place to protect religious liberty.[65]

This would likely result in what are now Establishment Clause cases being reframed as challenges to religious liberty under the free exercise provision. Ultimately the Court would be better positioned to "properly limit its rulings to issues which directly impact free exercise rights but do not diminish the state's authority to resolve the complex situational problems regarding church/state relations."[66]

Second, the degree of change that might be wrought by altering the incorporation doctrine would depend on how it was achieved. The boldest approach would be to overturn *Everson*, freeing states from any substantive constraints under from the Establishment Clause. This alternative would simply undo incorporation. But while various legal commentators have argued for this,[67] no member of the Supreme Court has done so. It is highly unlikely that the Court would take such a dramatic step.

Rather, the Court would be more inclined to modify or loosen incorporation, adopting a more deferential posture when state programs involving religion are at issue, thus allowing states latitude to carve out distinct religion policies of their own.[68] This more modest approach would allow for a two-track constitutional analysis of church/state issues. Review of federal action would continue under current doctrine. Meanwhile federal courts would continue to examine church/state issues stemming from state laws, policies, and programs pursuant to a different, and presumably looser, standard in doing so. Invoking this approach, Justice Thomas has avoided calling for an abandonment of incorporation, but rather contemplates differing Establishment Clause standards for the states.[69] State action should, therefore, be evaluated "on different terms than similar action by the Federal Government" with states at freedom "to experiment with involvement [in religion] . . . " States can "pass laws that include or touch on religious matters . . . " so long as they do not impinge upon free exercise rights or any other individual religious liberty interest.[70] Federal courts would remain the primary arbiters of church/state disputes but would be more intentional in balancing the demands of the First Amendment with the "federalism prerogatives of States."[71]

Under this scenario, the applicable law would vary depending on whether the program under consideration was federal or state in its origin and administration. Federal programs presumably would be decided by current Establishment Clause doctrine; state programs would not necessarily be free of legal regulation. Rather, the muting of the Establishment Clause in causes arising out of state-level programs would be accompanied by a corresponding turn to state constitutions to fill the legal void. Instead of ignoring their own constitutions in favor of reliance upon the federal Establishment Clause and federal court interpretations, state courts would look to their state's constitutional language and their own independent analysis and interpretation of that language.

Thus would religious liberty and non-establishment clauses contained in state constitutions "take on a life of their own instead of merely mimicking federal standards . . ."[72] State constitutions would matter again, as would the specific regional and state characters and cultures from which they sprang. States would adhere to restrictions, or act in the absence of them, in light of their specific values, historical development, and judicial character.

Modifying incorporation would not mean the deregulation of church-state relations. It almost surely would not open the flood gates for religious accommodation. Indeed, it might actually result in tighter restrictions on religious sector/governmental interaction. As courts turn to state constitutions to determine the necessary safeguards respecting religious accommodation, the shift would cut both in accommodationist and separationist directions, depending on the substance of the applicable state constitutional measure. It would produce stricter separation or laxer constraints, depending on the particular state constitutional approach. Many states would proscribe much of what is now proscribed by the incorporated Establishment Clause, and more.[73] Many state constitutions would present significant obstacles to the interaction by states with religion and religious actors. Those state constitutions often exceed the barriers imposed by the U.S. Constitution.[74] Given the number of states that explicitly address the funding of religious organizations, de-incorporation could result in an increase in the sum total of separation from the current state of the law.[75]

Reliance upon independent state constitutional analysis would be much more likely to yield a relatively coherent, more comprehensible body of constitutional jurisprudence in matters of church and state. State constitutional provisions are distinct in form and substance from the U.S. Constitution, addressing religion in far greater detail than their federal counterpart.

The ambiguity of the Establishment Clause would be replaced by provisions that address the legality of religion relative to government in detailed, explicit, and precise fashion. The application of state constitutions would be more straightforward, free of the obscure haze of federal law that clouds the realm of church/state relations.

State constitutions also are more easily and frequently changed. On the federal level, we are locked into an ambiguous Establishment Clause, immune to popular change, of which the courts have made a complete muddle. In contrast, the greater ease with which state constitutions can be amended means the legal relationship between religion and government can be navigated in ways which reflect the contemporary sentiments of the state and communities within the state. The role of religion in the public sphere would be returned to the arena of democratic processes rather than judicial mandate.

STATE CONSTITUTIONS: A "ONE WAY RATCHET" OR A DOUBLE-EDGED SWORD?

Both separationists and accommodationists who support a greater role for state constitutions would implement that change in ways that would push church/state jurisprudence more consistently in their respective directions. Those desiring a stricter separation between church and state do so via the "one-way ratchet" argument. They assert that the benefits of a loosened Establishment Clause would work only in a separationist direction. That is, state constitutions could be invoked only to strengthen disestablishment and individual religious liberties, and not to ease restrictions on government/religious interaction.

The First Amendment as incorporated through the Fourteenth has traditionally been understood as a floor or minimum level of protection against religious interaction with government at the state level. Under this approach, states are at liberty to impose regulations on church/state relations that are stricter than those necessitated by the Establishment Clause. But states cannot go in the opposite direction and allow greater engagement between government and religion than that permitted by the Establishment Clause. This view treats the U.S. Constitution as a threshold, creating a minimal set of limitations on the degree of church-state interaction.[76] With an increasingly accommodationist Supreme Court, separationists have fallen back on this one-way ratchet interpretation in hopes of gaining the benefits of more restrictive state constitutions without enduring the opposite effect in those instances where state constitutions are more permissive.[77]

Those on the other side contend that states should be free to diverge from federal interpretations of the Establishment Clause in either direction. Modified incorporation would subordinate the First Amendment in all cases where the states would apply their own religion clauses to states laws, policies, or programs. States with particularized language barring public revenues or assistance to religious institutions would rely on that language to bar a proposal to directly aid a parochial school or other FBO. Conversely, those states with more accommodating language or without any prohibitions on church/state relations altogether could allow greater interaction. The freedom to diverge from the Supreme Court's interpretation of the Establishment Clause would work in both ways, depending on the language of state constitutions.

CHALLENGES TO THE ENFORCEABILITY OF BLAINE AMENDMENTS

Meanwhile, on the accommodationist side, advocates stand ready to challenge the widespread use of state constitutional amendments as a barrier to church/state interaction. Decentralized church/state law will undoubtedly elevate state "mini-Blaine" amendments to a position of critical importance. The extent to which government actors pursue partnerships with religious social service providers will depend in no small part on the language and enforceability of the applicable state constitutional provisions. If taken literally, the constitutional amendments in many states would almost certainly preclude public money from going to private religious institutions, whether for education or social services. While the language and text vary widely from state to state, they typically are much stricter and more precise than the First Amendment in banning the dissemination of state funds to religious organizations or for religious purposes. If upheld, these amendments would likely stop the voucher movement (or any state-funded faith-based social service program for that matter) in its tracks.

The legality of these state mini-Blaine amendments may not be as clear as their language might otherwise seem to indicate. Proponents of vouchers and collaboration between government and the religious sector in other contexts have launched legal attacks based on allegations that state constitutions were amended primarily as a product of deep seated anti-Catholic animus that was commonplace in the late 1800s and early 1900s. As such, they should be unenforceable. A pro-voucher legal advocacy group has already brought lawsuits in a handful of states to test their constitutions, either to resolve them in a manner consistent with *Zelman* or to create sufficient conflicts in the law that the Supreme Court's intervention will be required. Challenges to the relevant state constitutional clauses were raised in the *Locke v. Davey* case, as well as a Florida case in which that state's voucher program was overthrown.[78] In neither case did the court address or consider the legal force of the respective state constitutional provisions. Hence this remains an open question.

Nevertheless, faith-based proponents remain eager to litigate what they consider to be vulnerable provisions, notwithstanding the clarity of the language barring aid to sectarian groups. Given the wide degree of divergence in the language of state constitutional religion clauses and the history behind their enactment, it is impossible to generalize on the likely legal outcome of legal challenges to them. Of particular interest will be the extent to which the Supreme Court will consider the historical motives behind state funding limitations. It is possible, but by no means certain, that courts might find anti-Catholic impetus for the enactment of state mini-Blaine amendments to be a discriminatory and hence unconstitutional barrier to funding of religious organizations.[79] This could have a dramatic impact on church/state relations as a matter of state religion policy.

CONCLUSION

The Supreme Court's decision in *Locke v. Davey* (2004) provides a preview of what a decentralized church/state jurisprudence might look like. The Court in *Locke* considered a Washington state scholarship program, under the terms of which recipients were precluded from applying their scholarship funds to certain college majors relating to theology or religion. Davey was granted a scholarship but had it revoked when he opted for a pastoral studies major. The Supreme Court rejected Davey's free exercise claim against the state. In doing so, it noted that while it would have been permissible under the federal Establishment Clause to include Davey and theological majors in the scholarship program, the U.S. Constitution did not *require* that the state include such religious uses for the funds. The Court emphasized the autonomy and authority of the state to make that choice, relying upon the Washington state constitutional provision banning public aid for religious instruction. That provision gave the state latitude to decide whom to include or exclude from the program. Moreover, the Court found it significant that Washington had developed a coherent and discernible body of law in its own right on the subject of religion.[80] In short, *Locke v. Davey* was grounded in principles of federalism and the autonomy of states to shape their own distinctive religion policy. "*Locke*, sounding in federalism, is thus entirely about the scope of state discretion in the zone between the First Amendment's religion clauses: that is, religion-specific actions which those clauses permit but do not require."[81]

The result in *Locke* struck a middle ground. On one hand, the decision was separationist in result, but without giving explicit support to the "one way ratchet" view. Instead, the decision reinforced "the constitutional legitimacy of state-level norms concerning the relationship between religion and the state."[82] But the Court also gave no indication that Washington State's provision was somehow suspect, though explicit challenges were raised before the Court.

The Court has thus far kept its cards close to its vest. *Locke v. Davey* anticipates a judicial mindset that is deferential to the impact of a state constitution and the traditions under that constitution, even if they diverge from the U.S. Constitution and the Establishment Clause. As faith-based policy continues to mushroom at the state and local level, and as it generates litigation along the way, the Court will have ample opportunity to reshape its church/state jurisprudence in ways faithful to the federalist arrangement. In the end, this can only hold out promise for an improved and principled constitutional approach to navigating the problematic relationship between religion and politics across America.

NOTES

1. *Elk Grove Unified School District v. Newdow*, 542 U.S. 1 (2004).
2. *Wash. Const.* Art. 1 § 11.
3. *Locke v. Davey*, 540 U.S. 712 (2004).
4. Fritz Mechthild, "Religion in a Federal System: Diversity Versus Uniformity," 38 *Kan. L. Rev.*, 39–79, 43 (1989).
5. See Mechthild, 44.
6. See also Mark Ragan and David J. Wright, *The Policy Environment for Faith-Based Social Services in the United States: What has Changed Since 2002? Results of a 50-State Study*, The Roundtable on Religion and Social Welfare Policy (2005), Appendix A. This report is available online at http://www.religionandsocialpolicy.org/docs/policy/State_Scan_2005_report.pdf.
7. See Alan G. Tarr. "Church and State in the States," 64 *Washington Law Review* 73–110 (1989) at 95–100 for a more detailed accounting of states' treatment of religious establishment. A sampling of state constitutions reflects their diversity. For example, California bars using public money for "the support of any sectarian or denominational school." *Cal. Const.* Art. 9, § 8. Michigan bars "tuition vouchers" from going to "nonpublic schools" where religious instruction takes place. *Mich. Const.* Art. 8, § 2. Other states bar public funds going to "the institutions of any religious sect or denomination," which would seemingly include social service agencies. *N.H. Const.* Art. 83; *Oreg. Const.* Art. 1, §5. Some states disallow public funds for "any charitable or benevolent purposes" or for "any denominational or sectarian institution or association." *Colo. Const.* Art. 5, § 34; *Pa. Const.* Art. 3, § 29. The Indiana constitution flatly states that "no money shall be drawn

from the treasury for the benefit of any religious ... institution." *Ind. Const.* Art. 1, § 6. Florida's law echoes the federal constitution in barring laws "respecting the establishment of religion ... " *Fla. Const.* Art. 1, § 3.

8. See Mechthild, 55. Nor are state constitutions limited to the "establishment" side of the religion coin; many of them have specific provisions protecting religious liberties as well, often doing so with much greater detail and clarity than the First Amendment of the U.S. Constitution (Tarr, 77–78).

9. *Everson v. Board of Education*, 330 U.S. 1 (1947)

10. Space constraints allow only the briefest encapsulating of the case against Establishment Clause incorporation. For a more extensive explication of the basis for the criticisms, see generally James J. Knicely, "'First Principles' and the Mismanagement of the 'Wall of Separation': Too Late in the Day for a Cure?" 52 *Drake Law Review* 171, 174 (2004); Daniel L. Dreisbach, *Thomas Jefferson and the Wall of Separation Between Church and State* (2002); Akhil Reed Amar, "Some Notes on the Establishment Clause," 2 *Roger Williams University Law Review* 1–14 (1996); Steven D. Smith, *Foreordained Failure: The Quest for a Constitutional Principle of Religious Freedom* (New York: Oxford University Press, 1995); William K. Lietzau. "Rediscovering the Establishment Clause: Federalism and the Rollback of Incorporation," 39 *DePaul Law Review* 1191–1234 (1990); Fritz Mechthild, "Religion in a Federal System: Diversity Versus Uniformity," 38 *Kansas Law Review* 39–79 (1989); Michael Malbin, *Religion and Politics: The Intentions of the Authors of the First Amendment* (Washington, D.C.: American Enterprise Institute for Public Policy Research, 1978); Phillip B. Kurland, "The Irrelevance of the Constitution: The Religion Clauses of the First Amendment and the Supreme Court," 24 *Villanova Law Review* 3, 14 (1978); Mark DeWolf Howe, *The Garden and the Wilderness: Religion and Government in American Constitutional History* (Chicago: University of Chicago Press, 1965); Joseph Snee, "Religious Disestablishment and the Fourteenth Amendment," *University of Washington Law Quarterly* (1954).

11. See Amar, "Some Notes," 11–12. See also Lietzau at 1200; "[T]he issue was properly left to the state and local governments and that the federal government should therefore have no legislative authority in the area."

12. Jed Rubenfeld, "Did the Fourteenth Amendment Repeal the First?," 96 *Michigan Law Review* 2140–2145, 2145 (1998). Rubenfeld states that "[d]espite the Fourteenth Amendment, states must and may deal in all sorts of ways with religion, favoring some religious traditions or disfavoring them, so long as they neither establish nor prohibit free exercise" (Rubenfeld, 2145).

13. See Lietzau, 1200.

14. See Rubenfeld, at 2143, citing Madison.

15. Ira Lupu and Robert Tuttle, "Federalism and Faith," 56 *Emory Law Journal* 19–105, 27 (2006).

16. See Lupu and Tuttle, "Federalism and Faith," 28.

17. See Lietzau, 1199.

18. See Dreisbach, 61.

19. See Knicely, 198.

20. See generally Akhil Reed Amar. "The Bill of Rights as a Constitution," 100 *Yale Law Journal* 1131, 1202–1208 (1991).

21. See Lietzau, 1199.

22. See Knicely, 195. The question remains whether the Establishment Clause was exclusively a structural or procedural provision aimed at protecting states' prerogatives. Some have acknowledged that thrust while contending that the Establishment Clause also reflected a substantive judgment in opposition to church/state interaction (See Steven K. Green, "Reconciling the Free Exercise and Establishment Clauses: Federalism and the Establishment Clause: A Reassessment." 38 *Creighton Law Review* 761 ([2005]). I intentionally avoid this question, both as beyond the reach of this limited essay and because it ought not to affect my analysis.

23. See Lupu and Tuttle, "Federalism and Faith," at 30, citing Smith.

24. See Lupu and Tuttle, "Federalism and Faith" 32.

25. Note, "Rethinking the Incorporation of the Establishment Clause: A Federalist View," 105 *Harvard Law Review* 1700, 1709 (1992).

26. See Note 1 for full citation. As Justice Stewart aptly put it in his dissent in *Abington Township v. Schempp* 374 U.S. 223 (1963), "it is not without irony that a constitutional provision evidently designed to leave the states free to go their own way should now have become a restriction upon their autonomy" (374 U.S. 223), Stewart, J. dissenting). For other instances of judicial statements on disincorporation, see Lietzau, 1215.

27. See Amar, "Some Notes," 3.

28. See Note, "Rethinking the Incorporation of the Establishment Clause," 1709. If the Establishment Clause both restricts federal power and specifically protects a popular prerogative in the states, then "it is logically impossible to turn such a protection on its head and make it a prohibition" (Porth, William C., and Robert P. George, "Trimming the Ivy: A Bicentennial Re-examination of the Establishment Clause," 90 *West Virginia Law Review* 109, 136–139, 139 1987).

29. See Elliott.

30. See Note, "Rethinking," 1710.

31. See Amar, "Some Notes," 11–12.

32. See Amar "Some Notes," 12.

33. See Rubenfeld, 2143.

34. Mary Ann Glendon, Comment in *Antonin Scalia, A Matter of Interpretation*, Amy Gutmann, ed. (1997).

35. *Everson* followed on the heels of the incorporation of other key First Amendment rights—speech rights in *Gitlow v. New York*, 268 U.S. 652 (1925), press in *Near v. Minnesota*, 283 U.S. 697 (1931), assembly in *DeJonge v. Oregon*, 299 U.S. 353 (1937), and religious exercise in *Cantwell v. Connecticut*, 310 U.S. 296 (1940).

36. Lupu and Tuttle, "Federalism and Faith," 39, 42.

37. Elliott.

38. *See* Knicely, 209–210, citations omitted. Amar, "The Bill Of Rights," at 1256. Amar cites extensive evidence from various members of Congress surrounding the passage of the Fourteenth Amendment that they understood the Bill of

Rights to represent "privileges and immunities of citizens" that could not be abridged by states. This would by implication seem to leave out of incorporation those provisions that were clearly not privileges held by citizens, but instead were meant to preserve certain distinct realms to the states free of the federal government, such as matters of establishment.

39. See generally, Snee (1954).

40. See Note 11 for examples of such criticisms.

41. *Van Orden v. Perry*, 545 U.S. 677 (2005); *McCreary County v. ACLU*, 545 U.S. 844 (2005); *Zelman v. Simmons-Harris* 536 U.S. 639 (2002); *Good News Club v. Milford Central School*, 533 U.S. 98 (2001); *Santa Fe Independent School Dist. v. Doe*, 530 U.S. 290 (2000); *Mitchell v. Helms*, 530 U.S. 793 (2000).

42. See Green, 107.

43. Most of these figures are taken from Ragan and Wright's *The Policy Environment for Faith-Based Social Services in the United States: What has Changed Since 2002? Results of a 50-State Study* (2005). This study was conducted at the behest of The Roundtable on Religion and Social Welfare Policy.

44. See Ragan and Wright, 7.

45. Ibid., 9–10.

46. Ibid., 10.

47. Ibid., 11.

48. Claire Hughes and Anne Farris, *Feds Hope to Inspire States to Advance Faith-Based Efforts*, The Roundtable on Religion & Social Welfare Policy (December 2006).

49. See Ragan and Wright, 18.

50. David K. Ryden and Jeffrey Polet, *Sanctioning Religion? Politics, Law, and Faith-Based Public Services* (Boulder, CO: Lynne Rienner Publishers, 2005).

51. See Ryden and Polet, 181–82; see also The Roundtable on Religion & Social Welfare Policy at http://www.religionandsocialpolicy.org/legal/. The Roundtable, sponsored by Pew Charitable Trusts, is a clearinghouse of faith-based policy and has a resources page on legal developments which tracks the latest in lawsuits and litigation.

52. See Lietzau, 1225.

53. See Lietzau, 1226.

54. See Tarr, 109.

55. One scholar contends that this realization was behind the Framers' federalist approach to church/state issues in the first place. "The framers . . . realized that in an area where passionately held values varied so radically, only local government could effectively handle the delicate policy questions that were implicated" (Lietzau, 1215–1216).

56. See Elliot.

57. See Lietzau, 1231.

58. See Tarr, 109.

59. See Knicely, 213.

60. See Lietzau, 1226.

61. See Knicely, 213.
62. See Elliott.
63. See Note, "Rethinking," 1717.
64. *Zelman,* J. Thomas, concurring.
65. "Presumably, if similarly situated organizations, religious and secular, were granted access to state aid, the more recently developed standards for neutrality and voluntary choice, and the absence of any imprimatur of state approval giving a particular religion favored or unequal status, would apply so long as there were no independently established Free Exercise or Equal Protection Clause violations" (Knicely, 220–21).
66. See Lietzau, 1233.
67. One illustrative voice argues that the federalist thrust of the Establishment Clause simply cannot be reconciled with its incorporation; hence we ought to directly acknowledge that they are "flatly inconsistent" and move to "selectively deincorporate" the Establishment Clause (Note: "Rethinking," 1712). In another law review note, Christopher Elliott similarly asserts that we ought to concede that the "history of the Establishment Clause is uniformly capricious with the Clause's incorporation and deincorporate it."
68. See Lupu and Tuttle, "Federalism and Faith," 51.
69. See Knicely, 207.
70. *Zelman,* at 678–79, 681, J. Thomas, concurring.
71. Ibid.
72. See Knicely, 222.
73. Ibid.
74. See Knicely, 223.
75. See Knicely, 224.
76. See Tarr, 80; see generally Mechthild, 1989.
77. See "Note: Beyond the Establishment Clause," 1985.
78. *Bush v. Holmes,* no. SC04–2323, Fla. S. Ct. (2005).
79. See Ryden and Polet, 182–184.
80. See Lupu and Tuttle, "Federalism and Faith," 78.
81. Ibid., 60.
82. Ira Lupu, and Robert Tuttle, *State of the Law 2005*. The Roundtable on Religion & Social Welfare Policy, 2005, at 92.

FURTHER READING

Joseph Snee offered the first systematic critique of Establishment Clause incorporation in "Religious Disestablishment and the Fourteenth Amendment," *University of Washington Law Quarterly* (1954). Akhil Reed Amar has posited one of the most convincing contemporary criticisms of the development of church/state jurisprudence in "Some Notes on the Establishment Clause," 2 *Roger Williams University Law Review* 1 (1996). Daniel Dreisbach's *Thomas Jefferson and the Wall of Separation Between Church and State* (2002) is an in-depth book-length analysis of the historical grounds for church/state relations and the distorting effect of the "wall of separation" metaphor. Professors Ira Lupu and Robert Tuttle offer a measured nonpartisan perspective on the bases for decentralizing religion policy in "Federalism and Faith," 56 *Emory Law Journal* 19 (2006). Professor Steven K. Green is one of the most stalwart defenders of Establishment Clause incorporation; for a representative work, see "Reconciling the Free Exercise and Establishment Clauses: Federalism and the Establishment Clause: A Reassessment," 38 *Creighton Law Review* 761 (2005). For an exhaustive source of information, legal and otherwise, on the faith-based initiative, see The Roundtable on Religion & Social Welfare Policy, Legal Resources Page, at http://www.religionandsocialpolicy.org/legal/. For an in-depth examination of how the faith-based initiative is playing out constitutionally, see David Ryden and Jeffrey Polet's *Sanctioning Religion? Politics, Law, and Faith-Based Public Services* (Boulder, CO: Lynne Rienner Publishers, 2005). Alan Tarr's "Church and State in the States," 64 *Washington Law Review* 73, 110 (1989) provides a useful summary of the treatment of religion in state constitutions and the possible implications.

8

The Limits of Free Exercise in America

Timothy J. Barnett

The limits of religious liberty in the United States are seen in an American ethos that blends a cultural heritage with a constitutional history. While the ideal of religious liberty has been esteemed in the nation across time and geography, the constitutional protection of religious liberty was not uniform at the nation's start, religious liberty being understood as the prerogative of the states since the colonial era. This dispersion of religious autonomy among the states was retained when the new union became federalized under the Constitution. Likewise, when the nation's Bill of Rights was ratified in 1791, religious liberty was constitutionally formalized as a state right and put outside the federal government's reach. Congress was restrained from making laws "respecting an establishment of religion or prohibiting the free exercise thereof," while the various states remained at liberty within the framework of their respective constitutions to shape the particulars of religious liberty in accordance with the democratic will of state majorities. Nevertheless, most Americans then and now view the basics of religious liberty—freedom of religious conscience and belief, religious speech, and religious assembly—as inalienable rights and essential aspects of human dignity and democratic legitimacy.

Since the 1930s, the increasing religious diversity in the United States has contributed to the realization that the lawful restraint of some religiously motivated actions is a necessary aspect of modern life in a large democratic republic. While religious belief can be protected with relative ease, religiously motivated conduct can be quite difficult to protect in some public contexts, especially where competing private claims or compelling governmental interests are at stake. When religious expression enters the public square, it is frequently constrained at the margins by statutory law so as to accommodate the core components of religious liberty for all—the exercise of conflicting liberties refereed by government so as to maintain public order and uphold the rule of law.

Modern religious diversity has produced a variety of conflicting views of what constitutes religion and the free exercise of religion. With this growing conflict in mind, this chapter will explore one of the most significant unsolved problems of free exercise jurisprudence—the identification and implementation of suitable means of protecting the free exercise of individuals and interests for whom community-level religious establishment (or quasi-establishment) is an essential aspect of free exercise. Many religious people believe they cannot experience their religion fully without living in the context of a community where participants voluntarily compromise their opportunities for individualism so that they can more fully experience a religiously informed way of life. This matter of constitutional justice is the overarching dilemma in the work that follows.

THE COMPETITION AMONG "RIGHTS"

In the current era, governmental constraint of religiously motivated conduct arises as a reflection of government's efforts to sustain a free market for religious activity or uphold the goal of governmental neutrality between religions. However, since the federal government began the process of incorporating the Fourteenth Amendment (through the Due Process Clause) against the First Amendment in the 1930s and 1940s, governmental constraint of the free exercise of religion operates to protect other constructed categories of rights against the possible incursions of religion. The essential rights categories that have been constructed include the rights of commerce, privacy, speech, freedom of choice, due process, and the equal protection of the laws. Equally important is a category of rights that the U.S. Supreme Court has constructed on behalf of government; namely, the right of government to pursue what it sees as its compelling interests. Hence, while religious liberty may be viewed by some traditional observers as a category of rights deserving preferential treatment based upon American history—the First Amendment singling out religion in its opening statement—the reality of American politics and constitutional jurisprudence is that many interests have become compelling to the national government in the context of politics.

The current era is one in which religiously motivated conduct traditionally associated with the agenda of a Christian majority is increasingly constrained by reason of other categories of rights now protected on behalf of competing interests. This has led some observers to speak of a "culture war," some bidding with nostalgia for a return of Christendom while others hope to bid farewell to even the cultural vestiges of establishment religion.[1] But this is less than half of the picture. When the national scene is viewed through a different lens, observers come to strikingly different conclusions. In some instances, the conclusion is that the federal government is increasingly accommodating religion, especially conservative Christianity. From this perspective secular interests are not only forced to subsidize religion that they disagree with but are also required to give way to it in the public sphere as a tacitly preferred governmental interest. Thus, there is considerable controversy over the limits of free exercise—a controversy rooted in theology, history, political theory, constitutional law, and the politics of power.

THE EARLY YEARS

During the American colonial era the statutory limits of free exercise in the colonies were, in part, reflections of English traditions reworked for application in new world societies. These traditional perspectives became combined with emerging ideas about human nature, religion, and the purposes and limits of civil government. While the early American colonies were organized under the auspices of European government, operationally they took the form of close-knit communities. The general understanding of rights and liberties in this context assumed that a set of greater rights came from God (explained, in part, by Nature) while sets of lesser rights were within the developmental province of human governments. The excitement of the times was that communities were choosing and cultivating their own governmental forms—what history recalls as the new advent of American democracy.[2]

Community-based rights and liberties in the American colonial era showed variation across the colonies. In a few colonies a mildly libertarian outlook produced forms of government in which many rights and natural liberties were reserved to individuals. But the larger number of colonies leaned toward communitarianism—a view of responsible liberty in which individuals delegate some portion of their liberties to the management of the community, the idea being to facilitate the development of a desired cultural environment. Massachusetts and Connecticut were prime examples of the communitarian approach while the Rhode Island of Roger Williams illustrated the more progressive or somewhat libertarian approach.[3]

By the time that Virginia's James Madison penned his famous *Memorial and Remonstrance against Religious Assessments* (1785), Roger Williams's model of religious individualism was in the first rank of theories of religious association and obligation. Yet, to some communitarians, the Williams model raised the specter of moral weakness combining with specious reasoning to produce injuries for individuals and communities alike. On the other hand, proponents of libertarian approaches to religion discounted the early colonial era belief that semi-closed religious communities possess the advantage of institutional experience and learning without which some individuals will make serious mistakes to their own harm and the harm of their neighbors. Indeed, progressive thinking during the era held that traditional religious communities offered the prospect of ignorance and malpractice that could not well survive open market conditions.[4]

The debate over the open and classically liberal community versus the relatively closed or Puritan-style community diverts attention from a more important free exercise issue: by what means do communities acquire their governmental prerogatives? Do communities 'capture' individuals and dictate their rights? Conversely, can 'free' individuals subordinate many choices to democratically composed communities? Do individuals have a right by Nature to release their rights by contract or covenant to the primacy of a community until they leave the community? These questions are centrally important to how governments and courts differentiate between religious establishment and the free exercise of religion.

The colonial record portrays much of what modern jurisprudence considers "religious establishment" as simply "free exercise" in the minds of individuals who understood themselves as retaining the natural right to subordinate individuals' rights to the judgment of a community. For example, the *Massachusetts Body of Liberties* (December 1641) contains many declarations of prohibited conduct as well as statements of rights, yet the package was viewed in those times as constituting liberty.[5] In colonial Massachusetts, many citizens found the prohibitions to facilitate a religious milieu where they were buffered from frequent exposure to various passions, pursuits, and pleasures they wished to avoid. As legal scholar Thomas Curry explains, "Congregationalists . . . claimed also that theirs was a truly mild and equitable system, hardly to be called an establishment, as John Adams noted. The Massachusetts Constitution of 1780 did not refer to the public system supportive of religion as an establishment of religion, nor did the law that eventually dismantled it make any reference to disestablishment."[6]

When the ideas of democracy, federalism and community are combined, the results can be likened to pursuing self-realization by living life on a chain of free islands. If one selects an uninhabited island, individualism is maximized but at the cost of the interesting choices and opportunities that come from being a member of a community. If one takes one's boat to a nearby-inhabited island, a different experience awaits: individual choices may be lightly or heavily constrained by the aggregate will of the democratic majority. Just because an individual chooses to live on a community-styled island where the options for individuality are few does not mean that self-realization is dampened, for in choosing and remaining on a particular island, one exercises individuality.

Throughout American history, the foregoing concept has been grasped readily by communitarians while remaining obscure to many libertarians, their lack of appreciation for the concept perhaps reflecting that they would not freely choose a constrained environment for themselves. While the modern U.S. Supreme Court cannot be fairly described as libertarian, it too has struggled to make room for free exercise that chooses some form of establishment as the outcome of its exercise. Indeed, this quandary continues to baffle the Court and tangle its decisions. Happily for the Constitution's framers, they avoided this quagmire by applying the First Amendment only to the national government. Hence, the states were free from any need to invent justifications for one form of neutrality over another, as the states were originally under no federal compunction of neutrality by which to determine the limits of free exercise.

The idea of community-level establishment as an expression of individualistic free exercise is nicely illustrated with classical music. If an individual wishes to worship the Supreme Being by means of a symphonic or orchestral performance—a musical *community* of wind, string and percussion instruments—government would be acting against that individual's free exercise if government were to make unlawful the organization of musical groups that achieve their ends through particular rules, norms, and disciplines that limit the musical autonomy of individual members. Individuals committed to playing nothing but solos or duets might feel sorry for members of highly disciplined orchestras, but this is a matter of taste, not liberty. In music, liberty, self-expression, and the discovery of joy are achievable in various ways, including the liberty of making music more profound by giving up the right to musical improvisation while in the midst of a musical community.

The message of the musical analogy can be seen in Thomas J. Curry's argument that to "posit that in 1789 the inhabitants of the New England states saw the church-state system in that region as a new kind of establishment is to misread the historical record."[7] The record lends itself more readily to the conclusion that many congregationalists saw as free exercise what modern Americans see as establishment. Again, music illustrates the point: people who have played in large orchestras know that great feats in orchestral music are dependent upon adequate authority for leaders, standards of excellence for participants, expectations of rigorous preparation, means of performance evaluation, protocols for disciplining or dismissing unproductive or failing members, crowd control, and a sense of community cohesion. Perhaps individuals experience merely limited aspects of certain religions in libertarian contexts where everyone marches to his own inner drummer.

The oddity is that much of what passes for regular American life would not exist if the U.S. Supreme Court aimed at disestablishment outside of religion. Business corporations, whether private or public, for-profit or not-for-profit, are organized with hierarchy, bureaucracy, specialization, and protocols of operation that in some cases create fairly inflexible expectations of performance and limitations on the free exercise of choice for employees. People with high-paying and low-paying jobs learn to show up on time, attend to their assigned work, submit to established authority, and work within an organized system. The same considerations apply to the operations of government, whether local, state, or national. While there are some business entities that are organized along the lines of creative anarchy and rampant individualism, the usual expectation of workers is that a good amount of autonomy is traded temporarily in exchange for the right to receive income from the organization.

Arguably, if the U.S. Supreme Court attempted to lay upon business the feats of disestablishment it laid upon the states in the latter half of the twentieth century, much of business would be in ruins. But the evolution of American culture allowed no such benefit of the doubt for religion. The nature of religious establishment at the state level was too encompassing. Furthermore, religion was vulnerable to expressing its agenda through monopoly. Indeed, had religious establishments been limited to the county, ward or precinct level—with every state federally mandated by the U.S. Constitution to maintain two-thirds of its local government jurisdictions completely free from establishment—disestablishment may never have gained the cultural momentum that moved the Court to find its free exercise trajectory. The intriguing aspect of this scenario is that establishment variations of religious free exercise would have received the opportunity to compete with other systems of choice. Ultimately, though, religion is itself to blame for its loss of power. Repeatedly, religious establishments and quasi-establishments were insufficiently adaptive, failing to offer people the higher dimensions of life and fulfillment that people seek when weighing the cost of reduced choice against the attractions of a community-shaped way of life. Indeed, modern gated communities have succeeded in attracting residents where traditional religious communities failed.

The disenfranchisement in the 1940s of state-level establishments of minor consequence coupled with the creation of national standards of free exercise enhanced some forms of religious liberty while necessitating the further decline of communitarian forms of free exercise. There are fewer constraints on religious liberty for most members of the majority and for religious minorities than there were fifty or one hundred years ago. But for communitarians spread across many diverse sects as well as for Americans desirous of seeing public, non-sectarian religion well maintained in the public square, the limits of free exercise are more noticeably felt and the wall of separation between church and state more institutionalized and buttressed between the cracks. How this came about is best revealed in the U.S. Supreme Court's jurisprudence.

THE NATIONALIZATION OF RELIGIOUS LAW

The idea of nationally-protected religious rights began developing as an outgrowth of constitutional innovation. For some, like James Madison, reason alone could support federally mandated disestablishment of religion at the state level, universal rights of conscience, and unfettered free exercise. Most Americans, however, were not so sanguine about elevating the federal government to define the operation of religious liberty across the whole land.

The prospect of a national Bill of Rights became the catalyst for political and theological debate over how the federal government should best go about protecting America's religious ethos and the operations of religion within the states. Many anti-federalists did not want a uniform national protection of religious rights. They were satisfied that the budding nation's best interests were served by merely protecting the prerogatives of the states in matters of religious liberties, regardless of whether states favored free exercise, plural establishment, or some other variation of establishment. Federalists, too, were divided on the question, some wondering if a string of problems in the state of Virginia over religion might spread to other states in the absence of federal protections against religious enthusiasts grasping the levers of the state.

Virginia was at the tail end of a protracted struggle between establishment interests battling for a state subsidy of religion that would have disproportionately benefited the Church of England and disestablishment advocates who wanted no state subsidy for any religion. This state-level struggle prompted Thomas Jefferson in 1779 to draft *The Virginia Act for Establishing Religious Freedom,* which was approved by the Virginia General Assembly in 1786.[8] While Jefferson's efforts in this document were primarily aimed against state coercion of financial contributions for the support of religion, the debate took place under the cloud of Virginia's much earlier experience with "Dale's Laws"—a set of English statutory laws used in early colonial Virginia that provided severe punishments for a broad array of moral failings and religious lapses.[9] Indeed, Virginia's early legal system made colonial Puritanism look like an escape to liberty (a claim made by early colonists in New England).

The religious conflict within Virginia weighed heavily on James Madison's mind, as evidenced in his 1785 *Remonstrance.* Furthermore, the dangers he associated with the unchecked passions of factions are described in numerous places in his contributions to the Federalist Papers. Thus, it is no surprise that Madison leaned to the federalist side at the time the U.S. Constitution was framed, his anti-federalist inclinations largely in hibernation until he served as vice president during the Thomas Jefferson presidency.

During the debates of the First Constitutional Convention, Madison did not favor a bill of rights, for he believed the structure and philosophy of the new constitution was a bill of rights in itself. However, when it became apparent that the Constitution would not receive sufficient support from constitutional delegates without the pledge of a bill of rights, he adjusted his position on the matter. Thereafter, he took the initiative to compose a positive statement of national religious rights in the Bill of Rights he proposed to the first federal Congress—his selection of rights reflecting his disquietude with establishment religion.[10] Congress, though, had other ideas, politely acknowledging Madison's concepts while moving on to contemplate a raft of proposals and revised drafts that eventually were reduced to a formula for state autonomy: "Congress shall make no law respecting an establishment of religion, or prohibiting the free exercise thereof."[11] Congress's choice of how to best protect religious liberty was ratified by the young nation as part of the First Amendment and alongside nine other rights declarations in the Bill of Rights. The result was a national situation much like the colonial system in regard to diversity of controls. The limits of free exercise were retained as the due product of state-level democracy, which in turn was allowed to reflect cultural traditions, the religious heritage of local areas, and regionally dominant ideas about civil society.

Underlying the constitutional declaration of religious rights, the Bible operated on the cultural level as a unifying document that made the states' management of religious matters look comparatively orderly. Indeed, even the U.S. Supreme Court found itself turning to the Bible for symbolic, historical, and substantive reasons from its early years until the 1930s.[12] Thus, while the First Amendment did not nationalize the limits of free exercise at its outset, it did create the beginnings of a civil religion with the implied doctrine that if federal government should stay out of religion, states should do so as well.

Exactly one hundred years after the ink dried on Thomas Jefferson's initial draft of *The Virginia Act for Establishing Religious Freedom,* the U.S. Supreme Court would decide its first case in which it would significantly alter the covenant relationship between the federal government and the people concerning the power of the government to make laws respecting religion. The bridge that allowed the Court to cross that Mosaic divide in *Reynolds v. the United States* (1879) was the emerging national visibility in the 1850s of an uncommon marital arrangement sufficiently disconcerting to enough Americans that Congress could label it "barbaric."[13] The cause of insult to the moral sensibilities of the nation's regular churchgoers was Mormon polygamy in the Utah Territory, carried on under the banner of prophetic revelation and divine mandate. In hindsight, a conduct more socially hazardous but considerably less stirring to the imagination may not have induced the high court to discover a free exercise dichotomy between beliefs and conduct until well into the twentieth century.

Following the U.S. Congress' disquietude arising from information about the growth of polygamy in the Utah Territory, the U.S. Congress created the Morrill Anti-Bigamy Act, which President Abraham Lincoln signed into law on July 8, 1862. The Act aimed at reducing the prospects for the union of church and state in the Utah territory by limiting the value of property that a church could own (excess property forfeited to the United States) and by banning bigamous marriage. The Act made bigamy punishable by imprisonment not exceeding five years and by fines up to $500. Furthermore, the Act annulled all actions of the Legislative Assembly of the Territory of Utah pertaining to spiritual marriage as well as polygamous marriage for the life now lived. Congressional action against marriage in the life to come as well as the here and now suggests that Congress was so moved by public outcry and its own moral sentiments that it forgot its place as an institution addressing temporal issues. But this is the historical pattern for lawmaking where religion is the alleged perpetrator of hazards or the purported victim of perceived threats.

The Morrill Act had about the same initial effect in the Utah Territory as did the Fifteenth Amendment (1870) upon African American voting in the South: little changed. Estimates are that the percentage of the families practicing polygamy in the Southern Utah city of St. George grew from 30 to 40 percent between 1870 and 1880. While such a level of polygamy was considerably higher in St. George than in many Mormon settlements, the observation is telling, not just about early Mormon culture but the federal government's ability to make a difference.[14]

Underfunded, the Morrill Act was little more than a shot across the bow of the Mormon ship, at least in its early application. A few years later, however, the patience of the U.S. government did expire when the Utah Territorial Legislature (essentially a Mormon institution due to its members' obligations to the Mormon Church) ruffled the feathers of the House Judiciary Committee in 1867 by asking Congress to repeal the Morrill Act. As explained by historian Jessie L. Embry, "Instead of doing that, the House Judiciary Committee asked why the law was not being enforced, and the Cullom Bill, an attempt to strengthen the Morrill Act was introduced. Although it did not pass, most of its provisions later became law."[15]

In the seven years following the Cullom attempt, several anti-polygamy bills were introduced in the U.S. Congress, none of them passing until 1874, when the Poland Act found success. This act of Congress limited the power of probate courts, empowered federal district courts in matters of civil and criminal jurisdiction, and made the Territorial Marshal a federal office. The effect was to put all cases involving polygamy into the federal courts where presidentially-appointed judges could prevent state-level courts from making end-runs around federal laws.

Confronted with the prospect that the Morrill Act could not be enforced in the Utah Territory, the Mormon Church decided to challenge the constitutionality of the Morrill Act and related laws. The church's strategy was to have George Reynolds, the private secretary to the church's president, Brigham Young, voluntarily stand trial for bigamy under section 5352 of the Revised Statutes of the United States.[16] Not surprisingly, the territorial district court's decision went against Reynolds, the court burdening him with a $500 fine and sentencing him to two years of imprisonment and hard labor. Reynolds appealed the lower court's decision to the Supreme Court of the Utah Territory, which upheld the lower court. Consequently, Reynolds appealed to the U.S. Supreme Court, the case reaching the high court in 1879, shortly after the death of the Mormon church's president, Brigham Young (1801–1877). *Reynolds v. United States* was destined to become a landmark decision for both federalism and the free exercise of religion.[17]

In *Reynolds*, a unanimous court upheld the Morrill Act (sect. 5352 of the Revised Statutes), declaring that laws are made "for the government of actions, and while they cannot interfere with mere religious belief and opinion, they may with practices."[18] After dealing with the procedural issues of the appeal, the Court focused on the substance of Reynolds's defense, namely, his claimed duty (and the duty of all male members of the Mormon church, circumstances permitting) to practice polygamy. Reynolds argued that this duty was enjoined by several of the sect's holy books, that there was precedence in the Holy Bible, and that the Almighty God had commanded the practice of polygamy in a revelation given to Joseph Smith, the founder and prophet of the church. While clearly skeptical, the Court acknowledged Reynolds's claim that were he not to practice polygamy, his refusal "would be damnation in the life to come." The Court also noted Reynolds's claim that bigamy had been duly sanctioned by the church pursuant to the doctrines of the church.[19] Still, the Court resisted.

Chief Justice Waite responded to Reynolds's position by noting that the issue was not the power of Congress to prescribe criminal laws in the Territories but the guilt of one who knowingly violates a properly enacted law on the justification that his religion causes him to believe the law is wrong. Waite acknowledged that the First Amendment to the Constitution "expressly forbids" Congress to pass any law for the Territories that prohibits the free exercise of religion. He then said, "The question to be determined is, whether the law now under consideration comes within this prohibition." He added that the "precise point of the inquiry is, what is the religious freedom which has been guaranteed . . . "[20] In this way, Waite focused this landmark case squarely on the question of the limits of free exercise, establishing precedence for marking the leeway of the Court's discretion in such matters.

The *Reynolds* decision suggested that in the absence of any definition of religion in the U.S. Constitution, the Waite Court could define the limits of religious exercise as subtly as judicial and cultural conditions allowed. It said as much in its decision. The Court's understanding of religion relative to civil society gave it the power to separate religious belief from religiously-motivated conduct, giving the former primary protection and only secondary and subjective protection to the latter.[21] The Court accomplished this work out of will as much as wit, owing to the fact that in the U.S. Supreme Court's first case involving the Free Exercise Clause—*Permoli v. First Municipality of New Orleans* (1845)—the Court upheld the original understanding of the First Amendment without the slightest concession. An excerpt from the case drives the point: "The Constitution makes no provision for protecting the citizens of the respective states in their religious liberties; that is left to the state constitutions and laws; nor is there any inhibition imposed by the Constitution of the United States in this respect to the states."[22]

The decision of the Waite Court was no different, in essence, from the work of state governments, except that state governments were not prohibited from making laws on religion while the national government was under that prohibition in the First Amendment. If there was bias or preference in the way a state court defined religion, the consequences were largely limited to that state's physical jurisdiction. The application of federalism put the state's decision into a marketplace environment where people could vote with their feet and move on if they disagreed with the state court. When, however, the U.S. Supreme Court defined religion in contradistinction to Mormon religious beliefs, there was no place left for Mormons to go short of emigrating out of the country. Without much delay the Mormon Church bent to the Court's will, helped by the realization that there was more at stake in building a Deseret kingdom than polygamy. Nevertheless, although Mormon leadership declared an amended position under coercive duress, many Mormons felt the Court could not overturn their prophets' earlier revelations. Little did they know that the Waite Court's decision would become a landmark.

As Carol Weisbrod observes, "Reynolds was never overruled and was sometimes reinforced" by the Court's logic. In *Minersville School District v. Gobitis* (1940), Justice Frankfurter declared that individuals have not been relieved "from obedience to a general law not aimed at the promotion or restriction of religious beliefs." And in *Smith* (1990), Justice Scalia in writing for the court majority claimed *Reynolds* as the first case employing the principles he asserted. Nevertheless, Weisbrod claims that *Reynolds* is most frequently recalled in the current era as an "example of persecution of a religious group by the federal government."[23] Perhaps the Court's awareness of that perspective explains, in part, the Burger Court's reluctance a century after *Reynolds* to dictate terms of community life to the Amish in Wisconsin.[24]

TWENTIETH-CENTURY PROTECTIONS AND LIMITS FOR FREE EXERCISE

While the Supreme Court's unanimous decision in *Reynolds* demonstrated the power of the Court to limit free exercise within a federal territory, the Court accomplished its purpose by focusing upon the dangers of polygamy to the public good rather than by exploring the issue of states rights. At the time of *Reynolds*, the Court knew full well that an 1833 landmark case on federalism, *Barron v. Baltimore*, had secured states' rights quite thoroughly from any constraints flowing from a liberal reading of the Bill of Rights. Indeed *Barron v. Baltimore* would continue to exert controlling precedence in the matter of states' rights for decades after *Reynolds*, delaying application of the Fourteenth Amendment to the First Amendment's religion clauses until well into the twentieth century.[25]

In 1938 the federal government gained a toehold in limiting the rights of states to manage religious affairs when Justice Cardozo declared for the Court majority in *Palko v. Connecticut* that some parts of the Fourteenth Amendment could be applied through the Due Process Clause to the First Amendment. While the case concerned first-degree murder and the question of double jeopardy under the Fifth Amendment, Cardozo used the framework of the case to open the door to the Court's oversight of free exercise, remarking as follows:

[T]he due process clause of the Fourteenth Amendment may make it unlawful for a state to abridge by its statutes the freedom of speech which the First Amendment safeguards against encroachment by Congress . . . or the free exercise of religion . . . or the right of peaceable assembly . . . In these and other situations immunities that are valid as against the federal government . . . have been found to be implicit in the concept of ordered liberty, and thus, through the Fourteenth Amendment, become valid against the states.[26]

Justice Cardozo went on to state in his opinion for an eight judge majority that the "line of division may seem to be wavering and broken if there is a hasty catalogue of the cases" but that reflection and analysis would resolve the questions by giving light to "a rationalizing principle." While the principle is not self-evident as claimed—Cardozo stating that the enlargement of liberty by latter-day judgments had included "liberty of the mind as well as liberty of action" (a seeming reversal of the belief-conduct dichotomy in *Reynolds*)—the Cardozo logic was sufficient to move the Court further toward the nationalization of free exercise shortly thereafter in *Cantwell v. Connecticut* (1940), a case that concerned the constitutional right of Jehovah's Witnesses to proselytize as they saw fit.

The Cantwell case resulted from the arrest of Newton Cantwell and his two sons in New Haven, Connecticut, for using a record player on a street in a highly Catholic section of the city to play a Jehovah's Witness record that castigated many religions, especially Catholicism. When the Cantwells' actions produced an outcry by passersby, local police arrested them. The Cantwells were tried and convicted for soliciting without a license, inciting a breach of the peace, and three other counts. After the Connecticut Supreme Court upheld the lower court decision, the U.S. Supreme Court heard the case on the Cantwells' appeal, deciding unanimously to invalidate the Cantwells' convictions on the grounds of free exercise.[27]

Writing for a unanimous court in *Cantwell*, Justice Owen J. Roberts returned to the dichotomy between belief and conduct, reiterating the holding from *Reynolds*: "We hold that the statute, as constructed and applied to the appellants, deprives them of their liberty without due process of law in contravention of the Fourteenth Amendment... [T]he Amendment embraces two concepts—freedom to believe and freedom to act. The first is absolute, but, in the nature of things, the second cannot be. Conduct remains subject to regulation for the protection of society."[28]

While Roberts acknowledged that government must be scrupulous in upholding vital freedoms, he also wrote that the "fundamental concept of liberty embodied in [the Fourteenth] Amendment embraces the liberties guaranteed by the First Amendment." He further declared that the Fourteenth Amendment "has rendered the legislatures of the states as incompetent as Congress to enact such laws."[29] Thus, while the Court maintained a belief-conduct dichotomy in some matters, it deemed the proselytizing efforts of the Witnesses an integral part of their religious practice and a legitimate activity protected by free speech in the Bill of Rights as well as the Free Exercise Clause in the First Amendment.[30] Eventually, the Court would simplify that jurisprudence by moving away from the Free Exercise Clause as a protection for religious recruitment, founding the right instead upon free speech.

Cantwell supplied the Court with justification for moving toward a wider federal authority over religion. A few years later in *Everson v. Board of Education* (1947), Justice Hugo Black was able to seize upon the Court's evolving thinking about the Fourteenth Amendment to dramatically expand the Court's reach. In writing for the majority, Black accomplished this feat with such stealth that even his associates were unsure of the ramifications.

In *Everson*, the Court majority incorporated the Fourteenth Amendment against the Establishment Clause, thus mandating that states build a wall of separation between church and state.[31] Justice Black baffled his associates by matching aggressive arguments on behalf of an impregnable wall between church and state with his justification of upholding New Jersey's subsidized busing of children to private religious schools. In writing for the dissenters, Justice Robert Jackson said that "the undertones of the opinion, advocating complete and uncompromising separation of Church from

State, seem utterly discordant with its conclusion yielding support to their commingling in educational matters."[32]

In evaluating Black's opinion in *Everson,* legal scholar Philip Hamburger asserts that Black knew exactly what he was doing—a conclusion that Black's separationist-oriented supporters reached in a tardy fashion after lambasting him for being disloyal to the wall of separation doctrine while lauding it.[33] In reality, Justice Black employed a strategy similar to the one used by Chief Justice John Marshall in *Marbury v. Madison* (1803) in which Marshall chose to lose the immediate battle with Thomas Jefferson, James Madison, and the anti-federalists so that he could acquire strategic cover in allowing the federalists to empower the U.S. Supreme Court with judicial review. The fact that John Marshall found it necessary to sacrifice the judicial appointments of a few members of his political party was a small price to pay for a permanent victory.[34] For Justice Hugo Black it was much the same: by upholding a comparatively inconsequential form of governmental assistance in New Jersey for bused students, he was able to gain strategic political cover for a much stronger principle of church and state separation. Working surreptitiously and yet for ends that he held in high regard, Black converted an incremental decision into a landmark opinion.

Justice Black's shrewdness was reinforced a few years later when the circumstances of *McCollum v. Board of Education* (1948) made it evident that the Court would need the support of minority religious groups—Baptists, Seventh-Day Adventists, Jews and Jehovah's Witnesses—just as James Madison needed the support of the dissenting Baptists in Virginia to win his seat in the first Congress under the new Constitution.[35] Indeed, in regard to the Baptists, the history of the movement is a running account of advocacy against state-level establishments so as to increase Baptists' religious opportunities.[36] With the Baptists, as explained by James T. Baker, freedom "permeated every cell of their being: freedom of religious choice (volunteerism), freedom of conscience (the priesthood of all believers), and freedom of all churches and sects from clerical or political dictation (the separation of church and state)."[37] But Baker also illustrates a conundrum for Baptists that their free exercise advocacy created:

Since 1791 Baptists have had to deal with the implications of their achievement. If the state cannot control religion, can a religious group accept gifts from the state in the form of tax exemptions . . . If church and state are separate . . . should religion try to influence political deliberations when they are perceived to be dealing with moral issues? In places where Baptists are an effective majority or plurality of the population, should they try to impose their will on what might be seen as a dissident, irresponsible, or immoral minority?[38]

While religious groups like the Baptists won rulings from the U.S. Supreme Court that facilitated a wider exercise of some types of religious liberty, their success in the courts weakened the ability of state and local authorities to prescribe moral standards and community norms associated with traditional Christian beliefs. Thus, in the same time frame that selected elements of religious liberty were receiving judicial reinforcement, the Court was backing away from its traditional view of the United States as a Christian nation—a view it had promulgated in various decisions through 1931.[39] Indeed, with as few as 25,000 Catholics in the United States in 1785 the nation seemed as Protestant as it did Christian, the then existent Protestant sense of morality being imprinted on state laws.[40] But the justices who decided *Everson* in 1947 saw that the old religious order was fading fast. It would take less than forty years from *Everson* before a Court Justice, William Brennan, would criticize the very idea of America as a Christian nation.[41]

While the high court no longer considers America a Christian nation, it does in some instances note that Americans are a religious people. One legal scholar, John Witte, has gone as far as saying the nation has "the soul of a sanctuary"—a suggestion of abundant religious sincerity flowing out of religious diversity.[42] The strong religious element in American culture has contributed to U.S. Supreme Court jurisprudence where the doctrine of measured accommodation for religion in public affairs has been preserved alongside concepts of walled separation. The result is a hybrid system that serves competing interests.

THE CHALLENGE OF DEFINING CONSTITUTIONALLY PROTECTED RELIGION

The ability of the high court to advance an evolutionary jurisprudence on the religion clauses following *Cantwell* and *Everson* was aided by the constitution's omission of any definition of the nature of religion protected by the First Amendment. Indeed, little in the civil religion of the United States has provided suitable aid in defining what elements of religion are constitutionally shielded. As legal scholar Bette Novit Evans explains, the words of the First Amendment mask a difficult dilemma, namely, how to "recognize a religion and to distinguish legitimate religious claims from spurious ones." The crisis according to Evans is that "every effort to make such distinction infuses the Constitution with some particular notion of a legitimate religion or religious practice, and that is precisely what the First Amendment should forbid."[43]

The meaning of the term "religion" has become supple enough in the last fifty years to allow the Court to work around the increasingly idiosyncratic nature of its cases. But flexibility has left the Court with the problem of neutral discretion and stable definition. Religious dissenters and nontraditional religious sects seem best aided by a broad definition of religion, especially when they try to secure constitutional protection for their religious beliefs or religiously motivated conduct. Conversely, as pointed out by Evans, "definitions broad enough to include educational, social service, and patriotic activities would leave many ordinary governmental functions vulnerable to the charge of violating the Establishment Clause."[44] This second perspective advocates a narrow definition of religion to prevent large swaths of American life from becoming walled off to religion.

The problem for the U.S. Supreme Court is that it is pulled toward a broad definition of religion by some of its reasonable objectives while being tugged toward a narrow definition by other considerations. Since a compromise definition satisfies neither of the Court's expediencies, the Court is tempted to provide no formal definition of religion so as to allow itself more maneuvering room. This inability of the Court to find an overarching definition for constitutionally protected religion strikes many observers as contributing to piecemeal rules for deciding cases under the First Amendment's religion clauses.

While the Court's line of reasoning from *Cantwell* to today demonstrates a great deal of intellectual labor, learned observers see a mixed result. One political scientist, Kenneth Wald, describes the Court's Establishment Clause work as a "tangled jurisprudence."[45] He argues that in many instances the Court's attempts to advance the free exercise rights of one litigant will gut the Establishment Clause protection supposedly enjoyed by another.[46] Another legal scholar, Steven Smith, states that a general theory of religious liberty is a "foreordained failure" because every theory is rooted in an imperfect conception of religion.[47]

Other voices concur. Thomas J. Curry claims that of all the clauses in the Bill of Rights, none generates more controversy among scholars today than the religion clauses.[48] Richard Collin Mangrum surveys the landscape of religious-based statutory and judicial exemptions, then states that under present establishment reasoning "the courts are left with the conundrum that religious exemptions may be required by the Free Exercise Clause even as they may be prohibited by the Establishment Clause."[49] To protect one clause under the ascendent jurisprudence the Court must do damage to the other clause. Mangrum also points out that the "status of religious-based statutory and judicial exemptions remain a perplexing constitutional issue," and the Court's work is irreconcilable with any principled analysis.[50]

Thomas Schweitzer states that there is likely no area of American constitutional law "as confused and inconsistent as the jurisprudence of the First Amendment's Establishment Clause," spawned by the Court's remodeling work in *Everson*.[51] Michael W. McConnell argues that the Court's majority opinion in *Sherbert* (1963) produced an expansionist reading for both of the religion clauses, making them "mutually contradictory."[52] McConnell goes on to explain that the conflict between the religion clauses became the central theme of case law and scholarly criticism for more than two decades following *Sherbert*."[53] Constitutional law scholars Lee Epstein and Thomas G. Walker label the Court's jurisprudence on both religion clauses as "unstable."[54]

Justification for these evaluations abounds in the post-*Everson* period. However, an effort to understand free exercise cannot focus solely upon so-called free exercise litigation because disestablishment cases oftentimes involve elements of free exercise.[55] The conundrum is that one person's idea of establishment is another's idea of free exercise. Seemingly aware of this, the framers of the U.S. Constitution laid no rule of universal application at the national level except that the federal government should stay out of the regulatory enterprise and let every state come up with its own—and necessarily biased—version of free exercise.

FORWARD FROM *EVERSON*

The Court's *Everson* decision made it evident that the nation's long march from confederation toward a hybrid federal-unitary governmental system was advancing briskly. Daniel O. Conkle explains that though *Everson* created a wall between church and state, "this wall of separation did not forbid neutral governmental programs that included religious as well as secular beneficiaries."[56] Neutrality, imperfections and all, was thus on its way to becoming a national jurisprudential principle in partial substitution for federalism of religion—the latter growing obsolete because it advertised, rather than concealed, its preferential nature.

One year after *Everson*, the Court had the chance to reinforce the neutrality rule it expounded in Everson, doing so quite forcefully in *McCollum v. Board of Education* (1948). The *McCollum* case involved a public school's religious education release time program where privately paid religious teachers (provided by an ecumenical religious council) offered on-premise religious classes for interested students. Uninterested students simply stayed in their classrooms and continued with their normal work. The Court saw this program as providing special treatment for the children of religiously motivated parents who requested their children's involvement. Hence, the

Court declared the program as "squarely under the ban of the First Amendment" that it had established in *Everson*.

The *McCollum* decision was a controversial 6–3 ruling that spawned efforts on the part of religious communities to find release time programs that would meet the Court's emerging standard of constitutionality. Four years after *McCollum* the Court revisited the release time issue in *Zorach v. Clauson* (1952) by evaluating a release time program where the religious classes were held at nearby religious centers instead of being convened on public school premises. Justice William O. Douglas intoned for the 6–3 Vinson Court: "We are a religious people whose institutions presuppose a Supreme Being."[57] Douglas continued, stating that when "the state encourages religious instruction or cooperates with religious authorities by adjusting the schedule of public events to sectarian needs, it follows the best of our traditions."[58] Thus, Douglas formalized a principle of accommodation by which neutrality could be administered in light of the religious character of the society when justified by the circumstances of the moment. Furthermore, in a harbinger of what was to come, he observed that the Court saw the line between acceptable accommodation and the unacceptable promotion of religion by government as an incremental problem of degree. The Vinson Court's core position in *Zorach* has never been explicitly overruled, the principle of accommodation continuing to find new supporters in the courts, academia, and the broader culture.[59]

In 1963, the U.S. Supreme Court articulated a view in *Sherbert v. Verner* that would stand for nearly three decades as the most important case in the Court's Free Exercise Clause jurisprudence.[60] In *Sherbert*, the Court developed the doctrine that a law or governmental practice that burdens or impedes the exercise of religion is legitimate only if demonstrably necessary to achieve a compelling governmental purpose. The consequence of this doctrine is that government is obligated to provide exemptions or some type of accommodation in situations where it can be shown that the governmental purpose is not compelling.[61] The doctrine creates new problems because exemptions or accommodations when granted may make it appear that government is giving one group preferential treatment over another, thus ensnaring the government with the Court's mandate of disestablishment.

Less than a decade after *Sherbert* the Court heard *Wisconsin v. Yoder* (1972), a case centered around the Amish way of life. While the Court largely upheld its compelling interest doctrine from *Sherbert*, this would be the last time the Burger Court would rule in favor of a free exercise claim apart from matters such as unemployment benefits.[62] In *Yoder* the Court held that "only those interests of the highest order and those not otherwise served can overbalance legitimate claims to the free exercise of religion."[63] Yet the Court made an effort to distinguish the uniqueness of the Amish way of life, suggesting the Court's declining interest in providing religion exemptions in the face of growing criticism that exemptions operated more or less as infringements of the Establishment Clause. Still, it would take until 1990 when the Court rolled back the *Sherbert* doctrine for the Court's thinking to become evident regarding how best to reconcile the two religion clauses.

One case that is remarkable in respect to free exercise and yet is generally considered under disestablishment doctrine is *Lemon v. Kurtzman* (1971). In *Lemon* the Court introduced a far-reaching three-pronged test to determine the constitutionality of government actions that reach religion. The first prong of the *Lemon* test involved the inquiry of whether a federal or state statue demonstrates a secular purpose. If the veiled purpose of a statute is to provide a benefit to religion, the act is unconstitutional. The second prong of *Lemon* seeks to identify the primary effects of legislation to see whether religion is advanced or inhibited— another exercise without bright lines. Finally, *Lemon*'s third test aims at finding any type of connection between state and church that might be judged an excessive governmental entanglement with religion. Here jurists are asked to exercise their discretion in regard to the ideas of "excess" and "entanglement"—an undertaking facilitative of judicial activism.[64]

For legal scholars, *Lemon* denoted the Court's resolve to operationalize the principles of disestablishment. As applied, *Lemon* served to make it harder for church and state to find cooperative enterprise at the local level, reducing the prospects for communitarian brands of free exercise. Nevertheless, the Court did not use *Lemon* as aggressively as some supposed it would, demonstrating in *Widmar v. Vincent* (1981) a continuing attachment for accommodation.

At issue in *Widmar* was the question of whether the state could allow people to use public facilities, such as schools, for secular purposes but not for religious ones. *Widmar* demonstrated, as Sanford Levinson notes, that "religious speech cannot, in the name of protecting against an establishment of religion, be selected out by the state for worse treatment than secular speech when the state generally makes its facilities available for public use."[65] While the Supreme Court chose not to reach the free exercise claim of the *Widmar* litigants but to decide the case upon the basis of precedents regarding the regulation of free speech, the Court's stance clearly indicated that some aspects of free exercise would not be significantly altered by the Court's doctrines of disestablishment.[66]

In the case of *United States v. Lee* (1982), the Court reasoned that not all burdens on religion are unconstitutional. As Bette Novit Evans explains, the litigant Lee claimed that "compulsory participation in the Social Security system interfered with his free exercise rights." But the Court held that the "state may justify a limitation on religious liberty by showing that it is essential to accomplish an overriding governmental interest." Chief Justice Burger declared that if Lee chose to enter into commercial activity, he had the obligation to abide by the scheme of taxation established by government.[67]

Justice John Paul Stevens wrote a concurring opinion in *United States v. Lee* that proved significant, signaling what the Court would do in later cases to deal with the increasing tensions within its jurisprudence. Stevens questioned the wisdom of a compelling state interest standard that essentially reversed the traditional burden of proof and required government to justify laws that litigants claimed to burden free exercise. Stevens pointed out that if the Court had granted an exemption to Lee, the Court would have placed the government in a position of having to regularly evaluate the relative merits of various religious claims. This situation troubled him, suggesting a stance incongruent with the Court's view that the Establishment Clause prohibits government from discriminating between religions so as to possibly provide some religions an advantage over others.[68] Stevens' thinking on the matter was a harbinger of a reorientation of Court thinking that would gradually lead the Court toward new doctrines less likely to raise the need for exemptions.

The important religious liberty cases following *Everson* tend to support Steven D. Smith's contention that no general principle of religion clause jurisprudence is possible in the post-*Everson* era. Agreeing with Steven Smith, Kenneth Wald writes that the Court split the two religion clauses into "mutually-exclusive categories" and then developed "a unique approach in each domain." Consequently, the "*Lemon* and *Sherbert* standards, as well as their more recent replacements, provide no real principles" to guide judges. Attempting to illustrate the point, Wald advances a hypothetical situation that looks like a case the Court heard in 1992, namely *Lee v. Weisman*. Wald suggests that if one student is allowed the free exercise of leading prayer at a public school graduation ceremony, the student's free exercise will infringe on another student's disestablishment liberty to escape religious pressure at the commencement ceremony.[69]

The Rehnquist Court decided to take a bold step in dealing with these conflicts in its highly controversial 1990 decision *Employment Division, Department of Human Resources of Oregon v. Smith*. Legal scholar Bette Novit

Evans observes that while *Sherbert* (1963) and *Yoder* (1972) characterized "the dominant understanding of the free exercise of religion" for a couple of decades, *Smith* came to characterize the emerging jurisprudence of the conservative Supreme Court as the 1990s began. In the *Smith* case, a 6-to-3 Court majority took the view that a state law forbidding the use of peyote rightly constrained Native American religionists from using the controlled substance for religious rituals. The Court's position on the state law allowed it to uphold the denial of unemployment compensation benefits to two Native Americans who had been dismissed from their jobs for peyote use. As Evans points out, "a five-member majority (Justice Sandra Day O'Connor concurred on other grounds) rejected the need to justify burdens on religious exercise by compelling state interest, and it ruled that religious exemptions to generally applicable laws are not constitutionally required."[70]

Smith is intriguing because it allowed government at all levels more latitude in church and state matters without trespassing on the Establishment Clause. However, something had to be sacrificed to accomplish this feat, evident in the waves of criticism from lawyers on the ideological Left and Right in the months following the decision. *Smith's* most considerable effect was to make it more difficult for citizens to litigate on the basis of claims that their free exercise rights had been infringed. While *Smith* was not a good business outcome for those practicing free exercise law, it did serve notice that the Court majority felt the subjectivity in granting exemptions as well as the potential entanglement with the Establishment Clause constituted more serious problems than a narrowing of opportunities for litigation based upon the constitutional free exercise guarantee.

Justice Antonin Scalia wrote the majority's opinion in *Smith* and experienced a public reaction not dissimilar from what Justice Hugo Black endured a half-century earlier in *Everson*. Referring to the public opinion climate that followed his *Everson* decision, Black quipped in reference to King Pyrrhus, "One more victory and I am undone."[71] Indeed, the savvy embedded in Black's decision would not be recognized by his supporters for some time, the same holding true for Scalia in *Smith*. While *Smith* seemed to undercut the prospects of free exercise for "religious practices that are not widely engaged in," as acknowledged by Scalia, the decision strengthened the prospect that major sects, like Roman Catholicism, could pursue their agendas with less need to continually defend against small sects' claims that their free exercise would be impinged. Thus, *Smith* had the effect of reducing litigation in the federal courts based upon controversy over the limits of free exercise. Also, it moved the high court's jurisprudence away from its *Sherbert* era deference to the free exercise of religious dissenters and nonconformists over religions more democratically popular at the state level. Scholar Bette Novit Evans explains:

According to Justice Antonin Scalia, the Free Exercise Clause is breached when laws specifically target religious practice for unfavorable treatment. Generally applicable laws, neutral in intent, do not in this view raise First Amendment problems. This requirement is met simply by a formal neutrality; it requires only that a law be religion-blind and not on its face discriminate against religion; it does not require religious-based exemptions... Moreover, the Smith majority ruled that the Free Exercise Clause does not require that laws burdening religious exercise be justified by a compelling state interest... Thus, when the majority rejected this standard, it made a significant reversal in constitutional policy about an issue neither raised nor argued by the litigants.[72]

Three years after *Smith*, Congress countered with legislation demanded by various religious interests and numerous constitutional scholars. Late in 1993 Congress enacted the Religious Freedom Restoration Act (RFRA), aimed at restoring the compelling state interest test and limiting government's ability to restrict a person's free exercise of religion only in instances where government uses the least restrictive means of furthering the compelling interest.[73] The Supreme Court, however, did not yield its position as articulated in *Smith* when the RFRA's constitutionality was raised to the Court's attention in *City of Boerne v. P.F. Flores, Archbishop of San Antonio, and the United States* (1997). In *City of Boerne* the high court ruled the RFRA unconstitutional on the grounds of separation of powers, the Congress not having the right to dictate to the Supreme Court its standards of jurisprudence even when both chambers of Congress were nearly unanimous in their voting.[74] *City of Boerne* ensured that *Smith* would continue to exert controlling precedence. Nevertheless, the jurisprudential landscape remains challenging as complicated by the fact that *Lemon* and other major cases not fully congruent with *Smith* have not been directly overruled.[75]

Shortly after deciding *Smith,* the Rehnquist Court tested its new doctrine in *Church of the Lukumi Bablu Aye, Inc. and Ernesto Pichardo v. City of Hialeah* (1993). The controversy involved the ritual sacrifice of animals for the Yoba religion. Using a strict judicial scrutiny standard, the Court found that the southern Florida City of Hialeah attempted to impede the Yoba adherents' free exercise of religion by creating city ordinances that were neither neutral with regard to religion nor of general application. The Court found evidence of tacit governmental hostility in the way the ordinances effectively singled out the religion. In the Court's view, the city's ordinances did not advance interests of the highest order nor were the ordinances narrowly tailored in pursuit of those interests. Furthermore, the Court observed that the ordinances did not advance legitimate and compelling governmental interests, resurrecting the applicability of *Sherbert* in the shadow of *Smith*.[76]

The Court's methodology in the case suggests a continuing effort to find definitions, tests, and doctrines by which to address the variables in free exercise cases. But organizing the Court's analytical instruments into intuitive categories is not easy. One legal scholar, Douglas Laycock, presents a useful model. Laycock sorts the Court's interpretative solutions on free exercise (as perceived by scholars) into four groups.

The first category is formal neutrality—an approach that says free exercise exemptions are forbidden. The category is founded on the idea that exemptions imply Court preference or perhaps the inadequacy of a jurisprudential system that requires adjustments to produce suitable results. The category is not, however, in much play because the two problems it seeks to avoid are less disruptive of Court interests than the prospect of fewer tools by which to fit justice to unusual cases.[77]

The second attempted solution is that exemptions are permitted but not required (permissive formal neutrality). This solution purportedly describes the Court's thinking until *Sherbert* (1963); it continues to explain the Court's approach in matters of traditional religious privilege. One example is the exemption of sacramental wine from state liquor laws.

The third attempted solution allows that exemptions that are required for matters of conscience—an approach evident in the years between *Sherbert* and Scalia's opinion in *Smith*. Support for this view is found in James Madison's argument that duties to God supercede duties to civil society. Most accommodationists go at least this far in urging exemptions for cases in which conscience might be infringed without them.

Finally, a fourth and more aggressive solution advocates exemptions for religious autonomy as well as conscience. The ideal of religious autonomy includes the notion that regulation that burdens religion discourages religion—a problem for the Free Exercise Clause. Nevertheless, numerous skeptics remain concerned that too much autonomy for religious organizations—exemption from taxation, zoning, employment, and other types of laws—gives these organizations a license to misuse the public trust.[78]

While Laycock's system has the attraction of intuitive progression along an axis of free exercise, the effort also illustrates the difficulty of categorizing theories, doctrines, rules, tests, precedents and idiosyncratic solutions in the context of undulating boundaries and variable definitions of religion. It is of little surprise, then, that many scholars find no clear way forward, generating a pessimistic expectation of the Court's jurisprudential future on the religion clauses. But there exists as much cause for optimism, since no other nation on earth has preserved as much religious liberty as has the United States while providing paths of political recourse for dissatisfied participants.

CULTURE AND THE LIMITS OF FREE EXERCISE

In the 1981 case of *Badoni v. Higginson,* the Supreme Court refused to give the Navajos a special accommodation in using a sacred Native American site. The controversy concerned the Rainbow Bridge—one of the world's greatest natural rock arches that had become increasingly accessible to tourists through the filling of Lake Powell on Utah's border with Arizona. The Navajos claimed a right of free exercise. The Court, conversely, focused on the Establishment Clause, claiming, in essence, that if it were to grant the Navajos an exemption for preferential use of the site (which had become a National Monument), it would be guilty of giving the equivalent of affirmative action to one religion.[79] The Court welcomed Navajos to continue using the site for religious purposes but not to the exclusion of tourism as regulated by the National Parks Service.

Cases like *Badoni v. Higginson* are suspect to some observers who believe that culture plays an outsized role in how the Court understands free exercise.[80] Edwin B. Firmage writes that the Mormon polygamy cases "reflect a refusal on the part of the federal judiciary, the Congress, and the executive branch to allow for a radically different vision of American society to coexist in a nation colored by the concept of traditional Protestant Christianity."[81] Melody Kapilialoha MacKenzie and Catherine Kau argue much the same thing with regard to peculiar aspects of Polynesian religion, stating that the "distinctiveness of Native Hawaiian religion—so different from traditional Judeo-Christian doctrines—makes it especially vulnerable and renders doubtful its continued protection under the Free Exercise Clause."[82] Joan Mahoney argues that laws concerning personal morality in the United States have been rooted far more in religious beliefs and norms than in any type of objective assessment of the secular purposes of the law—an argument increasingly in vogue on the political left.[83] Mahoney reinforces her argument by citing a comment by Justice John Paul Stevens in *Thornburgh v. American College of Obstetricians and Gynecologists* (1986), Stevens asserting that laws restricting abortion have no secular purpose but are instead moored to religious philosophies.

In essence, the Stevens and Mahoney argument is that people's lifestyle choices—abortion and gay marriage included—are impinged by the way religious belief seeps into the culture. As dominant religious beliefs transmit convictions about appropriate personal morality into society, these religious judgments can become secularized as in the form of culture; as such, they may escape censure under the Court's disestablishment rules. Since any establishment potentially limits someone's free exercise, culturally embedded religion serves to narrow the conduct side of religious free exercise for individuals whose religion is accepting of all behaviors entered into by consenting adults. This idea is no new innovation since part of the rationale of voluntary disestablishment in the states during the nation's formative years was predicated on the belief that the cultural dimensions of religion would remain evident in the designs of state law, creating an environment friendly to Christianity's ends without the need of state-supported churches.

One way to explore the question of culture's impact upon religion clause jurisprudence is to contemplate how the Court's understanding of the word "religion" has changed as American culture has evolved. During the nineteenth century, the Court understood religion as including a strong theistic element; that is, belief in a Supreme Being. The thinking reflected the religious culture and history of the United States as well as world history in general. As culture changed, the Court found it convenient to drop this theistic standard in its 1961 *Torcaso v. Watkins* decision. In that case it held that government cannot "aid those religions based on a belief in the existence of God as against those religions founded on different beliefs."[84]

Evidently, the Court was concerned that to prefer theistic religions over non-theistic religions would be paramount to creating an establishment on behalf of preferred religions over non-preferred religions. This type of thinking led to the Court's work in *United States v. Seeger* (1965), where it cited theologian Paul Tillich's work as cause to broaden its understanding of religion. Tillich's definition of religion allowed for almost anything that might concern "the depths of your life, of the source of your being, of your ultimate concern, of what you take most seriously without any reservation."[85] Maneuvering from Tillich, the Court suggested that it could accept as a religion a sincere belief that "occupies a place in the life of its possessor parallel to that filled by the orthodox belief in God . . . " Just seven years later in another conscientious objector case, the Court expanded the boundaries of religion even further, at least in regard to conscientious objection to military service.[86]

These examples suggest that although the Court did not allow in *Seeger* an exemption from combat duty under the Selective Service Act for objections that were merely "political, sociological, or philosophical," the Court has broadened the idea of religion greatly where it has served the Court's purposes or needs. The protection of non-theistic religion—sincere beliefs that occupy a place in one's life parallel to personal occupation with a belief in God—opens the door to the protection of self-defined religion that might include as its elements the right to abortion, self-cloning, homosexual marriage, polygamy, ritual drug use, animal sacrifices, and many other such things; granted, theistic religion can produce the same result.

Justice Scalia's opinion in *Smith* suggests a concern about the prospect of anarchy for the Court's religion clause jurisprudence if the meaning of religion is overly broadened. Scalia wrote, "We have never held that an individual's religious beliefs excuse him from compliance with an otherwise valid law prohibiting conduct the state is free to regulate." Scalia further cited *Reynolds* in arguing that a claim of religion ought not to give people liberty to become a law unto themselves.[87]

A related way to think about the intersection of religion with culture involves the notion of de facto religion—a term coined by Mark De Wolfe Howe in his 1965 book, *The Garden in the Wilderness*. Howe thought that the social reality of the United States demanded that religious interests be advanced by culture, quite notably by public language (e.g., "In God We Trust" on coins), the naming of cities (e.g., St. Paul), and the origination of religious holidays (e.g., Thanksgiving).[88] But there is more to de facto religion than symbolism: The American version of religious freedom is largely deferential to traditional religious norms. These background norms include moralistic assumptions regarding suitable behavior and the punishment of crime, many of the assumptions reflecting traditions such as ancient Israel's Mosaic code. As William Marshall explains, this de facto religion is "too much a part of the public culture to be excised," any such attempts potentially harming the fabric of society.[89]

The U.S. Supreme Court has long recognized the situation with de facto religion and has taken several paths in addressing the symbolic side of it. In *Marsh v. Chambers* (1983), the Court created an *ad hoc* exception for legislative prayer, recognizing that this type of religious activity was *noncoercive and embedded* in the character of the nation. In other instances, the Court has allowed religious practices that are *adequately secularized*—such as the placement of a Christian nativity scene into a broader context. In this situation a context of competing religious and non-religious symbols marginalizes any advantage for the de facto religion. A lesser frequently used third approach is to apply a *de minimus* scrutiny to the challenged action, the Court simply averting its gaze and claiming no serious constitutional concern. The Court could, as William Marshall points out, create a class of minor cultural establishments that are protected from strict scrutiny as an alternative means of accommodating de facto establishment of cultural religion.[90]

While the U.S. Supreme Court has not shown evidence of considering de facto cultural religion as a limit upon the free exercise of those who are unhappy with it, neither has it done much with plausible arguments on the opposite side of the ledger. For example, Michael McConnell notes that in early times, "[e]ach of the state constitutions first defined the scope of the free exercise right in terms of the conscience of the individual believer and the actions that flow from that conscience." McConnell then notes that none of the state constitutional provisions confined their protections to mere beliefs and opinions, their design suggesting the intention of countering any sentiment that religious conduct was unprotected. McConnell thus claims that free exercise has always extended to some forms of conduct, even if the scope of the protected conduct is vague.[91]

If America's de facto religion is not only symbolic but inescapably moralistic and preoccupied with the conduct of individuals and good of the community, the mere protection of conscience, beliefs, and formal religious practice is not suitably protective of the core of traditional American religion. A case can be made that to deny pious people with traditional religion the political wherewithal to experience the social and cultural aspects of their religious framework unduly limits the essence of their free exercise. The plausibility of creating local pockets of federalism to facilitate such ends, while protecting states from religious coercion or the loss of religious pluralism, could imply that some structural innovation is in order.

The foregoing logic is not dissimilar to that offered by Jewish scholar Amitai Etzioni when he states that to object to the moral voice of the community is "to oppose the social glue that helps hold the moral order together." He continues:

Relying on internalized values and consciences—expecting people to do what is right completely on their own—asks too much of individuals and disregards their social moorings and the important role that communities have in sustaining moral commitments. In effect, those who are so adamantly opposed to statism must recognize that communities require some ways of making their needs felt . . .[92]

If Etzioni's argument were refused a place on the table alongside others, it would be tantamount to elevating non-traditional religion as the de facto religion of the state. Indeed, this line of thought suggests that the Rehnquist Court's work in *Smith* may have been pragmatic in allowing a larger role in the political process in deciding some of the limits of free exercise of religion. That said, the political process is not always orderly or constructive of prudent outcomes. Indeed, the national political process in the late-nineteenth century might have produced a result far less hospitable to religion and to the interests of modern accommodationists had it not been for thirty-five holdouts in the U.S. Senate.

In the 1870s, the United States experienced a violent eruption of Nativism, a reactionary expression of hyper-Protestantism triggered by surging Catholic immigration and fears of power loss among traditional Americans. Reacting to the sentiments of the Protestant majority, the U.S. Congress, President Grant, both political parties and much of the nation prepared to alter the religion clauses of the First Amendment as a means of undercutting any prospect of the Catholic Church gaining political power through the operations of federalism or its private school system. The proposed corrective was widely heralded as the Blaine Amendment, named for its congressional sponsor, James G. Blaine of Maine.[93]

An aggressive endeavor, the Blaine Amendment would have impeded the growing power of Catholicism in America by laying a truly imposing wall of separation between church and state at every level of government. The proposed amendment read, "No State shall make any law respecting an establishment of religion, or prohibiting the free exercise thereof."[94] The replacement of the word "Congress" with the words "No State" simply anticipated what the Supreme Court would do seven decades later. But the amendment continued at some length, prohibiting state funds from ever being under the control of any religious sect or denomination, or even being divided between them (a potential blow to neutral accommodation).

In 1876, the proposed amendment passed the U.S. House of Representatives in overwhelming fashion but fell two votes short of the necessary two-thirds margin in the Senate. Had the Blaine Amendment passed and been ratified by three-fourths of the states, this emotionally charged adjustment would have become the nation's Sixteenth Amendment. As things worked out, the Eighteenth Amendment became the means by which the nation established its ill-advised policy of Prohibition. If the Blaine Amendment would have passed the Senate and been ratified in the states, the nation may have found itself later recanting that work of prejudiced religious passion just as it found it necessary to recant what it thought was prudence when it ratified Prohibition. The tumultuous episode serves as a reminder that good law tends to arise from reflection, understanding and judicious dialogue, the prospect for these advantages seldom as good as at the Founding.

CONCLUSION

The Supreme Court's meandering route between accommodation and separation has served the nation fairly well, protecting religious liberty for far more people and under more diverse conditions than many people would have thought possible. As the Court's history shows, religion cannot be adequately protected without the interplay of separation and accommodation—the construction of a modest wall and the preservation of prudently situated breaches in it. Of course, metaphors overly simplify the enormous challenges the Court faces in interfacing a nationalized Free Exercise Clause with a nationalized Establishment Clause.

Arguably, one of the most important tasks awaiting the Court is to find suitable ways of providing free exercise for individuals and sects for whom community-level religious establishment is an essential aspect of their free exercise. This particular challenge may require the nation's premier court to acknowledge more fully that for many religious people, religiously motivated conduct is not easily separated from religious belief. Scholars seem increasingly aware that this is a matter of constitutional justice and a concern that deserves greater scrutiny.

Knowledgeable Supreme Court observers disagree as to whether religion is being incrementally removed from the public realm or gradually re-accommodated. Both effects likely exist as the Court's work is played out on different fronts. Then, too, one's idea of what constitutes religion markedly influences perceived gains or losses for free exercise. Nevertheless, a mixed evaluation of what is transpiring in the Court's religion clause jurisprudence may suggest a happy difficulty in finding any political system with better prospects for managing enormous religious diversity. While there are other imaginable cultural conditions that might make it possible for the U.S. Supreme Court to construct a religion clause jurisprudence with better coherence, liberals, moderates, and conservatives have reason to hope that the evolving limits of free exercise will be hospitable to quality religion, civic virtue, and good government.

NOTES

1. Thomas J. Curry, *Farewell to Christendom: The Future State of Church and State in America* (New York: Oxford University Press, 2006). Curry believes the First Amendment put an end to Christendom (i.e., state-supported religion), the national government possessing almost no constitutional competency in matters of religion.

2. Stephen L. Carter, *The Dissent of the Governed: A Meditation on Law, Religion, and Loyalty* (Cambridge, MA: Harvard University Press, 1998), 61–66. Carter believes that a religious community can provide the benefit of organizing political resistance.

3. Gerard V. Bradley, *Church-State Relationships in America* (Westport, CT: Greenwood Press, 1987), 27.

4. Franklyn S. Haiman, *Religious Expression and the American Constitution* (East Lansing, MI: Michigan State University Press, 2003), 141.

5. Donald S. Lutz, ed., *Colonial Origins of the American Constitution: A Documentary History* (Indianapolis: Liberty Fund, 1998).

6. Thomas J. Curry, "Establishment Clause: Background and Adoption" in *Religion and American Law: An Encyclopedia*, ed. Paul Finkelman (New York: Garland Publishing, Inc., 2000), 165.

7. Ibid.

8. Jefferson's Act is variously named, another common title being the "Virginia Statute for Religious Liberty."

9. Stewart Davenport, "'Dale's Laws,'" in *Religion and American Law*, 119–120.

10. Thomas J. Curry, *The First Freedoms: Church and State in America to the Passage of the First Amendment* (New York: Oxford University Press, 1986), 198–199.

11. The quoted phrase is the opening statement of the Bill of Rights.

12. Patrick M. O'Neil, "Bible in American Law," in *Religion and American Law*, 30–34.

13. Jessie L. Embry, "Polygamy," in *Utah History Encyclopedia*, ed. Allan Kent Powell (Salt Lake City: University of Utah Press, 1994), 428–430.

14. Ibid.

15. Ibid.

16. The Revised Statutes of the United States preceded the United States Code as a means of organizing the acts of Congress.

17. *Reynolds v. United States*, 98 U.S. 145 (1879).

18. Embry, 428–430.

19. *Reynolds v. United States*, 98 U.S. 145 (1879).

20. Ibid.

21. Haiman, 93.

22. Michael McConnell, "*Permoli v. First Municipality of New Orleans*, 44 U.S. (3 How.) 589 (1845)," in *Religion and American Law*, 358.

23. Carol Weisbrod, "*Reynolds v. United States*, 98 U.S. (8 Otto) 145 (1879)," in *Religion and American Law*, 420–421.

24. See *Wisconsin v. Yoder*, 406 U.S. 205 (1972).

25. Michael Kent Curtis, "*Barron v. Baltimore*, 7 Pet. (32 U.S.) 243 (1833)," in *Religion and American Law*, 25–27.

26. *Palko v. Connecticut*, 302 U.S. 319 (1937).

27. Melvin I. Urofsky, "*Cantwell v. Connecticut*, 310 U.S. 296 (1940)," in *Religion and American Law*, 65–66.

28. *Cantwell v. Connecticut*, 310 U.S. 296 (1940).

29. Urofsky, "*Cantwell v. Connecticut*," 65–67.

30. Renee C. Redman, "Jehovah's Witnesses" in *Religion and American Law*, 245. According to Redman, the Witnesses have been involved with at least thirty-seven plenary decisions involving the First Amendment.

31. Tony Freyer, "*Everson v. Board of Education*, 330 U.S. 1 (1947)," in *Religion and American Law*, 173–175.

32. Philip Hamburger, *Separation of Church and State* (Cambridge, MA: Harvard

University Press, 2002), 461. Hamburger quotes U.S. Supreme Court Justice Robert Jackson.

33. Ibid., 461–470.

34. Thomas Dye, *Politics in America*, 6th ed. (Upper Saddle River, NJ: Pearson Education, 2005), 459.

35. John M. Mecklin, *The Story of American Dissent* (Port Washington, NY: Kennikat Press, 1970, repr.), 310.

36. Catherine Cookson, *Regulating Religion: The Courts and the Free Exercise Clause* (New York: Oxford University Press, 2001), 80–94.

37. James T. Baker, "Baptists in Early America and the Separation of Church and State," in *Religion and American Law*, 20–25.

38. Ibid., 24.

39. Davison M. Douglas, "'Christian Nation' As a Concept in Supreme Court Jurisprudence," in *Religion and American Law*, 74–75.

40. Ibid.

41. Ibid.

42. John Witte, Jr., *Religion and the American Constitutional Experiment*, 2nd ed. (Boulder, CO: Westview Press, 2005), xvi.

43. Bette Novit Evans, "Definitions of Religion in Constitutional Law," in *Religion and American Law*, 122.

44. Ibid., 123.

45. Kenneth D. Wald, *Religion and Politics in the United States*, 4th ed. (Lanham, MD: Rowman & Littlefield, 2003), 108.

46. Ibid., 112.

47. Steven D. Smith, *Foreordained Failure: The Question for a Constitutional Principle of Religious Freedom* (New York: Oxford University Press, 1995).

48. Curry, "Establishment Clause," 162.

49. Richard Collin Mangrum, "Establishments of Religion Created through Free Exercise Exemptions," in *Religion and American Law*, 169–172.

50. Mangrum, 172.

51. Thomas A. Schweitzer, "Public Aid to Parochial Education," in *Religion and American Law*, 382.

52. Michael McConnell, "*Sherbert v. Verner*, 374 U.S. 398 (1963)," in *Religion and American Law*, 459.

53. Ibid., 457.

54. Lee Epstein and Thomas G. Walker, *Constitutional Law for a Changing America: Rights, Liberties and Justice*, 5th edition (Washington, D.C.: CQ Press, 2004), 145, 213.

55. Robert S. Alley, ed., *The Constitution and Religion: Leading Supreme Court Cases on Church and State* (New York: Prometheus Books, 1999), 11. Alley's selection of free exercise cases is quite similar to mine starting with *Reynolds* and moving through *City of Boerne*.

56. Daniel O. Conkle, "*Zorach v. Clauson*, 343 U.S. 306 (1952)," in *Religion and American Law*, 576.

57. Ibid., 576.

58. Ibid., 578.

59. See Michael J. Perry, *Under God? Religious Faith and Liberal Democracy* (New York: Cambridge University Press, 2003), ix. Justice Douglas was joined in his opinion by Chief Justice Fred Vinson and Justices Reed, Burton, Clark, and Minton. Separate dissenting opinions were provided by Black, Frankfurter, and Jackson.

60. Michael McConnell, "*Sherbert*," 456–457.

61. Ibid., "*Sherbert*," 457.

62. Walter F. Pratt, Jr., "*Wisconsin v. Yoder*, 406 U.S. 205 (1972)," in *Religion and American Law*, 561.

63. Bette Novit Evans, "*Employment Division, Department of Human Resources of Oregon v. Smith*, 494 U.S. 872 (1990)," in *Religion and American Law*, 148.

64. Phillip Presby and Donald G. Nieman, "*Lemon v. Kurtzman*, 403 U.S. 602 (1971), 411 U.S. 192 (1973)," in *Religion and American Law*, 275–280.

65. Sanford Levinson, "*Widmar v. Vincent*, 454 U.S. 263 (1981)," in *Religion and American Law*, 556.

66. Ibid., 556–557.

67. Bette Novit Evans, "*United States v. Lee*, 455 U.S. 252 (1982)," in *Religion and American Law*, 547–548.

68. Ibid., 548.

69. Wald, 111–112.

70. Evans, "Employment Division," 147.

71. Hamburger, 462.

72. Evans, "Employment Division," 147.

73. Evans, "Employment Division," 151.

74. Melissa Day, "*City of Boerne v. P.F. Flores, Archbishop of San Antonio, and the United States*, 521 U.S. 507 (1997)," in *Religion and American Law*, 83–84.

75. Presby and Nieman, 279. Also, Evans, "Employment Division," 151.

76. Richard B. Saphire, "*Church of the Lukumi Babalu Aye, Inc. And Ernesto Pichardo v. City of Hialeah*, 508 U.S. 520 (1993)," in *Religion and American Law*, 77–80.

77. Douglas Laycock, "Theories of Interpretation: Free Exercise Clause and Establishment Clause," in *Religion and American Law*, 516–526.

78. Douglas Laycock, "Theories of Interpretation," 516–526.

79. Stephen K. Schutte, "*Badoni v. Higginson*, 638 F. 2d 172 (10th Cir. 1980), cert. Denied, 452 U.S. 954 (1981)," in *Religion and American Law*, 17–18.

80. See Philip Schaff, *Church and State in the United States* (New York: Arno Press, 1972), 37. Schaff argues that the limitations of religious liberty depend upon "the course of public opinion."

81. Edwin B. Firmage, "Mormon Free Exercise in the Nineteenth-Century America," in *Religion and American Law*, 324.

82. Melody Kapilialoha MacKenzie and Catherine Kau, "Hawaiian Native Religion and American Law," in *Religion and American Law*, 221.

83. Joan Mahoney, "Privacy Rights and Religious Influences," in *Religion and American Law*, 378–379.
84. Evans, "Definitions," 124.
85. Ibid., 127. Evans quotes theologian Paul Tillich.
86. Ibid., 128.
87. Ibid., "Employment Division," 148.
88. William Marshall, "De Facto Establishment of Religion," in *Religion and American Law,* 120.
89. Ibid., 121.
90. Ibid., 120–122.
91. Michael McConnell, "Free Exercise Clause in Historical Perspective: The 'New' American Philosophy of Religious Pluralism," in *Religion and American Law*, 194.
92. Amitai Etzioni, ed. *The Essential Communitarian Reader* (Lanham, MD: Rowman & Littlefield, 1998), 43.
93. Ibid., 296–299; 321–328.
94. See Richard Aynes, "Blaine Amendment," in *Religion and American Law*, 39–41.

FURTHER READING

Where does one start to learn more about free exercise in America? One could begin with the *Colonial Origins of the American Constitution: A Documentary History* (Donald L. Lutz, 1998). Lutz's collection of early documents is one of the best for opening up the primary literature on free exercise theory. Next, Robert S. Alley's 1985 book *James Madison on Religious Liberty* provides many writings by the so-called father of the Constitution as well as Alley's insightful commentaries. For a comprehensive yet accessible examination of the legal basis of religious liberty in America it is hard to match the 2005 second edition of *Religion and the American Constitutional Experiment,* by John Witte, Jr., Director of the Center for the Study of Law and Religion at Emory University.

Steven D. Smith's *Foreordained Failure: The Quest for a Constitutional Principle of Religious Freedom* (1995) provides a legally sophisticated examination of the Court's work on the religion clauses. University of Chicago Law Professor Philip Hamburger's 2002 book *Separation of Church and State* is credited with reinvigorating the debate about the importance of public religion in America. Michael J. Perry's 2003 Cambridge University Press book *Under God? Religious Faith and Liberal Democracy* reveals considerations that moved an accomplished separationist scholar to become a mild accommodationist. Finally, Paul Finkelman, editor of *Religion and American Law: An Encyclopedia* (2000) supplies a superb collection of erudite yet readable legal essays on the religion clauses. Arranged alphabetically by topic, the essays provide background information and perspective on the full spectrum of free exercise and disestablishment issues.

Appendix: Selected Cases

The following cases are discussed or referenced by the chapters in this volume. Only precedent-setting decisions or important clarifications are included in this appendix. Though not all the cases here are, strictly speaking, matters of church and state jurisprudence, all have important ramifications for the issues covered in the volume.

Abington Township v. Schempp (1963): A Pennsylvania law required public school students to read at least ten Bible verses and recite the Lord's Prayer at the beginning of the school day. Concerned parents argued that even with the allowance for exemptions, this practice violated the Establishment and Free Exercise Clauses. The Supreme Court, siding with the parents, declared the practice unconstitutional.

ACLU v. Leavitt (2006): The U.S. Department of Health and Human Services authorized funding for the "Silver Ring Thing," a religiously-based abstinence program. The ACLU charged that this funding violated the Establishment Clause and after an initial suit in 2005, reached a settlement in a 2006 case of the U.S. District Court of Massachusetts, thereby ending the funding.

ACLU v. Rabun County (1982): In this case, argued in the U.S. Court of Appeals, Eleventh Circuit, the ACLU challenged the constitutionality of a large cross erected on an 85-foot platform in the Black Rock Mountain State Park in Georgia. Due to the state-funded upkeep of the cross and the "noneconomic injury" it caused to those non-Christians using the park, the Court decided that the installation of the cross violated all three prongs of the Lemon Test (*Lemon v. Kurtzman*).

Agostini v. Felton (1997): A parochial school teacher challenged an earlier decision by the Supreme Court regarding whether or not public school teachers could teach secular subjects at parochial schools. The ruling by the U.S. Supreme Court reversed *Aguilar v. Felton* (1985). Not only can public school teachers enter parochial schools without necessarily violating the Establishment Clause, this decision means that not all entanglements of church and state should be assumed unconstitutional.

Aguilar v. Felton (1985): Since the 1960s, New York City had used public monies to pay teachers in parochial schools as a means of combating educational inequality. The Supreme Court found that the monitoring of publicly paid teachers necessary to ensure that they were not promoting religion amounted to excessive entanglement between church and state. The Supreme Court later overturned this ruling in *Agostini v. Felton* (1997).

Americans United for the Separation of Church and State v. Prison Fellowship Ministries (2003): Americans United brought challenge against Iowa corrections officials and Prison Fellowship Ministries, arguing that the Ministries' pre-release program for inmates constituted a violation of the Establishment Clause. A federal judge ruled that the program was completely religious in origin and focus and the prison system provided no secular alternative for non-religious inmates or those of other faiths. The judge ordered the Fellowship to repay all state-granted money. The case is currently under appeal.

Anderson v. Salt Lake City Corp. (1973): This case from the Tenth Circuit of the U.S. Appeals Court questioned the constitutionality of a monument to the Ten Commandments at a Salt Lake City courthouse. The monument also contained various symbols and references to Abrahamic religions and U.S. history. The Court found the monument to be constitutional in its recognition of the religious roots of the nation and further held that an "ecclesiastical background" did not make the monument necessarily religious in character.

Aronow v. United States (1970): In this challenge to the use of the national motto, "In God We Trust" as a violation of the Establishment Clause, the U.S. Court of Appeals for the Ninth Circuit upheld the motto. The Court argued that this motto has only a "patriotic or ceremonial character" and thus does not seek to advance religion or preference a particular religion.

Atkins v. Virginia (2002): The U.S. Supreme Court considered a Virginia case in which a mentally retarded man was found guilty of abduction, armed robbery, and capital murder and sentenced to death. Pointing to the Eighth Amendment, the court determined that such a sentence qualified as "cruel and unusual punishment" due to the man's psychological state. This ruling reflected a growing trend in state legislation to limit the death penalty in this way.

Badoni v. Higginson (1981): A group of Navajo members sued to protect sacred sites threatened by the planned flooding of Lake Powell for downstream water storage and recreational boating. Although affirming Native American claims to the land, federal courts found the state's interest in promoting economic prosperity more compelling than the concerns of the Native American groups.

Bowen v. Kendrick (1988): The Adolescent Family Life Act (AFLA) gave federal funds to service and research organizations that dealt with premarital teenage sexuality, including several religious organizations. Chan Kendrick represented several citizens, clergy, and the American Jewish Congress in claiming this violated the First Amendment's Establishment Clause. The Supreme Court decided against Kendrick by determining that support of religious organizations was not the primary goal of AFLA.

Bowers v. Hardwick (1986): The State of Georgia charged Michael Hardwick with violating a statute against sodomy after he was observed by an officer in the act of consensual homosexual sodomy with an adult in his bedroom. Hardwick appealed by way of questioning the constitutionality of the statute. The Supreme Court found that no constitutional protection for sodomy existed, thus allowing states to outlaw the practice. This case was later overturned by *Lawrence and Garner v. Texas* (2003).

Bush v. Holmes (2004): This ruling by the Florida First District Court of Appeals ruled that the state's Opportunity Scholarship Program (OSP) and school-voucher program as a whole were unconstitutional because they allowed state funding of religious schools. The state of Florida appealed to the State Supreme Court, which struck down the OSP as a violation of the state's Education Clause. It made no determination on the church/state issues involved.

Cantwell v. Connecticut (1940): Jessie Cantwell and his son, both Jehovah's Witnesses, were arrested for failing to obtain a solicitation permit and for disturbing the peace after proselytizing in a Connecticut neighborhood inhabited primarily by Catholics. The Supreme Court found that the arrest violated the Cantwell's First and Fourteenth Amendment rights, as their message did not constitute a threat of bodily harm.

Church of Holy Trinity v. U.S. (1892): In this case, the Church of the Holy Trinity in New York entered into a contract with an English preacher. Though such a contract with a foreign laborer was forbidden under U.S. law, the Church argued that the minister did not qualify as a foreign laborer. The Supreme Court agreed with the Church that the minister did not fall under the category prohibited by this law, thus emphasizing the spirit over the letter of the law.

Church of Lukumi Bablu Aye v. City of Hialeah (1993): As practitioners of Santeria, the Church of Lukumi Babalu Aye incorporated animal sacrifice into worship. Soon after the Church was established, the local city council in Hialeah County passed ordinances prohibiting the sacrifice or slaughter of animals outside of specific state-licensed activities. The Supreme Court found these ordinances to be unconstitutional because they were enacted specifically to be applied to this church. The statutes thus constituted an undue burden on religious exercise.

City of Boerne v. Flores (1997): Citing the 1993 Religious Freedom Restoration Act (RFRA), Archbishop Flores of San Antonio sued local zoning authorities for limiting his ability to expand his Boerne, Texas church. City authorities cited the historic preservation designation of the site of Flores' church as reason to restrict the expansion. The Supreme Court concluded that through RFRA, Congress had overextended its Fourteenth Amendment powers by making local ordinances subject to federal regulation. Only states may decide how to apply statutes such as RFRA.

Corporation of the Presiding Bishop v. Amos (1987): An individual was fired from a nonprofit facility run by the Church of Jesus Christ of Latter-Day Saints because he was not a member of the Church. He and other individuals brought suit against the Church alleging religious discrimination in violation of Title VII of the Civil Rights Act. The Supreme Court found the policy unconstitutional because the work of the facility and the job in question were secular activities.

County of Allegheny v. ACLU (1989): The ACLU of Greater Pittsburgh challenged the constitutionality of two local-government sponsored holiday displays in Pittsburgh, PA. The first display sat inside the County Courthouse and showed a Christian nativity scene with an explicitly Christian message displayed in front. The second was a large Hanukkah menorah outside the City-County building, placed there by a local Jewish organization. The Supreme Court disallowed the nativity display because of its location and its explicitly Christian message. The Court allowed the menorah because of its setting outside of the government building.

Cutter v. Wilkinson (2005): Ohio prisoners and practitioners of minority religions accused prison officials of violating the Religious Land Use and Institutionalized Persons Act (RLUIPA) of 2000 by not allowing them to practice their religion. Prison officials countered by claiming RLUIPA violated the Establishment Clause by advancing religious practice. The Supreme Court unanimously affirmed the constitutionality of RLUIPA in that the act ensured religious freedom for those inmates practicing both majority and minority faiths.

Engel v. Vitale (1962): In an attempt to standardize practice and minimize local conflict, the Board of Regents for the State of New York instituted a nondenominational and voluntary prayer to be said at the beginning of each school day. The Supreme Court determined that the prayer was unconstitutional despite its nondenominational nature and the allowance for abstention.

Everson v. Board of Education (1947): New Jersey instituted a law allowing for the reimbursement of funds to parents who sent their children to both religious and public schools on public transportation buses. Everson charged that this violated the Establishment Clause by enacting state support of religious schools. The Supreme Court upheld the constitutionality of the law by claiming the reimbursement was available to religious and non-religious individuals alike and did not constitute direct support of religious organizations.

Gilfillan et al. v. City of Philadelphia (1980): In 1979, Pope John Paul II visited the city of Philadelphia and, in preparation, the city spent $200,000 to construct a platform on which the Pope would deliver Mass. A U.S. Appeals Court ruled that this expenditure violated all three requirements of the *Lemon* Test (*Lemon v. Kurtzman*) and thus constituted a violation of the Establishment Cause. The local Archdiocese reimbursed the city for the funds and the Supreme Court denied a hearing of the case.

Good News Club v. Milford Central School (2001): The Good News Club is a Christian organization for preteen children that sought and was denied access to public school facilities for an after-hours program. The Good News Club sued, claiming that their First Amendment rights were being violated. Though earlier decisions favored the school, the Court found that since the school allowed other groups to meet in their facilities, they could not discriminate against a religious club.

Hein v. Freedom From Religion Foundation (2007): The Freedom From Religion Foundation sued the federal government after an executive order was issued by the President to form conferences within executive departments promoting Bush's new Faith-Based Initiative programs. A District Court ruled that the Foundation had no standing to sue as it was not directly affected or harmed by the order. The U.S. Court of Appeals for the Seventh Circuit thought otherwise and allowed for the suit on this Establishment Clause question. The Supreme Court agreed with the District Court in denying the right of citizens to bring suit as taxpayers against the Executive Branch.

Lawrence and Garner v. Texas (2003): After entering John Lawrence's house after a report of a weapons disturbance, Houston police discovered Lawrence and another adult man, Tyron Garner, engaged in a sexual act. They were arrested and charged with deviate sexual intercourse in violation of a Texas law. The Supreme Court argued that the law violated the Due

Process Clause and constituted an inappropriate involvement of government in private affairs, thus overturning *Bowers v. Hardwick* (1986).

Lemon v. Kurtzman (1971): This case was heard with two other cases involving laws in Pennsylvania and Rhode Island that funded teacher salaries and instructional materials for secular subjects taught in non-public schools. The Supreme Court concluded that these policies violated the Establishment Clause and developed the "Lemon Test" for determining whether a law violated the Clause. This test requires that a law must have "a secular legislative purpose," that the law must neither advance nor hinder religion, and that a law cannot lead to "an excessive government entanglement with religion."

Locke v. Davey (2004): In 1999, Washington State established its Promise Scholarship to provide college scholarships to top students. The state limited these funds by disallowing their use for theology programs. Joshua Davey earned a Promise Scholarship but declined the money in order to pursue pastoral ministries at a Christian college. Davey sued claiming a violation of his free exercise of religion. The Supreme Court denied Davey's suit, stating that government has a right to restrict its funding and only support non-religious programs of instruction as a means of avoiding state support of religious activity.

Lown v. Salvation Army (2005): The New York ACLU charged the Salvation Army with religious discrimination due to its restrictions on employees based on religious belief combined with its use of government funds to pay for its social service programs. A New York U.S. Circuit Court judge ruled that the Salvation Army could continue its policy and government funding provided the funds were used for non-religious activities.

Lynch v. Donnelly (1982): Daniel Lynch charged that the annual Pawtucket, Rhode Island, Christmas display in the city's shopping district violated the Establishment Clause by including a nativity scene as well as a Christmas tree, a "Seasons Greetings" banner, and a Santa Clause house. The Supreme Court disagreed and held that this display did not have a specific religious purpose but rather represented the history of the Christmas holiday.

Marbury v. Madison (1803): William Marbury and others sued the government to obtain jobs they were appointed to near the end of John Adams's presidency. Since the appointments were never finalized, Marbury and others were not able to fill their appointed posts. They sued in the Supreme Court, which found in their favor and established the principle of judicial review.

Marsh v. Chambers (1983): Coming out of the Nebraska state legislature, this case focused on the use of public monies to pay chaplains for prayers offered in the legislature's assemblies. The Court abandoned the requirements set up by the *Lemon* Test (*Lemon v. Kurtzman*) and, relying on the idea that historical customs have their own legitimacy in the public sphere, upheld the chaplaincy program.

McCollum v. BOE (1948): A coalition of Jewish and Christian organizations sponsored a period of voluntary religious instruction to take place during the regular school day and in public school facilities. The Supreme Court found that the use of tax-supported property and the working relationship between public school and church authorities violated the Establishment Clause.

McCreary County v. ACLU (2005): In this case, the ACLU sued three counties in Kentucky for displaying the Ten Commandments in public facilities, including courthouses and schools. The Supreme Court found that the Kentucky displays did violate the Establishment Clause because it appeared as if the government was endorsing religion.

McDaniel v. Paty (1978): Historically, many states have had prohibitions against ministers serving in various public offices. In 1977, Tennessee law still restricted clergy from some public offices, including their constitutional convention. McDaniel, an ordained minister, sued, claiming the prohibition violated his rights. The Supreme Court agreed, holding that while a prohibition was constitutionally permissible, Tennessee had not shown why it was necessary.

Minersville School District v. Gobitis (1940): The Gobitis children were members of Jehovah's Witnesses who were expelled for not saluting the flag, an act they found to be in conflict with Biblical command. The Supreme Court upheld the mandatory flag salute, arguing that national unity was an important consideration and that attempts to promote it did not automatically violate a citizen's freedom.

Mitchell v. Helms (2000): This case, like others, focuses on the use of public money in sectarian schools. At issue here was the provision of funds for library, computer, and other educational materials. The Supreme Court ruled that the fact that all schools, religious and secular alike, were eligible for such aid means that the government has been neutral in its services and has thus not violated the Establishment Clause.

O'Hair v. Blumenthal (1979): In this case, Madaly Murray O'Hair, then President of the American Atheists, sued the federal government to remove the phrase "In God We Trust" from currency. The U.S. Court of Appeals for the Fifth Circuit ruled against O'Hair, arguing that the motto was secular and served a secular purpose.

Permoli v. First Municipality of New Orleans (1845): Bernard Permoli, a Catholic priest in Louisiana, conducted a funeral service in a New Orleans church, in violation of an 1827 public health law regulating the transfer and display of bodies in the city. Permoli sued, arguing that his First Amendment rights were being violated. The Supreme Court found that the First Amendment protections did not apply to state laws, and thus left individual states free to regulate religious expression.

Reynolds v. U.S. (1879): George Reynolds, a member of the Church of Jesus Christ of Latter-Day Saints, was charged with bigamy in Utah. Along with certain procedural arguments, Reynolds held that religious duty obligated him to marry more than one woman at a time. The Supreme Court upheld Reynolds' conviction and drew a distinction between what religious people might believe and what they can practice in the public sphere.

Rosenberger v. UVA (1995): University of Virginia student Ronald Rosenberger requested a disbursement from the student activities fund to subsidize the publication of a Christian newspaper. The University refused on the grounds that it could not promote any specific religious viewpoint. The Supreme Court held that the University had acted in such a way as to penalize Rosenberger's speech, and further found that the University's publication policy was neutral toward religious content and did not therefore violate the Establishment Clause. The University, if it subsidizes any paper, must support a student religious publication on the same basis.

Santa Fe Independent School District v. Doe (2000): Two families brought a suit against the Santa Fe Independent School District's practice of allowing an overtly Christian prayer before home football games. While the case was pending, the school district changed the policy from requiring a prayer to permitting one. The Supreme Court held that the new policy violated the Establishment Clause because the prayer took place on school property at an official function, and therefore could appear to endorse religious practice.

Sherbert v. Verner (1963): A member of the Seventh Day Adventist Church was fired from her job for refusing to work on Saturday, which was, for her, the Sabbath. She was denied unemployment compensation by the South Carolina Employment Security Commission. The Court held that the state's attempt to restrict her unemployment compensation violated her rights to the free exercise of her faith.

Stone v. Graham (1980): This case challenged a Kentucky law that required the posting of the Ten Commandments in public school classrooms. The Court found that the law violated the first prong of the *Lemon* Test (*Lemon v. Kurtzman*) since the posting had no secular legislative purpose.

Torcaso v. Watkins (1961): After his appointment as Notary Public in Maryland, Roy Torcaso was denied his commission for refusing to affirm his belief in God. The Supreme Court unanimously found Maryland's requirement that public officials affirm a belief in God as a prerequisite for holding office to violate the First Amendment.

Updegraph v. The Commonwealth of Pennsylvania (1824): Abner Updegraph was found guilty of blasphemy for speaking against the truth of the Bible. The Pennsylvania Supreme Court reversed the jury's conviction based on the technicality that Updegraph's comments were not made in a profane manner. In its decision, the Supreme Court proclaimed Christianity as part of the common law of Pennsylvania and, thus, reasoned that certain instances of blasphemy should be punished.

U.S. v. Lee (1982): In this case, an Amish employer sued for relief from IRS imposed back taxes and penalties leveled against him as a result of his failure to pay Social Security taxes for his employees. Lee argued that his religious beliefs mandated that he not support government relief programs as they imply that the burden for caring for the sick and elderly fell to the public sector instead of the religious community. While the Supreme Court did find that his beliefs were "sincerely held," they maintained that not all burdens on religious expression automatically violate the law and some are, in fact, necessary for proper function of the government. Though Amish could exempt themselves from the Social Security program, they could not avoid the tax.

U.S. v. Seeger (1965): This case concerns the definition of religion as it related to claims for religiously based conscientious objector status. Federal law required that applicants for conscientious objector status be able to affirm a theistic, rather than a political, sociological, or philosophical, understanding of reality. The Supreme Court held that the opinions of the individuals themselves must be taken into account and thus that Congress could not define what was or was not religious in this setting.

Van Orden v. Perry (2005): Van Orden sued the state of Texas in federal court, claiming that a monument to the Ten Commandments on the grounds of the state capitol violated the Establishment Clause. The Supreme Court ruled that the Ten Commandments, though religious in origin, are part of American history and society and could therefore be included in public displays without violating the First Amendment.

Widmar v. Vincent (1981): This case concerned access to university facilities at the University of Missouri at Kansas City. A Christian club that had been allowed to meet in previous years sued when a new policy prompted school officials to deny permission for the club to have access to university facilities. The Supreme Court held that the Establishment Clause did not require school officials to deny access to school facilities on the basis of the religious nature of the club.

Wisconsin v. Yoder (1972): This case revolved around whether or not

Amish families could absent their children from school facilities after a certain age on the basis of religious conviction. The Supreme Court held that public schooling was in direct conflict with the Amish way of life and that the state of Wisconsin could not therefore compel students to attend after the eighth grade.

Zelman v. Simmons-Harris (2002): The Cleveland City School District's voucher plan offered publicly-financed aid for students to attend private, even religiously-sponsored, schools. A group of taxpayers sued, claiming that the voucher plan violated the Establishment Clause in that it provided public money for parochial education. The Supreme Court held that since the plan was part of the state's effort to provide an education for all children, and that since the decision as to where a given child would attend school was not made by school officials, the plan did not violate the First Amendment.

Zorach v. Clauson (1952): New York's policy of allowing release time from public schools for students to attend religious instruction elsewhere was found to be permissible by the Supreme Court. Since school facilities were not being used to promote religious instruction, and since no student was bound by school officials to attend such instruction, the program did not violate the First Amendment.

About the Editors and Contributors

THE EDITORS

ANN W. DUNCAN is a Ph.D. Candidate in American Religious History at the University of Virginia. She received her M.A. in Religious Studies from the University of Virginia in 2005 and her B.A. from Duke University in 2000. Her research, publications, and conference presentations have focused on intersections of religion and politics, American Christianity in wartime, and, more recently, motherhood and American Christianity.

STEVEN L. JONES is Associate Professor of Sociology at Grove City College and is the former associate director of the Center on Religion and Democracy at the University of Virginia. He received his M.T.S. degree from Duke University and holds a Ph.D. from the University of Virginia. A former fellow of the Center for Children, Families, and the Law and the Institute for Advanced Studies in Culture, his main areas of academic interest are political sociology and family, state, and church conflicts. He is currently finishing a book on patriotism and church schooling in America.

THE CONTRIBUTORS

TIMOTHY J. BARNETT holds an M.P.A. degree (1992) from Boise State University and a Ph.D. in political science (1998) from the University of Kansas. Dr. Barnett teaches at Jacksonville State University where his course offerings include religion and politics, legislative politics, the presidency, political parties, and public opinion. He is a former president of the Alabama Political Science Association and has written on the U.S. Congress as well as constitutional federalism, political economy, and First Amendment issues. His research interests include populist economic policy, civic virtue in religion, and sustainable natural resource policy.

RICHARD BOWSER is Associate Professor of Law at the Norman Adrian Wiggins School of Law of Campbell University. He holds a B.A. in Religion from Grove City College, an M.A. in Religion from Westminster Theological Seminary and a J.D. from Campbell University, where he was a member of the Campbell Law Review and an editor of the Religious Freedom Reporter. Before joining the Campbell Law faculty, Professor Bowser practiced law in Washington, D.C., concentrating in the areas of church-state law and tax-exempt organizations. He currently teaches courses in the fields of constitutional law, jurisprudence, and Christian legal thought.

ZACHARY R. CALO is Assistant Professor of Law at the Valparaiso University School of Law. He holds B.A. and M.A. degrees in history from The Johns Hopkins University, a J.D. from the University of Virginia School of Law, and a Ph.D. in American Religious History from the University of Pennsylvania. He has practiced law in Washington, D.C., and served as a Civitas Fellow in Faith and Public Affairs at the Brookings Institution and as a visiting scholar at the Pew Forum on Religion and Public Life. Professor Calo researches widely in the area of law, theology, and ethics, and is currently writing a book on John A. Ryan and the history of American Catholic social thought.

DOUGLAS L. KOOPMAN is Professor of Political Science and William Spoelhof Teacher-Scholar-in-Residence Chair at Calvin College, where he also serves as the program director of the college's Paul B. Henry Institute for the Study of Christianity and Politics, as well as the interim director of the Calvin Center for Social Research. He is the author, co-author, or editor of three books—*Of Little Faith: The Politics of George W. Bush's Faith-Based Initiatives* (2004) with David Ryden of Hope College and Amy Black of Wheaton College; *Serving the Claims of Justice: The Thoughts of Paul B. Henry* (2001); and *Hostile Takeover: The House Republican Party, 1980–1995* (1996). He received his undergraduate degree from Hope College in Holland, Michigan, and his Masters in Theological Studies from Wesley Theological Seminary in Washington, D.C. He also holds a Ph.D. in American politics from The Catholic University of America.

BARBARA A. McGRAW is Professor of Social Ethics, Law, and Public Life at Saint Mary's College of California and an author and speaker on the role of religion in public life, the moral foundations of the American political system, and the politics of pluralism. She holds a Ph.D. in Religion and Social Ethics and a Juris Doctor Degree, both from the University of Southern California, and is a member of the Bar of the Supreme Court of the United States. She is the author of *Rediscovering America's Sacred Ground: Public Religion and Pursuit of the Good in a Pluralistic America* (2003), and the co-editor (with Jo Renee Formicola) of and contributing author for *Taking Religious Pluralism Seriously: Spiritual Politics on America's Sacred Ground* (2005). Earlier in her career, she practiced law with the international law firm Skadden, Arps, Slate, Meagher, and Flom.

ROBIN MUSE is Assistant Professor of Law at the Norman Adrian Wiggins School of Law of Campbell University. She holds a B.A. and an M.A. in Church-State Studies from Baylor University and a J.D. from the Norman Adrian Wiggins School of Law where she was a member of two appellate advocacy teams, a Legal Research and Writing Scholar, and president of the Christian Legal Society. Before joining the faculty at Campbell, Professor Muse served as a law clerk to Judge John M. Tyson of the North Carolina Court of Appeals. Professor Muse currently teaches Legal Research and Legal Writing, Appellate Advocacy and Judicial Writing.

DAVID K. RYDEN is Professor of Political Science at Hope College in Holland, Michigan. He earned a B.A. from Concordia College in 1981, a J.D. from the University of Minnesota Law School in 1985, and a Ph.D. from The Catholic University of America in 1995. Over the past few years, his research has focused on faith-based initiatives and the *Bush v. Gore* Supreme Court decision. His research has resulted in numerous articles and three books, including *Of Little Faith: The Politics of George W. Bush's Faith-Based Initiatives, The Constitution in Context,* and *Sanctioning Religion? Politics, Law, and Faith-Based Public Services.*

MARY C. SEGERS is Professor of Political Science at Rutgers University in Newark, New Jersey, where she has served since 1970. She received her B.A. in history from the College of Mount St. Vincent and her Ph.D. in political theory from Columbia University. Professor Segers was a National Endowment for the Humanities Fellow at Princeton University and a Ford Foundation Lecturer in Women's Studies in Religion at Harvard Divinity School. She received the Charles Pine Award for Teaching Excellence at Rutgers-Newark in 1998. She also served as Fulbright Distinguished Chair in American Studies at the University of Warsaw in Spring 1999. She is the author of nearly 50 scholarly essays and seven books. These volumes include *Piety, Politics and Pluralism: Religion, the Courts, and the 2000 Election* (2002); *A Wall of Separation? Debating the Role of Religion in American Public Life* (1998), which she co-authored with Ted Jelen; *Abortion Politics in American States* (1995) and *The Catholic Church and Abortion Politics: A View From the States* (1992), both co-edited with Timothy Byrnes; *Church Polity and American Politics: Issues in Contemporary Catholicism* (1990); and *Elusive Equality: Liberalism, Affirmative Action, and Social Change in America* (1983), co-authored with James Foster. Her most recent book is *Faith-Based Initiatives and the Bush Administration: The Good, the Bad, and the Ugly* (2003), co-authored with Jo Formicola and Paul Weber.

W. JASON WALLACE is Assistant Professor of History at Samford University in Birmingham, Alabama. He earned his Ph.D. in European and American Religious History from the University of Virginia. Dr. Wallace studies the relationship between religion and politics in the West, and his research interests include the role of religion in American public life.

Index

Abington Township v. Schempp, 291
abolition, 22–24
abortion, 209, 210–11, 212, 213, 281–82
Abrams, Elliot, 146–47
absolute government, 27–28
absolute power, 6, 7
accommodation, principle of: Douglas and, 275; interplay with separation, 285–86; one-way ratchet argument and, 247–48; overview of, 51–54; Supreme Court and, 179, 181, 242. *See also* neutrality doctrine
ACLU v. Leavitt, 184, 291
ACLU v. Rabun County, 91, 291
Adams, John, 2, 14, 21, 29, 113–14
Adams, John Quincy, 21
Adams, Samuel, 14–15
Agostini v. Felton, 181, 291–92
Aguilar v. Felton, 181, 292
aid to religiously affiliated schools, 54–55
Albanese, Catherine, 70
Alito, Samuel, 149, 169
Alley, Robert, 66
All Saints Church, 200, 203–7
Amar, Akhil, 234
American Life League, 211
American Party, 117–18
Americans United for Separation of Church and State, 199, 220 n.1

Americans United for the Separation of Church and State v. Prison Fellowship Ministries, 187–88, 292
Amish, 268, 275–76, 299–300
Anderson v. Salt Lake City Corp., 88–89, 292
animal sacrifice, 279–80, 294
anti-Catholicism, 116–17, 123–24, 186
Armstrong, George D., 23–24
Aronow v. United States, 88, 292
Atkins v. Virginia, 151, 292
autonomy, religious, 280

Backus, Isaac, 44
Bacon, Edwin, 204, 205, 206, 207
Bacon, Thomas, 23
Badoni v. Higginson, 281, 293
Baker, James T., 271
Baptists, 271
Barron v. Baltimore, 269
Bellah, Robert, 65, 66
Bercovitch, Sacvan, 67
Berger, Peter, 143
Bible, 265
Bill of Rights: approval of, 57 n.8; debate over, 263; jurisdictional view and, 232–33; Madison and, 37 n.81, 264–65
Black, Hugo, 270, 271, 278
Blackmun, Harry, 150

Black Rock Mountain State Park, 91
Blackstone, William, 18
Blaine, James G., 228, 285
Blaine Amendment, 186, 248–49, 285
blasphemy cases, 18–22
Blum, John, 82
Bonomi, Patricia, 68, 69
Bork, Robert, 155
Bowen v. Kendrick, 181, 293
Bowers v. Hardwick, 293, 296
Bradford, William, 107, 108
Brennan, William, 272
Breyer, Stephen, 150
Bryan, William Jennings, 81
Buckley, James, 202
Burger, Warren, 89–90, 91, 92, 277
Burke, Raymond, 211–12, 215, 217
Bush, George W., 65, 92, 93, 103. *See also* faith-based initiatives
Bush v. Holmes, 293
Butler, Jon, 68, 71

Calhoun, John C., 118–19
Campbell, Lewis D., 118
Cantwell v. Connecticut, 269–70, 293
Cardozo, Benjamin, 269
Carter, Jimmy, 89, 126
Catholic Church: anti-Catholicism, 116–17, 123–24, 186; colonial experience and, 105; electioneering and, 208–14; immigration and, 78; in medieval period, 5; Nativism and, 285; pluralism and, 85; voting instructions and, 217–18
Chandler, Chan, 216
Chandler, Joseph, 118
chaplain, legislative sessions and, 70
charitable choice language, 176
Chase, Salmon P., 77
Chemerinsky, Erwin, 48, 153
Chesterton, G. K., 65
Christenson, Gordon, 150
Christian Coalition, 198
Christian Echoes National Ministry, Inc., 198
Christianity: American, 69, 111–12; in ancient Rome, 32 n.12; Civil War and, 76, 77; common law and, 19; declaration of rights and, 19–21; general principles of true or genuine, 20, 21; influence of, on American culture, 128–29; millennial, 96 n.23, 110; Revolutionary War and, 71; slavery and, 22–24; Social Gospel movement and, 78; Supreme Court and, 272
Christian right, arguments of, 2
Christmas display, 52–53, 91–92, 294, 296
Church at Pierce Creek, 200–202
churches, taxation and, 196–97. *See also* electioneering by churches; *specific churches*
Church of Holy Trinity v. U.S., 293
Church of Jesus Christ of Latter-day Saints, 294, 298
Church of Lukumi Bablu Aye v. City of Hialeah, 279–80, 293–94
church-state law: definition of, 136; federalism and, 227–28, 236–38; *Locke v. Davey* case and, 249–50; policy appeal of decentralizing, 241–44
City of Boerne v. Flores, 279, 294
civic public forum, 25–26
Civic Republican views of religious liberty, 45–46
civil religion: Civil War and, 75–78; in colonial America and new republic, 67–75; diversity and, 78–80; First Amendment and, 264–65; overview of, 64–67; World Wars and, 80–84
Civil Rights Act, 189
Civil Rights movement, 125–26
Civil War, 75–78, 119
Cleveland, Sarah H., 155
Clinton, Bill, 104, 146
colonies: Catholic Church and, 105; civil religion in, 67–75; established churches in, 42; free exercise in, 259–63
Commission on International Religious Freedom, 145–46
Committee on Public Information, 82
common law tradition, 17, 18, 19
common school movement, 117
Communion Wars, 210–14
communitarianism, 259–60, 261, 263
community-level religious establishment and free exercise, 258, 261

compelling state interest test, 277, 278, 279
conduct, constraint of religiously motivated, 258–59, 266–68, 278, 286
Conkle, Daniel O., 274
conscience: exemptions for matters of, 280; freedom of, 9, 15–17, 25
conscientious objector status, 282, 299
conscientious public forum, 26–27
conservatives and international human rights law, 154–55
Constitution: Article VI, 57 n.5; freedom of conscience and, 16–17; political/legal system and, 14; principles of, 128; religious tests and, 72; as values-based, 27, 28. *See also* Bill of Rights; state constitutions; *specific Amendments*
Constitutional Convention, 264–65
constitutional interpretation: of faith-based initiatives, 177–78; international law and, 149–55
constitutionalism, 242
Continental Congress, 68, 69–70, 71
Corporation of the Presiding Bishop v. Amos, 189, 294
County of Allegheny v. ACLU, 52, 294
court oaths, 86
covenant theology, 106–7, 109, 111
culture and limits of free exercise, 281–85
culture war debates, 1–4, 30, 127, 171–72
Curry, Thomas, 260, 262, 273
Cutter v. Wilkinson, 53–54, 294

Dale's Laws, 264
Daschle, Tom, 209, 211
Davis, Jefferson, 119
death penalty, 151–52, 292
Declaration of Independence, 2, 13, 71, 112
Declaration on the Elimination of All Forms of Intolerance and of Discrimination Based on Religion or Belief (U.N.), 140–41
de facto religion, 283–84
defining religion, challenges of, 142, 272–74
deism, 12
Delahunty, Robert, 150

Delaware Declaration of Rights, 20
democracy: construction of, 94; faith-based initiatives and, 171; individualism and, 261; republicanism and, 14
de Tocqueville, Alexis, 65, 75
Dickenson, John, 16
direct aid to religious institutions, 180–81
disestablishment of religion: Establishment Clause and, 231; founding generation and, 43; move to, 69; Supreme Court and, 262–63
diversity, religious, in early republic, 109–10
"divine right," 5–6, 8
Douglas, William O., 275
Dreisbach, Daniel, 233
Drinan, Robert, 141

economic rights, 152–53
education. *See* schools
Edwards, Jonathan, 69, 110
Eisenhower, Dwight D., 85–86, 122–23
electioneering by churches: ban on, 197; cases of, 200–207; enforcement of ban on, 198–200; moral issues in, 207–18
Elk Grove Unified School District v. Newdow, 227, 234
Ellison, Keith, 129–30
Embry, Jessie L., 266
Employment Division v. Smith, 157–58 n.16, 277–79
endorsements, political. *See* political endorsements
Engel v. Vitale, 48, 50–51, 88, 294–95
England: Anglican Church in, 6, 105–6; common law tradition in, 17, 18
Enlightenment: political theology of, 7–11, 110–11; views of religious liberty in, 45
E Pluribus Unum motto, 72, 122
Epstein, Lee, 274
equal dignity, 22–24, 26
equality principle, 47
equal justice, 14
Establishment Clause: accommodationists and, 51–54; critics of Court's work related to, 273–74; federalism and, 229–31; framing of, 231–33; Free Exercise Clause and, 89, 195–96, 233;

Establishment Clause (cont.)
  incorporation of, 234–36; interpretation of, 177–78; modified incorporation of, 244–47; neutrality doctrine and, 54–56; states and, 228; strict separationists and, 48–51; Supreme Court and, 48–56, 84, 87–93. See also Religion Clauses in First Amendment
establishment of religion, 17–18, 42
Etzioni, Amitai, 284
European Court of Human Rights, 153, 154
Evangelical views of religious liberty, 44–45
Evans, Bette Novit, 272, 273, 277–78, 279
Everson, Mark W., 198, 199, 200
Everson v. Board of Education: church-state jurisprudence and, 157 n.2; Court forward from, 274–81; Establishment Clause and, 84, 178, 230, 231; as expanding reach of Court, 270–71; incorporation of Establishment Clause and, 235–36; overturning, 245; overview of, 295; strict separation and, 48–50
experiential religion, turn toward, 110

faith. *See* public expressions of faith
faith-based initiatives: challenges to, 168–69, 240; constitutional interpretation of, 177–78; culture war debate and, 171–72; federalism-centered approach and, 238–41; future judicial approach to, 183–88; hiring freedom and, 188–90; history of, 172–73, 176–77; multiple, with one goal, 169–71; status of, 168, 190; in 2000 election, 167–68
Farr, Thomas, 147
fast days, 73–74
federal courts and church/state disputes, 245–46
federalism-centered approach: church/state jurisprudence and, 236–38; Establishment Clause and, 229–31; faith-based policy and, 238–41; overview of, 227–28; philosophical advantages of, 243; policy appeals of, 241–44; textual grounds for, 229

Ferraro, Geraldine, 208–10
Firmage, Edwin B., 281
First Amendment: civil religion and, 264–65; disestablishment of religion in, 43; opening sentence to, 42; religious freedom and, 142. *See also* Establishment Clause; Free Exercise Clause; Religion Clauses in First Amendment
First Great Awakening, 12, 17, 69, 110
First World War, 80–82, 122
flag salute, 297
Flake, Floyd, 208
formal neutrality, 280
founding fathers, 72–73, 112–15
founding of America, 4–7, 12–17
Fourteenth Amendment: due process clause to, 269; free exercise and, 245; incorporation of Establishment Clause and, 234–36; religion clauses and, 42; slavery and, 38 n.101
Franklin, Benjamin, 35 n.59, 45, 114
Freedom from Religion Foundation v. Hein, 188
free exercise: in colonial era, 259–63; culture and, limits of, 281–85; *Reynolds v. U.S.* and, 266–68; twentieth-century protections and limits for, 268–72
Free Exercise Clause: Establishment Clause and, 89, 195–96, 233; as fundamental liberty, 245; Scalia and, 279; *Sherbert v. Verner* and, 275
free will, 7
fundamentalist religious groups, interaction with government by, 173–74

gay marriage, 211, 281–82
genocide and religious identity, 141–42
Germans, demonizing of, 82–83
Gilfillan et al. v. City of Philadelphia, 90, 295
Ginsburg, Ruth Bader, 150
Gladden, Washington, 78
Glendon, Mary Ann, 235–36
globalization, 149
God: American, 65–66; in Declaration of Independence, 71
Goldberg v. Kelly, 162 n. 103
Goldsmith, Jack, 155

Good News Club v. Milford Central School, 237, 295
Gore, Al, 103, 167, 208
government: absolute, 27–28; discontent with in 1970s, 174–75; fundamentalist-mainline split in interacting with, 173–74; as social contract, 9–10, 14, 25
great awakening. *See* First Great Awakening; Second Great Awakening
Great Society programs, 174–75
Guiness, Os, 94
Guluizza, Frank, 54

Hamburger, Philip, 271
Harrison, William Henry, 116
Heflin, J. Thomas, 124
Hein v. Freedom From Religion Foundation, 295
Henkin, Louis, 137
Herberg, Will, 65, 85
Herndon, William H., 121
Hertzke, Allan, 146
hiring and religious groups, 188–90
historical context for founding of America, 4–7
holiday displays, 52–53, 91–92, 283, 294, 296
Hoover, Herbert, 124
Howe, Mark De Wolfe, 283
human beings, nature of, 6–7
human rights movement, 135, 138, 143–44
Hutcheson, 85–86, 94

ICCPR (International Covenant on Civil and Political Rights), 139–40, 142, 143
identity politics, 126, 208–14
incorporation of Establishment Clause, 234–36, 244–47
individualism, 261
"In God We Trust" motto: *Aronow v. United States,* 88, 292; Communism and, 122–23; Eisenhower and, 86; 50th Anniversary of, 93; Lincoln and, 77, 120–21; *O'Hair v. Blumenthal,* 88, 297; T. Roosevelt and, 79–80; Supreme Court and, 88

Inhofe, James, 200
Internal Revenue Service (IRS), 196, 197–207
International Covenant on Civil and Political Rights (ICCPR), 139–40, 142, 143
International Covenant on Economic, Social, and Cultural Rights, 152
international law: church-state law and, 135–36; constitutional interpretation and, 149–55; debate over, 155–56; religious freedom in, 138–44; status of, 137
International Religious Freedom Act (IRFA), 137, 141–42, 144–49
irrelevant, founders' intent as, 3–4
IRS (Internal Revenue Service), 196, 197–207
Islam and religious freedom, 141
Israel, as Puritan ideal, 108
issue advocacy, 205, 221 n.10

Jackson, Andrew, 73–74
Jackson, Robert, 270–71
Jefferson, Thomas: on absolute government, 27–28; Declaration of Independence and, 112; Enlightenment tradition and, 45; religion of, 12, 112–13; on religious liberty, 15; religious tests and, 70, 72; rhetoric of, 74, 113; on truth, 16; *The Virginia Act for Establishing Religious Freedom,* 264; wall of separation metaphor of, 3, 233
Jehovah's Witnesses, 269–70, 293, 297
Johnson, Lyndon, 174–75, 197
Jones, Walter B., 200
judicial review, principle of, 296
jurisdictional view of Establishment Clause, 231–33

Kau, Catherine, 281
Kennedy, Anthony, 151, 153
Kennedy, John F., 87, 125
Kerry, John, 208–9, 210–11, 212, 213
Killea, Lucy, 224 n.43
King, Martin Luther, Jr., 125–26
Know Nothing Party, 117–18
Koh, Harold, 138
Krol, John, 210

law: conflating with morals, 214–15; of consistency/no hypocrisy, 26; moral dimension of, 24, 28; of no harm, 26; religious, nationalization of, 263–68; rule of, 14. *See also* church-state law; international law
Lawrence and Garner v. Texas, 153, 293, 295–96
Laycock, Douglas, 280
Lee, Richard Henry, 15
Lee v. Weisman, 277
legislative sessions, prayer in, 70, 91, 283
Lemon test: *ACLU v. Rabun County* and, 291; dilution of, 183; "excessive entanglement" prong of, 179; free exercise and, 276; *Gilfillan* case and, 90, 295; *Marsh v. Chambers* and, 296–97; *Mitchell v. Helms* and, 237; "primary effect" prong of, 185; prongs of, 276, 296
Lemon v. Kurtzman, 54–55, 179, 296. *See also* Lemon test
Levinson, Sanford, 276
Levy, Leonard, 64
libertarianism, 260, 261
liberty, 17–22
lifestyle choices and religious belief, 281–82
Lillich, Robert, 150
Lincoln, Abraham, 76–77, 119–21, 265
Linder, Robert, 66–67, 72, 81
Little, Daniel J., 201
lobbying, 196–97
Locke, John, 7–11, 13, 28
Locke v. Davey, 186–87, 228, 249–50, 296
Lown v. Salvation Army, 190, 296
Lynch v. Donnelly, 52–53, 91–92, 296
Lynn, Barry, 216–17, 222 n.13

MacKenzie, Melody Kapilialoha, 281
Madison, James: First Constitutional Convention and, 264–65; free exercise and, 280; on government, 29; religion and, 3, 45; religious tests and, 72; rhetoric of, 74–75, 114; *1785 Remonstrance,* 264
Maher, Leo, 224 n.43
Mahoney, Joan, 281

mainline religious groups, interaction with government by, 173–74
Mangrum, Richard Collin, 273
Manifest Destiny, 75, 78–79
Mann, Horace, 117
Marbury v. Madison, 271, 296
Marshall, John, 271
Marshall, William, 283
Marsh v. Chambers, 91, 283, 296–97
Martin, William, 147
Maryland, 109
Massachusetts Bay Colony, 107, 109
Massachusetts Constitution, 260–61
Mayflower Compact, 107
McCarrick, Theodore, 212–13
McCollum v. Board of Education, 271, 274–75, 297
McConnell, Michael W., 52, 274, 284
McCreary County v. ACLU, 93, 237, 297
McDaniel v. Paty, 89, 297
McKinley, William, 79
measured accommodation doctrine, 272
millennial Christianity, 96 n.23, 110
millennialism, 71
Miller, Perry, 67
Minersville School District v. Gobitis, 268, 297
Mitchell v. Helms, 181, 183–84, 237, 297
Mondale, Walter, 209
Moore, Roy, 127–28
moral issues in church electioneering: overview of, 207–8; relation between law and, 214–15; voting instructions, 215–18
morality and religion, 94
Mormon Church, 265–66, 268
Morrill Anti-Bigamy Act, 265–67
multiculturalism, 126
Murray, John Courtney, 85

nationalization of religious law, 263–68
National Prayer Breakfast, 86
Native Americans, 278, 281
Nativism, 285
natural law tradition, 20
natural religion or natural theology, 111, 112
nature, law of state of, 8–9

Neuman, Gerald L., 155–56
neutrality doctrine: hiring and, 189; *McCollum v. Board of Education* and, 274–75; overview of, 54–56; Rehnquist Court and, 171, 183; Supreme Court and, 179; types of neutrality, 280. *See also* accommodation, principle of
new republic: civil religion in, 67–75; politics, religion, and, 109–15
Noll, Mark, 75, 76
non-coercion test, 53
non-theistic religion, protection of, 282–83

Obey, David, 215
O'Connor, John, 182, 210
O'Connor, Sandra Day, 168–69, 183, 185, 237–38
Office of International Religious Freedom, 145
O'Hair v. Blumenthal, 88, 297
original sin, doctrine of, 6
Otto, Rudolf, 56
Owens, Marcus, 198–99, 204, 205, 206

Paine, Thomas, 14, 45
Palko v. Connecticut, 269
participate, duty to, 27
partisan, political compared to, 218–19
peace, times of, 80, 83
Penn, William, 44
people: founding of America and, 12; Locke and, 9, 10
permissive formal neutrality, 280
Permoli v. First Municipality of New Orleans, 267–68, 297–98
Perry, Michael, 143
"pervasively sectarian," meaning of, 181–82
peyote, use of, 278
Philpott, Daniel, 138, 144
Pierard, Richard, 66–67, 72, 81
Pilgrims, 106–7
Pledge of Allegiance, 86, 123
Plyler v. Doe, 162 n. 103
Poland Act, 266
political endorsements, 195–96, 214–15, 218–20
political theology, 5–6, 7–11, 110–11
polygamy, 265–67

pope, 5
practices of religion. *See* conduct, constraint of religiously motivated
practices that appear religious, 63–64
Pratt, Robert, 187
prayer: in legislative sessions, 70, 91, 283; in school, 50–51, 88
president, role of, 66–67
progressives and international human rights law, 153–54
prophetic role of churches, 218–19, 220
publications, religious, 55–56
public confession, practice of, 104–5
public debate, participants in, 16
public expressions of faith: in early republic, 112; by founding fathers, 112–15; in nineteenth century, 115–21; as source of controversy and division, 127–29; in twentieth century, 121–28
public forum, 25–27
public order and safety, and religious freedom, 142–43
public schools, debates over, 116–17
Puritans: Church of England and, 105–6; civil religion and, 67–68; covenant theology of, 106–7, 109, 111; European history and, 108–9; Massachusetts Bay Colony and, 107–8; views of religious liberty by, 43–44

Rainbow Bridge, 281
rational religion, 12–13, 17
Rauschenbusch, Walter, 78
Reagan, Ronald, 90, 104, 175
reason, Locke and, 11
Reedy, George, 197
Regas, George, 203, 204, 206
Rehnquist, William, 168
Rehnquist Court: *Church of Lukumi Bablu Aye* case and, 279–80; Establishment Clause and, 187; as "faith-friendly," 190; neutrality and, 171, 183; O'Connor and, 169, 182; *Smith* case and, 277–78, 284
release time issue, 274–75
religion: challenges of defining, 142, 272–74; Court's understanding of, 282–83; de facto, 283–84; establishment of, 17–18, 42; experiential, turn toward,

religion (*cont.*)
 110; as force in society, 41; Locke and, 10–11; meaning of term, 32 n.5; morality and, 94; rational, 12–13, 17. *See also* civil religion; disestablishment of religion
Religion Clauses in First Amendment, 42, 46–48. *See also* Establishment Clause; Free Exercise Clause
religious freedom. *See* religious liberty
Religious Freedom Restoration Act, 279, 294
Religious Land Use and Institutionalized Persons Act, 53–54, 294
religious law, nationalization of, 263–68
religious liberty: Civic Republican views of, 45–46; Enlightenment views of, 45; Evangelical views of, 44–45; exporting, 144–49; as first liberty, 14; founders on, 14–15; historical context for, 4–7; in international human rights law, 138–44; limits of, 257, 277; meanings of, 47–48; Puritan views of, 43–44. *See also* Establishment Clause
religious organization, definition of, 197–98
Religious Right, 2, 103, 127
religious test, 57 n.5, 70, 72, 87
republicanism and democracy, 14
Republican Party, 127, 225 n.50
revival, religious, 12–13, 115–16
Revolutionary War, 69–71, 76
Reynolds, George, 266–67
Reynolds v. U.S., 265, 266–68, 298
rhetoric: of Adams, 113–14; of Bush, 92; of Eisenhower, 123; of founding fathers, 112–15; of Jefferson, 74, 113; of Kennedy, 125; of King, 125–26; of Know Nothing Party, 118; of Lincoln, 76–77, 119–21; of Madison, 74–75; power of, 64–67; of F. Roosevelt, 83–84, 122; on slavery, 118–21; of Washington, 72–73, 114–15; of Whig Party, 116; of Wilson, 81–83, 121–22
rights: community-based, 259–60; competition among, 258–59; declaration of, and Christianity, 19–21; emergence of concept of, 7. *See also* Bill of Rights

Roberts, John, 149, 169
Roberts, Owen J., 270
Robertson, Pat, 127, 198, 222 n.13
Romney, Mitt, 130
Roosevelt, Franklin D., 83, 122, 124
Roosevelt, Theodore, 79–80
Roper v. Simmons, 151–52
Rosenberger v. Rector & Visitors of the University of Virginia, 55–56, 298

sacred ground: in debate today, 29–31; definition of, 21; framework, principles, and purpose of, 24–29
salute to flag, 297
same-sex marriage, 211, 281–82
Santa Fe Independent School District v. Doe, 237, 298
Santeria, 294
Scalia, Antonin, 278, 279, 283
scholarships, 186–87
schools: aid to religiously affiliated, 54–55; common school movement, 117; prayer in, 50–51, 88; public, debates over, 116–17; transportation to and from, 48–50, 84
Schwietzer, Thomas, 273
Second Great Awakening, 75, 115–16
Second World War, 83–84, 122
Section 501(c)(3) organization, 196, 197
secular, meaning of term, 31 n.5
secular left, arguments of, 2–3
separationism: clearly religious activities and, 181; *Everson* case and, 178; interplay with accommodationism, 285–86; *Locke v. Davey* case and, 250; in 1960s and 1970s, 241–42; one-way ratchet argument and, 247; political endorsements by churches and, 219–20
separation of church and state: historical context for, 4–7; international law and, 135–36; interpretation of, 178–80; Religion Clauses and, 46–47; selective blurring of, 63–64
separation of powers, 14
September 11, 2001, 92
Shapiro v. Thompson, 162 n. 103
Shattuck, John, 147
Sherbert v. Verner, 274, 275, 298

Sheridan, Michael, 212, 215–16
slavery, 22–24, 118–21
Smith, Alfred E., 124–25
Smith, Steven, 273, 277
Smolin, David, 148
Snee, Joseph, 236
social contract, government as, 9–10, 14, 25
Social Gospel movement, 78, 172
social services programs, history of, 172–76. *See also* voucher programs
sodomy, 153, 293
sovereign nation-state, birth of, 138
Spanish-American War, 79
Stanford v. Kentucky, 151
state constitutions: church/state jurisprudence and, 227–28; free exercise and, 284; mini-Blaine amendments and, 248–49; modification of Establishment Clause and, 245–47; one-way ratchet argument, 247; religion policy and, 229; religious freedom and, 257
states: faith-based initiatives and, 239–40; as laboratories of policy innovation and experimentation, 243. *See also* state constitutions
Stein, Sidney, 190
stem cell research, 211
Stevens, John Paul, 277, 281
Stone v. Graham, 90, 298
Stout, Harry, 76, 77
Stout, Jeff, 94
strict separationists, 48–51
Strong, Josiah, 78–79
Strossen, Nadine, 150, 152–53
Supreme Court: Christianity and, 272; definition of religion and, 273, 282–83; disestablishment and, 262–63; Establishment Clause and, 48–56, 84, 87–93, 178–83; free exercise cases and, 280–81; incorporation of Establishment Clause and, 235–36. *See also* Rehnquist Court; *specific cases*

Tandem Project, 143
Ten Commandments, displays of: in Alabama, 127–28; *Anderson v. Salt Lake City Corp.,* 88–89, 292; *McCreary County v. ACLU,* 93, 297; *Stone v. Graham,* 90, 298; *Van Orden v. Perry,* 92–93, 299
Terry, Randall, 222 n.13
Thanksgiving Day, 73, 77
Thomas, Clarence: Establishment Clause and, 245; *Everson* case and, 237; federalism movement and, 231; *Locke v. Davey* and, 228; *Newdow* case and, 227, 234
Thompson v. Oklahoma, 151
Thornwell, James H., 23
Tillich, Paul, 282
tolerance of religious beliefs, 9, 11
Torcaso v. Watkins, 87–88, 89, 282, 298–99
transportation to and from school, 48–50, 84
Treaty of Tripoli, 114
Treaty of Westphalia, 138
Tushnet, Mark, 154

United Nations Charter, 138–39
United States v. Lee, 277, 299
United States v. Seeger, 282, 299
Universal Declaration of Human Rights (UDHR), 135, 138, 139
Updegraph v. The Commonwealth of Pennsylvania, 18–19, 299

Van Buren, Martin, 116
Van Orden v. Perry, 92–93, 237, 299
Virginia, 263–64
voting instructions, 215–18
voucher programs, 180, 184–85, 238, 248–49

Wald, Kenneth, 273, 277
Walker, Thomas G., 274
War of 1812, 74–75
Washington, George, 14, 65, 72–73, 114–15
Webster, Daniel, 119
Webster, Noah, 21, 70
Weisbrod, Carol, 268
welfare programs, history of, 172–76. *See also* voucher programs
welfare reform, 176

Whig Party, 116
White, Ronald, 76
Whitefield, George, 12
White House Office of Faith-Based and Community Initiatives, 168, 188
Widmar v. Vincent, 276, 299
Williams, Roger, 2, 44, 260
Wills, Gary, 93–94
Wilson, Woodrow, 81–83, 121–22
Winthrop, John, 68, 107–8
Wisconsin v. Yoder, 275–76, 299–300

Witte, John, 56, 144, 272
World War I, 80–82, 122
World War II, 83–84, 122

Yoo, John, 150
Young, Brigham, 266

Zelman v. Simmons-Harris, 180, 184–86, 237, 238, 300
Zorach v. Clauson, 275, 300